The Sierra Nevada

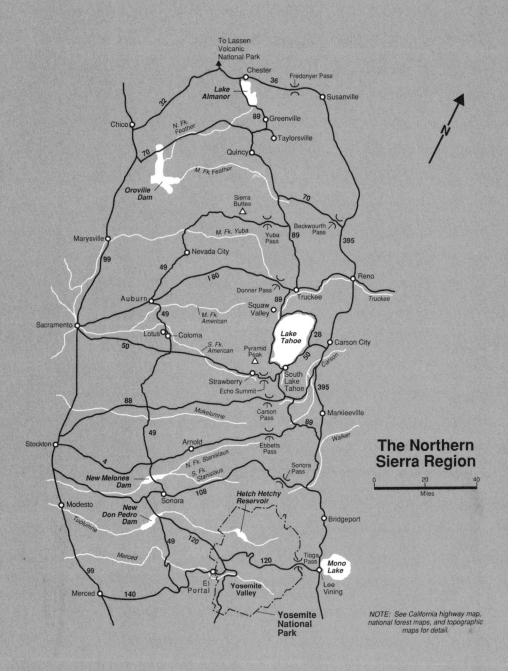

The Northern Sierra Region

NOTE: See California highway map, national forest maps, and topographic maps for detail.

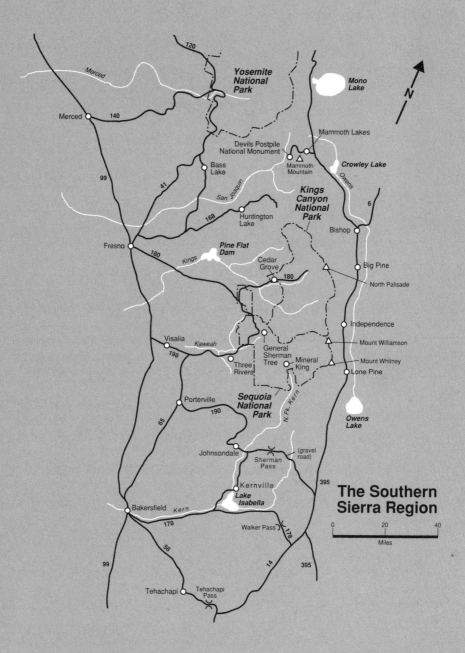

The Southern
Sierra Region

Also by Tim Palmer

Rivers of Pennsylvania
Stanislaus, the Struggle for a River
Youghiogheny, Appalachian River
Endangered Rivers and the Conservation Movement

The Sierra Nevada

A Mountain Journey

Tim Palmer

ISLAND PRESS

Washington, D.C. ☐ Covelo, California

ABOUT ISLAND PRESS

Island Press, a nonprofit organization, publishes, markets, and distributes the most advanced thinking on the conservation of our natural resources—books about soil, land, water, forests, wildlife, and hazardous and toxic wastes. These books are practical tools used by public officials, business and industry leaders, natural resource managers, and concerned citizens working to solve both local and global resource problems.

Founded in 1978, Island Press reorganized in 1984 to meet the increasing demand for substantive books on all resource-related issues. Island Press publishes and distributes under its own imprint and offers these services to other nonprofit organizations.

Funding to support Island Press is provided by The Mary Reynolds Babcock Foundation, The Ford Foundation, The George Gund Foundation, The William and Flora Hewlett Foundation, The Joyce Foundation, The J. M. Kaplan Fund, The John D. and Catherine T. MacArthur Foundation, The Andrew W. Mellon Foundation, Northwest Area Foundation, The Jessie Smith Noyes Foundation, The J. N. Pew, Jr. Charitable Trust, The Rockefeller Brothers Fund, and The Tides Foundation.

For additional information about Island Press publishing services and a catalog of current and forthcoming titles, contact Island Press, P.O. Box 7, Covelo, California 95428.

Cover photo: Marie Lake from Selden Pass

All photographs by Tim Palmer

Library of Congress Cataloging-in-Publication Data

Palmer, Tim.
  The Sierra Nevada.

  Bibliography: p. 313
  Includes index.
  1. Nature conservation—Sierra Nevada Mountains (Calif. and Nev.) 2. Natural history—Sierra Nevada Mountains (Calif. and Nev.) I. Title.
QH76.5.S54P35   1988   333.78′4   88-13019
ISBN 0-933280-54-8
ISBN 0-933280-53-X (pbk.)

MANUFACTURED IN THE UNITED STATES OF AMERICA

Contents

Preface

The lay of the land and the clarity of light offer something incomparable here. The qualities of the Sierra Nevada are recognized by people who know the mountains and by people who know only the names: Yosemite, Tahoe, Sequoia, Squaw Valley, Mammoth, American, Merced, Kings, Kern, Whitney, Cathedral, Palisades, Enchanted Gorge, Sky Parlor Meadow. The list could go on and on, lighting memories or wishes, stirring curiosity, wonder, and excitement.

It is America's longest unbroken mountain range. Outside Alaska, the Sierra includes our highest peak, deepest canyon, and longest wilderness. The sequoia trees are the largest living things on earth. Many people say the Sierra backcountry is the most spectacular in the United States. Here is an entire range of superlatives, but also one with people and communities, with subtle beauty, economic importance, and seemingly impossible challenges to resource managers and government leaders.

Three national parks cover 1.6 million acres and eight national forests include 8.1 million acres in this rugged region, 400 miles long and roughly 50 miles wide discounting foothills (generally below the 3,000-foot elevation, these would add another 10 to 30 miles to the Sierra's width). The mountains cover 12.8 million acres—larger than New Hampshire and Vermont combined—in parts of eighteen counties in California and two in Nevada. Yosemite, our third major national park, has been a pacesetter in parks and recreation management. The Sierra provides prototypes and archetypes for wilderness use, river preservation, water quality, wildlife protection, land development in alpine settings, and the dilemmas of exploitive versus sustained uses, of short-term versus long-term expectations. These mountains are at the forefront of resource management as a science, an art, and a political practice.

Millions of people visit the Sierra Nevada each year: Lake Tahoe alone sees 12 million, Yosemite nearly 3 million, Sequoia and Kings Canyon national parks, 2 million. National forests account for 25

million visitor-days annually—one-eighth of the recreation on all
national forests in the nation. Mammoth Mountain, with 1.5 million skiers a year, is the most used ski resort in the country, Heavenly Valley is one of the largest in the area, and Squaw Valley is
one of the most challenging. The South Fork of the American River,
with 130,000 rafters and kayakers in a season, is one of the two
most popular rivers in the West for whitewater paddling, and it
receives half of the whitewater use in the state.

The entire population of California, greater than that of Canada
or the rest of the western states, lives within a day's drive of the
mountains. These people have an important stake in what happens
here, and so do people nationwide—76 percent of the Sierra is
owned by the citizens of the United States. Timber harvesting, cattle grazing, dams, diversions of water, mining, and urban development are important uses—though sometimes they benefit few
people and often they conflict with recreation, wildlife, fisheries,
and an undefinable mystique that sets the Sierra Nevada off by
itself.

The original conservation debate in American history was John
Muir's attempt to spare Hetch Hetchy Valley from a dam in the
early 1900s. Since then the Sierra rivers have been a hotbed of
dispute. The struggle to save the Stanislaus was arguably the most
intense river conservation battle ever. In recent years, the Tuolumne and Kings were regarded by the nationwide organization
American Rivers as the most important endangered rivers in
America.

Lake Tahoe has been the subject of one of the most concentrated
efforts for integrated resource planning in the United States, and
Mono Lake is emblematic of conflict over the allocation and use of
water. The 1984 California Wilderness Bill included more acreage
than any other addition to the wilderness system since its incep-
tion, except for Alaska. This landmark bill and its outcome are an
important part of the story of the mountain journey in this book.

Throughout the region, new threats to the natural environment
are growing, and many of the old threats have not disappeared. The
forests are being clearcut on a massive scale, with the support of
industry, labor, and the Forest Service, but not without objections
by literally tens of thousands of other people. These historic mountains, long a battleground of competing uses, have reached a new
era of transition and conflict, and the changes hold major consequences for special landscapes and communities. Like the rest of
California, this is a place of political extremes, inescapable attention, and revealing compromise.

No other mountain range combines the Sierra's qualities, public lands, nearby population, path-breaking politics of land and water protection, and ongoing intensity in the struggle for scarce resources. The Appalachians, Rockies, Basin and Range, Cascades, Coast Ranges, and Alaskan ranges are all different, yet all share some of the current state and future fate of the Sierra.

Here is a place to see the issues of modern resource management, the cooperation and lack of it, the success and the failure of planning for diverse uses in an outstanding natural landscape. Since Yosemite was first set aside in 1864, the Sierra has been a forerunner. What happens here often happens elsewhere; lessons learned here can provide models—good and bad—for other places and for the future.

Regarding that future, many people are involved: conservationists, residents, park rangers, wildlife and fisheries biologists, recreation businesspeople, planners, civic leaders, politicians, foresters, and resource professionals of all types. Yet few have the chance to know the entire range or to see the similarities, the differences, the connections, the consequences—to see the whole thing.

Being curious about these mountains, about the people who live and work here, and about the use and future of this extraordinary place, I set out on a journey through the Sierra Nevada.

1

The Storm

THE STORM DOES NOT SEEM DANGEROUS. The wind has quit, and the temperature holds steady at twenty-four. But beyond any doubt and regardless of any wishful hopes or sunshine yearnings, I'm being buried in foot upon foot of snow, and I'm beginning to ask myself, What am I doing here?

This is not the howling blizzard of Montana tales but a peaceful, silent whiteout, big flakes like in crayon drawings from the second grade, billions of flakes animating the air. It is alive. Within a few hundred feet of me, the earth and sky are indistinguishable; they become one.

The snow piles higher, day and night. Snow buries boulders pushed here by glaciers, buries trunks of fallen sugar pine that resemble the path a whale-sized mole might make. The storm inters streams that are not dead, and they carve treacherous tunnels that can cave in and drench a winter traveler. Wind slices across the high ridges, and though I can't see it from here, a blur of snow flies almost horizontally into the maw of the canyons beyond. Yet some snow clings to the leeward side of the ridges and builds cornices—overhanging drifts that will break with the sound of a dynamite blast and trigger avalanches of incredible violence, the bane of wilderness skiers.

It was snow that impressed one of the first non-Indians who saw these mountains. The missionary Pedro Font wrote from the mouth of the Sacramento River, "About forty leagues off, we saw a great snow-covered range [*una gran sierra nevada*] which seemed to me to run from south-southeast to north-northwest." The Franciscan was only describing what he saw, but the name stuck. The year was 1776; while a society in Philadelphia produced the Declaration of Independence, the Sierra Nevada remained unexplored by white people.

Now, more than 200 years after the first writer took note of the area, I will see what is here and what has happened to the place. I'll discover why the Sierra is important to many people. How does this range affect people, and how do they affect it? What will happen to this extraordinary part of the earth that reaches so successfully toward the heavens? Here is a land loved by some, enjoyed by many, but still unknown or barely known to most people. I am here to learn about these mountains and about our care and management of them.

The storm is a good place to start; it offers beginnings of many kinds. When the white reservoir melts, we have water for the abundance of Sierra life and even for San Francisco, Los Angeles, and other cities. According to Larry Price, in *Mountains and Man*, 48 percent of the runoff in California is from the Sierra Nevada. Snow wears the uplifted range to the sculptured forms that we prize and travel thousands of miles to see. Snowstorms created the glaciers that carved Yosemite Valley, the unlikely sides of Unicorn Peak, and many of the eroded places now filled by 1,500 lakes. Sixty small glaciers remain, and today's storm recharges them.

With the softest snow came the creation of hard-rock canyons— meltwater rampaged downward and eroded the chasms of the Feather, the Kern, and thirteen other major rivers in between. Much of the fertile sediment, thousands of feet deep in California's Central Valley, was washed from the Sierra by water. The runoff slowly transports the mountains and the continent to the sea.

I sit in my van at the end of the plowed section of the Ebbetts Pass road—Highway 4. The storm began last night, and just now the snow topped the running board: two feet. I think it might let up soon, but I may be surprised. Late winter storms in mid-March surprised even Snowshoe Thompson, the intrepid mailman who skied across the Sierra and back for twenty years beginning in 1856.

One hundred feet beyond my rusty-colored van, the world disappears in an atmosphere of solid white, but for most Californians, this storm is merely rain. I imagine it: soaking wet and stacked for hundreds of miles out across the sea, the clouds transfer water from ocean to land, blowing in and spattering their soggy load on the beaches. Above the oak-veneered hills of the Coast Ranges, green with the juicy grass of March, the clouds climb and the rain pounds harder, greasing the bare dirt. East of the hills in the seventy-mile-wide Central Valley, the rain eases to a steady gray curtain.

At the 1,000-foot level in the foothills, the rain beats on scrubby oaks and ceanothus, on toyon and chamise, collectively called chaparral—tough, low cover that survives the summer heat of that furnacelike land because the roots and stems drink their fill now. The gray green digger pine is the forerunner of what some people have called the greatest conifer forest in the world, which the rain enters at 3,000 feet—the elevation where, to me, the foothills end and the mountains begin. Drops glisten from cedar, ponderosa pine, then sequoia, and the forest responds to the climate by thickening into a scented belt of green that continues nonstop for thirty miles to the spot where I watch.

For each 300 feet of climb, the clouds grow one degree colder (if it were not raining or snowing, the temperature would drop one degree for each 200 feet). Today, 5,000 feet is the divider: here spring turns to winter when rain turns to snow. Where the fir begins to replace the ponderosa pine, snow clings to limbs but melts when it hits the carpet of needles or the pavement of hardened lava. A little higher, the snow melts only to slush. But up here at the end of the road, the storm yields nothing but snow, nothing but white.

Where I sit, the storm realizes its greatest potential. Two more inches in an hour. The snow loads the needles of the lodgepole pine and bends young trees to the ground. Some will never recover and will grow with bizarre U-shaped contortions in their trunks. Animals take refuge in the air pockets made by the doubled-over lodgepoles. At high elevations, the hemlock are weighted until lower branches sag and touch the ground; upper branches shed their load by drooping to dump clumps of snow, making tiny craters under the trees. Juniper cope with the snow differently: they support the weight on muscular limbs that tremble not at all. Fir trees are pointed and shed snow like steep roofs.

Today's weather is a starting place. It is vital to the Sierra and to all who live here—vital to most people who live in California because of the water they will receive. Beyond being vital, the storm is beautiful and mesmerizing. John Muir sat out storms like this. Without a van. "The winds will blow their own freshness into you, and the storms their energy."

Inspired by the Old Man, I decide to go for a walk. I leave the skis but untie the snowshoes from their resting place against the ceiling. Skis in two feet of fresh snow are just snowshoes anyway, except on steep hills, which today I will avoid.

I head east on the road, which I recognize not by looking down at the ground but by looking up at an avenue of sky cleared of trees. After a while I veer to the right through the woods and follow a draw that seems to parallel the road. It's a simple plan, not likely to get me lost. This ravine drops to Lake Alpine.

The snowshoes push a wake of powder flakes to the sides, and with each step I sink deeply. Fresh snow can be 90 percent air, sometimes more. Even while I walk, fresh snow piles up on my shoulders and cap. The world is flattened in white; with no sunlight and no shadows, I see no depth, no bumps, no gullies, even though they are plentiful. Never level, the land surprises me by dropping away unexpectedly or rushing up to meet my snowshoes too soon. This unevenness would cause lurching descents on skis, but at my turtle pace on snowshoes it doesn't matter. Not a track do I see; every other living thing has burrowed in. Red fir encircle me, snow clinging to their rough armor of reddish bark. The countless trunks fade into a nothingness of white. It's a small world, showing nothing of the larger view.

Only in my mind's eye do I see beyond this storm-filled beginning. I imagine this scene repeated from Lassen Peak south, across the peaks and meadows, south to the highest mountains, then coasting down out of the storm to Tehachapi Pass, where the southernmost Sierra join the Coast Ranges or vanish into desert. The Sierra's northern latitude is that of Denver and Philadelphia; the southern latitude is that of Albuquerque and Cape Hatteras. Ebbetts, one of ten major passes in the Sierra, is less than halfway, north to south. Here Jedediah Smith made the first white man's trip over the mountains in 1827. The great fur trapper and explorer had been banished from California by the Spanish at San Gabriel, but after leaving the mission, he sneaked off to the north. Twice he tried to cross the Sierra—once at the Kings River and once at the American River—then with two men he followed this route up the North Fork of the Stanislaus and crossed the snow-covered heights that he called Mount Joseph. Two horses and a mule died. Through his career of ten years, Smith's outward search was for beaver to trap, but he wrote that his pursuit was "the love of novelty common to all."

As the range became better known, Carson Pass was opened, named for Kit Carson. Because it is lower, Donner Pass became the favorite and remains so today, carrying Interstate 80—the only four-lane highway over the mountains.

Storms like today's are what made the passes difficult. Because settlers pushed from Missouri to California in one season, they hit the eastern escarpment of the Sierra in the fall and faced deadly risks of being snowbound while they crossed. Some, of course, didn't make it, the Donner party being the most celebrated of the luckless.

I stop to tighten the straps on my snowshoes. At Lake Alpine, which is frozen, I emerge from the woods, turn right, and enter a maze of buried boulders that are mounds of white, some ten feet high. I hear a faraway rumble. *Is* it far away? I stop walking, stop moving, stop breathing. The rumble is gone, and the only noises are snowflakes and my heartbeat, accelerated by the sound of the avalanche.

Just down the mountain from here is a place called Tamarack (the local name for the lodgepole pine; real tamarack do not grow in the Sierra). Tamarack holds the North American record for snowfall in a single month: thirty-two and a half feet in January 1911. In a typical winter, thirty-seven feet falls there, though the Sierra record is seventy-three and a half feet in 1906–7. In the United States, only the Olympic Mountains and the North Cascades receive more snow than this range.

If this storm turns out like the one in 1983, I'm in trouble, snowshoes or not, kerosene heater or not. Up to fifteen feet fell, drifting to thirty feet, closing Interstate 80 for days. Thousands of westbound trucks were halted in Reno. Avalanches were among history's worst in the Sierra. At Alpine Meadows ski area near Lake Tahoe, a woman was buried five days in a smashed building. Searchers found her miraculously alive, though badly frostbitten.

That was extreme weather, but in this range, the extreme is commonplace. At 14,494 feet, Mount Whitney is the highest peak in the country outside Alaska, but it is only sixty miles from Death Valley—the lowest depth at 280 feet below sea level. (Note: When I find different elevations listed for a peak, which happens often, I use U.S. Geological Survey figures.) North to south, the Sierra is the longest continuous range in America. (The Appalachians run for 2,000 miles, the Rockies for 3,000, and the Cascades for 700, though these ranges are not continuous but are composites of smaller ranges with gaps in between.) Sequoia trees—one is thirty-six and a half feet in diameter at its base—are larger in volume than any other living things on earth. Kings Canyon is the deepest canyon in forty-nine states—8,240 feet at one point. From its headwaters to Pine Flat Reservoir, the Kings River has the greatest undammed vertical drop in America. Lake Tahoe—1,685 feet deep—is one of the two largest mountain lakes. Tahoe and Mono Lake are two of

America's oldest lakes. America's southernmost glaciers are in the Sierra. Yosemite Falls is the seventh highest in the world, Feather Falls is the sixth highest in forty-nine states, and El Capitan is called the largest granite monolith anywhere.

The preservation and use of the Sierra are also extreme. The first time that the federal government set aside parkland for its scenic and natural values was at Yosemite. Later it became our third major national park; Sequoia was the second. The largest state water system takes its supplies from the Sierra, and the largest project of the federal Bureau of Reclamation dammed Sierra rivers for farms and cities. Millions of homes were built with fir, cedar, and pine from these mountains. Yosemite is one of the most popular national parks and has the most overnight visitors. Lake Tahoe is one of the most visited lakes in the West, and the southeastern Sierra is one of the most used recreation regions on the continent. Two dozen ski areas draw millions of visitors, climbers prize Sierra granite as the finest rock climbing in the world, and many river runners regard the Tuolumne as the best whitewater in the West.

The Sierra stage has been set for controversy for a hundred years. Milestone after milestone in the conservation movement occurred here: the establishment of national forests, the federal reservation of Yosemite as a state park, the designation of Sequoia and Yosemite as national parks, the debate over damming the Tuolumne River and flooding the Hetch Hetchy Valley, the establishment of Kings Canyon National Park, the efforts to designate wilderness areas, and debates over dams on the San Joaquin, Feather, Stanislaus, American, Tuolumne, Merced, Kings, and Yuba—on virtually all the rivers. And there is more: conflicts over road improvements at Tioga Pass, highway plans that would have transected the southern Sierra, the Mineral King ski resort proposed by Walt Disney and subsequent plans at Horseshoe Meadows and Peppermint, the export of water from Mono Lake, logging and in particular clearcutting, the grazing of cattle and sheep to the detriment of wildlife, the urbanization of Tahoe and Mammoth. There is interesting history in all of this, but more than history—the debates continue. In fact, they rage.

What of the mountains today? I will keep one eye on the past and watch for connections that are mostly ignored as our civilization roars on, but history is not my main interest. I'm looking for events that are happening now, for a community that is alive. I'm looking for people, for landscapes, for adventures, and for the tension and balance inherent in a culture that tries to use these mountains in ways that are apparently exclusive of each other. Are they?

The trees thin out and I can see a universe of white. On other days, I would see the Dardanelles and maybe Iceberg Peak, but today my image of the mountains is limited.

There are many popular images of the Sierra: John Muir's vision, "So glorious a morning"; the view of Half Dome and the tent cities at Yosemite's campgrounds; the skiers' head-wall runs at Squaw Valley and the sunny bowls at Mammoth; the beaches and casinos at Tahoe; the sign "Chains Required" on Interstate 80; the white-water splashing you in the face on the American River's South Fork and the Kern's North Fork; the sequoia with the hole cut through it for a road, the view from Lone Pine to Mount Whitney, elegant at sunrise. And more images: a logger's paradise, a gold miner's bonanza, a mountain cowboy's vacationland. These images are not false—most of them exist or used to exist—but some of them have led to false impressions. That sequoia tree with the hole cut through it fell over in 1969, killed by what people had done to it. Many people think that the Sierra Nevada does not extend north of Donner Pass, but it does. Some people think that the Sierra is made wholly of granite, which is a myth born of Ansel Adam's photographs and weekends in Yosemite; in reality, many square miles are covered with volcanic and metamorphic rocks. People think the mountains are staid and static, but they are growing and changing at one of their fastest rates ever.

Professionals have images as well: a park ranger's ultimate challenge (Yosemite), a resource planner's nightmare (twelve thousand letters expressing divergent opinions about just one plan for only one of eight national forests), a wildlife biologist's triumph (the reintroduction of bighorn sheep), a fisheries biologist's determination (to oppose destructive hydroelectric dams), and on and on.

The images are only narrow glimpses of what is really here. Behind each image lies a world of contradictions, manipulations, history, and a larger setting that frames the scene and often causes it to look very different. And most interesting: behind each image are people who have changed the place to look the way it does, or people who have prevented changes because they prefer the Sierra the way it is.

In Congress, the California Wilderness Bill would protect important parts of the Sierra the way they are—as wilderness. Other proposals would make the Tuolumne a national wild and scenic river and Mono Lake a national scenic area. What happens to these bills this year—in 1984—may provide clues about the way we will take care of the Sierra Nevada and more: our care for these mountains may offer a clue about how we will care for the rest of the earth.

The crunch and fluff of today's snow is so different from what I first felt in this range, but the unknown out here reminds me of my earliest adventures in the Sierra. In 1968 I hitchhiked across Nevada and met the mountains near Reno when the setting sun fired a yellow glare from behind the peaks. The next morning I caught a ride over Tioga Pass, then another into Yosemite Valley, where I stared up in the usual amazement.

I hiked to the Grand Canyon of the Tuolumne by way of Glen Aulin. For three days I wandered down that brilliant river and breathed a liveliness I had never known. Right away I felt the extraordinary combination that makes the Sierra unique: it is spectacularly wild and I think the most beautiful range in the country, but it is also easy to enjoy, with good weather, few mosquitoes, water clean enough to drink (back then), and trails that are easy to follow. A guidebook calls the Sierra climate the mildest and sunniest of any major mountain range in the world. It has been said many times, but truly, this is the gentle wilderness. I dove into granite-rimmed pools where turquoise deepened to the richest blue depths. I climbed out of the Tuolumne and onto smooth, hot boulders, the scent of cedar and pine everywhere. I sat in my sleeping bag while the stars populated a violet sky darkening to black. Transported in body and in mind, I was not the same when I returned to the civilized world. In sixteen years I have never recovered from the Tuolumne, and I ache to go back to Glen Aulin.

After I ran out of food on that walk, I hitchhiked back to Yosemite Valley, where I met the limits of welcome adventure. My pack was stolen and was later found on a dead man thought to be me. Ever since, I have expected both the best and the worst from these mountains: the remarkable spiritual power of Yosemite and a seemingly uncontrollable crime rate; the clarity of Lake Tahoe and the plastic city of gambling casinos rising from parking lots for thousands. The extremes can be enraging, captivating, ugly, and fascinating, and the edges between them are friction filled. Here is the view of mountains-as-cathedral and the view of mountains-as-money. In the minds of some, the two views merge. And beyond the extremes, here is the ordinary life, simple and complex, passionate and drab, hopeful and futile, full of dreams, full of regrets, and never—on close view—ordinary. A lot happens on this 400-by-50-mile plot of up-and-down ground.

Right now my goal is simply to snowshoe back the way I came, and I'm having a hard time even at that. I see little of my route ahead. Below me the ground is not solid but soft and fluid. Behind me, snow covers my tracks as if I had never been here at all.

2

The North

FROM A LOG CABIN AT ELEVATION 4,000 feet where I had waited out the winter, I drove away toward Ebbetts Pass, freshly plowed and open for another spring, summer, and fall. Within the Sierra's chaos of granite and pine, peaks and lakes, loggers, rangers, and urban refugees, I will take the easy path to order. I will begin at the top of the map. From the wet forest in the north, I'll creep south toward the desert; from the lowest mountain pass, toward the highest peak; from sawmills where the mountains begin, to windmills where they end.

On a day that must have been like this, John Muir wrote, "Another glorious Sierra day in which one seems to be dissolved and absorbed and sent pulsing onward we know not where." Muir came to the Sierra in 1868 at age twenty-nine, adopted Yosemite Valley as his home for six years, popularized the mountains and the wilderness by talking and writing about them, invented the political nature essay, served as the first president of the Sierra Club, led the successful fight to protect Yosemite as a national park, and led the losing fight to stop the damming of the Tuolumne River. He is recognized as the father of the American preservationist movement, from which came wilderness protection. He was the first person to widely publicize the Sierra and to praise its values, and the only spokesman the full range has ever had. Although flowery by today's

9

standards, his descriptions of the mountains and his emotional response to them have never been equaled. To ignore Muir would be like walking and canoeing from Saint Louis to Astoria without the journals of Lewis and Clark. Muir gives me a foundation, a baseline, so to speak, because he wrote about many places that I will visit.

This is the season to begin traveling. It is spring, and the breakup of winter has released more than ice water, crocuses, and skunk cabbage. Fishermen in great numbers cast for trout of questionable numbers. Suburbanites and city dwellers, self-imprisoned for months, venture onto mountain roads, some still littered with needles and branches that fell with the snow and remained after the snow melted. The number of these people will increase steadily from now until August. Short-sleeved skiers at Mammoth revel in the unexpected pleasure of eighty-degree days, but the other ski resorts are closed. The season advances northward fifteen miles a day and climbs the mountains a hundred feet a day. With warm winds, yellow green spikes of grass, and white blooms of dogwood, surely this is the most vivid season.

In mid-May, the snow in the high country melts four inches a day, and the rate increases with the growth of sun cups—bowl-shaped depressions in the snow. Three-fourths of the snowpack melts in April, May, and June. The streams are full of cold whitewater—this is the time to see waterfalls. Forty percent of the Sierra runoff occurs this month, 35 percent in June.

People who live in the mountains relax on days that grow longer. Chains coated with road salt lie rusting in a dusty brown heap in the trunk. The sunshine dries winter's dampness, and the breeze dilutes the nostalgic but too-pervasive scent of wood smoke. For some mountain people who have been out of jobs, it is time to go to work—the economy stirs as new homes are built where deer lived last year. Loggers cut in valleys that until now were frozen shut by winter. The high passes to the south remain barred, and the back roads lie deep in drifts or muddy ruts, but the roads to the north are open.

The adventure of traveling—of creeping up on a new horizon—never fails to excite me. The weather is clear and the future is bright, but I feel the comfort that I attribute only to my van. On the roof rests my Mad River canoe, looking like the pounded veteran of 160 different rivers and hundreds of trips. The inside of my Ford van is intricately complex, for it is a vehicle, a home, and an office. A paintless table, three feet by two feet, fits in front of the picture window behind the driver's seat. This is where I write.

Probably a thousand things are packed in here by the time I

count four kinds of tape, sockets in a set of wrenches, and eighty books. Most of the gear is under the bed. Up front, at the cook's fingertips, are a box of pots and pans, three boxes of food, and a cooler. Behind is the largest item—a fourteen-foot raft (deflated)— along with a wooden rowing frame, two tents, a hundred feet of rope, tire chains, a tow chain, a hacksaw and a bucksaw, a camp shovel, three waterproof ammunition cans packed with boating gear, life jackets, and camping stuff. Equally buried are a kerosene heater, two pairs of ski boots, winter clothes, and more. A bicycle rests across the van against the back doors.

Anything that would be propped in a basement corner is tied to the ceiling of my van. Rings screwed into the roof beams hold cross-country and downhill skis, snowshoes, oars, paddles, an ice axe, and ski poles. Nearly everything I own is within reach. The words *compact, convenient,* and *complete* describe my home. It's claustrophobic to others but therapeutic for me. Smallness and order are a way of life. I think that all of this has metaphysical overtones, but I don't know what they are.

Heading north at noon, I speed through Reno. I'm tempted to traverse this gambler's oasis blindfolded like fifteenth-century travelers who tied handkerchiefs over their eyes while they crossed the Alps to spare them the ugliness of mountains. Yet I cannot think of a city—even Seattle, Salt Lake, or Boulder—that has such fine mountain country so close. I pass Reno up for now; my goal today is the northernmost Sierra.

How many people who have heard the names Yosemite, Sequoia, and Tahoe can name a town, a river, a county, or a national forest in the northern Sierra? This region is the most populated by year-round residents yet the least known to outsiders. After a two-hour drive through the northwestern corner of the Great Basin desert, I enter Susanville, not in the Sierra but at its edge. Mountains shining with snow climb from the town's border.

I buy groceries, turn west, and cross Fredonyer Pass, whose ponderosa pine, tall, straight, and long-needled, blanket gentle slopes. The summit is a generic hilltop. Meadows stretch wide and green, fenced for cattle. At Westwood, the Red River Lumber Company operated the world's largest pine lumber mill in the 1920s. Frame houses line the streets, and a few three-story commercial buildings remain, a visual feast of peeling paint—call it lack of maintenance or call it nature taking over. Heavy equipment rusts at the town fringe; railroad tracks sprout weeds, nature's pioneers in abandoned lots; and backyards are graveyards for stripped jeeps and mechanical refuse. I return to my search for the mountains' northern beginning, somewhere near here.

Old accounts, including John Muir's, have the Sierra reaching north through the mound- and cone-shaped peaks of Lassen and Shasta. But those clearly belong to the Cascade Range—the line of volcanoes, including Hood, Saint Helens, Adams, Rainier, and Baker, that run to Canada. Lassen is the southernmost of those peaks, so by going there and working southward, I know I will find the Sierra's northern limit. But where?

Until Mount Saint Helens exploded, Lassen was the continent's most recent volcanic eruption. In 1915, boulders and ash were blown from the 10,457-foot peak. Bulldozer drivers have recently exhumed the road from winter's burial under many feet of snow, and I park at the high point. Tracks to the summit lure me up this plug volcano, created by molten earth forced up like toothpaste from a tube that solidified before spilling down the slopes. My steps crunch on an icy crust that is melting under the morning sun. Two hours later, I step on top of Lassen.

Mount Shasta, seventy miles north, captures my eye because of its symmetry, isolation, and 14,162-foot height. Until 1864, Shasta was thought to be the highest mountain in the United States. Lassen is the only place in the world where a person can see all four types of volcanoes—plug, strato, shield, and cinder cone—at once. But more important to me, it is the only place where I can look down on the whole width of the northern Sierra. To the south the Sierra is split where forks of high country bend and nearly embrace a great mitten-shaped basin holding Lake Almanor.

Geology of the Sierra Nevada does not state exactly where the Sierra begins. The rule of thumb says merely "south of Lassen." Dick Nambo, a ranger in Lassen National Park, said that a Cascade-to-Sierra "transition zone" lies from Lake Almanor to Quincy, fifty miles south of here. In that direction I see layers of blue ridges. An ocean of volcanic rock runs south as far as my eye carries me. It does not help to look for the gray granite of Sierra Nevada picture books—the "celestial city," as Muir called it—because brown lava dominates much of the northern Sierra.

Popular boundaries place the range's northern limit far south of here. In the book *Sierra Nevada,* too large to put on a shelf, all of the 127 photographs were taken from Yosemite south. (Yosemite is 200 miles south of Lake Almanor.) *Gentle Wilderness*—an earlier book and my favorite—contains 80 photos; all but one are from Yosemite south. The northern Sierra has been shortchanged on publicity, maybe to its benefit.

Almanor, sprawling in midview, is one of California's largest reservoirs, formed by a hydroelectric dam. To the southwest, the North Fork of the Feather River winds in a 2,000-foot-deep canyon. Bill

Westmoreland, of Lassen National Forest, said, "Many people call
the Feather River Canyon the start of the Sierra. Others say that
where the granite starts, that is the beginning." The first granite
surfaces in thin bands north of the canyon at a mountain called
Ben Lomond.

Finally I found a geologic map which I declared the Word. It
shows orange-coded volcanic rocks for twenty miles from Lassen
to Lake Almanor, where a collage of pink- and blue-coded rocks
emerge from the south. These marine deposits, formed in the Paleo-
zoic period, mark the beginning of the Sierra Nevada. The map
exposes a fact I would rather not have known: the range's northern
limit lies buried under a reservoir.

Damp, moss-filled forests will mark my springtime entry into
the Sierra; at the end of autumn, the Mojave Desert will mark my
exit—from pine martin to gila monster, Douglas fir to Joshua tree;
Central Valley vineyards on the west, sagebrush on the east. The
mountains separate these regions; high country splits the land. The
mountains are a wall, but more central to my interest, the mountains are a land apart, an island within the continent.

Geologists regard the Sierra as a unit, and so do authors such as
Verna Johnston, who wrote about natural history, and Robert Reid,
who wrote about local literature. The case for unity is strong. The
high crest is continuous for 400 miles, broken only subtly by passes.
Many of the rivers are similar, crashing off the western slopes from
snowfields that last until midsummer. People in the range share an
economic heritage of logging and cattle. Throughout the range, the
major sources of money are now recreation and tourism; the Sierra
is a playground for urban California, for urban America. Federal
land predominates, covering 76 percent of the land.

But awareness of unity—the recognition of the Sierra as one
place—is rare. A cafe owner in Quincy has nothing to do with one
in Bishop. A poker dealer at Lake Tahoe wears a gold chain; a horse
packer at nearby Bridgeport wears chaps. I would guess that most
people in Groveland have never visited Taylorsville, have never even
heard of it. A congressman simultaneously favors saving Mono Lake
and damming the American River. Attitudes and decisions regarding the mountains often have little to do with geography.

Yet the image of the mountains may make a lot of difference in
what is done to them. If a place is not seen as part of a larger,
familiar universe, it is never really a place at all in the minds of
powerful strangers. If the identity of a place, however strong, is not
realized, then that identity will survive only by luck or neglect.

Many people don't travel through the mountains and see the
similarities. Like the rest of California, the mountains are split

between the two megalopolises. From here to Yosemite is the back-
yard of San Francisco; from Yosemite south, the mountains belong
to Los Angeles. Maps of congressional districts look like they were
cut by a jigsaw that ignored the lay of the land and divided the
mountains into political fiefdoms, some being colonies, some having home rule.

Near Lake Almanor's north shore—as close to the Sierra's northern boundary as I can be without scuba gear—I undertake the most
crucial chore of the day: I search for a campsite. I turn right, then
left. The road is composed of lava chunks from some arm of Lassen
that reached down to overlay the Cascades onto the Sierra in the
transition zone mentioned by the ranger. Low gear brings me to
railroad tracks. I cross, stop at the water's edge, strip, and plunge
into Almanor, so cold my scalp aches. This swim is my ceremonial
opening of the new season. I lie in the sun on a poor excuse for a
beach—not sand but rocky soil. Before the reservoir was filled, this
was only a hillside.

Later I reboard the van and lurch on the rutted road to a level
place behind a row of power poles planted at the high-water line.
The lake is full, showing little mud, though the level fluctuates
eighteen vertical feet, depending on the Pacific Gas and Electric
Company's sale of hydroelectric power, produced by pulling the
plug on this 28,000-acre tub.

Before this place was covered with water, it was called Big Meadows. The Lassen Emigrant Trail, used by settlers and gold miners
bound for the Central Valley, passed nearby. After the Maidu Indians were pushed out and killed, the meadows became "some of the
best dairy farms in the state," according to local history. But in
1902, engineer Julius Howells convinced Los Angeles bankers to
finance a hydroelectric dam that was begun in 1913—the same year
that John Muir and others lost the fight to save Hetch Hetchy Valley
from damming, and the year that Los Angeles completed the Owens
Valley aqueduct to divert Sierra water south. Muir's fight was the
first major attempt to save an American wilderness, and Owens
Valley residents later blasted the hated aqueduct with dynamite,
but no such controversies ensued here at Almanor.

The Great Western Power Company's reservoir was only one-fifth
the size of today's Almanor, whose name was derived by the company's president from those of his daughters: Alice, Martha, and
Elinor. In 1930, the Pacific Gas and Electric Company bought the
dam and raised it to the height I see. PG&E calls Almanor the "key
water warehouse" in a system of nine hydroelectric plants on the
North Fork of the Feather.

Being a "warehouse" seems to detract little from real estate values. Here is the hottest property in Plumas County. One owner subdivided 650 lots. Steve Allen, of the county planning staff, said, "Our heaviest growth is on the Almanor Peninsula; nothing else comes close." In 1970, 400 people lived there; in 1980, the population was 1,600 (the county population ranks fifty-second among the fifty-eight counties in the state).

A carload of people parks behind me. Two men of average build, a slender woman, an overweight woman, and a child walk to the rocky beach under the power line. The men fish. After dark they leave, and in the morning I find a plastic bag and four cans. I decide to go to town for breakfast.

Chester is divided by the North Fork of the Feather. East of the river the architectural style is eighty-year-old frame with false fronts; maintenance has seemingly been deferred since the logging boom after World War II. Ayobb's Ace Hardware's sign says, "Free hunting and fishing information." The Funeral Chapel's walls are armored with old white shingles. Even here, a video shop awaits business. As if aware of the main street's status—essentially a borderline between the two greatest mountain ranges of the far West—Lassen Drugs occupies the north side, and the Sierra Motel occupies the south side. The pink Big T supermarket advertises deals in windows plastered with butcher paper: "Potato Chips 89¢"; "Jumbo Franks $1.39 lb." Sawmill waste from Collins Pine, the largest lumber company in the county, rises as smoke nearby.

The North Fork of the Feather scribes the western boundary of the old half of town. The stream used to flood frequently, sometimes before people had shoveled out the previous flood's mud, so a 200-foot-wide diversion ditch, locally called the Panama Canal, was dug to intercept extra water and bypass the business district.

West of the Feather River is the second half of Chester. Gas and motel rooms are offered along the roadside swath of free enterprise intended to move dollars from tourists' pockets to local ones. To catch the eyes of people moving fifty miles per hour, the signs and buildings are brightly colored. The two halves of Chester evoke the economic forces behind the local economy: logging and highway tourism.

At the Copper Kettle, pickups fill the parking lot. A poster of a double hamburger decorates the wall by the coatrack. Three calendars advertise local businesses. Three copper kettles and twelve exhumed bottles are antiques in the 1950s decor. The prices, too, are behind the times. The special of the day costs $2.50 and is biscuits and gravy.

The cafe opened at five o'clock, when business was brisk with loggers and mill workers. Those who remain employed. In the northern Sierra, entire mills were shut during the last two years, and the number of workers shrank to a fraction of what it had been.

Now, a quarter after six, the loggers are gone. At a table next to me are four men. One, in a T-shirt and red cap, is overweight, with a bushy beard. The second has short, slicked-down hair parted near the middle, and a trimmed mustache. The third is clean-cut—his hair may be blow-dried. The fourth wears a flannel shirt, a beard, and hair greased into a duck's tail. They talk about industrial hoses. When a young man walks in with a baby in his arms, a woman says to the infant, "Come to Aunt Mary."

I take yesterday's *Chester Progressive* from the table now vacated by the four men. I see pictures of a young couple—new owners of the Snack Shack—and of three men in suits who opened a broker-age firm. Help wanted: someone to cut mill slash, someone to collect delinquent mortgage accounts, a waitress-maid, a part-time childbirth educator, a part-time high school custodian ($6.60 per hour), a special education aide ($5.30 per hour), a preschool teacher, nurses, a medical receptionist. A catskinner. Some of these jobs are in Red Bluff, seventy miles away.

Three men who have each been thrown forcefully to the ground by animals appear on the sports section's front page, totally consumed by news of the rodeo. Page 2 features a man clutching a twenty-four-inch brown trout from the Middle Fork of the Feather. A handsome new pro at the Graeagle Tennis Club is one page ahead of a three-year-old holding a two-pound catfish.

After breakfast I drive slowly through town. I don't want to cause anyone any trouble. I crowd the curb of the main street's four lanes and allow impatient commuters and snorting log trucks to roar by. One pickup stubbornly clings to my bumper, and when I turn the van around, it turns also. I stop. The driver double-parks by me. He is a large, bearded man, and I wonder what he wants at 7 A.M.

"What part of Pennsylvania are you from?" he asks. Because I have no other permanent address, I register my van in Pennsylvania even though I am seldom there. I laugh because his question is one I hear often. People have been leaving my old home state and moving west for a hundred years. Twenty years ago, looking for a better job, this man moved to California, but he still stops to greet people from back home.

He came here for work in the lumber industry. Now, lumbermen are laid off by the thousands. Is history repeating itself? The forests of the East were cut and the slash burned in 1910, when loggers moved to Wisconsin, Oregon, and California. They mine the land for trees. Timber production in California has declined steadily for twenty-two years, with more decline projected. Timber corporations are moving to underdeveloped countries and to the South, which vice president C. W. Bingham of Weyerhaeuser said would "provide the next major region for forest development." The Sierra timberland shows all the promise of ripped-up Appalachia. Chester, California, and Charleston, West Virginia, have much in common: rich resources once regarded as inexhaustible and now nearly gone. However, in the Sierra, the destruction is not as complete. Here, some opportunity to change the course of environmental history may remain.

To see a modern timber sale, I get directions from a man at the Forest Service office and drive into the mountains above the Feather's North Fork. Because the slopes are extreme, logs are winched up the hill by steel cables. Men load logs where bulldozers scraped a fifty-foot-wide road for trucks. Frayed cables lie on the ground. Damaged logs, abandoned, make two piles ten feet high. As the logs are pulled up by cable, they gouge trenches in the mountainside. These ditches fan out from the loading site like spread fingers and run down the mountain like furrows dug by old-time farmers, who plowed up and down the hills instead of on a contour. The place is a mess, likely to deteriorate after rains, when water will rip down the eroded fingers. This cable site is supposed to be an example of modern technology avoiding past problems of dragging out logs behind bulldozers, a practice that I know is worse than what I see.

Who is tending the mountains of the northern Sierra? Under no protest, Los Angeles investors flooded the Big Meadows. PG&E and the state blocked salmon runs on the Feather River. Now the Forest Service sells old-growth timber, on steep slopes, for clearcutting, and the equivalent of whole hillsides wash downriver to become mud at the bottom of Oroville Reservoir. Ranger Dick Nambo at Lassen said, "There's not much interest in the environment up here. People just figure the place will take care of itself. Farther south you'll find more interest in the future." Yet somewhere the ideas of sustainability and stewardship must survive or must be growing in a new environmental culture.

Twenty-five miles south of Chester I reach Greenville. A business district radiates one block from Ayoob's Department Store. Smoke perfumes the air at the Copper Hood, a bar, dark but open in the morning. A customer sips on a beer. As my eyes adjust, I face a slogan on a tin plaque: "Marriage isn't a word, it's a sentence."

About fifty slogans decorate the walls and ceiling. A storefront poster advertises Bob Pettit for county supervisor. Bob says, "Let's Grow Together."

Beyond the business district, rocks dumped by trucks line the shores of Wolf Creek. Someone parked a bulldozer in the stream and left it. Homeowners have groomed backyards and cultivated gardens watered by hoses during the dry spring and summer. A chiropractic office, always prominent in logging towns, fronts on the main street. Volunteers are active in Greenville: a new sidewalk was poured by the Rotary Club, and the front page of the *Indian Valley Record* features eight men and one woman laying pipe for a park.

In Ayoob's, I browse down only one aisle before a short, bald man says, "May I help you?" Later Michael Ayoob asks, "Where're you headed?"

"Quincy."

"Why go there?"

"To see it. Something wrong with Quincy?"

"They get everything."

"Like what?"

"Like business."

The topic drifts to gold. Ayoob says, "There's a new mine some people want to start up near Bucks Lake. Hire twenty men. I hope it goes through." With a customer who is dissecting a handgun on the sporting goods counter, he debates the validity of lode claims versus placer claims when both are declared for one site.

South of Greenville, I pass the Louisiana Pacific sawmill at Crescent Mills, where sullen pickets stand guard. A sign says, "Strike Headquarters LPIW." That is the Lumber Production and Industrial Workers Union. A yearlong strike is coming to a conclusion that might have been expected in the mid-eighties: the employees are losing their jobs.

The TV series "Bonanza" was filmed near Lake Tahoe, but Taylorsville would have been a more authentic site. It is southeast of Crescent Mills, and cattle, not logs, seem to be the economic staple. At the tavern, three horses are tied in front of three men who sit on a bench and drink.

A half mile beyond is Indian Creek and a swimming hole that draws hundreds during the rodeo—the event of the year, held across the road. This stream and the North Fork of the Feather are the northernmost Sierra waterways, both dammed near their sources. Above here, Indian Creek flows past Grizzly Peak—a roadless area that local people proposed for wilderness protection. The Plumas National Forest and the Tahoe Forest are the only national forests

in the Sierra without designated wilderness areas. That will change
if the California Wilderness Bill passes this year. It includes new
wilderness areas in all eight Sierra Nevada national forests.

Below Taylorsville, Indian Creek enters a gorge 1,000 feet deep.
At Indian Falls I bushwhack, slide, grab oak limbs, and dance around
poison oak, not always successfully. At the twelve-foot falls, truck-
sized rocks decorate the shores, and fir and pine rise on the steep
canyon sides. Today it is eighty degrees, so I jump into a pool scoured
deep by the falls. It's Saturday, and four teenagers arrive with beach
blankets and a radio.

Instead of the luster of a granite-rimmed pool in the southern
Sierra, this place has the rural flavor of a country swimming hole.
Indian Creek is typical of the north: streams, lakes, and mountains
make an outdoor paradise for people living here, yet most of the
attractions do not draw tourists. North of Lake Tahoe, the highest
mountain in the Sierra is Lola, only 9,143 feet. Most are much
lower. Here are no national parks, no large ski resorts. Fishing and
hunting—not skiing, hiking, or whitewater boating—are the prime
recreation activities. John Muir wrote little about the north, his
most memorable passage describing a windblown experience near
the Yuba River, where he climbed a tree to enjoy "the passionate
music of the storm."

The north is omitted from Sierra hype and lore, but here is the
Feather River, carrying nearly twice the volume of the next largest
river in the Sierra. The superlative Feather is not the North Fork
but the Middle Fork. From Graeagle it drops for forty miles in one
of the least penetrable and most spectacular canyons in America.
Rough as a washboard, a dirt road reaches the river at Milsap Bar,
and below there the water cuts 1,000 feet deep into Bald Rock Canyon. Blizzards of whitewater scour bars of rocks the size of medicine
balls, red, gray, black, and white. The Fall River, a tributary, plunges
over 640-foot-high Feather Falls, sixth highest in forty-nine states.

The Middle Fork was a landmark in American river conservation. In 1968, Congress designated it as one of seven initial national
wild and scenic rivers, stopping dams that had been proposed and
prohibiting federal permits for other harmful projects. Also in the
Sierra, part of the North Fork of the American was later added to
the national rivers system. This year, the nation's greatest current
struggle for a river rages on the Tuolumne River, which will be
dammed if it is not added to the wild and scenic rivers system. If
the Tuolumne is not saved this year, two dams will be built.

In spite of the wild and scenic river designation on the Feather's
Middle Fork, the Plumas National Forest supervisor issued a gold
mining permit for Continental Quicksilver Inc., from Arizona, to

dredge a mile-long belt of gravel above Milsap Bar. The supervisor said that the project was not "controversial enough" to warrant an environmental impact statement. The Northern California Flyfishers and Friends of the River appealed and halted the dredging. In 1981, the chief of the Forest Service rejected the miners' application because of doubts about the "validity" of the claim.

The gold pan and miner's pick are symbolic of early California, though most miners worked not in the mountains but in the western foothills through the Mother Lode—a 100-mile-long belt of rock, rich in gold, near the 1,000-foot elevation. New proposals, however, involve several open-pit mines in higher country, including a site near Greenville. With equipment suitable for strip-mining coal in Kentucky, miners would dig the ore, then separate the gold with the use of mercury. Unavoidable by-products are tailings piles and ponds where waste would theoretically be contained.

Even when gold brought $900 an ounce, the real treasure of the Sierra was not that soft yellow metal useful for tooth fillings and jewelry and little else. All of the bullion originating in California is trivial compared with the runoff from these mountains. Millions of people know nothing of the Feather River yet depend on it daily— 2 million acre-feet of water a year are channeled from here to California's thirsty southern empire, part of which would otherwise shrivel to dust. (One acre-foot equals 325,900 gallons, enough for a family of five for a year.) The Feather River delivery system is the centerpiece of the nation's largest state water project, in which Oroville Dam, at 770 feet the tallest American dam, stores water before it is shunted 600 miles south. Northern Californians opposed the approval of bonds for a project so lopsidedly beneficial to Southern California. *San Francisco Chronicle* editors called the plan for twenty-one reservoirs "The Water Hoax." But the majority of Californians live in the south, and in 1960, voters approved $1.75 billion—at that time the largest bond issue of its kind.

Feather River water is piped to Napa, Solano, Alameda, and Santa Clara counties, but most flows through the California Aqueduct to the San Joaquin Valley, then to the Los Angeles area after 3,300 feet of lifting by pumps that draw more electricity than any other consumer in the state. Hydroelectricity provides some of this energy; at Oroville an underground plant is large enough for the state capitol building. Other parts of the State Water Project are Davis, Frenchman, and Antelope reservoirs, which flood Sierra streams for recreation and for fish and wildlife "enhancement."

While the Middle Fork is mostly inaccessible and dammed only at its lower end, the North Fork canyon was used for the Western Pacific Railroad in 1903 and for Highway 70. PG&E owns dams from Almanor down and calls the North Fork of the Feather "one of America's major sources of hydroelectric power." Counting reservoirs on tributaries, the system can produce 719,800 kilowatts at nine plants. The U.S. Fish and Wildlife Service recommended that a minimum of 600 cubic feet per second be left in the river for fish, but the state required only 50 to 75 cubic feet per second (roughly the size of a stream twenty feet wide). Even these token requirements were often not met. Salmon had been blocked by the dams, then trout populations were decimated by the low flows and warm water resulting from the dams.

The North Fork story is a common one. Urban and agricultural Californians have adopted entire Sierra basins as resource colonies: cities on the east side of San Francisco Bay dammed the Mokelumne twice and want to dam it again; San Francisco dammed the Tuolumne; Los Angeles diverted the Owens River and streams that had nourished Mono Lake; PG&E operates dozens of dams; and county irrigation districts and water districts have dozens more. No major river and few minor ones flow unchecked. Largest of all developments is the federal Bureau of Reclamation's Central Valley Project, including New Melones Dam on the Stanislaus—625 feet high and one of the most intensively fought dams in history. At the American River, the Bureau still proposes Auburn Dam at a site that became a symbol of the limits to big water projects. I will hear many stories about many rivers between here and the Mojave Desert, but at this northernmost waterway of the Sierra, the two forks of the Feather show both the protection and the exploitation of mountain resources.

Even from Highway 70's approach to town, I know that Quincy is different. The Ford dealership and a few other businesses were built in the meadow, but otherwise, Quincy appears compact. The town is shaped like a squashed circle; on one side, fields with cattle; on the other side, green mountains. The courthouse,with its pillars and fortresslike door, dominates the center; a lawn and maple trees surround the building. Small shops line the main street. In this town I can walk from store to store, from home to school. Seasoned by the years, houses are two stories and frame, some roofs are tin, and they remind me of New England. So does the three-story wooden schoolhouse, recycled for offices. At the movies I pay $2.75 for a short, a cartoon, three previews, and the feature. Popcorn is unsalted, but smoking is allowed. There are no traffic lights in all of Quincy, and, for that matter, in all of Plumas County.

What do people do? Countywide, 900 work with lumber and wood products, 900 with retail trade, and 1,850 with government. Fifty work in agriculture. Here in Quincy the proportion of retail trade and government are higher than in the rest of the county.

From bulletin boards I learn that a Reno Philharmonic quartet will play in the High Sierra Motors Showroom. The Morning Thunder Cafe will host an "evening of short films." Preschool, child care, senior citizen socials, timber harvesting plans, parenting classes, quilt shows, and environmental reports for subdivisions are announced. Fiddlers will compete on July 7.

In all the Sierra (in this book my boundary excludes the foothills and the low-elevation Gold Rush towns, such as Nevada City, Placerville, and Angels Camp), Quincy looks like the most traditional small town, though it has attracted untraditional people.

When Wayne Dakan steps out of his twelve-year-old van on this Sunday morning, I know I have come to the right place. On the telephone he described himself as "an old man with a beard." That he is, wearing denim overalls from many campaigns, a flat-brimmed straw hat, and boots broken in perhaps during Eisenhower's presidency. I cross Highway 70 to meet him, and his first words are, "Don't get yourself run over now."

Like a prospector, he has trimmed his gray beard, which covers up enough face to accentuate the twinkle in his eye. Wrinkles signify plenty of experience. His mostly bald head is not revealed until much later; the straw hat may as well be glued on. "Tell you what now," he offers, even this first direction carrying the touch of the raconteur, "you just follow me." I get in my van and follow him.

We pass homes and industrial shops of East Quincy, we pass a sawmill, and we turn onto a flat with scattered houses. One is much smaller than the others. We park. Two men in their thirties, Jeff and Curt, sit on lawn chairs where Wayne left them in the diminutive shade of the house. They are planning an Earth Day celebration for next April, and they came to consult with the old-timer.

The twenty-by-fifteen-foot, shingle-clad home was fashioned around a veteran travel trailer. Wayne says he will show me around, so I step inside. The first thing I encounter is a microscope, standing on a table as ready as a television. Books cover one wall. Fat volumes on botany dominate. A paperback copy of *Extinction* sits on a wooden box.

Water is heated out back on a solar unit that Wayne built. He also made a solar oven, which "isn't quite hot enough to bake bread." Wayne never owned a TV but says he has a place for one: "Right there." He points to his home's foundation, where a hole has been plucked out to gain access to a clogged toilet drain, which Jeff may unplug after formulating a strategy for Earth Day.

Wayne hauls out folding chairs and seats me by Jeff and Curt, starts our conversation, then steps indoors with a slam of the screen door. He returns with a frosty quart of Stroh's. After we pass glasses around and divide the quart, Wayne deposits the empty in his recycling bin.

He was a botanist but also a railroad worker, a gold miner but a philosopher, a fugitive from convention but a disciple of cooperation bordering that of a commune. He was a nomad who roamed the country but a man with roots fifty years deep in the Sierra.

"Yes, this is home," Wayne says. I ask how he got to know the place. "Know it? Ha. Listen now. These mountains, you never really know them. After fifty years, I'm still finding stuff. New plants, though I thought I'd seen 'em all. You go up a little higher and it's a different place. Different season—why, it's another world."

The old man is outraged by what he has seen. "On the North Fork of the Feather you were allowed to catch ten pounds of fish. That all disappeared with the power plants and Oroville Dam. If you catch a fish, you don't dare eat it because of PCBs." Landslides demolished a PG&E power plant at Caribou, and toxic chemicals were washed downstream. Presumably they are not poisoning the Los Angeles water supply at the other end of the river.

Wayne does what he can and stirs up a good bit of trouble. From the wastewater ponds of a sawmill, he filled two bottles with the odd-smelling, colorful water. At the next county supervisors meeting, he set the samples down on the table and asked, "What are you going to do about *that?*" It is uncertain what the supervisors did, but Wayne says that the company's response was clear. "They built a five-foot-high chain link fence around the ponds to keep me out.

"We're like a bull in a china shop. The fisheries are gone, and the timber is almost gone. Look at that woods." Wayne casts a weathered hand at the hillside. "Those trees are nothing compared to what we had. Scalpin' a hill like that is scrapin' the bottom of the barrel. They're not only taking timber but the land, too."

Wayne elaborates little about his earlier life, dismissing his stories as those of an old man, but I learn that he was born in 1911 on the plains of Nebraska and grew up on dry farmland near Pendleton, Oregon. His mother and father each had three children by earlier marriages, then they had four more. "Too many," Wayne says. "I decided to never have children and to never get married." He pauses. The twinkle in his eye is relit. "Just took honeymoons." However, as we talk, Wayne refers with pride to his "kids," whom he says I should meet.

"It was a day-long horseback ride to the Columbia River," Wayne recalls of his childhood. "At Celilo Falls, there I'd stand on the

Oregon side of the river, not an instant I didn't see a salmon swimming upstream. Ah, it was something. It was a sight. Then they built all those dams and killed that. Through the last generation we've added a billion new people to the earth and they're hungry, but on the Columbia we eliminated one of the greatest sources of food: the salmon. Not only the Columbia. The Feather, too."

When the Depression came, twenty-year-old Wayne went "on the tramp" with tens of thousands of men and wintered in the Central Valley of California. I ask if it was like Steinbeck's *The Grapes of Wrath*. "Ah, it was here, it was here.

"Carl Malone was an old Wobbly [the International Workers of the World, or IWW]. They trained me, the Wobblies did. It was the depth of the Depression, but we did fine. We didn't need much." A farmer hired Wayne and in three weeks left him in charge while the family camped in Yosemite. (Vacationers increased sharply at Yosemite throughout the Depression.) Wayne could have stayed on the farm. For that matter, he could have stayed on the family farm in Oregon, but always he moved on.

Why catch another freight? "To see it," Wayne says. "It's the way young people are. They want to see the country. Now they go to Mexico. It was fun." The old eyes look out at the hillside of ponderosa pine, they look beyond to a high ridge of the Sierra Nevada, and they look back at me. Wayne answers my question: "We were always looking for something better. We never found it, but we kept looking anyway."

A friend told Wayne, "Head on up to Quincy," so he caught the Western Pacific (now the Union Pacific) in the spring of 1936, jumped off at Keddie, walked six miles to town, and said, "This is the place." Wayne survived the late thirties by mining. "I know more places where there's no gold than anyone in this county, but I found some. I scraped up a living for a few years."

After the war, Wayne was a signal maintainer on the Western Pacific Railroad for twenty years and lived in a boxcar apartment. He looks back on the job as an extended travel privilege. "I got my transportation from Oakland to Salt Lake City on those two streaks of rust." When the train stopped, Wayne "botanized." This avocation has lasted forty years so far with no sign of letup. Why botany? "I wanted to know what these plants were, and nobody could tell me."

Wayne has compiled a list of Plumas County vascular plants for the Forest Service. "You might want to see a little bit of what grows around here," he suggests. Later in the week, he will show me the unusual plant life of Butterfly Valley.

"I think we ought to go over to Morning Thunder and get some lunch," Wayne says. "There are some people I'd like you to meet."

We climb into my van but don't go far. At a bridge in a pasture Wayne calls out, "Stop here." The water underneath is stagnant.

"See that? When the limit was twenty trout, you could catch 'em right here. Ah God, you could live on 'em. Now all you can catch is an old rubber boot. When they cut the forests, they ruined the watershed. The soil, it's gone. Washed away when the roots of the trees rotted. May as well have hauled it away on trucks and dumped it in the Feather River. No sooner it rains than the water flashes off the hillsides. Any water that's left, they divert to irrigate pasture, suck out every last drop and overgraze until there's nothing left, until the ground is trampled, packed down. It's a sad thing if you know what it used to be.

"What you see here, this won't last. Greece used to be 60 percent trees, now it's 15 percent trees; the rest is like desert. We're headed down that road. Right here, right now, we have to turn a corner, but I don't know if we ever will."

In the shade of a sugar maple I park, and we walk two blocks to Morning Thunder. Three black kids speed past on bicycles and wave at Wayne. Here in Plumas County black people comprise 1.7 percent of the population. Through most of the Sierra, they comprise zero. "The sawmills brought 'em in thirty years ago for cheap labor. From Louisiana. Good folks, been here longer'n most." We speak to the photographer Philip Hyde, who lives nearby.

When we approach the restaurant—an old building with a wooden veneer like many of California's "natural" food cafes—two people on the porch yell, "Hey Wayne," and he answers, "Well well well. You kids learning anything?" To me, he says, "Some of my youngest kids." They are students of Mike Yost, a forestry teacher at Feather River College. "Mike brings all his students out to meet me. Mike, he's a good boy. This college, it's been a wonderful thing for us up here in the boondocks."

We step inside, into new realizations. Wayne is known by all. He says, "There's Lew."

"Reverend Dakan," Lew Persons says, as he slides over in the booth. Morning Thunder is the community center, and in the next hour, our table will become the hotbed of environmental activism. Lew's love is kayaking, but he works for a local utility company advising people about saving electricity. "I'm lucky. I get paid to do work that I believe in."

Rose, our waitress, has a direct and peaceful eye to customers. Her hair is pulled back; she wears a long skirt and Birkenstock sandals. She studied art, then took the Morning Thunder job because it was how she could live in Quincy. "The job is part-time, there's social contact, it fits my life-style, and I don't take it home with me."

A bearded, heavyset man enters. "Ah, there's Michael. Hey Michael, I'd like you to meet a friend." The bearlike man looks familiar. His face is on a poster. He is running for county supervisor. Michael Jackson and his dark-eyed, five-year-old daughter Julie sit down.

People talk politics. "Michael, he's going to make it," Wayne says and winks. Michael won the most votes in the primary, though he is a harsh critic of unplanned growth, the spokesman for new wilderness designations, and a newcomer—this in a Republican town where logging has been an economic mainstay for three generations.

"The old guard has controlled local politics since the old guard was young," Michael says. "This town is run by the Rotary Club." He clarifies, "It's run by five men, and two of them are the judge and the newspaper editor. My campaign, it's run by a bunch of women. There's a strong populist movement; people are beginning to see the connections between the despoiling of human resources and of natural resources. Even the redneck element sees the idea of fighting the state senator, Rotary Club, and chamber of commerce as something that's not all bad. I'm just an old redneck myself. If they don't think you're bird-watchers, there's a real affinity between loggers and the new environmentalists."

Michael sips the strong, fresh-ground Thunder coffee. "A change has happened up here. A thirty-five-year-old logger wants to know if he'll have a job in twenty years. He wonders what his kids will do. Many people see the timber industry for what it is: the dying gasp of a bygone era. 'What next?' they ask. The biomass fiasco taught us all a lot. It brought us together."

A corporation from Southern California prepared to build an electric power plant fueled by trees. I can see the appeal—all that sawdust, bark, and scrap from the two mills, when they operate— but Wayne says, "Scrap wouldn't begin to cover what they'd need. They'd burn everything."

Michael says, "County zoning restricts the height of a structure, and that was the only apparent snag for them—they had to get an exception for their smokestack. But the thing that really turned it around was the threat of an initiative to ban the plant." The environmentalists collected 2,000 signatures, far more than half the voters.

With pride Wayne says, "Usually you need money to fight that stuff, but we just have people."

The corporation wanted to straighten residents out on this, so it called a public meeting. After a cordial reception and a description probably designed by public relations specialists, old Wayne stood up, respectfully removed his hat for rare exposure of his bald head, and spoke: "That's very good, and I thank you for clearin' up some misunderstandin's. But seems to me what you have is a siting problem, and I think I can help you out." After the raconteur's pause, he added, "I say put it on the back side of the moon." This broke the ice, and a flood of opinion washed over the night.

Toward the end, a drunken logger who had arrived late stood up and slurred a testimony intended as three words: "Biomassmyass." Other than an alliance with a drunk, I still don't see how the biomass proposal brought loggers and environmentalists together.

Michael explains, "Right now there are seventy men in Plumas County cutting firewood for a living, hauling truckloads to Tahoe. With the biomass plant, someone else'd be in there cutting and chopping down all that fuel for a Southern California corporation."

Wayne adds, "This ponderosa pine makes wonderful sawlogs—yellow pine they call it at the lumberyard—but who would ever see a tree that big again? Loggers who now cut timber would be replaced by mowing machines that strip young trees and anything that grows." One of those seventeen-ton biomass harvesters can cut an eight-foot swath and is called Jaws 3.

Here is Mike Yost, the forestry teacher, and our conversation speeds off in tangents dealing with forestry, soils, education, and kids today. Other people arrive.

After an hour, Lew and several friends return with us to the tiny house, where the temperature has climbed five degrees. Wayne's remedy is Stroh's. We line up in a row, sitting with our backs to the wall because the house isn't tall enough to throw a midday shadow large enough for a more social arrangement. Michael and Julie arrive.

Here at this humble home, the talk is of the mountains. A whole community of people seems to be based on the saving of this place. Lew notices the distant haze. Wayne says, "Smog—you can cut it with a knife. Didn't used to be here. Started, I'd say, 'bout seventy."

Seeking a new home, Lew moved here from Davis five years ago. His perspective is born of urban California, youth, and, I would say, innate hopefulness. "It's not as bad as Wayne makes out. There's still a lot of good stuff in this part of the country." Here is a pattern: new immigrants see the good—they see the ways in which their adopted land is better than the place they fled, while the old immigrants remember how much better it used to be, and so they are not able to shake the loss of the Good Life.

Lew says, "Where else in the Sierra have local people turned down a biomass plant, turned around a county growth plan, and stopped the Forest Service from spraying herbicides? Now we're going to keep the county from damming Indian Creek."

A dam would be built above Indian Falls and water ditched for two miles to make eleven megawatts of electricity. The Friends of Indian Creek plan to pick up where the biomass opposition left off. The dam is proposed by the Plumas County supervisors, though its own planning commission classified Indian Creek Canyon as an outstanding scenic area. Michael attacks the supervisors' role as "a socialistic endeavor interfering with private enterprise; the government's meddling at taxpayer expense in the provision of services best provided through entrepreneurial means."

Wayne says, "Makin' power isn't the county's job." The old man leans back, hands folded at his belly. "Ah, my kids, they're doing fine." He reaches for his Stroh's, sips, turns to me, and winks.

Little Julie has exhausted Michael's list of things for her to do and approaches him with unprecedented resolve. "Dad, I'm getting out of here, and I mean *now.*" I admit, the stories and the Stroh's can go on only so long. What do you do on a hot Sunday afternoon in Quincy? Go to Spanish Creek and jump in.

Our caravan is an odd one of bicycles, a compact car with a dented trunk, and a rusty pickup—a singular group rattling at various speeds toward a common goal. I can see it all from my bicycle in the back, and I think: since John Muir, people have sought to protect the Sierra, but that effort has come mainly from the outside. Muir lived in Martinez for most of his career. The Sierra Club was formed by twenty-seven San Francisco Bay Area residents, such as William Keith, an urban artist, and Warren Olney, a lawyer. David Brower and Richard Leonard, leaders in mountain protection for half a century, live in Berkeley. Those people did not live in the mountains, though their concern was what saved many places that I will see. To those people, the Sierra offered enjoyment and a spiritual value; they wanted to let the mountains be. On the other side were people who saw an empty land that promised money if wealth were extracted. Included were the leaders of Los Angeles, San Francisco, Louisiana Pacific, Disney Enterprises, and agribusinesses. Both groups battling for the Sierra were from beyond the mountains. But Wayne and his kids are living here. Their movement is from within. Michael says, "This isn't my playground; this is my *home.* Well, it's both."

"In the past," said Steve Allen, of the county planning staff, "environmental protection was imposed by the state and federal governments. Now it's something that the people want to do. Ten years ago when we changed the zoning, people said it was too restrictive. Now we're changing it again, and people say it's not restrictive enough."

Although much of the Sierra is too devoid of people to ignite a good flame of cultural conflict, Quincy is a microcosm of California in this sense: it houses the extremes. Michael says, "Imagine Selma, Alabama, in 1956 meeting Berkeley, California, in 1969." Here the liberal meets the redneck, the newcomer meets the old guard.

In the race for county supervisor, Jim Gossett opposes Michael Jackson. Formerly the owner of High Sierra Motors—the Ford/Mercury garage just outside town—Gossett was born in Hot Springs, Arkansas, where his father filed saws in a lumber mill. When the logs were gone, it was time to move on, and the Gossetts came to Quincy when Jim was in seventh grade. That was during the 1940s, when large trees abounded in the Sierra, when loggers cut pine and fir feverishly to feed the postwar boom.

Jim entered the car business in 1954. Today he is in his late fifties, tan and handsome. We meet in the High Sierra showroom where he must frequently answer the telephone—I think he is covering for someone who is on lunch break—but after each call, he shows no stress from the interruption and casually, skillfully returns to the subjects of our talk. I ask him what the big issues are in Quincy.

Gossett does not hesitate: "Of course, the economy. We're coming off a recession, especially in the lumber industry." The Louisiana Pacific and Sierra Pacific mills were both closed because of labor disputes and slumping demand. "Now they've reopened, but that's still one of the biggest issues. We can't expect any big new industries; there's a heating problem in winter, and the work force isn't large. Some small, clean industries would be good.

"Of course, there's the environment, too. People who have been here a long time just want to live in the mountains. They like it. And the people who've come here, they're even more adamantly against anything that's going to change the place."

Jim Gossett opposes the biomass plant, but that is where agreement with the environmentalists ends. "Of course, I'm a businessman, and I always hoped to see some growth. I'm against wilderness proposals. The Forest Service already says that they won't log on about 5,000 acres near Bucks Lake. They just got the other wilderness of 45,000 acres through on the Middle Fork of the Feather." (He apparently refers to national wild and scenic river status granted by Congress in 1968.) "I'd say that without new wilderness areas, there are all kinds of places to go hiking." He favors the Indian Creek hydroelectric project. "If we don't do it, someone else will. It can be done without harming the environment. I don't think a development boom will ever be a problem here. We've never had to fight to keep growth away."

Of all the people I meet in Quincy, only one adult was born here, and he is different from the typical mold of native Anglos. Robert Moon's grandfather was shipped from China to work in the gold fields. One day he slipped away from camp. "There were so many Chinese, the bosses couldn't keep track of them all," Robert says. The canyon road up the Feather River did not yet exist, so Moon arrived via the old route over Spanish Peak. He bought a horse-drawn wagon and hauled food from the Central Valley to the mining camps of the upper Feather River. His family joined him, and they lived on land at Spanish Ranch, outside town, where Robert was born in 1926.

He worked in advertising near San Francisco. "Ten years in the Bay Area convinced me I was doing it all wrong. Fifty weeks there and two here is not the proper ratio." He moved back to Quincy, started an agency, and now directs the chamber of commerce.

"The largest changes started after World War II. A county population of 10,000 during the Gold Rush had dwindled to 4,600 in 1900, slowly climbed to 8,000, then jumped to 11,500 in the 1940s. The pace certainly has quickened in the last ten years. In 1970, there were 500 retail trade permits; in 1980, there were 1,000. Yet new employment opportunities are scarce. One of the big concerns is that there aren't enough jobs to keep kids here. Unemployment is high, mainly due to the cyclical nature of logging. Many other people would like to come here, but the question is, 'What am I going to do?'

"Growth versus the quality of life is the hottest political issue. Realistically, we're never going to be very large. In my lifetime we will not see drastic changes. It's not feasible, and the mood of the people is such that they'd never go for unlimited growth."

Plumas County houses 7 people per square mile. For comparison, Los Angeles has 2,000, California, 128, and Wyoming, 3.4. Gossett and Moon may be right; even with progrowth drumming for business, Quincy may not change much. But I'm not sure. The chamber of commerce's glossy brochure advertises that the area is "less than a half-day's drive from San Francisco." The county population jumped from 11,707 in 1970 to 17,365 in 1980 to 18,500 in 1983. More than 1,900 acres are zoned industrial, 80 percent of the land is vacant, and much of it is called "prime." Sixty-nine percent of the county is national forest, but this leaves about 500,000 private acres, enough to effect changes of unimaginable magnitude. Current zoning allows 150,000 people. Yearly visitors to the county number 500,000, and that could grow. "People are attracted for the mountain recreation without the crowds of Tahoe," said Steve Allen of the planning staff.

For this little town with some similarities to Appalachia and some to Shangri-la, the future is unknown.

It's time to see some land, and Wayne Dakan is going to show me. I drive to Butterfly Valley, Wayne's botanical showpiece, where he has hosted groups, including the California Native Plant Society. Much of the valley was logged but not clearcut. Rolling hills support a second growth of ponderosa, sunny clearings full of shrubs, and some large trees.

Right away we encounter an ancient Douglas fir, a giant, now rare in this area. "Look at that guy," Wayne says. "Ah, I'd certainly hate to see that one cut down. They left it as a seed tree, but then they go through a little later and cut the seed trees too. It's just another name for clearcutting, and it's bad stuff." He taps the ground with his walking stick and says, "When I'm all done, bury me at the roots of a life like that."

Our next diversion is a glade where weathered boards lie on the ground. Wayne is related to everything in this adopted homeland of his. "Here's where I spent one whole grand summer. I ranged around, botanized all over." I've heard of people having difficulties adjusting to retirement; Butterfly Valley was Wayne's solution ten summers ago. We come to a squaw plant. "The Indians ate the roots. They're small, but those people had a lot of time. They weren't making payments on any automobile."

Wayne abandons the path and tramps up the hill to a bog where pitcher plants grow. Their stems rise to knee height, then fan broadly, something like a threatening cobra. The top of the stem funnels into a tube. Insects are drawn to the opening, where they become trapped by hairs that point down to a gullet that is the base of the stem. The American pitcher plant can even eat small lizards and frogs. Later we find the sundew, two inches high, also a bug eater.

Wayne's list of Plumas County plants includes hundreds, and he knows each. He has mastered the pistils, stamens, leaf scars, and other details of taxonomy, but it's the big picture to which he constantly returns. He points at an abandoned railroad grade. "Anytime you build roads, you lose soil." The tracks had diverted the natural flow of water—a "sheet" flow across the forest floor—and caused it to gouge out a ditch. Forty years of storms have scoured deep, with no end of erosion in sight.

"Hey Wayne, why are the trees in the Sierra almost all evergreens?"

He answers, "It's not too cold for deciduous trees, but it's too dry during the summer."

Where a ponderosa pine has shaded out undergrowth, my guide

picks up a handful of soil and says, "In one teaspoon there are millions of fungi and bacteria, thousands of algae, and other stuff besides. Thousands of years of birth, life, death, fertilization go into that handful of dirt. Then, with herbicides and pesticides, it's gone." Wayne thinks that no one knows all the effects of chemical warfare against insects and shrubs. Fungal hyphae, for example, encase the root hairs of conifers and produce hormones that stimulate tree growth by absorbing minerals and making them available to the tree. "The Forest Service sprays out of helicopters, like swatting a fly with an atomic bomb." An old man with a beard is talking about clearcuts, erosion, and herbicides, and it all raises questions: What is the best way to care for these woods? What do loggers' productivity and a healthy landscape have in common?

"This is where life comes from." Wayne motions to the land around us. "If this isn't healthy, we won't be here. And we're raising hell with it; we have as much to worry about as the California condor."

There is no letup. Wayne talks about fire. "See this?" He grabs a dead limb of lodgepole pine, part of the tangled undergrowth. Cross-country travel would be an exercise in ripped clothes. "Thick as the hair on a dog's back in winter. Used to be small fires walked through the woods every now and then, cleared out the dead stuff and pruned things back a bit. Talk to Mike Yost about fire in the forest. Mike, yes, Mike is a good boy."

Wayne and I pull into the driveway at Mike's Taylorsville home. His wife, Sally, is also active in environmental and community affairs, but Mike is the expert on forestry. He says, "The biggest problem in the Sierra is the lack of fire."

That is the difficult beginning to the forester's argument—difficult because fighting nature is what our civilization has done since the Stone Age, and even among people who recognize a need to live in harmony with the earth, certain things that the earth does seem wrong. Certainly fire is one of them.

At a formative age, I was introduced to Smokey the Bear. I wanted to be a smoke jumper when I grew up. During my first week working for the Forest Service in 1969, I faced two requirements: pass a driver's test and graduate from fire school. A dream of sorts came true when I fought fires in Oregon and Idaho. Fire was the greatest enemy of the forest. Now I meet Mike Yost and learn that control of fires may be the greatest enemy and that ecology is more complicated than Bambi, running from the flames, ever led me to believe.

Mike says, "On average, every acre in the Sierra Nevada used to burn once in seven years. The forests were parklike—large trees with open areas around them."

John Muir wrote, "The inviting openness of the Sierra woods is one of their most distinguishing characteristics."

Yost continues, "Large ponderosa pine have thick bark that resists fire, and they drop their lower branches to protect the crowns from flames. Ground fires—usually caused by lightning—burned fallen needles, fallen branches, and a few young fir. Larger trees remained unharmed. In 1910, the government began putting out fires.

"The result is an incredibly inflammable understory. Even with all our efforts, we don't stop all fires, and when one starts with this kind of fuel buildup, we're looking at disaster. Fire climbs to the crowns and burns thousands of acres. The heat is so intense it incinerates the soil. Then hardly anything but manzanita will grow because the nitrogen is gone.

"We spent $2 million fighting the Babcock fire near here. Then the Elephant fire came a couple years later. The rate of these hot fires is such that within fifty years, much of the forest resource of the Sierra will be ruined for generations."

Wayne interjects, "That burned summer of '38," and points eastward to a mountain that wears scrub growth still.

"The solution," Mike says, "is prescribed burns, where the undergrowth is burned out on purpose. This would be cheaper than fighting the big fires."

In a 1959 *Sierra Club Bulletin*, H. H. Biswell called for prescribed burns of ponderosa pine. In 1963, wildlife scientist A. Starker Leopold reported to the National Park Service regarding the Sierra: "Much of the west slope is a doghair thicket, . . . a direct function of over-protection from natural ground fire." In 1968, Sequoia and Kings Canyon national parks began a program of fire management, but only a small fraction of the whole has been burned. Chief ranger Bob Smith said, "We've hardly made an inroad on 250,000 acres of woodlands." In all the national forests in the Sierra, only 34,221 out of 8.1 million acres were burned in 1982. In the Stanislaus National Forest of nearly 900,000 acres, an average of 3,500 acres are burned annually in prescribed fires.

Even after twenty-five years of scientific study, acceptance of controlled burns is difficult. One old ranger snapped at Mike Yost, "I didn't *study* fires, I *fought* them." But the American Society of Foresters supports controlled burns. Yost says that the general public's attitude against fire is the main reason that more acres are not burned.

Fire is Mike's specialty, but he says, "There are many issues, and they're all connected. Look at clearcutting." This is where all trees in an area are cut. It is the common way to achieve "even-aged management," meaning that trees of the same age are grown on one tract. One alternative to clearcutting is select cutting, where only mature trees are taken, with the rest left to grow in uneven-aged management.

The Forest Service has its reasons for clearcutting, but none of my friends in Quincy think much of them. Clearcutting depends on the killing of competing undergrowth by heavy doses of herbicides. In the Sierra in 1983, the Forest Service sprayed 15,000 acres with 37,400 pounds of herbicides or pesticides; uncounted acres of private land were also sprayed. A temporary ban is now in effect while a court-imposed environmental statement is written, but the Stanislaus National Forest reported, "The use of pesticides on the Stanislaus Forest is expected to increase substantially in the future. Increased use of pesticides, primarily herbicides for vegetation management but including rodenticides, insecticides, and fungicides—will probably generate some public controversy."

The issues of forest management are complex beyond the range of whole shelves of books, beyond the forestry profession's experience since that imperfect, emotion-filled science was introduced to the country by Gifford Pinchot in the late 1800s. Regarding clearcutting, I talked to three other people.

Gordon Robinson began working as a chief forester for the Southern Pacific Land Company, California's largest private landowner, in 1939. He managed 2 million acres for maximum timber production and saw that plenty of trees were cut. When he was fifty-five his wife said, "Gordon, it's time to do what you really want to do." For the next twelve years he worked as the forestry specialist for the Sierra Club. Now he is retired, white-haired, impulsive, animated, prone to laugh loudly but at other times to fall silent in thought. He talked about regeneration.

"Once they clearcut, it's often too hot to get any trees to come back. Southwestern slopes fry in the sun. I don't know of a successful reforestation of red fir following a clearcut." This is the dominant tree on many high Sierra slopes. "The Forest Service plants pine. They want to convert to species bringing the most money to industry.

"Openings are needed for sunlight, but they use that as justification to mow hundreds of acres. They can make shelterwood cuts for small openings. No one has to cut the whole outdoors to get the trees to grow."

Robinson claimed a litany of ills from clearcuts: erosion speeds up, some research showing a fiftyfold increase lasting for one to ten years until new trees take hold. Nutrients are washed to sea hundreds of thousands of times faster than they are formed. Wildlife needs dead or hollow trees and combinations of shelter and small openings. Woodland soils, which are thirty times more porous than many open-land soils, are compacted by clearcutting, and recovery may require three to ten years, if it occurs at all. "This," Robinson says, "when the Multiple Use–Sustained Yield Act of 1964 calls for harvesting without impairment of the productivity of the land." The National Forest Management Act of 1976 also requires that timber be cut only where it can be restocked within five years. Citing a Forest Service study, Robinson says that the difference in cost between clearcutting and select cutting in 1976 was $1 per thousand board feet—negligible, considering that bids ran $150 and more per thousand board feet (he says that in the mid-eighties the difference is about the same, although the bids are much higher).

Many of the clearcuts are at steep sites where logs are pulled out by cables instead of bulldozers. The cables do result in less erosion than bulldozed roads, but Robinson says that the angle of repose (the steepest angle at which soil will stabilize and not slide down) is less after the trees are cut and the roots begin to rot. "We'll be seeing serious erosion for many years after those areas are cut." Robinson's advice for steep slopes: let them be. "If a slope is so steep that they need cables, it shouldn't be logged at all."

In Quincy, where Bob Jesen is in charge of planning for the Plumas National Forest, I hear another view. "Timber harvesting is probably more important on this national forest than on any other in the Sierra. We still have a large inventory of old growth." The average yearly cut on the Plumas Forest is 250 million board feet, enough to cover as much as 10,000 acres or fill 37,500 logging trucks. Some local municipalities favor increased cutting because 25 percent of the Forest Service's revenues are returned to local counties. According to the Forest Service publication *Facts about the National Forests in California,* about half of the $168 million in Forest Service receipts statewide are for timber and forest product sales.

I asked what major changes will occur with the Forest Service's new management plans, required by the National Forest Management Act. "One of the largest changes will be more clearcutting." Most of the remaining big trees are on steep slopes and are hauled out by cables. "With cable systems, you may as well clearcut because you damage everything anyway when you pull the logs up. Another reason is that some trees can grow in the shade and some can't. Firs do well, but sugar and ponderosa pine need sunlight. If we select cut, we end up with a white fir forest, and most people feel that a mixed conifer forest is superior." The Stanislaus National Forest *Planning News* calls clearcutting "the most successful and economical harvest method for most conifer species."

I asked Zane Smith, regional forester in charge of all the national forests of California, why do plans call for more clearcutting? "The principal reason is silvicultural. In the Sierra Nevada, we practiced what appeared to be uneven-aged management, but it wasn't. We removed certain trees, but only shade-tolerant trees came up. Not much was growing underneath the trees that we left, so we may as well cut it all at once."

Another reason is "national priorities." Smith said, "We have goals for timber production, and we attempt to meet those goals. That drives us to using the commercial forest largely for commercial purposes."

A forester's professional performance and promotion are based in part on meeting quotas of timber to be cut. The goal for the national forests of California was 2.1 billion board feet per year. Smith was successful in lowering that to 1.9. He said, "I'm listening to people in California, and they're saying, 'We want more natural landscape and more wilderness.'" However, the goal still represents an increase over the current rate of cutting—about 1.7 billion board feet. "The board-foot targets are a terribly powerful thing affecting every one of us," Smith said. "A forest supervisor knows he is expected to make his or her target. But nothing in our charter gives license to break our land ethic. Some foresters don't make the case for less cutting, or they make it poorly, and that's just as bad as not meeting the production quota."

Throughout the Sierra, the volume of timber under contract for cutting has climbed from 2.4 billion board feet in 1979 to 3.3 billion in 1983, even though many of the sales do not earn a profit. Under the "residual pricing system," timber is often sold even when the income is inadequate to cover administration of the sales. Deputy Regional Forester Bob Cermak reported that in 1979 about 10 percent of the California sales were deficit, an amount that grew to 57 percent in 1980.

Gordon Robinson would like to see a total reorientation of timber management. "The central problem is a deliberate manipulation of 'multiple use' to the timber industry's benefit. Where they clearcut, the land is lost to all other uses. That is not multiple use. Uses of the forest should be integrated; timber management should accommodate wildlife, recreation, and watershed protection."

Zane Smith said, "In multiple use there is a range of choices, and, yes, we're often on the dominant use side, especially regarding timber and wilderness. We are polarized into two groups: those who are preservationist and those who are development-oriented. Our policies sometimes tend to polarize people. I believe that in the future we will move toward uses that accommodate other uses more effectively."

Robinson is not happy with the environmentalists' strategy either. "Conservationists abandoned goals for overall timber management. They tried for policy reforms in the early 1970s but failed. They dropped those reforms in order to get more wilderness acreage. It's easier to get wilderness designated than to get good overall management, and one reason is that if you understand all this double-talk on management, you're probably employed by someone who doesn't allow you to talk." Robinson says that wilderness is fine, but it's not enough. "If we don't have improved management on the national forests, they'll be ripped off, and we'll see irresistible pressure to cut in the national parks and wilderness areas by the turn of the century."

I enter Morning Thunder for one last lunch before leaving Quincy. As soon as Rose, in her exquisite calm, delivers a menu, Wayne ambles in. Then Mike, the forester. Then Lew, the kayaker. Then Michael, the candidate. The table is full, and here we go again. But it's different today.

Confidence fills the air. These men are bright-eyed and expectant. Senators Pete Wilson and Alan Cranston announced a compromise to the California Wilderness Bill that would designate 1.8 million acres of new national forest wilderness statewide, and included is the Bucks Lake tract—the only large roadless area remaining in the Plumas National Forest.

The California Wilderness Bill has been debated since 1979, and people such as Russell Shay of the Sierra Club have lobbied constantly. With both senators' support, the bill may pass, and if it does, it will be the largest addition ever to the wilderness system, except for Alaska. The bill will be important from here to the southernmost miles of my journey.

Wayne says, "We're winning 'em all. We're going to turn the corner yet." These people have a sense of belonging that's contagious. Already I feel that this place is home. "We stopped 'em at biomass. Now we're getting Bucks Lake. When the vultures watching over your civilization get sick and die, it's time to reconsider a few things, and maybe we're doing that now."

While the others are reminiscing about Bucks Lake and already plotting something new, the old man sits and tips his straw hat back. "Ah, yes. All my kids. That's where there's hope. If only we have enough time."

For Quincy, I've run out of time. There is much more to see, and only four months until the snows come again. I camp at Silver Lake, whose level was raised in 1870 to supply water to hydraulic mines along Spanish Creek. Then I drive to Bucks Lake, a PG&E reservoir built in 1929. I canoe to the northern shore and hike into the proposed wilderness area. Nineteen thousand acres will be protected if the California Wilderness Bill passes. Gray boulders mark the first large outcrops of Sierra granite I have seen. I camp at the Bucks Creek campground, and even though it's Friday, only two sites are used.

Among the eight national forests in the Sierra, Plumas ranks third in size but seventh in amount of recreation use. Much of this is by hunters, who visit Plumas the most.

Southward. Graeagle is a historic village where families picnic at a small reservoir. Southwest of Graeagle is the village of La Porte, where Snow Shoe Sally was the first horse known to wear snowshoes. Brochures claim that the world's first competitive skiing took place here in 1867, when men on twelve-foot-long boards clocked eighty miles per hour.

To the south the mountains rise higher, as they will for 150 miles. The Sierra is not the only range to rise at its southern reaches. The Appalachians' highest peak is Mount Mitchell in North Carolina. The Rockies reach their height in Colorado, where Mount Elbert is the second highest peak in forty-nine states.

It is not just elevation that increases as I travel south. Forget the old maxim of Jack London tales that wilderness lies north. That is true of the Rockies, true of the Cascades, true of the Coast Ranges, but it is not true here. The Sierra is wilder to the south, though the change occurs with some glaring interruptions.

I drive past the Lakes Basin of fifty lakes, and as I shift to low gear on a hill spiked with stunted fir, the Sierra Buttes abruptly fill my eyes. If the green fields, dammed creeks, and logging towns have left doubt about the geologic map's revelation that I'm in the Sierra, the question now melts like snow in this month of June. The Buttes point 1,000 feet skyward to 8,587 feet.

I've seen some detail; now I scramble up to see landmarks from far away. My Sierra exploration will repeat this pattern: look close, then climb high for the big view. Each craggy outlook is a reward, each an epilogue. Each, except the last, is also an enticement, a window to unknown lands ahead.

The slopes are saturated with color. I look at my flower guide and find three kinds of Indian paintbrush. Mule ears and arrowhead balsamroot dominate—showy yellow composites. To the north flows the trout water of Salmon Creek; to the south, beneath folds of green, the Yuba's North Fork. In its lower reaches the Yuba yielded more gold than any other river in the United States, but hydraulic mining washed silt downstream and raised the river bed as much as a hundred feet. Central Valley farmers rallied against hydraulic mining, prohibited in 1884 under one of California's first laws for the protection of the environment.

Among river basins in the Sierra, the Yuba is the third largest in volume of water, though eighth largest in basin acreage. Oakland—125 miles away—began using electricity from a Yuba dam in 1899.

At the top of the metamorphic buttes, a fire tower stands locked and empty. In one sweeping view, I can see the northern Sierra. Beyond the first ridge lies the Middle Fork of the Feather, hidden in its canyon, but at its headwaters I spot Beckwourth Pass, 5,212 feet, the lowest and northernmost Sierra pass. James Beckwourth, whose father was a Revolutionary War officer and whose mother was a black slave, became a mountain man, guided John C. Frémont, and discovered the pass in 1851. He spent $1,600 building a trail, hoping for support from businessmen in Marysville, but he recovered little and lamented, "Those who derive advantage from this outlay . . . devote no thought to the discoverer."

Until now it had escaped me, but like an apparition, Lassen floats in the far, faraway view. Seventy miles away, the mountain seems not to rise from the earth but to hang from the sky. I see nothing but its snow, reflecting the morning light. It is an ethereal volcano; the earth and sky are blended unexpectedly. The sky-dwelling mountain captures my gaze. For minutes I stare almost without blinking. The view shows how far I've come. Beneath Lassen's slopes, buried in mist or haze or smog, lies Lake Almanor, which in turn buries the meadows that are the northern beginning of the Sierra Nevada.

I look north until I am saturated, until the scene is printed for me—the distances realized, the details revealed, the hidden canyons accepted as hidden and beyond me. Still, it's difficult to turn away; beginnings are hard to leave. Just when I get comfortable, it's time to go. Quincy. But look the other way; look to the unknown. I face south. Beyond the Yuba's green canyon, I see faint ridges of the American River basin, like a watercolor. Towering beyond is the snow-covered granite of the Desolation Wilderness, the northernmost of the spectacularly glaciated Sierra.

Hand-chiseled graffiti shows that E. H. Yothers was here at the Buttes' summit in 1880, Sam Kasper in 1935. "John 81" is chiseled into the cement blocks on which the fire tower sits.

As the air is pushed up from an elevation of 50 feet in the Central Valley to 8,000 feet at the Sierra crest, it cools and cannot hold its moisture. What was invisible vapor down below becomes droplets in clouds, now billowing upward. Their rapid rise creates electrical charges that cause lightning. Will it storm? The Buttes are the lightning rod of the northern Sierra. I think that I'll be back down at a safe elevation before an afternoon thunderstorm strikes, but I don't really know when a storm might arrive. As Wayne said, no one ever really knows these mountains.

One last look toward Almanor completes my exploration of the north. Below me, some land lies in peace, some hums with conflict and controversy. In those green folds, Wayne Dakan lives out his life; Julie Jackson begins hers.

Wayne said, "You'll be back."

Although peopled, although sprinkled with small towns, the north remains isolated, a backwater, a refuge. Before the big wilderness of the southern Sierra begins, the roads will be busier, the cities nearer, the conflicts more intense.

At Almanor I began, and now I turn toward another lake, toward towns that are nothing like Chester or Quincy, toward a place that people call the Jewel of the Sierra, though it houses a culture that is perhaps the antithesis of mountain life. Where I'm going next is one of the most contested landscapes in America. I will cross Yuba Pass, turn right in the village of Sierraville, and roll down the Little Truckee valley to Lake Tahoe.

3

The Deep Blue Lake

IT IS THE SECOND DEEPEST LAKE IN THE UNITED STATES, the tenth deepest in the world. It holds more water than all other California lakes and reservoirs combined and could flood a flattened Nevada and California to a depth of eight inches. It could supply everyone in the nation with fifty gallons of water a day for five years. But the most remarkable thing about Lake Tahoe is its color—a twelve-by-twenty-two-mile eyeful of blue.

Lake Tahoe shines in the deepest, richest blue imaginable. It reflects the blue of the Sierra sky perfectly because the water, which reaches a depth of 1,685 feet, is transparent and lacking colors of its own, such as brown or green. "Lake of the Sky" is another name for this watery blue place, east of the Sierra crest, one-fourth the distance along the range from north to south, 6,229 feet above sea level. Worldwide, only one other large lake—Crater Lake in Oregon—holds water as clear as Tahoe's. In past years, a dinner plate could be seen 120 feet deep.

Lake Tahoe has been called the "gem of the Sierra" by many people and "the fairest picture the earth affords" by Mark Twain. Because of the clarity of water, he called his boat rides "balloon voyages." Seeking a timber claim to the shoreline in 1861, he built a "brush" house and joined the first generation of ravagers when his untended campfire ignited a blaze that forced him into his boat and charcoaled entire mountainsides—if what he wrote is true.

The changes people have wrought at the lake are as remarkable as the lake itself. Lake Tahoe is the most troubled place in the Sierra, the most settled, and the most visited, receiving one and a half times the tourists of the country's most popular national park (not Yosemite but Great Smoky Mountains). Any notion I picked up in the northern Sierra that the range is a frontier, a refuge, or an enclave for the counterculture halts at eighteen-story high-rises and streets lit with neon—sprawling strips carbon-copied from ugly places elsewhere. All of that will steal my attention, but first, I want to see the lake.

In the early morning calm, neither wind nor motorboats roughen the water, and through its surface—not a mirror but a window—I see the intricacies of rocks that lie deep. I want to reach down and touch them, but they are fathoms deeper than I could dive. In my canoe, which I launched at D. L. Bliss State Park on the south-western side of the lake, I'm out for my own balloon voyage.

Near shore the water is tinted a minty green. Suddenly, beyond a submerged shelf of rock, Tahoe turns so blue that it startles, bluer than anything I've ever seen. This pigment must be the original blue from which all others are derived by dabbing in white or black or yellow, by adding seaweed or pollen or silt. A few of nature's colors are extravagant: golden rivers in deep canyons, red sunsets in the desert, orange autumns in the Northeast, the yellow green springtime in the Appalachians, and here, the blue in Tahoe.

The shore is piled high with sharp rocks or it rises in cliffs to a tangle of white fir and Jeffrey pine. Above them rise whole moun-tainsides of evergreens, and above them, granite slopes, and above them, snow-covered peaks, and above them, a blue that compli-ments the one at the bottom of this seven-layered sandwich of won-ders for the eye.

Thanks to those who made this a state park, and to those who stopped a proposed four-lane highway, the lake right here looks about the same as it did to John C. Frémont. He was supposedly seeking a river called the Buenaventura, thought to run from the Great Basin Desert westward to the Pacific Ocean, and he lost thirty-three horses and mules crossing the Sierra in 1844.

Frémont was the first white man to write that he saw Lake Tahoe, which he first called Mountain Lake and later, Bonpland, for a French botanist. The lake had other names: Lake Bigler, Truckee Lake, and Maheon Lake. Also Tula Tulia and Largo Bergler—the Lake of Beer. Only Bigler, named for California's proslavery governor in the early 1860s, was seriously used, and "Largo Bergler" stemmed from this name because the governor drank a lot. A Geological Survey cartographer preferred the Indians' name, which means "big water" or "high water" or "water in a high place," and in 1862 the name Tahoe officially appeared.

My paddling rate is about a stroke a minute. Why hurry on a tonic-filled day like this? I move closer to shore, where I watch my utterly smooth passage over rocks larger than houses, over cliffs, over an entire topography. When I sit still, it is strange: the rocks slowly swell and shrink because of the lake's pulse of waves, so far apart that I notice them only when I look straight down to the rocks, whose edges wobble distortedly.

Two miles brings me to Emerald Bay, carved by glaciers and claimed by Kodak as the second most photographed natural site in America (Niagara Falls is the first). The bay runs one mile toward the Sierra escarpment and the Desolation Wilderness. At Fanette Island, I lift the canoe onto rocks and climb to the Tea House, a stone masonry whim built along with a Scandinavian mansion called Vikingsholm at the head of the bay. I notice a change in the breeze and relaunch.

Motorboats buzz near me. A lumbering tour boat bears an amplified commentator who talks to the entire bay whether it wants to listen or not. The wind picks up, and now foot-high waves challenge me by slapping the sides of the canoe. I zip my life jacket.

Into a wall of wind I enter the main lake, a treadmill of a rapid. The full force of the northerly blow blasts me in front, shoving me off course and plowing swells against the canoe. I brace by pushing down on the paddle to raise the right side and keep waves from breaking into the boat. Foot by foot I labor north to the beach where I began so effortlessly. Here I'm protected from the wind and enjoy the full effect of the miracle that gives mountain life its life: the new season.

It is summer. The sand is hot, the air dry, the sun intense because less air blocks the rays at this high elevation. Up here the sun is four times as intense as at sea level, and it will shine all day. Except for afternoon thunderstorms in the high country, rain rarely falls in the Sierra in summer.

I lie on the beach. This is the easy season, and all of life, including the bug world, celebrates. Yet the easy life is illusionary because its season is short. In two months, a lot must happen. Annual plants must sprout, grow, flower, and seed (in alpine tundra areas, only 2 percent of the plants are annuals; perennials have a head start because they do not have to germinate, sprout, and grow each year). Many of the baby animals must grow to be adults, and some animals must gain enough weight to keep them through the fast of winter— large bears, for instance, must gain a hundred pounds. The future and its demands are out there, but today is today and the pleasures of the season fill me: few clothes, a warm breeze, the fragrance of flowers and fir, rough soil under bare feet, long days, cool nights, misty mornings.

The afternoon is hot, but the water is more than cold. It is frigid in late June. So what. I wade in and dive forward. This water is frighteningly cold below the first foot or two. I swim back to shore.

What I've just done—"swimming and water sports"—is the most popular recreation activity in the Tahoe basin if you discount riding around in cars and camping, which to me are simply matters of logistics and housekeeping, not real recreation. Downhill skiing is the second most popular activity, and cross-country skiing, third. Sierra trivia: skiing is the top recreational use on four of the eight Sierra national forests (Tahoe and Eldorado, which border Lake Tahoe, Stanislaus, and Inyo). Gambling was not counted as recreation in the Forest Service's data.

Sitting here on the beach, I face the Carson Range—an eastern arm of the Sierra and the only part of the range in Nevada. When earthquakes lifted the mountains, the bottom fell out of Tahoe, making a graben (from the German word for "grave"). The lake used to be much larger; geologists have found stranded beaches several hundred feet up the mountainsides. The ancestral Tahoe was two million years old—one of the oldest lakes in the United States.

Only one-seven-hundredth of the lake's water flows down the river each year; a drained Tahoe would require seven hundred years to refill. Below the outlet is a gentle reach of the Truckee River, where five-mile-long raft jams of fun-loving people fill the channel every summer weekend.

Twelve miles to the northwest of Tahoe but clearly a satellite to its economy, Truckee was a mining and railroad town, population 1,025, elevation 5,820, where one-third of the existing structures were built before 1900. The town holds onto its old character, a railroad station, and a sawmill. Traffic idles thickly, and the tourists stroll on the Old West boardwalk. At the Squeeze In, a cultural center of sorts where restroom graffiti includes poetry, mathematical formulas, and denouncements of the president, breakfasts are the best this side of Quincy's Morning Thunder. The Bar of America stands like a fortress, as it must be; many hundreds of people crowd elbow-to-elbow in a get-down ritual every weekend. The Truckee River—an advanced canoe run—riffles through town on the other side of the tracks.

Everyone knows that rivers flow to oceans. But they don't here. This river flows to Nevada. All of the Nevada-bound Sierra rivers—

the Truckee, Carson, and Walker—flow to lakes and evaporate, but first, water is diverted for beef.

In some years, ranchers took all the water, and during droughts they coveted the seven-century accumulation in Tahoe. In 1912, a consortium of downstream irrigators tried to cut a deeper channel in the Tahoe outlet. An injunction halted the theft. During another drought ranchers dispatched a crew with a steam shovel under cover of darkness. Violence with lakefront landowners was averted when a deputy sheriff charged the operator with that classic Old West catchall, disturbing the peace. The government stepped in with an engineering fix: the Bureau of Reclamation built a dam to raise the level of the lake and now manipulates the top six vertical feet of water, releasing it to suit the needs of cattle.

Ranchers were forced to recognize that the river's source—Lake Tahoe—could not be stolen away from influential landowners, but the ranchers were never forced to recognize that the water's destination—Pyramid Lake—was also important.

Indians had depended on Tahoe water for their sustenance and economy longer than anybody. Because of ranchers' diversions, Pyramid Lake, formerly a biological bonanza holding world-record Lahonton trout, had dropped eighty feet and had all the promise of a dust pit. The Paiute Indians sued, their case went to the Supreme Court in 1983, and they lost. Although some water is allocated to Pyramid Lake, it will continue to shrink unless something else is done.

The wildness on the southwestern side of Tahoe, where I paddled the canoe, is rare. Buildings are scattered or packed on most other shores. At the outlet town of Tahoe City on the northwest side of the lake, I find shopping centers, condominiums, restaurants, motels, and homes. Development runs continuously northward to Nevada's state line, where casinos begin and development continues.

Thirteen miles north of the lake, Interstate 80 is the only four-lane highway linking the northern three-quarters of California with the rest of the continent to the east. The road drops eastward to Reno and climbs westward to Donner Pass, 7,239 feet.

Within a ten-minute drive of Tahoe are some of the finest ski areas in the Far West, including Squaw Valley and Alpine Meadows. At Donner Summit, Sugarbowl, one of the less expensive areas, has excellent runs and the deepest snow. Heavenly Valley (at the south shore) is the second most visited ski resort in the Sierra. More than a dozen resorts make Tahoe one of the most popular ski regions in the world.

Moving from the north to the northeast side of the lake, I come to Incline Village, where builders notched terraces of condominiums into mountainsides. The east shore includes the lake's largest reach of open space—the windswept shores of Lake Tahoe State Park. At the southeast shore is Stateline, the casino capital of the lake, followed by South Lake Tahoe, the real estate, residential, and fast-food capital.

Sixty thousand people live in the basin year-round, 42,500 of them on two-thirds of the land that is in California. More than 12 million visitor-days are estimated per year. The average daily visitation is 33,000. For comparison, Yosemite Valley sees 20,000 people on a busy day, though in a much smaller space. The Forest Service's Tahoe Basin Management Unit, which comprises parts of several national forests, records 2.8 million visitor-days a year, far more than any other Forest Service site in the Sierra and perhaps in the nation. In his excellent book, *Tahoe, An Environmental History*, Douglas Strong states that the lake is visited by more people than any other natural scenic wonder of similar size in the United States. Tourists can pick from 13,000 motel and hotel units. The South Lake Tahoe area alone houses 33,000 people and sleeps 9,000 visitors. It is by far the largest urban area in the Sierra Nevada.

At twelve major casinos on the Nevada side, "gaming" involves 60 percent of the lake's visitors. The Western Federal Regional Council reported that gambling accounts directly or indirectly for 78 percent of the jobs, 41 percent of the houses, 31 percent of the tax revenues, and 43 percent of the sewage at Tahoe. Stateline is Vegas-by-the-Lake, where casinos follow the Reno and Las Vegas model of slick metallic and electric glitter.

Business booms at Harrah's, an eighteen-story monument to the industry of chance. It's only nine o'clock at night, but already the jungle of slot machines is crowded. Pumping a one-arm bandit with silver dollars, one expressionless woman looks eighty, an untended cigarette dangling from her lips. Many people hold drinks in one hand, exercise a machine with the other, and assume the mechanical characteristics of the machines they have come to Lake Tahoe to visit.

This recreational palace of jangling change glitters with metal, lights, and mirrors. The air is smoky. Waitresses wearing little offer me drinks. Dealers in white shirts and vests look serious, efficient, and anonymous. The gamblers only look serious. I guess that the median age is fifty, and the dominant class is lower-middle, though most ages and all of the middle classes are represented.

In the restroom a man from Modesto says, "Lost a bundle so far, but I'll win it back." With his wife and a group of friends, he came by bus and will stay three days.

I loaf in a lobby area. A black woman in a dress that clings to her appealing shape walks by me once, smiles, and walks by again. At a stand-up lunch counter, I buy a taco and eat next to a woman of about sixty, with teased blonde hair, who is from Fresno.

Through a glassed-in area I can see a musical preview, not by the expected Wayne Newton but by Paul Revere and the Raiders, sporting Minuteman hats with Three Musketeer plumes, wearing glittery colonial costumes, playing rock and roll for people who are no longer young. They take it in sedately. The shows are at 10:30 P.M. and 2:30 A.M.

People come from all over the United States to spend a week in places like this. Now the activity increases like the movement in a stirred-up anthill. There are no windows, no clocks. I feel watched, and I am. Security guards roam everywhere, and in most casinos, the management has watchers behind one-way glass in the ceiling to guard against cheating. Like the billboards say, "Harrah's, it's another world."

To avoid traffic, the weather, and perhaps daylight, an underground walkway connects this casino with Harvey's. There I see a preview of a "sizzling review"—three women wearing less than any teenager at the swimming pool and wiggling in front of a backup band. They do not have the bellies of the billboard bodies that lure men and perhaps women to Lake Tahoe from all over California.

I've seen what I can see, and I leave. For hard information, and to disprove or confirm what I have seen of this unusual culture, I later return to talk with a Harrah's spokesman, who left teaching for better pay. Autographed pictures of John Denver, Kenny Rogers, and Willie Nelson hang on his wall. I learn that the hotel's 540 rooms are full most nights, and that the restaurant serves 10,000 meals a day. I ask how much the typical person spends here. "There is no data available." The median age of customers? "All ages." How many people visit the casino? "That is confidential." How much are the gross receipts in an average year? "That is something our competition would love to know."

I've heard that a majority of the people who gamble at Lake Tahoe never see the lake. The PR man disagrees: "People come for different reasons. Some enjoy gaming and that's all they do, but others might go outdoors in the daytime. The hotel was designed to give every room a view of the lake. I think that the natural beauty of the area appealed to Bill Harrah when he started business here."

Harrah began with a bingo parlor in Southern California, moved up to a casino in Reno, and in 1955 bought the Gateway Club at Tahoe. When he was ready to construct this eighteen-story building, he proposed thirty-one stories, but people thought such a high-rise would conflict with the Sierra skyline. Harrah's and the adjacent gambling palaces are by far the tallest buildings in the Sierra Nevada.

Bill Harrah died in 1978, and now the business is owned by Holiday Inn, a corporation that owns one hotel for each fourteen miles around the equator. A survey recently ranked this place among the top three hotels in the United States; accommodations are right up there with the winners in Dallas and Beverly Hills.

Gambling at Tahoe is a strange arrangement. Nevada, with neither many people nor restrictive laws, provides the fun, and California, with plenty of people but with laws against this kind of thing, provides the clientele. The state line just happens to run through some of the continent's most extraordinary natural beauty.

Bob Twiss, chairman of the department of landscape architecture at the University of California at Berkeley, has worked on Lake Tahoe for many years, including a term as chairman of California's Tahoe Regional Planning Agency. "People at the casinos don't associate Tahoe with the Sierra," he says. "They hear John Denver sing and think they've had a mountain experience."

The Sierra has undergone sequential eras of exploitation and use—mining, logging, road building, water development, and tourism—but the gambling at Tahoe is in a class by itself. The PR man may be right, but the people I talked to seemed to be oblivious to the mountains. I would say that the slot machine–blackjack brand of recreation has little to do with the natural resource, except for its inadvertent destruction of it and one other point: it seems that the lake and mountains provide a recreational atmosphere that, even if unused and unnoticed, has an appeal—a cleaner image than the gambling cities in the desert.

Because the casinos seem to have profited by the image of the lake even if no one sails, rows, fishes, canoes, motorboats, swims, sunbathes, or wades, I ask the casino spokesman, "What responsibility does the management recognize for solving the lake's problems, which are a result of so many people coming here to gamble?" He says that he cannot comment.

Howard Norcroft also knows about gambling, and he's willing to comment on everything: "Why do people gamble? They lost their money once, and they've been trying to win it back ever since." Howard, whose name has been changed for the purpose of this book, has been a poker dealer for nine years, one-third of his life. "I guess you could say it all started with the Grateful Dead, though

I hate to lay *this* on *them*. I came up from LA to hear the Dead in concert at San Francisco, and these guys I was with said, 'Hey, let's go to Tahoe.' I lost all my money and stayed.

"Living up here, I figured it would be great. I could gamble any time I wanted and cruise around this beautiful place. But I'd play until I couldn't borrow any more money. I'd lose $1,500 in a night. I got real depressed, over and over. During eight years I lost $50,000."

Howard is five foot seven, with a compact, muscular body. He's going bald, with a drooping blond mustache. He wears a Hawaiian shirt, shorts, and a gold chain, and he talks easily in his two-bedroom home under pine trees.

"My girlfriend and I bought this house together, but my gambling was a problem. After she left I figured that if I quit, maybe she'd come back. So I quit. Then she started going with my boss at the casino. I got Valium from a friend and took it every day before work. I went to a psychologist. I went to Gamblers Anonymous. As of today, I haven't gambled for a year and ten months and four days.

"Things are better now, but I hate the job. I see what people do there, the way they spend money. It kind of stands for all the vices: gambling, drinking, drugs. But the pay's real good and easy.

"Who gambles? All kinds. The real rich and people on welfare. Most people don't do anything with the lake. They see the mountains on the way. I know people who have motorboats and say, 'Later I'll take the boat out,' but they don't. They stay in the clubs.

"Living here, it's not a community. People rent for a month or a year, then they're gone. Over at Arnold, on the other side of Ebbetts Pass, my brother-in-law had a bad injury, and the neighbors got together and cut him and my sister a truckload of firewood. Here, maybe a few people would call you up and say, 'Hey, you know that money you owe me? There's no hurry to pay it.' "

Part of Howard's therapy is running. "It's a release. They say it's bad for the back, bad for the knees, and bad for the ankles, but it's good for the mind, and I guess that's what counts." While we run on trails from his neighborhood to Fallen Leaf Lake, Howard tells me about a book he has written and hopes to have published: *Real Poker Players Don't Eat.*

When we arrive at Fallen Leaf Lake, we are hot and sweaty, so we jump into the clear water with a view of snowfields. I tell Howard that I'm planning a backpacking trip up there. "I feel like going in tonight and throwing down the deck and throwing down the chips and coming up and joining you. But it's tough to leave here. The summers are great. Look at this." He holds out his hands at the scene. "A lot of people can't imagine living in a place this nice."

When we return, Howard says he will take me to breakfast at the Red Hut, which is hutlike but widely regarded as a social center of South Lake Tahoe.

Throughout breakfast, people walking by say, "Hey Howard," and he says, "Hi." One person will ride to the next Grateful Dead concert with Howard. Another person wants tickets to the Dead concert after the next one. When we finish, Howard grabs the check. "This is Tahoe, where money doesn't mean anything. Spend it. This is why I work, I guess, for a good time with friends now and then."

To show me some landmarks, Howard drives toward Stateline. The return trip is ten miles of asphalt-framed glitter without the designer touch of the casinos. Uncontrolled signing advertises unfettered tourism with undiscriminating taste. Along with gambling, it seems that people come to Tahoe to eat: McDonalds, Kentucky Fried Chicken, Taco Bell, Rico's Pizza—All You Can Eat $2.95, Snowflake Drive-In. Only in California: Izzy's Burger Spa. And people come to drink: Tahoe Keys Liquor, Tahoe Bottle Shop, Liquor Barn—Huge!

There are indigenous and exotic-sounding places to sleep: Sierra Lodge, Swiss Chalet Village, Condor Lodge, Flamingo Lodge, Ponderosa Motel, Bonanza Motel, Jack Pot Inn.

Some people go outdoors and no doubt appreciate nature at Tahoe: I see signs for Sierra Tahoe Jeep Rental, Magic Carpet Golf and Arcade, and Trout Fishing No License Required.

Quickie marriages are a long-term growth industry, and now we are getting to the winners of the sign contest: A Touch of Love Wedding Chapel, Chateau L'Amour, Love Building, Weddings $69 Total, Lake Tahoe Tourist and Wedding Information Center, Amour DuLac Weddings No Blood Test No Need for Nevada. A couple was recently married at the top of the Heavenly Valley gondola. A friend of Howard's who is something of a fitness nut will be married between the bicycling and running events of the next triathlon.

Not only marriages but also social problems are rampant. A July 9, 1984, *Sacramento Bee* article is titled "Tahoe Glitter Traps Those Fleeing Personal Problems" and documents epidemic levels of alcoholism, drug abuse, and child neglect.

Until the mid-fifties, what I see probably did not exist even as a gleam in a realtor's eye. Tahoe was isolated, hidden by a mountain barrier that seemed to guarantee peace, a resort area for the few—not particularly the wealthy, but the few—who were willing to make the journey because they enjoyed the lake and the mountains. Then gambling expanded from Reno. Then the 1960 Squaw Valley Olympics marked a leap into the California mainstream that was never to be reversed. Fleets of bulldozers carved Interstate 80 into Donner Pass; contractors labored overtime in a futile effort to finish the highway for the winter games. They destroyed the streams near the road, then the road made the development of north Lake Tahoe inevitable, then people and their by-products overloaded the lake with pollution. The economic interests at South Lake Tahoe lobbied for their share, so Highway 50 from Sacramento was upgraded. The mountain barrier that had blocked settlers until 1841, that had posed monumental difficulties to the railroad, and that saw the first four-lane highway only in 1960 was now reduced to scenery beyond road cuts and to the occasional nuisance of tire chains.

No amount of concern for the future would stand up very well against the forces turned loose with commuter tourism. Along with gambling and easy access, California's population boom indelibly shaped the fate of the lake. Each day in the 1960s, 1,500 people immigrated. At Tahoe, open space disappeared, and development sped down a collision course with the quality of the environment that brought people—including Bill Harrah—here in the first place.

In *The Mountain States of America,* journalist Neal Price, known for level-headed analysis, wrote about the development at Tahoe: "It is all an obscene abomination, perhaps the most appalling assault on God-given natural beauty anywhere on the American continent."

In 1950, 2,500 people lived at Tahoe; in 1980, 60,000. In the 500-square-mile basin, half of the meadows were damaged or destroyed, along with a third of the streambanks and three-fourths of the marshes. From 1970 to 1978, the population grew 118 percent. Twenty-eight thousand acres were converted to urban use, including some that hadn't even been land.

Using techniques perfected in the seaward expansion of Newark, New Jersey, 5 million cubic yards of earth were dredged from Tahoe's marshlands during a five-year-period and piled into mounds of dirt where cattails used to grow; thus was the Tahoe Keys subdivision created. In 150-foot-wide canals, homeowners tie cabin cruisers to the back porch. This Venice-in-the-Sierra with channels in highly erosional muck arose where the Truckee River had entered the lake, where the Truckee Marsh had been the basin's finest wetland—a wetland that had purified water by filtering silt from the incoming runoff. Today the subdivision includes about 1,400 houses and a marina-based commercial district with the rope-and-anchor flair of Monterey.

The Dillingham Development Corporation built the project and hopes to build more, so I call it on the phone. An answering service tells me, "They are usually not here. I can give you their number

in Pasadena." I arrange to meet at the local office with Bernie Frizzie, the Tahoe Keys manager. He is reluctant to talk because he does
not know my angle, though I'm sure he suspects it. He is a lawyer,
formerly with the military, and he reasonably sidesteps some questions. His response to my question about the initial dredging is:
"That happened before Dillingham entered the picture.

"The project has certainly been good for the local economy. The
Keys served a useful purpose—it didn't require the kind of money
that was needed before. The less expensive homes sold for $19,000."
These ranch houses are now $100,000 or more, though most houses
at the Keys are considerably more. "This served as a place for the
upwardly mobile middle class.

"Nowhere I've been do environmental concerns, for better or
worse, approach those at Tahoe. You need four agencies to clear
anything you do. The intent is good—to save this basin—but the
regulatory environment is out of hand. Every single family home
must be approved, every porch must be approved. Under the current controls, we'd never be allowed to dig the first ditch. After the
dredging was done, we were required to spend $3 million on a water
recirculating system to filter out the dirt stirred up by the
motorboats."

In 1976, government agencies halted development of the Keys,
this subdivision-on-fill being the ultimate in destruction of sensitive lands where, even with a filtration system, even with a gen-
erous and indeed award-winning commercial treatment, the impacts
on Tahoe were great. Dillingham sued and in 1982 was allowed to
proceed with a smaller plan.

It's spilled milk today, but the Truckee Marsh almost escaped its
upwardly mobile fate and can be added to that list of deals that
everyone wishes they had made: in the 1950s, the Forest Service
could have acquired 750 soggy acres for $75,000. Going further
back, not only the marsh but also most of Tahoe could have been
saved as it was. Since the first proposal for a national park in 1900,
attempts for federal protection failed, up through 1982. Richard
Leonard, a leader of the Sierra Club through most of this century,
explained: "The Sierra Club never pushed very hard for protection
of Lake Tahoe. No one ever said so, but I guess we thought it was
hopeless. We knew that there were other things we could accomplish in the national parks to the south."

The current question for people who do not regard Tahoe as
hopeless is this: how can we save what is left? Like much of mountain life, Tahoe is hardy to the elements but fragile to the touch of
people—and thus is easily ruined. Slopes erode when disturbed,
soils are shallow, and the growing season is so short that plants
stabilize soil slowly or not at all once it's dug up.

Measured against other places—say, similar real estate bonanzas in the San Francisco Bay Area or Southern California—planning for Tahoe has been successful. If developers had had their run on an open field for the last two decades, the South Lake Tahoe syndrome would be found in north, west, and east Lake Tahoe also. But to keep the quality of Lake Tahoe requires more than treatment of sewage, more than steering development away from floodplains and mud slides—more than the traditional approaches to land protection.

The nontraditional approaches began in 1959, when local leaders organized the Tahoe Area Council, which led to formation of the Tahoe Regional Planning Commission. In 1963, the first basin plan essentially granted sanctions to what was happening anyway. Local zoning—not required to conform to the plan—allowed more than 600,000 people—another San Francisco. While both sides argued esoterically about land use and home rule, water quality plummeted.

With professionalism beyond reproach, Dr. Charles Goldman, of the University of California at Davis, had begun testing the water in 1959. His data base is now one of the world's most complete for a lake. "Soon after I began my work," Goldman said, "I was taken by the beauty of that environment but alarmed at the rapid rate it was being degraded. Nobody would believe it. I tried to be both an activist and a scientist, though it became evident that I had to stand back from the politics. Once people began seeing the green margin of algae around Tahoe in the spring, they were convinced we had problems."

Dr. Goldman was hired to study the biological effects of a proposed sewage treatment plant, and in 1963 he convinced government leaders to export all the waste to discharge sites beyond the basin. "If they hadn't, Tahoe would now be a cesspool." Here is one of few populated watersheds in America with no sewage discharge in its basin. North shore waste runs to a treatment plant at Truckee; south shore effluent, to Alpine County. A more difficult problem remains. Unless it is checked, the erosion of soil spells sure death to Lake Tahoe as we know it.

Forty percent of all precipitation in the basin lands on the lake. The other 60 percent hits land, and runoff washes sediment from construction sites, road cuts, and other disturbed areas. The real problem is not the silt but rather the algae that thrive on nutrients that arrive with the silt. Some erosion is natural, but not much; the U.S. Geological Survey estimated the sediment yield from the Incline Village condominiums at twelve times the rate from undeveloped land.

Between 1970 and 1978, nutrients from erosion increased by 20 percent, and algae grew by 150 percent. From 1969 to 1983, free-floating algae doubled, increasing at an average annual rate of 5.5 percent. In 1983, Goldman found that the lake's clarity was 75 feet, compared to 100 feet in the 1960s. In thirteen years, 25 percent of the clarity had been lost. A straight-line projection showed that the lake would lose most of its transparency in forty years.

The League to Save Lake Tahoe had been organized in 1957 by six property owners who were concerned about a proposed bridge over Emerald Bay. Supported by many enthusiasts from the San Francisco Bay Area, the league adopted the issue of water quality and the slogan "Keep Tahoe Blue." "It was a brilliant strategic move," said Paul Sabatier, of the University of California at Davis. "Water quality concerns made a strong justification to bring state and federal governments into the land-use matter and provided hard scientific information in a normally mushy matter of land use, aesthetics, and the quality of life."

County supervisors from within the basin were influenced by the land development go-getters, some of whom were themselves. County supervisors from outside the basin (a majority in every county that touches the lake) saw Tahoe as a gold mine that could generate tax revenues. Local protection efforts were doomed. Jim Bruner, director of the league, forced state attention on the issue: "Tahoe doesn't belong to local politicians, bankers, and realtors. It belongs to all of us."

The league lobbied successfully for the creation of the bistate Tahoe Regional Planning Agency in 1970. With authority to regulate development, the TRPA was one of the nation's first regional agencies established for environmental protection. It was intended as a model of planning and cooperation, but it became a case study of local versus state belligerence.

Local government representatives, who were almost always in favor of development, controlled the TRPA with six of eleven members. Three officials, representing less than 0.5 percent of the California population, outvoted representatives appointed by the governor, who represented more than 20 million people. Because the agency held the authority to stop developments, the stakes were high, and the TRPA director received phone calls threatening him and his children.

Between 1970 and 1978, the agency approved 10,000 new housing units and all requests by major casino-hotel owners. *Los Angeles Times* editors wrote that the TRPA seemed unable to plan anything but "gambling casinos and shopping centers."

A California TRPA had been formed to regulate land use in California until the bistate agency was organized, and in 1974, Governor Brown and the legislature strengthened the CTRPA. This corrected some problems but simply moved others. "Developers went over to Nevada to build multifamily units," said Paul Sabatier, who studied the intergovernmental dynamics of Tahoe. Only a stronger bistate or federal agency could solve the problem.

In a bold move, California Resources Secretary Huey Johnson called for a national recreation area, and in 1979 Congressman Vic Fasio introduced a bill for a national scenic area. Pressed with the federal presence, Nevada agreed to the alternative: a stronger bistate compact. Negotiated by California State Senator John Garamendi, the new TRPA banned new casinos, temporarily halted large developments, and increased the number of TRPA agency members.

The ban excluded four casinos that had already been approved. Caesar's was constructed on one of these loophole sites. One was bought by the Forest Service and one by a county, precluding development. Harvey's high-rise expansion was delayed when an extortionist's bomb blew up part of the existing casino, but the expansion was resumed and will bring 2,000 new employees and perhaps 6,000 residents to the south Tahoe area.

The new TRPA offered a promise of protection, but progress was blocked by the 1982 California gubernatorial election of George Deukmejian, whose actions are a study of how to make a good agency ineffective. He removed the strongest conservationists, Dwight Steele and Carlyle Hall, from the TRPA and appointed Alexander Haagen III, a Manhattan Beach developer whose father contributed $55,000 in cash and free office space to the governor's campaign.

Under Governor Jerry Brown, California had pushed for protection, while Nevada, under Governor Robert List, had supported development. Then the roles were reversed (Nevada Governor Richard Bryan has been an environmental advocate). Protection shifts with the whims of state officials.

The greatest success may be at the federal level. Through an ingenious scheme, the Burton-Santini Act allows the government to sell desert land near Las Vegas and use three-quarters of the money to buy land at Tahoe, much of it subdivided but not yet developed. Thus, after one of the most intensive planning programs in the nation and after legislation that twice granted a bistate agency rare powers over land use, final protection comes down to the expensive process of the federal government buying the land it originally owned but lost through homesteading schemes as ludicrous as Mark Twain's "brush" house.

Public land in the basin increased from 42 percent in 1954 to 75 percent in 1984, but even this is not enough to save Tahoe. Six thousand subdivided lots are so steep that, if they are developed, erosion from the sites could increase by a thousand times.

The antagonists to the League to Save Lake Tahoe and to other groups trying to preserve the Sierra and Tahoe is the Sierra Tahoe Preservation Council, which is fighting regulations and acquisition. The group says that erosion comes from roads that are already built and that the government should correct problems developers created in the past, not restrict lot owners. Jim Bruner said, "We should fix current problems, but we're throwing good money after bad by allowing more development."

Another battle will be fought this week. Tom Martens, the new director of the League to Save Lake Tahoe, will testify in hearings about a lawsuit by the league and California Attorney General John Van de Camp. Fighting for Tahoe's protection, Van de Camp claims that the TRPA's plan is inadequate to meet environmental "thresholds" already established by the agency. The suit has temporarily halted many developments.

"Air quality is the next problem," Martens said. While the lake turns from blue to green, the distant pine trees turn from green to blue, and on some days, the lake is buried in smog. Nitrates from air pollution add to the lake's nutrient loading. Thomas Cahill, of the University of California at Davis, stated that carbon monoxide, hydrocarbons, and lead at Stateline reach higher levels than in Los Angeles. Cars are the problem. In 1981, 11.8 million people arrived by car and 500,000 by bus. A regional plan calls for a 10 percent reduction in auto travel in twenty years, but how this will happen is unknown, just as the entire future of the lake is unknown.

"Tahoe is symbolic," Martens said. "It's one of the last things you can save in California. There is no other lake like this, yet it stands for many other places."

Bob Twiss called the mid-eighties an "era of chaos" for Tahoe. "If the TRPA continues to deteriorate, it will lead to another proposal for a federal takeover, and the whole process of improving the TRPA will start again."

Defenders of the TRPA say that yes, 95 percent of the applications for developments are approved, but because of requirements, many bad projects are never submitted. Also, the agency requires large lots, erosion control, and protection of natural features.

Charles Goldman said, "If the TRPA would do what they're supposed to do, we could turn Tahoe around in our lifetime. The problem is not yet irreversible. We must work something out. We have to be optimistic or there isn't any hope for anything."

Jim Bruner is not optimistic. "The California appointees have made the agency ineffective. I think that the usefulness of the TRPA is over. It has followed a steady path to urbanization. The agency was a noble experiment that failed. We need to come up with a new solution, and the land acquisition programs will let us do that. After the vacant land is bought, the main pressure group against protection will be gone. Then, national safeguards for Tahoe will pass Congress."

Today's Tahoe is a picture of rootlessness, but near this environment of condominiums and casinos, I will find a man who seems to belong to the place itself.

I drive to Fallen Leaf Lake, several miles from Tahoe, then higher on a dirt road studded with rocks. The road ends, and still I have not reached the place where Jim Hildinger's parents carried him in a wicker basket when he was two weeks old. I park, walk half a mile, and emerge at a shimmering lake guarded by cliffs that curve up slopes that could be the Alps.

At Angora Lakes, where this century could be forgotten, I find rustic cabins, a beach of golden sand, swimmers in trunks and bikinis, and people sipping lemonade. Quiet laughter splashes through at random; now and then an oar clunks on a rowboat, a person jumps into the water. Voices are only a murmur. Here lies the first sunbathers' beach I've visited in years where no radios are screaming. The scene—water, trees, sun, glistening bodies, no road, no cars, no radios, ringed by mountains—is distinctly paradisaical.

At one of the cabins I find Hildinger with a broom, sweeping the cedar deck where the lemonade is sold. A thin man, active and quick, he is close to sixty. He shows me several cabins he and his father, Bill Hildinger, built. In one, Jim says, "Here's where we play." With friends, students, and professionals, Hildinger plays the violin.

In 1917, the first year that cars crossed Donner Summit, Bill Hildinger drove to Tahoe in a Model T Ford. For $5 he leased this recreation site from the Forest Service. In 1930, he opened a resort; some of today's thirty-eight guests are the children of families that have returned for thirty seasons.

Jim didn't go to public schools until seventh grade. His family stayed here through winters, ten feet deep in snow. For a while they lived in Los Angeles, where Jim studied music. "In 1946, my dad paid $1,154 for a new Chevy and $5,000 for my violin." The unusual mix of music and the Sierra has occupied Hildinger's life.

"I was offered a job teaching music in Pasadena in 1958, but when a job opened at South Lake Tahoe, I was here the next day. In Southern California I spent one and a half hours a day in a car; at Tahoe, four minutes. My life expanded by nearly one and a half hours a day.

"No cars here at my cabins—that's one of the things people like. They plan their week so that they don't need to go out to the road."

A girl comes in for lemonade and says, "Hi, Mr. Hildinger."

"My first chair clarinet," he says to me. "Even after they graduate, students come to visit, some in their forties. This is roots, real roots."

Clouds build over the Sierra crest. "In Los Angeles it was awful— nothing ever happened. Here, the sky changes. The storms blow in hard, then it clears." Other changes have been less welcome.

"We never dreamed we'd see these crowds. This is a small lake; 300 is the maximum number of people for sanity. Add one more and they all go crazy like in experiments with rats.

"At Lake Tahoe that has happened on a bigger scale. The 1940s were quiet. In the fifties it began to grow. Roads were built. People stayed year-round. The change was welcome because you could make a living, but then it got out of hand. People destroy what they come to see when they come in numbers too great.

"At Lake Tahoe, people used to hike or ride horses. Some painted. They sat on the beach and talked. Now they drive around the lake, step out of the car to take a picture, and go to the clubs. The type of people has changed, and they bring their thoughts and lack of thoughts with them. Now I have to deal with five radios a day on the beach." Hildinger requires the listeners to turn the radios off.

"I love to sail, but not in the summer. There're too many people. I put the boat in the water in October." The lake never freezes because of its depth and winter turnover of water.

For years Hildinger worked to reverse the tide of development. "In our system of capitalism, something always seems to get exploited in order to make money. Here it's the lake. You can't blame the casino people, they're only doing a job. The people to blame are local officials who let it happen. They saw all those tax dollars coming in and couldn't turn them down."

What can be done? "Stop the growth. And in the future, even if it's a hundred years away, move gambling out of the basin. There will be so much demand for accommodations at Tahoe that the economy will survive without the gambling. You can gamble in Reno, Ely, anywhere. But there is only one Lake Tahoe.

"It sounds simple, doesn't it? We should save Lake Tahoe. You write letters to editors and speak up at meetings, but eventually you get threatening phone calls in the night. Things could get worse. Look at the election of Reagan. Not the man so much as the attitude that exploitation is okay." Recognizing that the federal government's $50 million in direct aid through public facilities for Tahoe's growth may have contributed to the problems, President Jimmy Carter created a federal council with authority over only federal projects at Tahoe. President Ronald Reagan abolished this in 1981, calling it unnecessary interference, though it interfered only with the wasting of tax dollars and with the profits of those on whom the waste was spent.

"Maybe we just can't do it. We don't have the ability or the willingness to deal with this many people."

We walk the length of the beach. "If I had it to do over again, I might not be a music teacher." Jim picks up a discarded cigarette butt and drops it into a bucket. "I wouldn't be a politician, but something close to politics. Maybe a writer, expose all that stuff."

"It's not too late," I say.

"No. I don't care any more. I'm older now. I want to take pictures and play my fiddle.

"My wife and I wondered, 'Where should we go to retire?' We thought, and we looked, and we learned something. There is no better place to go. You find our problems all over. That's why we have to find a better way."

The problems of Tahoe are in many ways the problems of the Sierra, and everyplace is lacking in better ways. Many communities are now like Tahoe was in 1958, and the attitudes of local governments are the same: let us alone; we want our share of development. Landscape architect Bob Twiss said, "If no planning is done at the state level, then decisions are made in the offices of banks and realtors. The lesson of Tahoe is that when economic pressures are strong, local governments will not reflect broader public interests. We need a central Sierra council to look at the whole mountain region. A Central Sierra Planning Council was tried, but the counties pulled out before accomplishing much.

"The Sierra doesn't have the identity that it needs to stimulate region-wide action," Twiss added, "but mountain communities share many problems and similarities. At Tahoe, 17,000 new homes could be built on lots that are already created, and it's that way all over the Sierra. Counties are unable to deal with major projects, like hydroelectric dams or toxic waste disposal sites, but a joint state and local group could do the job.

"It's tough to see the cumulative effect of hundreds of separate decisions, but together, they create big changes. After we realize that the air is polluted or the lakes are dead, it's too late. That's what's so hard about planning. What you see today is a result of decisions made twenty years ago. Maybe Tahoe can be a lesson for other communities."

Fifty airline miles southwest of Tahoe, along the Ebbetts Pass road, Arnold is one of my favorite communities in the Sierra—in the evergreens above the foothills, yet low enough for mild winters. The manager of the bank provides small-town service without delay. Neighbors talk to each other in the grocery store. Last winter, while I lived in a friend's log cabin along Love Creek, the woman in the post office at nearby Avery held my general delivery mail and retrieved it with a smile. "The pace here is slower than down below," said Brenda Bullard. "People coming up from the cities need about six months to tone down."

Up above Arnold, the Mount Reba ski area at Bear Valley is excellent, and the Calaveras sequoia grove predated even Yosemite as the Sierra's first tourist destination, but Highway 4 has no attraction such as Lake Tahoe. Even so, the changes underway could give Arnold similar problems.

Within a five-mile radius of town, more than 6,000 lots have been sold. Calaveras County, with not one stop light, is the second fastest growing county in California on a percentage basis (Nevada County in the northern Sierra is first). Population of the greater Arnold area increased 100 percent in the 1970s. Projections call for another doubling to 10,000 people by 1990. Privately owned lands have the development potential of Tahoe.

"That won't happen here," predicted Brenda Bullard, who's job is to sell real estate. "We've welcomed controls. We primarily sell empty lots in ready-approved plans, and we resell homes in the subdivisions. People buy homes for retirement, but in ten years they don't want to shovel snow anymore, so the turnover is high."

Not all realtors are as concerned as Brenda with the way Arnold looks, and the coming years could see enough prosperity to convert Highway 4 into something routinely ugly. To arrest this, a scenic highway plan was drawn up by a local committee and county planners, calling for tighter zoning, screening, protection of natural features, limited signing, and rustic designs for businesses and homes seen from the road. "This is our way of balancing growth with protection of the area," said Tom Manning, chairman of the committee.

Arnold may be able to direct its fate and keep some of its mountain flavor, but the job won't be easy. Four new dams are approved near town, and the construction boom could bring Alaska pipeline problems. "You can only develop so much until the place is like everyplace else," said Wendy Corpening, who lives along Love Creek on land bought by her parents long ago. "Then the reasons for coming no longer exist. Everybody loses."

Thirty miles away, in the foothill town of Sonora, planning consultant John Mills said, "There are four kinds of people. The old-timers, who don't want regulations. Second, people who move into the country and in six months wonder, 'Where's the day-care center?' Then, the true urban refugees, living in old cabins or new homes where they finish one room a year. They don't want to see a lot of new development. Finally, the boomers—contractors and laborers. They are motivated by dollars, and they hold the convenient philosophy that everybody has the right to develop land. They combine with the old-timers, and they have control."

In Madera County, at the edge of Yosemite National Park, 20,000 lots have been created in the Sierra and its foothills. Throughout California, the population of rural counties grows at three times the rate of urban counties. The state population of 25.6 million grew a phenomenal 8 percent from 1980 to 1984, and many people search for a modicum of escape by owning a cabin in the mountains.

"People like to build in the same elevations where the deer spend the winter," said Joe Harn, who works for the Forest Service in San Francisco. "Habitat is reduced, and fences go up. Often, on-site sewage systems don't work properly. Ground-nesting birds are wiped out by cats and dogs."

In a four-volume doctoral thesis, John Harper wrote, "It strongly appears that the mountain subdivision is the single most ominous, long-term menace to public enjoyment of the Sierra Nevada as it is known today."

Compared to planning and land-use regulations at Arnold and elsewhere, Lake Tahoe is exceptional. If this were not the cleanest lake of its size in America, the successes would seem exemplary. But in 1983 TRPA voted to relax the ban on development of sensitive lands such as steep slopes, to allow subdivisions that had been blocked since 1975, and to increase the amount of land that can be excavated. Like visitors who throw dice, the local and state governments have gambled without fear of loss, and to reclaim the damage and save the lake now requires extraordinary public costs. Today's problems could be blamed on the government's own conflicting goals: provide easy access and keep the lake clean. We can go to the moon, but we cannot save a lake once a road leads to it.

Charles Goldman said, "Tahoe can be a model of holistic management. We have the resources and affluence in the basin to address the problems. If we can't solve them here, then what chance do we have of solving anything?"

The possibility remains that we can do it, that people like Goldman, Bruner, Martens, Hildinger, Twiss, and others can win. If we keep the lake blue, we will show that a large resource can be used by people and still retain the quality that makes it unique in the world.

I'm ready to leave South Lake Tahoe and its conundrums. I will enter a different world in the Desolation Wilderness, west of Tahoe, above the crowds and the cars. Here is one of the nation's most popular wilderness areas; in 1971, it was one of the first where the Forest Service required a camping permit.

From the trailhead at Glen Alpine I climb two hours, then hide my pack and walk to the top of Mount Tallac, where all of Tahoe stretches below me, immense and blue, streaked with silver or gold, depending on the angle of light on waves. From 3,500 feet above the lake, motorboats are specks, and the thousands of buildings seem insignificant. But the lake is still blue, and that *is* significant.

To the north, I see wild country that will be protected as the Granite Chief Wilderness if the California Wilderness Bill passes. To the west is Pyramid Peak, 9,983 feet high, cone-shaped, still snowy in early July. Pyramid is a landmark. On a clear day in Sacramento, 50 feet above sea level, you can climb up—say to the eighth story of an office building or to a freeway overpass—and you can see Pyramid.

The range runs ruggedly south. The distance I see is overpowering yet alluring. I want to cover the distance, to see everything, yet to always see more of it, more mountains waiting for me.

Desolation shows the Sierra's northernmost expanse of vast, glaciated granite. Named for its grainy texture, granite is a light gray igneous rock made of quartz and feldspar, with dark specks of hornblende and mica. One of the harder rocks, it breaks with sharp corners or weathers to smooth surfaces covering entire acres. The granite began as molten rock 100 million years ago and hardened underneath the earth's surface—a slow process that allowed the development of the large crystals that cause the coarse texture. In many places, lava was deposited on top of the granite. Where the brown lava has weathered and washed away, the granite shows. Really I should call this granitic rock because granite is a name used by geologists for only some of what I see. Within a family of rocks that look about the same, granite is the lightest in color and density. In the Sierra, there is more granodiorite than granite, but I, like most people, call it granite anyway.

Even up here, people have rearranged the flow of water. Medly Lakes had drained eastward into the Truckee River and Lake Tahoe, but a dam was built in 1875 and later enlarged to create Lake Aloha, draining west to Pyramid Creek and Horsetail Falls, which I regard as one of the most spectacular falls in the Sierra and in America. The water flows into the South Fork of the American River, then into the American River, the Sacramento River, and San Francisco Bay.

The American is the Sierra's second largest river in volume and the fourth largest in basin acreage; it is also the most historic river and the one most used for recreation. After these headwaters burst out of the Desolation Wilderness, they gather tributaries on their way to some of the nation's most popular whitewater, where people get a close-up view of rapids and a river's power. The direction of my journey is south, but I'm free to wander, and now I'll go west to see this river. From the base of Pyramid, I'll follow the American's canyon route across the Sierra.

4

Rivers

"THERE I WAS, CHAINED TO A SWIVEL CHAIR, watching a parade of fools wasting money by the megabucket, and there wasn't much I could do about it. I tended to think in the long term, and they thought in other terms."

After seventeen years in the Senate Office of Research, where Bill Kier was involved in nearly every substantial question affecting the environment of California, he was fired, and that is how he arrived here in the mountains, west of Lake Tahoe, along the South Fork of the American River, a mile below the Pyramid Creek confluence, in a historic lodge. Ten miles up Highway 50 is Johnson Pass (Echo Summit), the fourth highway pass over the Sierra from north to south.

The political veteran's voice is a curiously compelling monotone. He has mastered the art of speaking softly so that people will listen, and a lack of expression understates, verifies that something is so. It is a deep voice but soft, unhesitating but unhurried, and above all, orderly. The most unreasonable situations—such as Governor Ronald Reagan signing a state wild and scenic rivers act—become reasonable because Kier has the historical perspective; he can go back to the beginning.

He stands about six two, and he has blue eyes. The suits and ties hang deep in a closet; he wears a blue chamois shirt and faded jeans. Beyond all of this, Bill Kier is an excellent, lighthearted host. An older couple wander in. Bill welcomes them and suggests that they look around upstairs until they find the room of their dreams.

We talk in front of the fireplace at the Strawberry Lodge, where a blaze of lodgepole pine crackles on a cool summer evening. Old furnishings surround us in this hotel, whose predecessor was started in 1858.

Out back, the South Fork of the American rushes by as nicely as any trout stream I can name. Not far from here, in 1844, Kit Carson jumped into the river to save his boss, John C. Frémont, who had fallen in. Carrying a hundred-pound mail bag, Snowshoe Thompson skied up this route from 1856 to 1869, averaging 36 miles a day on the 180-mile round trip. Other mail carriers on this route were the boys of the Pony Express, who are deep in the lore of the West though their enterprise lasted only seventeen months. Their gallop down the Sierra's west slope was the finale of a long trip. The first transcontinental telegraph came this way. The latest proposal in this vein is a high-voltage transmission line to carry electricity from coal-burning power plants in Utah to the Sacramento Municipal Utility District, but the local Eldorado County people say, "Over our dead bodies."

"You see," Kier says, "I had developed a fantasy that government should work in greater harmony. So I took on that goal when I became the director of the Office of Research. I brought the highway engineers together with the land-use planners, the boomers with the wildlife biologists. I wanted to look at things like the role of public investment in private gains taking.

"Look at Lake Tahoe. You build a new road, you get more people, you sell more real estate, and the lake goes to hell. The public paid at the beginning, the public pays at the end, and in between somebody makes a killing." Bill says that dams show the phenomenon even more clearly, and his voice settles into a calm that tells me that he is about to launch into an analysis of that anachronistic, power-clutching, self-serving system known as the politics of water. But first I am interested in Bill Kier's unlikely climb from Sacramento to Strawberry.

"Believe me, I have respect for the political system, and enormous respect for some senators, but when other senators came in hyperventilating and wanting an immediate solution to some political problem, I had trouble hyperventilating with them."

Kier had walked into a trap. "I had done that Californian thing: with every promotion, Helen and I had moved into a larger home in Land Park until the swimming pool was like something off the cover of *Sunset*. My response to the problems at the office included Gordon's Gin and putting on weight. I realized that all I was doing was going to the Capitol and getting this computer-generated paycheck. Life had become a set piece. What are you doing in a situation like that? One thing you are not doing is learning new skills. You're middle-aged plus, and one day you think about that, and an intelligent or even unintelligent person says, 'Twenty-five years of life left—I want to do something different.'

"So when it finally comes down to the day I was sacked, when it came down to the minute I left the Capitol, to that last step out the door and into the sunlight, I hesitated, and looked down the steps, and I had a hard time suppressing a grin.

"So here sat the Strawberry Lodge. I had been in the place once, when I was sixteen. A friend in the Bay Area had heard that it was for sale. I became fascinated with the prospect for a different kind of life. I talked to a realtor who gave me a lot of reasons to stay away from Strawberry Lodge. Rich and I drove up to see the few things that were functional and the many things that were not, and the next day we bought it."

During that spring of 1983, not only the Kiers but also the Sierra Nevada measurably aged near Strawberry Lodge. As if political forces were not enough, geologic forces had to be reckoned with. Above Route 50, a sizable chunk of mountain slid from beneath a leaking hydropower flume. Strawberry Lodge was on the back side of the slide, which stopped all traffic for months. The former senate research director drove around the long way, and, isolated from the world by mud, he began work on his drafty enterprise and challenging new career.

First of all, this meant short-order cooking and tending bar. At 6 A.M. Kier fired up the grill for his first clients: bulldozer operators employed at the slide. "All day I tried to get water heaters heating and commodes flushing, then I tended bar at night. That was the worst. I've never been a part of the bar culture. I spent $6,000 out of my pocket and wondered, 'Can we keep up the pace? Will my marriage survive?' One year ago this place was a bad dream with no light in sight. Thirty creditors were ready to bring action, from a sheriff's sale on down. People with rules and regulations were nitpicking with me. What you see here was a capitalistic venture in the finest American tradition." The lawn sprinklers out back need to be moved. "Come on along," Bill says, and we walk near the river.

Bill's career in government began with rivers. He was a biologist for the state Department of Fish and Game, and at twenty-five, he was California's authority on stream flow requirements for fish and recreation. Although the political pragmatist ruled most of his career, he still looks at streams with the eyes of a biologist. He overturns a stone and identifies mayfly larvae, a favorite food of trout.

The mayfly and the trout both require a certain amount of water, at a certain temperature, with seasonal variations that the chain of life has adapted to over the millennia, but a pipe that would divert the water for a pittance of electricity could end the mayfly, the trout, and the chain. "A private hydroelectric developer, Joseph Keating, proposes to build a dam just above here on the South Fork, along with a dam and diversion that would affect 4,000 feet of Pyramid Creek below Horsetail Falls." Bill sets the stone back where he found it.

One of his jobs was to enforce water quality regulations on the Yuba River and Donner Creek during the construction of one of America's most-used public works projects: Interstate 80. "With the contractors, we were in and out of court like through a revolving door." After those streams were ruined, he evaluated water quality and the fishery at Lake Tahoe in 1960, when the boomers were moving in. The sprinklers have been moved. Bill says, "Let's go eat."

We pick a table with a view of the South Fork. Three couples and one family are eating. I ask about the clientele.

"My dream here is to have a family resort for outdoor purposes." Bill points to the front of the lodge. "Pyramid Peak is that way, three miles. Right over there," and he points across the river, "is Lovers' Leap, a world-class climbing rock. The Desolation Wilderness is a fifteen-minute walk from here. Sierra Ski Ranch offers great downhill skiing ten minutes away, and you can cross-country ski out the back door. Fishing, hiking from right here—people can use the mountains in many ways." Salad is served.

"The way people use the mountains has changed. Let me tell you about the history of recreation in California." This covers a lot of ground, but the gist is that opportunities once rare are now enjoyed by many. The outdoor experience was made easier and in the process was "trivialized." The effects go beyond renting a jeep at Tahoe or watching TV in a Winnebago at Yosemite. In Kier's story, fact grows to trend, trend to concept. Ultimately, at the end of our salads, the theme sits down right here at Strawberry Lodge: "We will never see a big chunk of the market because a lot of people are looking for rental jeeps, rental ski jets, rental video games, rental gold to pan, and rental fish to catch.

"Technology has removed us from real contact with life. Let's get back to it. People from Los Angeles call up five times asking if they need tire chains in the winter. Of course they need tire chains. Somehow people think everything will be taken care of." When the almond chicken is served, Bill excuses himself, and in a demeanor suitable to the Capitol, confers with his son about tomorrow's 6 A.M. pickup of garbage.

Bill talks while we eat. "Look at river running. The sport was so little known in the 1960s that New Melones Dam on the Stanislaus went through without an objection until 1970. Today, on the South Fork of the American, there are fifty commercial outfitters and 130,000 people a year going paddling." This means busy weekends and perhaps a trivialized experience. Instead of talking around a campfire on the evening of overnight river trips, some outfitters bus customers to bars and hot tubs. Crowds of rafters are taking us not only to permit requirements to float rivers but also to an economic boost of $10 to $12 million a year along the South Fork alone—and to a new political base of people who care about rivers. This last point is no small thing and is in conflict with a sacred cow in the politics of the West.

"Let me tell you the history of water development in California." Kier begins with gold miners, wheat farmers, and Ham Hall, one of the first visionaries to see the Golden State as a plumber's dream but a biologist's nightmare—also an economist's and taxpayer's nightmare.

There is so much water in the snowmelt of the Sierra that you could build an urban region of 12 million people—which is larger than each of forty-two entire states—and put it someplace where there is almost no fresh water, simply by tapping the rivers of the Sierra. Not only have Ham Hall's followers done that but—far more grandiose—they have also plugged and metered the Sierra rivers to irrigate an agricultural industry that takes 85 percent of all water used in California.

"Water, that's the story of this state. Follow this stream," Bill says, pointing out back as we finish dessert. "Take a look at it and at what some people are planning. You'll be amazed at what you find."

Amazing. The kayak in front of me disappears, though it is only a hundred feet away and nothing lies between me and it but water— and gradient. The boat has dropped into a hole.

Holes form below big rocks over which water pours forcefully. After some abuse, the kayak pops up from the innards of the washing machine and pitches downward again, glittering in triumph while I drop into the hole.

Because I row a raft, I'm not consumed, chewed, and swallowed, merely consumed. The curling wave breaks over the front of my fourteen-foot-long inflatable boat while I push on the oars, a wall of spray slapping me in the face. I emerge where additional thrills are waiting: wrap rocks, pinning rocks, pillow rocks, pour-overs, rooster tails, haystacks, hydraulics, keeper holes, suck holes, under-cut rocks, gardens of rocks, and places in between where the exhil-arating descent—like nothing else in life—yields to the peace of Eden.

The three kayakers paddle ahead of me. The sides of the canyon are steep, clearly out of people's element and into that of goats. I'm about fifty miles below Strawberry Lodge; I'm even below the pon-derosa pine belt that I consider the lower limit of the mountains. I float through the foothill belt of digger pine—gray green trees with forked trunks and cones spiked like war clubs that thrive in the hot hills on as little as ten inches of rain a year. As I descend, oaks will become dominant; the roots of the blue oak reach as deep as seventy feet for water. Chaparral is common, and openings are tan with grass cured by summer sun. In the coolest pockets, a few ponderosa survive. Before 1849, pine were more plentiful. The deforestation of the foothills preceded similar problems now appearing at higher elevations.

I feel out of my element at the low elevation, but the river has drawn me down. The river is a product of the mountains, a gift from them, so I've come to see it. This day in early July is a hundred degrees, but the South Fork of the American drenches me, refreshes me with the snowmelt of Pyramid Peak.

Here is the way to see this country: I lounge back on the seat of my Avon Adventurer raft. Where but on a river can you have easy travel, constantly changing scenery, abundant wildlife, and moments of utter peace followed by consuming struggles for life? It is not especially risky, but rowing a raft results in "real contact with life," as Bill Kier would say.

Jedediah Smith named this the Wild River for good reasons. John Sutter later renamed it after a group of Canadian miners called Americans by the Indians.

My friends the kayakers are Grant Werschkull, Jonas Minton, and Bill Center, whom I've known since 1980. Grant was the director of a group working for the protection of California's only major undammed river, the Smith. Now he works for the Nature Conser-vancy. Jonas works for the state Department of Water Resources devising ways to conserve water, action that he says can forestall the need for most new dams far into the future. He has built his case on facts and has won the respect of even the current administration.

Bill began working as a river guide on the Stanislaus, and through the group called Friends of the River, he met Robin Magneson—a guide from a whole family of guides—and got married. They run a company called California River Trips and own a campground at Lotus, where we will get out of the water.

This river is Bill's pleasure, his livelihood, and more. I think of Quincy as Wayne Dakan's territory, Tahoe as Jim Hildinger's territory, and the South Fork of the American as Bill Center's territory. In his thirties, he has already sharply influenced the future of this canyon.

As a way of getting by, I put all of life's hazards into either a high-consequence or low-consequence category and act accordingly. This sorting has worked so far. Most encounters are low-consequence, and most of today's rapids are not troublesome, yet rafting is demanding enough that it leads me to a greater appreciation of the vital things. Like breathing. Ahead of us, the forces of nature rumble. The distant thunder is water against rock.

We have nearly reached Sutter's Mill at Coloma, where John Marshall discovered gold in 1848, beginning that rapacious era of American history full of genocide, raped land, silted rivers, murders, extinction of species, theft, and greed known as the Gold Rush. The Gold Rush is now celebrated as colorful, though to many people at the time, it was probably no more colorful than the My Lai Massacre, Legionnaires' disease, or the last blue whale. The metal they looked for had so few uses that, after it was collected, much of it was simply locked up in a building in Kentucky. Looking at the long term, the Gold Rush is what got California off to the wrong kind of start, and a heritage of greedy digging in these river canyons has been hard to shake. The rumble I hear is the big rapid, Troublemaker.

I have heard many stories about this drop—flipped rafts and so forth—but I have never seen it. I still don't see it because it drops down out of sight. Following a hurricane of turbulence, the river crashes into a wall on the left where that old law of physics seems to be debunked: matter appears to be destroyed without a trace. The water disappears. It must angle like a bent elbow to the right. This may be a high-consequence drop, a rapid where I would stop and scout if I were alone. I will watch the kayakers, who, as usual, are ahead of me, and I'll adjust my course when I see what the river does to them.

Things are happening quite quickly now; between me and Troublemaker there is only a short straightaway and the kayakers. Bill yells to me, "Most people don't stay far enough to the left on this. Go far left."

While he shouted the instructions to me, Grant and Jonas paddled into an eddy on the left, where they now relax. Bill joins them. Suddenly there is nothing between me and Troublemaker but the front of my boat and an accelerating current.

From my low vantage point, the rapid has been unseen until this split second. Now, under significant stress, I would take the rapid on the far right. But Bill says go far left. The untrustworthy subconscious works on this information and says to take the rapid left of center.

My immediate problem is a lot of water, 3,000 cubic feet per second or more—much more than normal for this run. This problem is all of the runoff from Pyramid Peak on down, every bucketful trying to get through this pinched-off bend that is called Troublemaker for good reasons and has not been renamed by someone like Sutter. I am off into the unknown.

The top of the rapid sucks me in. So that I just might have time to maneuver once I see around the corner, I pull on the oars, which slows my speed because I face downstream.

At the brink, I see my problem. Until now, it was hidden by a smooth lip of water, but beyond that lip, lying in odd and treacherous proportions, is a hole—a big one. With a desperate pull on an oar, I set the raft straight so that I at least hit this frothy grave— it looks like the standard six feet deep and long—straight on. I might have missed it if I had drifted far left or extreme right. I might have busted through if I had pushed on the oars for momentum. If, if.

In an instant—the instant that the rear of the raft gouged the bottom of the hole—I see blue sky and feel water. Then I feel the hardness of my raft but then only softness, an otherworldly sensation of floating. I see white, then darkness. I know I'm in a maelstrom, but my world is dead silent. I've undergone a change that was so immediate, complete, and uncontrolled that I don't know which way is up. The main problem is that I cannot breathe.

What happened? The raft tilted up almost perpendicular to the river and rolled me feet skyward. Then I was trashed to the floor of the rear chamber of my boat, which was instantly filled by the Wild River and then refilled perhaps several times per second by the jet of the river aimed directly at me. As new water washed the old water out, it washed me out even more easily because I float. So why am I not floating now?

Only when the current lets my life jacket bring me up for air do I know what happened. My eye level is no higher than the river's surface, which plays by dunking me. I learn two things: first, my loyal raft is next to me. Maybe I can climb on top and ride the rest of the rapid on the floor of the overturned boat. With an overdose of adrenaline, I learn the second thing: Troublemaker Rock—at this high flow reduced to an enormous pour-over—is life's next obstacle. The danger is that I will hit it, and then the raft will hit me, bruises being the least consequence, being pinned to the rock by my own boat gone berserk being the greatest consequence—the Big Consequence.

"Feet up, feet downstream," I think, but I'm dragged under as if a rope around my foot is pulled by some giant down there. Fate somehow sends me around the rock, and below it the American vomits me to the surface.

"You okay?" a deep and calm voice asks from somewhere in my blurred, troubled world. What? I know I'm alone; no one could possibly have accompanied me through this encounter. Swimming Troublemaker is one of those solitary things to do. Just then my boat hits me from behind, so I grab it and discover that it's still right side up. I pull myself in, jump onto the seat, spit water, grab the oars, and row. People on shore cheer.

"Okay?" the deep voice repeats, and there alongside me is Bill Center.

Rowing through Troublemaker without having to save my life would have been enough of a challenge for me, and I suppose that operating a river business was enough of a challenge for Bill and Robin Center, but they also had to save their river.

"We had just found out that Robin was pregnant," is Bill's introduction to this important chapter in the environmental history of the Sierra. "Then that night we went to a meeting and learned that four hydroelectric dams were proposed." This latter item was bad news. The Centers were strongly attached to the river; their lives were being planned around it. "We returned home, and I went out to the pump house to start the gasoline generator, and someone had stolen it. We had no water. The next day we decided to forget our problems and go kayaking, and at Triple Threat I dropped my wedding ring in the river." This all stacked up to a mean streak of bad luck, but the Centers could handle themselves. Bill and Robin returned with a snorkel and mask and found the ring in ten minutes, they bought a new generator in two days, gave birth to Rebecca in seven months, and stopped the dams in four years.

The Eldorado Irrigation District had proposed to flood most of the twenty-mile reach from Chili Bar to Folsom Reservoir, excluding only a four-mile section for Sutter's Mill, protected by state law. While engineers drew up plans, the county attempted to nip opposition in the bud by banning rafting, but the river belongs to the public, not the county. The county failed, and the South Fork became

the most floated whitewater in California. If there was a lesson in
my swim through Troublemaker, it was to follow Bill Center's advice,
and the state legislature learned this also.

Bill claims only a compromise. "With the dam sponsors, we
developed a carefully crafted agreement that allows development
of an upper river project, with dams and diversions on the South
Fork, Silver Fork, and other streams above Chili Bar. We didn't
want to stop all of the projects; there would have been too much
bitterness. We live here, and we're determined to have community
support for the river."

After a long battle led by Assemblyman Howard Berman, the
legislature passed a bill that Governor Brown signed, prohibiting
for ten years the study of dams on the popular reach from Chili Bar
to Folsom Reservoir, which receives half of California's whitewater
use. Before the one-decade moratorium expires, permanent protection for the South Fork must be gained.

Bill, Grant, Jonas, and I land at Bill's beach, elevation 700, and
even with all the people—three groups are unloading boats—I feel
refreshed. What is it about rivers? They are full of life and movement. Now that recreation has "come to the masses," as Bill Kier
said, rivers are sought by people escaping the monotony of their
workday lives. But rivers are also sought by the West's most powerful individuals, corporations, and governments, which would
rather create more monotony to get a fast dollar out of the fast-
flowing water.

The water development industry repeats a California gospel: we
need more water and more power from more dams. The gospel has
been followed: 1,200 large dams have been built in the state. Dams
block every major river in the Sierra. On Forest Service land alone,
in the Sierra alone, 467 dams of all sizes have been built, preempting other uses and preempting wildlife from those streams and
valleys. Many of these are for hydroelectric power, but national
forest watersheds in the Sierra also supply 130 municipal water
systems. Federal and state water projects take vast quantities of
water from the Sierra Nevada and Northern California in a normal
year and deliver it to the Central Valley and Southern California.

I deflate my raft, while at my feet flows the South Fork of the
American, formerly a threatened river, reprieved through the work
of the Centers and other people. But the threats go beyond, to other
branches of the American and to other rivers of the Sierra, where
there are only so many Bill and Robin Centers working to save what
is left.

In the northern Sierra, a hydroelectric developer proposes to
divert water from Feather Falls, and dams are proposed on Indian

Creek and the Yuba River, including the South Fork above Highway
49. South of the American River, the East Bay Municipal Utility
District proposed damming the Mokelumne River above Highway
49, the most popular canoeing run in the Sierra. The North Fork
of the Stanislaus and its tributaries, which flow through high
meadows, granite canyons, evergreen forests, green pools, and white
rapids, will be dammed four times for hydroelectricity by a Calaveras County project approved in 1983.

Within a deer's migration of Yosemite National Park, irrigation
districts propose dams on the South Fork of the Tuolumne and on
the Clavey River—one of the largest undammed streams in the
Sierra and one of the most extreme kayak runs for the expert pad-
dler. An irrigation district proposed to dam the South Fork of the
Merced up to the park boundary. Another dam would divert the
Merced's main stem immediately below Yosemite, leaving a nearly
dry riverbed of sixty cubic feet per second for four and a half miles.
In 1855, the town of Mariposa devised a plan to dam Yosemite
Valley, and now Mariposa County would like to dam the Merced at
another outstanding site below Briceburg. South of Yosemite, the
Kings River is, in my opinion, the most beautiful of all the foothill
rivers, but it may be flooded by Rogers Crossing Dam. On the east
side of the Sierra, a map of proposed hydroelectric projects shows
a trail of dots up every major waterway.

The utter loss of rivers, streams, valleys, canyons, parks, forests,
homes, towns, historic landmarks, meadows, wildernesses, and
habitats flooded by the dams is not the only problem. Statewide,
40 percent of the natural flow of streams is diverted, leaving some
waterways bone dry and many lacking the essentials for life. Ten
percent of the native fish species are extinct; since 1940, populations of bass, salmon, and steelhead have declined as much as 80
percent. Statewide, more than 90 percent of the riparian habitat is
gone, and in the Stanislaus National Forest, for example, 200 of 325
wildlife species depend on this critical waterfront zone. Also, vast
acreage is becoming saline as a result of improper irrigation, the
fisheries of the Sacramento Delta are beleaguered by diversions,
and safety problems from leaking, aging, and poor planning—of
dams as major as Shasta Dam—are a plague to us and to future
generations.

Our civilization needs more water development, say the water
developers. They don't say that conservation of agricultural water
can save up to 40 percent of the water now used or that a mere 5
percent savings in agricultural water could increase residential
supplies by 50 percent or that Marin County cut use by 60 percent
without new hardware or that new dams cost two to twenty times

more than the cost of saving an equal amount of water or that undeveloped hydroelectric potential already exists for 2 billion kilowatt-hours a year at 212 existing dams without building new ones. Better scheduling of irrigation can save water at a rate of $10 per acre-foot when new development of water costs $100 to $200 an acre-foot. The irrigation management service, composed of only several people in the California offices of the federal Bureau of Reclamation, helps farmers cut their use of water by 15 percent simply by scheduling irrigation when the crops need it most. The conflict over water in the Sierra tends to describe the top end of the scale of environmental conflicts. Perhaps, as at Troublemaker, my vantage point from the river impairs my view, but it seems that we should at least be sure we have good reasons before we dam any more sections of rivers—for example, the other two forks of the American.

To see the North Fork I drive across crooked Highway 49 to Auburn, then up the dull, efficient grade of Interstate 80 to Colfax, then drop to the river by tortuous twists where it's important to remember that uphill traffic has the right-of-way. Above here, national wild and scenic river designation prohibits a dam planned in the 1960s at Giant Gap. Below here, nothing protects the river, so the plans are to flood it. Auburn Dam is the only "superdam" still seriously planned in the United States.

Two men mine gold below the bridge. At the base of a boulder they have dug a hole, and the contents are dumped into a sluice box, an artificial riffle with descending steps. Water pumped from the river rinses the lighter material to the end of the box. Eventually this waste will be flushed into the river. The miners scoop the grit remaining in the box into pans, and, with circular motions that throw off water and lighter waste, they eliminate all but the heaviest thimbleful of grains. One speck glints in the sunlight. The boss adds a sip of water, then rinses all the sand from the pan, leaving two flakes of gold, each paper thin and smaller than a pinhead. He says, "Two dollars o' gold ain't worth the trouble."

Agreeing, I hike downstream. The river runs clear, squeezed between boulders that create rapids. Green pools are perfect for a summer dip.

I drive to other sites. At Murderer's Bar on the lower Middle Fork of the American, motorcyclists have beaten a large riparian acreage to a pulp. At many places, mining equipment and scars remain from a hundred years ago, but dwarfing every other scar is the Auburn Dam site.

Near the town of Auburn, the American River canyon has been dug up as thoroughly as a West Virginia strip mine. For the height of a skyscraper, the trees, soil, and loose rock have been stripped and replaced with cement—the dam's foundation. Roads, bulldozed into the radical slopes, zigzag in straight lines like diagrams of static.

If it is built, Auburn would be the fifth tallest dam in the United States, by far the most expensive, and closer to a large city than any other large dam, even though earthquake faults mark the region like cracked glass. So far the Bureau of Reclamation has spent $320 million here—the taxpayers' investment in a foundation, a bridge, and a lot of scars.

The 685-foot-high edifice would have been the world's largest double-curvature, thin-arch dam—curved in both height and width. Then there was an earthquake, and geologists warned that 750,000 people in the Sacramento area would be flooded or worse if the dam ruptured. Auburn was the supersonic transport of the dam world; faith in dam-building technology died here when construction was halted in 1975.

The U.S. Geological Survey reported that a three-foot movement of earth was possible during an earthquake at the site. The Bureau of Reclamation said a one-inch slip was possible. The secretary of the interior called for a dam to withstand nine inches of movement. The engineers' marvel was redesigned to a fat, unarched, concrete-gravity dam, while costs soared $10,000 a month when inflation was high.

The critics, including Friends of the River and Protect American River Canyons (PARC), say to quit, that the waste to date is not as bad as the waste to come—$3 billion in all. Yet the Bureau of Reclamation and politicians remain serious.

To recover the government's costs, irrigation water would have to be sold for $350 to $900 an acre-foot. The fact is, the Bureau of Reclamation sells much of its water for $3.50 an acre-foot. This token is sometimes all that farmers will pay, and if the farmers don't buy the water, then how can the Bureau of Reclamation justify its projects? Auburn Dam would provide irrigation at a cost that would likely be 80 percent or more subsidized, including tax revenues from farmers in other regions of the nation, who go broke because of the subsidy to the California farmers and agribusiness giants. In California, many farmers receiving federal water pay 5 percent of its cost, the consumers of electricity pay 33 percent, and the taxpayers cover the rest, which may exceed $10 billion at the turn of the century.

The dam would reduce downstream flood levels, but the state Department of Water Resources found that modification of the existing Folsom Dam would yield 88 percent of the flood control benefits at 8 percent of Auburn's cost. Proponents of the Auburn dam claim that flat-water recreation would benefit. But the project and a related irrigation canal would cut flows to ankle depth in the American River in Sacramento—one of the country's most popular urban rivers, where 4 million visitor-days a year are recorded and where healthy flows are essential to 14 percent of the state's beleaguered king salmon. Not the least of costs: forty-eight miles of wild canyons are popular for hiking, fishing, rafting, kayaking, and more but would be permanently flooded. Otis Wollen, a PARC leader who lives near the river, said, "Those canyons are rich places and have much to offer to me, and my children, and everybody."

President Jimmy Carter sponsored a study of Auburn that called the costs prohibitive. Interior Secretary Cecil Andrus declared the project so expensive that it would have to be reauthorized by Congress. President Reagan's reclamation commissioner, Robert Broadbent, said, "Auburn is the last major dam remaining to be built." Yet funding is not recommended. The Bureau seeks nonfederal participants to pay a share. Local representatives have introduced reauthorization measures. In a new "value engineering study," the Bureau of Reclamation is spending $250,000 to consider a cheaper dam downstream.

As an alternative, Friends of the River, the Planning and Conservation League, and PARC propose using 43,000 acres of public land in the canyons as a national recreation area for the 2.8 million people living within 100 miles.

It is hard to imagine that a project of such dubious benefits and certain costs as Auburn will be built, but worse has already happened on a Sierra river—and not for any lack of people who were fighting to protect the place.

Dams cause the rivers and canyons not just to change but to disappear, and so among the fights to save mountain places, none has the intensity of the dam fight, and no dam fight has been as intense as the struggle to save the Stanislaus. Fourteen dams had already been built on that river, fifty airline miles south of the American. In the 1970s, a nine-mile section remained as California's most popular whitewater, the nation's river most used by handicapped people, and the West Coast's deepest limestone canyon. The mix of wilderness, whitewater, and people who enjoyed that paradise of a river produced an emotional clout unequaled in other fights to save rivers.

To build a project that serves real needs is one thing. To spend $376,158,000 on a dam that would generate power only two and a half hours a day, that would water crops only through subsidies of many hundreds of millions of dollars during the next fifty years, that would control floods more effectively if the reservoir were not filled, and that provide for additional flat-water recreation when ample is available for the next half century—all of this seemed absurd to people who loved the canyon more than any place on earth. The California Resources Agency found that the dam could be most economically used at a low level that would spare the nine-mile wilderness canyon.

Jerry Meral, a canoeist and Environmental Defense Fund biologist, formed Friends of the River to pass a statewide initiative against the dam in 1973. A prodam organization funded by the construction companies being paid by the government to build the dam advertised, "Save the River, Vote No." This was a vote to save the dam, and it won. Sixty percent of surveyed voters thought they had voted to stop the dam, but they had in fact voted to build it. Friends of the River waged a campaign for state scenic river designation, filed lawsuits, and testified before the state Water Resources Control Board, which had already acted to delay the filling.

In 1979, when the Army Corps of Engineers closed the dam's gates, Friends of the River leader Mark Dubois chained himself to a hidden rock near the water's edge. In announcing his plan to the Corps, he had written, "The life of the 9-million-year-old Stanislaus Canyon is far more significant than my short tenure on this planet." The canyon was not filled; one person's actions had apparently made a difference, and this is a powerful thing today, or at least it was a powerful thing in 1979. Hundreds more people joined the fight.

In 1980, a bill to add the Stanislaus to the national wild and scenic rivers system narrowly missed passage in a congressional committee. High runoff in 1982 and 1983 buried the nine miles of river.

Some people who had tried to save the Stanislaus found jobs in state and federal resource agencies, where they worked for change. Many pursued new environmental causes, and many were ready to fight again for another river.

The Tuolumne—the next river south of the Stanislaus—is the Sierra's fourth largest in volume and a highlight of the Sierra. The river winds through Tuolumne Meadows, cuts deep into the Grand Canyon of the Tuolumne—one of the most exquisite canyons in the United States—then cuts deeper into foothill canyons of whitewater. The river included Hetch Hetchy Valley, and in the 1980s, this waterway again became the site of the nation's greatest contest between river protection and development.

Among the earliest travelers on the river was Jerry Meral, who in 1968 paddled in a C-1 (a canoe that is decked like a kayak) with kayaker Dick Sunderland. The launching site for the eighteen-mile trip is called Meral's Pool. One year later, outfitter Marty McDonnell guided customers down the wild Tuolumne, recognized as the West's most challenging whitewater that could be run throughout the summer. In the early 1970s, Bob Hackamack explored the river from his home in Modesto and wrote a Sierra Club report calling for national protection.

These men formed a nucleus of supporters that would grow to include a movie star, a freshman congressman, and hundreds of people in a fight that duplicated in many ways the Tuolumne's earlier Hetch Hetchy fight, which historian Roderick Nash called "the first great conservation controversy in American history." Eighty years ago that fight was led by the Old Man himself.

John Muir had worked to establish a Yosemite National Park that incorporated the headwaters of its rivers. Along the smoothly winding Tuolumne, great meadows in a luxurious setting stretched through Hetch Hetchy Valley and supported enormous oaks. Waterfalls of tributaries crashed down, rimmed in the refuge of high granite cliffs. The main difference between Yosemite Valley and Hetch Hetchy was that few people had seen Hetch Hetchy.

The site did not escape San Francisco engineers, who sought water and power. Three times the federal government rejected the city's application to build a dam, but after the 1906 earthquake, advocates rode a wave of public sympathy. More important, in Gifford Pinchot, the water developers found an ally.

Credited with no less than the reform of resources management in America and the naming of this work "conservation," Pinchot was a friend of President Theodore Roosevelt who had been trained in the German forestry of maximum wise use of resources. This meant wise for people, in an economic sense. Against the protection of Hetch Hetchy, Pinchot argued, "I am fully persuaded that . . . the injury . . . by substituting a lake for the present swampy floor of the valley . . . is altogether unimportant compared with the benefits to be derived from its use as a reservoir." Pinchot recommended even the flooding of Tuolumne Meadows in the park if San Francisco wanted the water.

Roosevelt appointed a friend of Pinchot's, James Garfield, as the new secretary of the interior, and he approved the city's plans in

1908. This was a setback for Muir, but the case was not closed. The Sierra Club had been organized to protect the mountains in 1892, and it was prepared to fight against the dam that could bury the valley, the wilderness, and the park.

In 1969, Jerry Meral was in Central America doing zoological research when he opened a letter from his paddling partner, Dick Sunderland, who said that San Francisco and other groups proposed to dam the Tuolumne, this time below the national park, in the outstanding whitewater canyon that began at "Meral's Pool" and included "Sunderland's Chute," "Hackamack's Hole," and McDonnell's livelihood. With the Turlock and Modesto irrigation districts, the city proposed two dams on the Tuolumne and one on the Clavey River, a tributary. The dams and diversions would destroy seven miles of the Clavey and twenty-seven miles of the Tuolumne.

In a stroke of political genius, Bob Hackamack persuaded Representative John McFall, otherwise the dam builder's dam builder, to sponsor legislation in 1975 calling for study of the Tuolumne as a wild and scenic river—a designation that would ban the hydroelectric project. This move bought seven years of time.

The Forest Service completed the national river study and confirmed that here was the finest of western whitewater, including Clavey Falls, one of the nation's great rapids. Here was one of the finest California trout fisheries, with 1,000 pounds of fish per acre—three times that of the state's best fishing lake. Here were 200 kinds of wildlife, the habitat of endangered species, wintering grounds of the national park's two largest deer herds, and hundreds of archaeological sites, all within five hours of 5 million people. Out of 1,600 citizens who responded to the study, 1,400 wanted protection.

In 1979, President Carter recommended wild and scenic status, but Congress did nothing. Friends of the River concentrated on the Stanislaus, and the Sierra Club focused on national priorities, such as Alaska. "We figured Carter would be reelected, and the wild and scenic recommendation would go through," Jerry Meral said. Instead, President Reagan appointed new secretaries of agriculture and the interior, and the change was the same one Muir had seen when Garfield was appointed.

Meral recalled, "Even in 1980, we figured we'd be okay because of Burton." Phillip Burton, known for parks protection, chaired the House interior subcommittee. Dale Crane, head of Burton's subcommittee staff, had no doubts that his boss wanted the river protected but said that Burton was waiting for the right time. Meral saw time running out. "I looked at the date the moratorium would expire—1982—and I said, 'Burton or no Burton, we could lose this thing.' " In 1981, Meral, Hackamack, McDonnell, and others organized the Tuolumne River Preservation Trust.

As with Hetch Hetchy, few people had seen the Tuolumne canyon, but unlike John Muir's fight, river supporters in 1981 could draw on the popularity of the Stanislaus and American. They could draw on lessons learned and on people with skills and determination, but time was short. The moratorium on Tuolumne development would expire in a year, and then nothing would stand between the dam builders and the wild Tuolumne except these people, searching for some elusive political strategy to save their river and for a politician who would champion their cause.

John Muir and his friends made Hetch Hetchy the first nationwide battle to save a wilderness, the first to save a national park, and the first to save a river. They gained endorsements from diverse groups, and Muir wrote for the prestigious *Century* magazine. Over this single issue in the Sierra Nevada, Muir began to change the consciousness of millions. Going beyond the basic argument that a national park should not be ruined by flooding part of it, he imparted a spiritual awareness of the land: "Dam Hetch Hetchy! As well dam for water tanks the people's cathedrals and temples, for no holier temple has ever been consecrated by the heart of man."

Alternatives existed, but Hetch Hetchy was the cheapest. Federal officials were not concerned about the costs to the nation, only about the costs to San Francisco. Scores of newspapers, including the *New York Times*, published editorials against the dam, but western politicians and media endured as a unified bloc in favor of damming.

Within the newly formed conservation movement, the Tuolumne became the battleground. Muir argued for preservation of the finest natural sites as wilderness; Pinchot argued for development that would serve highly tangible needs. He wrote, "The first duty of the human race is to control the earth it lives upon." The philosophical split over a river in the Sierra continues to this day in all regions of the United States.

Any remaining hopes that the federal government would protect its park were dashed when Franklin Lane, former lawyer for San Francisco, was appointed secretary of the interior. The Sierra Club took the battle to Congress, where some men spoke eloquently for Hetch Hetchy Valley, but even William Kent, who had donated Marin County redwoods to the government and named his park Muir Woods, supported the dams. The *San Francisco Chronicle* printed a Washington edition with an artist's drawing of a recreational reservoir and delivered a copy to each congressman on the day of the vote in 1913.

The Raker Bill passed, allowing the Tuolumne dam and another dam on Eleanor Creek, also in the park. John Muir died within a year. O'Shaughnessey Dam flooded Hetch Hetchy Valley under hundreds of feet of water and still does.

For director of the Tuolumne River Preservation Trust, Meral and the others hired John Amodio, who had worked as the leader in efforts to expand Redwood National Park. He brought a knowledge of politics that was crucial to the Tuolumne campaign, and he advanced on many fronts: securing a commitment from the undecided Senator Pete Wilson, refining information, and broadening the base of support. Amodio knew there was no chance of an early national river designation, so he lobbied for a one-year extension of the development moratorium. Until Congress's adjournment at midnight, Amodio and staff from the American Rivers Conservation Council, the Sierra Club, and the National Aububon Society dealt feverishly but fruitlessly.

Without congressional action, the dam builders' legal gate opened, and the Federal Energy Regulatory Commission granted a permit for dam studies that cost millions and irrevocably hardened the resolve to build. A bad situation worsened. In the spring of 1983, Phillip Burton died of a heart attack. He had been one of the most powerful men in Congress, and Amodio had counted on him to carry protection for the Tuolumne.

The odds against protection were grim. The dam builders' lawyer was Lee White, former chairman of the Federal Power Commission (predecessor of the Federal Energy Regulatory Commission). In 1983 and 1984, the dam sponsors would spend $140,000 a month lobbying. The Tuolumne River Preservation Trust's budget was $200,000 a year.

Under Governor Brown, Jerry Meral had become the deputy director of the Department of Water Resources, which contracted a study by University of California economist Richard Norgaard, who found that the costs of the hydroelectric project would outstrip benefits. With this study and others, the state and the Tuolumne Trust showed an alignment of personal values and economic values in favor of the river.

Meral testified to Congress that the hydroelectric power was superfluous because energy demands were rising less than 1.4 percent per year, and that the state Energy Commission had identified other, preferred, options for generation. Only 0.5 percent of California's electrical load would be served by the project, and the benefits would go to irrigation districts whose power rates were already among the lowest—40 percent below the national average. Alternatives were as simple as the replacement of old refrigerators with efficient new ones, which throughout California could save six times the output of the Tuolumne dams.

Alexander Gaguine, a Stanislaus veteran, organized grass-roots campaigns and wrote action alerts. "You've Been There!" was an irresistible plea to people who had rafted the river. Along with the other outfitters and hundreds of private donors, Marty McDonnell funded the campaign. River guide Don Briggs—also a filmmaker and activist from the Stanislaus—convinced the national media to cover the Tuolumne. Every newscast and every article made it easier for fence-riding politicians to support the river.

Pinchot had derided Muir's paradise as "a swampy floor of the valley," and now, in San Francisco, the general manager of the Hetch Hetchy system said that the Tuolumne was "just another hot canyon—a kind of Disneyland." But in a crucial move, Tuolumne Trust president Alvin Greenberg and others convinced San Francisco mayor Dianne Feinstein and the supervisors to back out of the project and to support wild river designation. This left the two irrigation districts isolated.

Jack Burby, an editorial writer for the *Los Angeles Times* who had rafted on the Stanislaus, investigated the Tuolumne and wrote, "The districts make a frail case of need. . . . The loss of one of the few remaining semifree rivers within reach of millions of Californians is too high a price for the sake of lower power bills for a few thousand customers." The tide that had destroyed Hetch Hetchy and the Stanislaus was turning—if only it would turn fast enough.

John Amodio said, "We're taking a moderate tone and stressing mainstream values. Even the name *trust* appeals to conservative interests. We don't deny the other uses of the river, which is already providing almost 10 percent of the state's population with drinking water and 2 percent of the electricity generated in California. We maintain that the balance has been reached on the Tuolumne. We are not the extremists. The other side is the extremist, wanting to develop every last river."

After being guided down the river by Don Briggs, actor Richard Chamberlain became a principal lobbyist, twice flying to Washington, speaking on television, and writing about the river of the Sierra: "We have the power to destroy this, but never, never in our wildest imagination could we ever recreate it."

Amodio said, "No one else could have made the emotional appeal with such success." In the modern political arena, environmentalists must play under the developers' rules and win on economic grounds, yet Chamberlain showed that the emotional response to a wild river remains timeless in its appeal.

In the mold of the Stanislaus campaign, volunteers in Tuolumne County wrote letters, raised money, and guided newspeople down the river so they could see what was at stake.

Any notion that the river people were a ragtag band of paddlers was dispelled at a $125-a-plate formal dinner at San Francisco's Hotel Meridien honoring Richard Chamberlain and key supporters Justice William Newsom and Richard and Rhoda Goldman. Amodio said, "The dinner was a psychological coming of age, showing us to be in the mainstream, important, and respected."

The campaign reached a new intensity to gain the support of Senator Wilson. At Bill and Robin Center's camp on the South Fork of the American, Friends of the River volunteers persuaded hundreds of rafters each weekend to write to the senator. Ten thousand letters were more mail than he received about any other issue of his career. Charlton Heston and former California Resources Secretary Norman (Ike) Livermore—both supporters of Wilson—urged him to protect the river. In the House, Sala Burton had been appointed to her husband's vacant seat, and she led the effort to pass the California Wilderness Bill, but the Tuolumne was still in question.

Then, from the local area, freshman Congressman Richard Lehman came forward with a bill to designate a Tuolumne national river. Lehman, who came from a farming family, was aware of the benefits of water projects, but about the Tuolumne dams he said, "It is not a case of a project that is needed; it is simply a case of greed." Yet Lehman's bill lacked momentum.

The strategy for congressional action became clear: in June, Senators Pete Wilson and Alan Cranston added Lehman's language to the Wilderness Bill that had been gaining momentum for five years. With both senators' support, the bill was expected to pass the Senate by unanimous consent. The Tuolumne Trust counts support from a majority of California House members, yet a majority is not enough because one powerful member can delay action or halt it altogether.

During these midsummer days, when the prospects for protection look better than ever, the entire package for river and wilderness designation could be lost. Merced Representative Tony Coehlo chairs the powerful Democratic Congressional Campaign Committee, from which he appropriates campaign allowances to fellow congressmen. Although he supports protection of the South Fork of the Merced River, he favors the plan to dam the Tuolumne. Congress's decision on the remaining vulnerable reach of this river and on all the proposed wilderness areas will come this fall.

Three days on the Tuolumne are firing me up. This time I'm in a raft powered not by my own oars but by seven paddlers: Jerry Meral, who is now the director of the Planning and Conservation League; his wife, Barbara, who is a kayaker and teacher of deaf children; Doris Grimm, an archaeologist and a friend from the Stanislaus; Jennifer Jennings, who was a Friends of the River leader in the 1970s and is now a lawyer for the Department of Water Resources; Kevin Wolf, who organizes raft trips for Friends of the River; John Amodio; and me. All of these paddlers know the river well, and they show it off with pride. Several other boats carry gear and are rowed by guides, including Don Briggs, who is making a film about the river. We camp above Clavey Falls, definitely a high-consequence drop.

In the morning, we wander up the stream-sized Clavey River to a waterfall and pool, and I climb farther to an eight-foot waterfall that empties into a rock tub of dark, unknown depth. I swim through it and sit on a submerged rock at the foot of the falls. The sound, the spray, the coolness, and the negative ions that are plentiful at waterfalls fill me with an extraordinary, mindless pleasure. Bubbles engulf me; they mount over my arms and chest, almost to my shoulders, where they burst, and I feel carbonated.

I hold my hands so that I barely see them through the white foam—air and water, a blending of the elements. Each of the thousands of bubbles is a crystal dome—round, shining, reflective, perfect—but as I raise my cupped hands, a few bubbles burst, then many, until I have taken the combined air and water out of the river, and the magic is gone. I hold only water—clear but flat and still.

Back at camp we eat, load the rafts, and run Clavey Falls without falling out or flipping.

Three days on the Tuolumne. The river is robin's-egg blue at dawn, transparent with an amber bottom during put-in, green where we paddle over deep pools, glaring silver after lunch, aerated white where the gradient is steep, yellow ocher beneath cliffs, orange during the horizon's light, deep blue at twilight, and violet before it turns to streaked gray on black. Then it is only heard. The colors shine differently from any colors on land; they are water colors, river colors. They are distinct, but they match, and to me they say something about the blending of the entire mountain range into a harmony, a wholeness, connected by things like this river. Today I enjoy my descent of the Tuolumne, but I look forward to the opposite—the ascent. Where does all of this come from?

The three-day run has taken us from Meral's Pool, elevation 1,430, to a reservoir at elevation 816, where the river dies behind New

Don Pedro Dam. We step onto the muddy shore, a hot piece of dirt, dry and dusty above the lap of the waters. My friends and I unload. They are fighting for the life of the Tuolumne, and the next two months will make the difference. They and others will go back to telephones, copy machines, airports, and endless meetings, to public speeches, action alerts, backslapping, dealmaking, fund-raising, letter writing, and the defense of their own names. Maybe I should join them and fight for the mountains instead of just exploring them on this six-month lark, or however long it takes. I may finish a trip but find no place to which I can return. But I can't do it. I guess we each do what we can do.

I came down from Pyramid Peak to the foothills for good reasons—so I could see the complex and unresolved American River, the memorable but deceased Stanislaus, and the exuberant but threatened Tuolumne—yet I am unhappy at the bathtub-ring, sticky mud shore of New Don Pedro. I have left the mountains, and I'm paying the price in altitude sickness. I'm too low. The river was an energetic life force, but now that I'm away from it, the foothills' heat and the glare are oppressive.

Such sun. Sun that burns, bleaches, dries, then dries beyond dry; sun that glares from water, rock, cliff, face, and feet. The July foothills serve an overdose of sun. Here at the murky edge of a reservoir, styrofoam bait cups bob on waves from whining motorboats. My remedy is simple: climb.

I say good-bye to my friends. I do not see enough of them. Who knows when I'll see them again? Maybe at the end of my journey. By then, maybe they will have reached the end of their journey to save the Tuolumne.

In second gear, the van climbs the hill toward the small town of Groveland. Then I drive higher, up into a grove of ponderosa pine that smells like a hot, resinous forest, then higher to a dark thicket of fir that refreshes me, where I breathe easily before I coast down again on a road that clings to the edge of canyon walls, that penetrates the mountain through three tunnels. It is a road with the promise of something special, though it shows scarcely a glimpse of the incomparable landscape to come—a place that is perhaps the greatest wonder in all the Sierra, perhaps in all America. Yosemite Valley lies just ahead.

5

Yosemite

TO ENTER THE VALLEY HOLDS ALL THE PROMISE of leaving the rest of the world behind. This is not unusual for mountain places, but to find it in a lush and lazy Eden—where summers are hot and winters are mild, where cliffs and waterfalls are some of the most spectacular in the world—is nothing less than extraordinary. If there are powerful places on earth, this is one of them.

Here is the Merced River, glassy through yellow green meadows where deer graze. A waterfall drops 1,430 feet (Niagara drops 320). El Capitan, 3,600 feet high, is called the largest face of granite in the world—gleaming, smooth as a bedsheet, sweeping down to forests where a glacial moraine had blocked the river. Half Dome, sliced in two from top to bottom, rises 4,800 feet above Mirror Lake. But Yosemite is more than all of these parts.

In the mountains there are expansive places where you can look out and see who's coming, places ringing with freedom and excitement, which are essential to the spirit. In perfection, these are summits—places of prospect. Mountains also provide refuges in sheltered valleys—places turned inward and enclosed—and they meet a need of the body. The ultimate refuge is the cave. In *The Experience of Landscape*, geographer Jay Appleton theorized that the two landscape qualities of prospect and refuge are not just important but they are so important that awareness of them has been genetically transferred. Over the generations, people who live in places with both qualities were the people who survived.

Both prospect and refuge are offered in rare combination in Yosemite Valley. The valley encloses you, and after you are in there, it opens up. From the meadows or from rock shelves above the valley floor you can see far, but still the granite rim protects you.

The feeling remains something like that described in 1851 by L. H. Bunnell, who was among the first white men credited with entering the valley: "An exalted sensation seemed to fill my whole being, and I found my eyes in tears with emotion." No tourist, Bunnell was the doctor in the so-called Mariposa Battalion, which was looking for Indians to kill. Other members of the group found the valley "a gloomy enough place," and to this day, Yosemite affects people differently.

You know when you enter the valley. It's a world apart, surrounded by spellbinding mountains. Some of the magnetism comes from a wealthy blend of opposites: prospect and refuge, horizontal and vertical, soft meadow and hard rock. It's the innards of the continent and it's an island. It's easy living beneath the most rugged mountains. It's a place that I can reach with little effort, but it is apart from the mainstream of civilization. Or is it?

In 1968, I hitchhiked here after backpacking in the Tuolumne canyon. In Chicago, the Democratic National Convention was underway. Yosemite Village was loud with tourism, congested with cars. The campgrounds were full, so I set my pack along the river and talked with two young campers. They had loafed in the valley for months, moving now and then to "give the rangers the slip." I didn't blame them for wanting to stay.

Trusting, tired, and hungry, I left my pack near the river and walked to the village with only my surplus gas-mask bag that held my camera, film, and notebook. For $2.50, at Degnan's smorgasbord, I ate a glutton's number of courses, then sat outside until dark. I took a shortcut back to the campground and became confused. All the campgrounds and all the loops of roads looked alike.

Finally I arrived at my riverfront. I saw the tree that I had leaned my pack against, but no pack. I looked under another tree. I walked circles around a dozen trees, then I walked upriver, and, faster now, I walked downriver. The pack was gone.

With no place to go, I lay down on a flat spot and fell asleep, but not for long. I woke up cold. Remembering that bums back home had stuffed newspapers in their clothes for insulation at night, I walked to the yellow-lit restroom and pulled off yards of toilet paper and stuffed it inside my shirt.

A man walked in. Groggy, he squinted at me. "What are you *doing?*" I told him. "Good grief, sleep in my car."

At dawn I began the search. My pack had a $6 frame, my brother's canvas rucksack tied on, a sleeping bag, a wool shirt, a rubber poncho, shorts, and small things—not much, but that wasn't the point. The point was that I had nothing else.

The two young men with whom I had talked slept in, but next to them, an elderly couple was starting breakfast. I asked if they'd seen my pack. The woman said, "Sit down and have a cup of coffee. How about some breakfast?"

She poured the coffee, broke the eggs, turned them, peppered them, served them, sat down, looked at her husband, looked at me, and said, "I think I know what happened."

The two men next door had friends nearby. "Only yesterday one of them told me they were going to Big Sur, and I couldn't understand much of what he was talking about, but he needed a sleeping bag and some clothes. I think he wanted a handout. Well, last night they were talking to those two right there and walking around. We wondered what they were doing. "At about seven they pulled out." A white van with a blue emblem on it—I decided that if I didn't find it in Yosemite, I'd hunt in Big Sur.

After talking futilely with the two men who I now thought gave my pack away, and finding no evidence in their camp, I walked to park headquarters, where a ranger completed a form that he filed with hundreds of others. He said they would write me if they found my gear, "but don't count on it." He said that rangers were too busy to look for the white van, so I walked through every campground.

With no gear for sleeping out, no suspects, and no money for new supplies, I had no choice but to leave Yosemite Valley less than a day after I had arrived. I hitchhiked to Sacramento. A friend, Wendy, whom I had met while hitching across Nevada, could put me up for a night. From there I would hitch to the coast. But Wendy wasn't home, I never made it to Big Sur, and I never thought I would see my pack again.

In September I was at college when my father was called by the local sheriff. He had received a call from the Tuolumne County sheriff, who explained that rangers in Yosemite had found a body. The man had fallen from the top of a waterfall and wore no identification except on his pack: Tim Palmer, Beaver, Pa.

The late sixties was a time of chaos for Yosemite, and like my current paranoia about hiding my pack when I'm not wearing it, the Park Service of today was shaped back then. Crowds increased yearly, and rangers wished that they could just be rangers: none of them had come to the parks to deal with drunks, drugs, and the criminal element. Park Service managers felt powerless to address fundamental issues, such as too many people.

Campgrounds were free and first-come, first-served, and conflicting claims were sometimes settled in brawls. Without bus service in the valley, everyone drove their cars, but not everyone could park. So they drove around and around, or they parked anyway, blocking traffic or abandoning cars in the meadows. The valley was buried in campfire haze thicker than Los Angeles smog. Seven hundred people were once camped at Little Yosemite Valley—a backcountry site. Between 1967 and 1972, backcountry camping increased 184 percent, from 78,000 to 221,000 overnight visits (Shenandoah National Park increased 400 percent and Rocky Mountain National Park, 730 percent in ten years). America boomed with growth, and the idea of limits was foreign, backward, un-American, unprofitable, impossible.

Yosemite attracted unusual individuals. One man drove around in a van with a ten-foot antenna—God was going to contact him by radio in the valley. Harmless. Not harmless: a man bulging with muscles hidden only by a loincloth who resisted arrest when rangers from several patrol cars confiscated his three-foot sword.

As if the park's problems were not enough, the troubles of the nation spilled out of Washington and Chicago and Berkeley and entrenched themselves everywhere. With people's political involvement—emotional, physical, confrontational—came a rebounding need for escape. For the first decade since the 1800s, more people moved to rural areas than to urban areas. Those who could not flee on a permanent basis fled for a day—they came to the mountains.

Young people by the thousands, full of hatred of authority, laden with contradictions, traveled to Yosemite to escape. Rangers and tourists saw them as a threat to the valley, and prejudice against the long-haired, the voluntarily poor, the unbathed, and the unclothed strengthened. Rangers called longhairs "maggots," and the kids called the rangers "fascist pigs." Many of the longhairs were not relaxed, peaceful, nature-loving hippies who smoked some grass but rather motorcycle-gang types and youths who were prone to violence when on downers and alcohol. A collision was inevitable. From two different witnesses I received two different stories about the Stoneman Meadow riot on July 4, 1970.

"It was not an unforeseen incident," said Bob Roney. A large man, Roney is about thirty-five and bearded. His job is to create slide shows and films, and this interview occurs behind the Park Service warehouse in a windowless trailer that is a studio, full of tape recorders and movie projectors, with film cuttings on the floor. His long-haired assistant works excitedly on a film editing job. Roney is thoughtful and direct, selecting words carefully.

"The year before, a bunch of kids were drinking beer and partying on Sentinel Beach. My impression was that they were isolated and not bothering anyone. We went in and made arrests. One ranger identified children of park employees and told them to swim across the river.

"Then there was the night before. On July 3 they said the disturbance was at Stoneman Meadow, across the river from Lower Pines campground. Basically we made a parade, a show of force. First there were ranger patrol cars, then pickups, then the fireguards." Roney, a fireguard at the time, pauses so I can imagine this unlikely Soviet-May-Day-style procession through a campground. "People lined both sides of the road and booed the rangers.

"Then came the big night on the fourth. We heard that a riot was going on, that people were injured, so I took my first aid kit. We arrived after most of the action. At the intersection there was glass all over the road. It was dark and kids were running around in the meadow. We came to a sheriff's car that had been rolled over, the windows broken. The fireguards were each issued a can of Mace and an axe handle. We had absolutely no training. I was a real straight-arrow, but some of the guards were acidheads and beer drinkers. Two of them were drunk and started a Mace fight behind the Visitor Center. Guarding the Visitor Center was our main job. That's where the rangers brought the kids who were arrested."

The fireguards were not on the cavalry charge, but Armand Quartini was. A high school teacher and football coach in San Francisco, Quartini had applied for a ranger's job in 1968 and was hired in expectation of violence. "The superintendent said that they were having trouble with the hippies, and knowing that I had played linebacker was a big plus in getting the job. Every summer night, '68 through '70, we made fifteen to twenty-five arrests. It all culminated in the riot.

"There were hundreds of kids in the meadow, making a racket, bothering people. They made obscene gestures, did everything you can imagine. We tried everything we could think of to get them out. We talked to their so-called leaders. Then we put loudspeakers on the vehicles, told them it was an unlawful assembly, and that they'd have to vacate. They booed." About forty rangers were called in, including the chief ranger and district ranger. About twenty horses were saddled.

Anyone who has been spoken to through a bullhorn knows that the instrument was seemingly designed for the incitement of riots, but through a bullhorn a ranger announced that anyone found in the meadow at 7:30 would be arrested. The kids answered that they were going to free Yosemite from the establishment. At 7:30 there were perhaps 500 kids in the meadow.

"We lined up on one side of Stoneman Meadow," Quartini recalls. "The chief ranger said that when he gives the command, the horses will go first, then the rest will follow and make arrests."

- So it was. In this crown jewel of the national park system, on Independence Day, the year of Earth Day, the chief ranger gave the order to charge, a phalanx of twenty horsemen galloped toward the center of a mass of hundreds of wild and spacey kids, and twenty infantrymen in ranger suits ran behind with Mace and big flashlights and orders to arrest the kids who remained.

People scattered, but the horses—pack stock—were easily intimidated, and the kids ran around behind the horsemen to close ranks. Hundreds of kids surrounded the foot rangers. "They had taken garbage cans and filled them with rocks and bottles, and now they started throwing them at us. We retreated. They won that first battle."

The superintendent considered asking for the National Guard, under the Kent State model that had killed four students only three months before. Instead, he broadcast an SOS, and within hours, local law officers arrived from California and Nevada. "By 11:30 we had a force of 200," Quartini says, "and those men knew how to handle themselves.

"The rangers met in the Visitor Center, where the chief ranger announced, 'We're going to arm you. Anyone with an aversion to weapons may leave.' " At least a few rangers' children were probably among the kids. Three or four rangers left, and the others, presumably without aversions, received weapons. No one knew what was going to happen when this army of rangers, sheriff's deputies, and local cops returned with guns that presumably tipped the balance of power away from the kids.

"We didn't go to the meadow," Quartini says, "but to the campground—that's where a lot of the kids were by then—and we broke up all groups of more than six people. We made 174 arrests, and 174 of them were physical, I mean down on the ground. Hundreds of other people chose to leave that night.

"I didn't see any ranger brutality, but the publicity was bad. A former state senator from Florida was the father of a girl who was there, and he had a letter put in the *Congressional Record*, and it damaged the Park Service's reputation. We weren't hitting people with night sticks. Oh, there was some of *this*." and Quartini makes the motion of ramming a club into a person's gut, "but no hitting."

Quartini thinks that the rangers did what they needed to do. "It broke the back of the hippie element. If we hadn't gone in, they might still be there."

Roney, Quartini, and others consider the riot nothing less than a turning point for their agency. "The next day, the effect was felt throughout the National Park Service," Roney says. "The initial reaction was raw power. The superintendent hadn't been able to buy a pistol, but now Washington asked him, 'How many shotguns do you want?'" The National Park Police sent forty-five enforcement specialists to Yosemite. "The event represents a major turnaround in what it means to be a ranger. The traditional role was forever changed."

Quartini agrees: "It was the beginning of the focus on law enforcement in the Park Service. Training began a week after the riot."

In 1971, the Park Service turned toward permissiveness. Few people were arrested. "It was ridiculous," Roney says. "Some volunteer rangers on shuttle buses were literally thrown out onto the pavement by partying kids. The rangers walked on eggshells, but law enforcement eventually became more professional, and in the next few years they saw that they could make the problem go away without busting heads.

"Gradually a harder line on law enforcement was readopted," Roney says. "Today it has swung again to that side."

Quartini, who has no regrets about strong-arming during the riot, feels that enough is enough. "Rangers should be here to help people enjoy the outdoors, not to arrest people." I ask if the current attitude is to get tough. He answers, "Well, sometimes it is."

Roney adds, "I'd like to see a return to at least a facade of the traditional ranger role." He says that if I stick around awhile, I will probably see what he means.

Trouble for the rangers in that difficult era, 1968–75, came not only from hundreds of youth but also from the heart of the establishment, including Hollywood and the president of the United States.

In 1973, the Music Corporation of America (MCA) bought the Yosemite Park and Curry Company, a commercial monopoly operating the lodges, restaurants, gas stations, bars, horse stables, and gift shops. At the same time, professional management of the park slipped to an abysmal low because of directives from the top. Richard Nixon appointed Ron Walker, his advance man who had arranged for public appearances during the 1972 campaign, as head of the Park Service. At a time of unprecedented stress, the agency that had remained distinguished even in times of gross government mismanagement was led by one of the few nonprofessional directors in its history.

The Yosemite superintendent was instructed to cooperate with MCA. Its largest subsidiary, Universal Studios, filmed a television series called "Sierra," and while the park faced an entirely new era in matters of visitation, crime, environmental awareness, back-country use, and almost everything, a TV show that producers later aborted stole priority. Universal Studios closed roads, paid rangers to act, and took over entire campgrounds.

When the cliffs were the wrong color for the TV show, Universal painted them darker, and that was the limit. Photographs of the "painted rocks" were broadcast nationwide. The paint was soluble in water and would wear away, but the principle was the thing. Environmental groups were outraged, an entire park plan was eventually halted because it catered to MCA, and Congress launched an investigation into concessionaires. In 1976, the report was issued: "National Park Service Policies Discourage Competition, Give Concessionaires Too Great a Voice in Concession Management." Today, this experience is behind MCA and the Park Service. Each presumably learned important lessons.

In 1968, I abandoned Yosemite without my pack, and though it has taken me sixteen years to resupply, I'm back with a lot more gear than I used to carry, and with more than my old sense of adventure. Now I have questions. How has the place changed? Yosemite is arguably the most important site in the Sierra Nevada. What is its future?

One thing has not changed: I'm still unable to find a legal campsite. Finally, one opens up at Sunnyside, a walk-in campground where John Muir stayed.

Muir had planned to go to the Amazon, but he got sick and went to California instead. Inspired by a brochure probably written by J. M. Hutchings, the first promoter of the valley, Muir arrived at Yosemite in 1868. He lived near Yosemite Falls, he cut wind-felled logs in Hutchings's sawmill, and he stayed six years. Why he ever left is a question unanswered to my satisfaction. From this Yosemite experience, Muir grew to be a spokesman for the Sierra and the protector of the range from this point south. From this Yosemite experience, Muir changed no less than the course of American history by starting the environmental protection movement.

Since the 1950s, Sunnyside—also called Camp 4—has been the home of rock climbers. This patch of woods is the center from which the Yosemite climbing culture was born and thrives. All the great climbers camped or lived here for weeks, months, or years. Dirty and disgusting to some tourists and lodge operators, a few "climbing bums" have survived on leftovers at the Curry Company cafeteria. Many have dropped out of colleges or graduate schools and abandoned profitable opportunities in the dominant culture. These people live to climb and have created a culture of their own. As Chris Jones wrote in *Climbing in North America*, "Camp 4 was their spiritual home, their bastion against the outside world."

Site 25 is occupied by climbers who receive free rent and an hourly wage for rescue services when rangers need help. Grant Hiskes has been saving people for five years. Last season he worked on twenty-five rescues, evacuations from El Capitan during snowstorms being the most exciting. I ask Grant if he has seen Steve Schneider, the archetypal full-time climber and an old acquaintance. I learn that he has moved to Tuolumne Meadows, where it's cool and less crowded.

Sunnyside strikes me as an anthill of all nations outfitted by REI. This is not my idea of camping, but, like the others, I will do almost anything to be in Yosemite. John Muir sawed logs, the wealthy pay $121.50 a night at the Ahwahnee, and I elbow my way onto a dusty space at Sunnyside.

The bright thing here is Nancy Mertz, the ranger who issues camping permits. She does an outstanding job, proven by the fact that each person who talks to her smiles, in spite of their nationality, language, sex, or ten-minute wait.

As the average visitor entering the valley, I would not go to Sunnyside unless maybe I knew Nancy was there. Sunnyside is too strange and inexpensive, and you have to walk a hundred yards from the car to sleep in a colony of strangers. No, I would check in at one of the three lodge complexes, where 4,000 people stay each night in everything from wall tents at $17.75 to the Ahwahnee, one of America's great resort hotels. Or I would hunt for my diminutive, smoky campsite, $7 a night, reserved many months in advance through that contemporary symbol of mass gatherings—Ticketron.

After checking in, I would take the free shuttle bus to the Visitor Center and Yosemite Village. The village has gift shops, a grocery, a delicatessen, Bank of America, a pizza shop, an ice cream stand, a hamburger stand, and an Ansel Adams store featuring prints and art. I would walk on one of the most popular nonurban paths in America: the trail up the Merced River to Vernal Falls, where 200,000 sightseers a year create bridge jams. In the evening I would eat at one of six restaurants or more likely at the cafeteria, and I'd go to a program where a ranger-naturalist (interpreter) talks and shows slides. These excellent presentations draw 50 to 400 visitors.

Who are these people? More than three-quarters are Californians. Half graduated from college. Nine of ten are white, and I would say that most of the others are Asian. About 2.5 million people come to the park each year, a fairly stable number since the mid-seventies, though the number is climbing again and will soon reach 3 million. Seventy percent of the park's use is in Yosemite Valley. February is the loneliest month, with 70,000 visitors in the park; in August there are 500,000. The reasons for coming to this place visited by P. T. Barnum in 1870 and Ralph Waldo Emerson in 1871 show as much gradient as the granite walls. The Lake Tahoe syndrome has set in; chief interpreter Len McKenzie said, "Many people come for things they don't need Yosemite for, and it's a party atmosphere for some."

Park superintendent Bob Binnewies said, "Many thousands of people get their first view of the Sierra in Yosemite Valley. At Glacier Point they have an easy opportunity to see more of the range, and still more at Tuolumne Meadows. They might return the next year and hike. Yosemite allows that kind of progression."

"Yosemite Valley is paradise," one visitor said.

"It's a zoo, too crowded," said another (this is the sixth most used national park in total recreation visits).

The Yosemite master plan calls the valley "one of the grandest natural settings that exist anywhere in the world."

Queen Elizabeth said that this valley was the highlight of her trip to America.

After sleeping out in the snow on Glacier Point with John Muir, President Theodore Roosevelt called his Yosemite experience "the grandest day of my life."

What do people who live here think? "It's unusual, to say the least," ranger Steve Hickman said. "A good bit of the spectacle wears off, and you're left with a small community where everyone knows your business, nothing is nearby, and tourists overrun you. But the schools are excellent, here and in Mariposa, where the kids go after sixth grade. It's a great place to raise children; twelve-year-olds go on overnight camping trips by themselves."

Bob Binnewies said, "Yosemite is an exceptional place to be a park superintendent. It clearly ranks as one of the world's masterpieces of nature, and statistically, the park is in a class by itself. It has the largest overnight visitation of any national park [2 million; Yellowstone is second with 1.3 million]. It's open year-round. It's under the eye of the media more than any park, except maybe Yellowstone in the summer. The demands for search and rescue, law enforcement, and emergency medical attention exceed anything in the Park Service." Binnewies came to Yosemite in 1979, "by pure luck," when Bill Whalen, President Carter's director of the Park Service, made an "impulsive offer." Binnewies had started working in the parks in 1961, and when Whalen appointed him, he was a vice president for the National Audubon Society.

Dick Riegelhuth, with an enviable lifetime of Sierra experience, is in charge of resource protection in Yosemite, and he said, "The park is not only an exceptional place but vitally important to other places. It's a model, a pacesetter. When you protect this park, you protect the parks of the world."

"Yosemite Valley is not unlike a small city of 12,000 people," said Don Fox, the park's landscape architect and planner. The population swells to 22,000 on busy days. Here are 1,000 buildings counting permanent tent frames, 30 miles of roads, 2,000 employees and dependents, lodging for 4,000, and camping space for 4,500. The park's budget is $9.3 million. A jail holds sixteen, and the magistrate is busy all the time.

Is this what a national park—the finest national park in the opinion of many people—is supposed to be? "There has been an erosion of the Park Service's role and mission," said Fox. "We've not been aggressive in defining what a park should be." History supports Fox's views. To understand Yosemite, it helps to look at planning in the past.

There was little of it. In essence, though not in name, Yosemite was the first national park in the world (Yellowstone, in 1872, was the first park to be called national, kept by the federal government when Wyoming was still a territory). Yosemite's protection came in 1864, after John Conness convinced colleagues that the land was "for all public purposes worthless." It was the first time Congress acted to preserve scenic values.

President Lincoln's act ceded the lands to California, and the governor appointed Frederick Law Olmsted, the father of American landscape architecture, as chairman of the Yosemite Valley Commissioners. He said, "The first point to be kept in mind is to preserve and maintain the natural scenery as exactly as possible." The legislature, however, suppressed the plan, leaving decisions to political appointees and concessionaires who already had a stranglehold on the valley.

California allowed squatters to settle, dams to be built, trees to be cut, and fences to be strung for cattle and 300 horses. In 1890, Congress made Yosemite the nation's third major national park, only days after Sequoia was designated. Park status theoretically protected the basins of the Merced and Tuolumne, where meadows were being eaten root-deep by sheep, but the valley remained under state mismanagement. Prodded by Muir and others, California gave the valley back to the federal government in 1906, and much of the land was gradually reclaimed.

Second only to effective administration, transportation was the key to park management. To reach Yosemite in the late 1800s, people boarded a boat in San Francisco, then rode by stagecoach for sixteen hours from Stockton to Coulterville and on horseback for thirty-seven hours to the valley. When the government considered allowing cars in the park, James Bryce said, "There are plenty of roads for the lovers of speed and noise. . . . If you were to realize what the result of the automobile will be in that wonderful, that incomparable valley, you will keep it out." But he had no say; he was the British ambassador to the United States.

Cars were allowed in 1913, and the push to accommodate them was on. Roads were built and more were planned. Park service director Stephen Mather supported a road through spectacular backcountry from Glacier Point to Tenaya Lake via Nevada Falls (the road was never built). Even in the 1950s, Sierra Club leader William Colby supported new highways, including southern Sierra routes over Kearsarge Pass and in upper Kings Canyon.

Mission 66, a funding program for parks development from 1956 to 1966, brought new facilities, but as Don Fox said, "It made no effort to look at the whole area." In Washington, D.C., the kickoff dinner for the Mission was cosponsored by the American Automobile Association. The idea was, the more parking lots the better.

Yosemite became the victim of a madness that tried to accommodate whatever anybody and everybody wanted to do. The theme seemed to be that new is good, more is better, and new and more is best, and under this wisdom Yosemite became a symbol of park development gone berserk. More commercial buildings were constructed. Conservationists' criticism of valley management had been growing since 1950, when Ansel Adams called for a master plan, and 1952, when the *Sierra Club Bulletin* referred to Yosemite's "fatal beauty" and smog.

The late sixties brought a new era in planning after the Yosemite Park and Curry Company asked for permission to convert its rental tent sites to permanent buildings. The tents expand the range of lodging downward to people who cannot afford a room. Also, to construct buildings would forgo options for other uses of the land. Before considering the request, a plan would be drawn, and with it came the first serious look at the future.

At Lake Tahoe, the need for planning was obvious, but the delivery was plagued with intergovernmental strife. No less need existed in Yosemite, and if planning should work anyplace, it should work in a national park where the politics, ownership, and goals are simplified, theoretically.

"In the middle of this planning effort came Earth Day," said Don Fox, "and the idea of minimizing impacts." The criticized centerpiece of concern was the automobile, no longer a prerequisite for the American dream but suddenly a source of the American nightmare. Traffic jams became the national symbol for stress and life out of balance. In Los Angeles it was bad enough, but in Yosemite Valley, domination by cars was wrong, simply wrong.

In 1971, the first plan called for no less than the elimination of cars from the valley. Foresta, near Route 120, would be a staging area where people would switch to buses. Costs were high but could have been reduced.

In the cultural blink of an eye, while everyone carped over details of the plan, the countercultural optimism that said you could really do something—that you could really change something—met a quiet demise. The great imaginative thrust of the early 1970s was choked by the status quo, and the momentum to restore Yosemite Valley to a precar condition—an Edenlike condition—was lost.

Planners whittled at the problem: the roads to Happy Isles, Mirror Lake, and the Ahwahnee Meadow were closed, totaling several miles. Shuttle buses, started in 1969, offered an alternative, though no solution, to traffic jams.

When a new plan was begun, a new problem took over—commercialization. Now MCA wanted three new High Sierra camps for backcountry lodging, expansion of Tuolumne Meadows development, more lifts at Badger Pass (started in 1935, it is California's oldest ski area), and a cable car from Curry Village to Glacier Point, where a hotel would be built. Conservationists furiously attacked the plan. "The park has its own values; we don't have to make a Disneyland out of it," said Becky Evans of the Sierra Club. Assistant Interior Secretary Nathaniel Reed agreed that the plan "appeared to be written by MCA." The future of the valley hung in the balance during yet another attempt at planning.

In 1978, a new plan carried the humble goal of "rectifying an overzealous attempt to civilize the park." Regaining some initiative against cars, planners called for a parking lot at a gravel pit in the lower end of the valley, not visible from major viewpoints, where people coming for one day would leave their cars and transfer to buses. Visitors staying overnight would drive to their room or campsite but would not use their cars once they checked in.

Rangers somehow believed that their work load would increase if dependence on cars was decreased. Although crowds were approaching 30,000 people on a busy day, officials thought that the visitors' experience would somehow be ruined if they didn't have their cars on hand. On his days off, the chief ranger lobbied against the transportation proposal at the Park Service's San Francisco headquarters.

The government would see what the public thought of the plan. Sixty-three thousand copies were sent out, and the Park Service received "the largest amount of public input of any plan done by the federal government." An extraordinary 40 percent of people surveyed returned a questionnaire, and, according to Don Fox, an "overwhelming majority" called for cutbacks in cars. A final plan was written that reflected the public desire to "restore the natural scene as nearly as possible."

In spite of this mandate, the superintendent approved the plan in 1980 without the day-use parking lot at the lower end of the valley and without the driving restrictions, though the document clearly states, "The intent of the National Park Service is to remove all automobiles from Yosemite Valley and Mariposa Grove and to redirect development to the periphery of the park and beyond."

The elusive thrust of the plan had shifted from cars to employee housing. In Yosemite Valley, Park Service summer housing would be reduced from 210 to 70, and concessionaire housing from 1,240 to 400. Much of the replacement housing would be built in El Portal, sixteen miles down the Merced Canyon (this has been proposed since 1958). Some people fight the move because it will create yet more transportation demands of shuttling employees back and forth. MCA objects to moving valley workers but has relocated its warehouse and administrative offices, with forty employees, to Fresno.

The plan marks the "first big step" toward a park "uncluttered by . . . stumbling blocks of commercialism, machines, and fragments of suburbia." More than 200 overnight lodging units, and 116 campsites will be removed (in the late sixties there were 1,500 campsites; the cutbacks will leave 800, most with a capacity of six people). The golf course at the Ahwahnee Hotel was reclaimed by the meadow in 1981. In trade for the lodging cutback, the plan allows more development of outlying areas, such as Wawona and Tuolumne Meadows, for a net reduction of only 10 percent in accommodations.

About the seemingly forgotten efforts to reduce cars, Don Fox said, "We don't have a solution. It's going to take a major attitude change. We hope that more people will leave their cars at home and take public transportation to Yosemite." But the concessionaire's contract is problematic. Until 1993, MCA has the exclusive right to run buses in the park. Anyone organizing bus service must negotiate not with the Park Service but with MCA. Fox said, "It eliminates competition and discourages new solutions to the problem."

Another official said, "Restrictions won't work. We have a very conservative group of rangers, who will not enforce additional regulations." Yet I've seen rangers who are all but rabid in their pursuit of violations as minor as a registered camper sleeping in a van instead of a tent at Sunnyside.

Bob Binnewies says that the goal of eliminating cars is "on the horizon and possible, but not overnight." For two holiday weekends, he has imposed a limit of 5,000 cars in the valley at one time—a number determined by parking space, and slightly less than the worst days of crowding in the past.

Rather than implementing proposals for reduced use of cars, the Park Service is launching a new research effort to determine the "carrying capacity." Like the existing plan, the new study will require years of work. Meanwhile, traffic is thick rolling up one side of the valley and down the other.

Progress in planning has come in fits and starts and has largely been limited to short-term solutions, but many people agree that Yosemite is a better place than it was twenty or even a hundred years ago. Dick Leonard, a pioneer in Yosemite rock climbing and the Sierra Club's honorary president said, "A lot of people complain and say they'll never go back to Yosemite, but it's better today than it was." On his first trip, he and his troop of boy scouts walked in at night because the dirt road was dust, "six inches deep." Look at the old days: the fire fall—an extravaganza of flaming logs shoved over the rim at night—was stopped in 1968 because it was unnatural. Before that, the Glacier Point hotel operator threw live chickens off the rim for tourists to watch, and a Howitzer was kept on hand for echoes. The Howitzer, chickens, hotel, fire fall, and dust are gone. The Park Service cites the removal of several buildings among other accomplishments in implementing the plan; however, a major new structure is to be built—a jail.

The development or restoration of the valley is Don Fox's problem, but what people do here is Armand Quartini's problem. He has seen changes since he was hired with linebacker credentials in 1968, and even more changes since he camped here in 1933. "It was a happier time back then. Now there's a lot of stress." While we talk at the dispatch center, I overhear a ranger on his radio at the Crane Flat gas station. "We're going in." In the station is a stranger with a gun.

In a typical Yosemite year, fifteen people will be killed in accidents, many due to what Steve Hickman called visitors' "lack of awareness of natural hazards—gravity and cliffs." Rangers will be called 100 times for search and rescue and will catch people at 700 class 1 offenses serious enough for incarceration.

Dealing with today's problems, Quartini is probably as personable as the rangers of the thirties. He calls himself the "pleasant paisano," except when people leave food out for the bears (there are 350 in the park) or when drunks are rowdy. Then he is the "dangerous dago." He tells jokes and sings songs. He even sang to Queen Elizabeth, who responded, "Very cute, Mr. Ranger." Quartini says, "A lot of good things happen here.

"In the morning I get dressed, put on my hat, look in the mirror, and say, 'Good morning, ranger.' I want to go out with the image of a ranger—to help people have an enjoyable experience. But during the day you lose track of that idea." Quartini gestures frequently and now raises his hands as if the problem is a mystery, but it is not. Rangers deal with nearly 3 million people a year.

Steve Hickman, a Yosemite ranger since 1966, said the greatest challenge is to "keep in sight why I joined the Park Service. So many people have a positive experience, but 90 percent of my contact is with people who have a negative experience." Hickman works with law enforcement, safety, search and rescue, and miscellany, such as a human bone that a hiker brought in last summer. He and other rangers told me, "These problems are not what I joined the Park Service for." But not all the rangers feel that way.

For nearly a generation, since the riot in 1970, the Park Service's hiring and training practices have recognized a new reality. Guns, nightsticks, and Mace are important weapons where odd hats and an outdoor demeanor drew enough respect in the old days. Are new rangers a different breed?

"We're fighting that very thing right now," Quartini says. "Rangers today—you graduate from the police academy, they give you a gun, a book, and a vehicle, and say, 'Go out and do the job.' The guy runs into the same problems he'd run into on a beat in Fresno. It's easy for them to begin acting like policemen. I believe in educating the people if it's possible to give them that option."

The debate of ranger versus cop started long ago. In 1967, when I worked for the Park Service at Crater Lake in Oregon, one ranger was outcast as "the cop" because he would rather write tickets to Californians going forty miles an hour than show people something special about the lake. Now Yosemite is in the vortex of the conflict.

Bob Binnewies said, "The valley is an extremely demanding place in terms of law enforcement. It's a lot to ask a ranger to keep a positive perspective when he's dealing with a drunken driver who hit a kid and then throws up in the patrol car. In the last ten years, there's been a significant shift to hard enforcement, but I think that's a temporary aberration. We're going to achieve a good balance. The trend is toward a new kind of professional within the parks: a ranger trained in law enforcement but with the visitor's enjoyment in mind."

At noon I leave the Yosemite library and sit on a bench. This pedestrian mall that used to be a parking lot for 250 cars is a good place to watch people.

"I think it would be neat to conceive a baby up here," says a young woman to her partner. I think that few of the young adults who visited here fifteen years ago came with babies in mind. It seems that babies have been conceived all over. Little kids are everywhere.

"It's too long a drive," one man says to another. "Up and back is too much for one day."

"You know how long it took us to get hot dogs and a piece of pizza? Twenty minutes!" A survey found that shopping and eating out were the only activities to which many visitors give poor ratings. Do people come to Yosemite to shop and eat out?

Vince Kehoe, director of the Yosemite Institute, walks to the post office. The institute is one hope for the future. A staff of environmental educators spreads the Yosemite message to school kids, delinquents, the elderly, and others. The institute's message is "A better understanding of the natural environment will create a positive impact on the future character of the world."

"Lisa! Is that you?"

"Tim!"

On the Stanislaus River, in 1979, I met Lisa Nemzer while writing a wild and scenic river study. She helped with the chapter on plant life. Now she teaches for the institute. She guided raft trips in Idaho earlier this summer. Next spring she doesn't know where she will go. She spends a lot of money on transportation and shrugs her shoulders at the future.

Off on the side, a ditch-digging crew wearing the olive drab pants of the Park Service clinks and chunks into the dirt, aiming to exhume a water line. There is something unusual in the swing of their picks. They are women. There is no discrimination in hiring practices here, but for some reason virtually all the rangers I need to interview are men.

Here comes Lee Stetson. Holding a cup of coffee and a *Los Angeles Times*, he sits on the bench next to me. Wrinkled, half-bald, and wiry, wearing a shaggy beard, faded jeans, and a brown brim hat, he looks like John Muir. To tens of thousands of people, he is. His one-man show, "Conversations with a Tramp," sells out three times a week in the valley, and in the winter, Stetson's impersonation of Muir is the first choice of entertainment for environmental groups from Seattle to Washington, D.C.

"Hi, Lee."

"Hi. Have we met?"

We meet. Stetson is a professional actor, and I clumsily inquire if he believes in what he's doing—spreading the gospel according to the Old Man. He answers, "Look, you can't state rock-bottom truth every night and not get attached to it."

It's time to work, and I'm plagued by this vexing issue of cars. If I were coming to the valley for a day, I would not complain about riding a bus. If I camped or roomed overnight, which is what more than two-thirds of the visitors do, I would have no problem parking my van for the duration. No cars and no driving—it would be fun, like taking a boat to the other side of a lake. We have used cars for seventy years out of several million of human existence. Is it too much to leave the gas guzzler behind for a day? I can see that the average visitor might rather drive. The average visitor wants pizza faster. Of *course* people say they want to drive. Those who disagree have left. The average visitor is not the average Yosemite enthusiast; many live in exile, avoiding the valley because of cars, crowds, and development.

While supporting the shuttle bus system as it exists, most park officials I talk to do not think buses can replace cars. "To keep cars out would be to keep people out," said assistant valley ranger Steve Hickman. But buses deny no one access; buses are the vehicles used by people who are too old to drive, too handicapped to walk, and too poor to own a car. Critics of car cutbacks also say new technology is needed. But why wait for technology while here sits a road and a fleet of vehicles capable of bringing in sixty tourists at a time? We need a rack on the bus for coolers, and a parking lot down the road instead of here in the world's masterpiece of nature, where 200 square feet are consumed to park each car. A large percentage of private cars have been banned from other parks: Mount McKinley, the Shark Valley portion of the Everglades, and Devils Postpile National Monument right here in the Sierra. Not to mention Jim Hildinger's resort near Lake Tahoe. The town of Zermatt, Switzerland, is restricted to rail access. Tourist destinations as busy as Nantucket Island, Massachusetts, and Williamsburg, Virginia, succeed phenomenally without cars. Why not Yosemite?

Congressman Richard Lehman, representing part of the park, said, "I think Yosemite is at a real juncture in the way it's managed. There are too many people, too many cars, and too much pollution. Anything we can do to get the cars out of Yosemite, or at least limit them, is going to help."

What could be done? Incentives to not drive could be tried—say, a free entrance permit but a fee every time drivers pass a checkpoint instead of walking, bicycling, or riding the bus. Fringe parking areas near Yosemite entrance gates could be combined with free admission to people who ride the bus and steep entrance fees for those who drive. I will see what Ed Hardy thinks.

Ed Hardy is a tall, muscular man, middle-aged, wearing short hair and, today, a Hawaiian shirt. Except for a water glass, a plant, and a piece of paper, his desk is bare. On the wall behind him is a certificate from the United States Marine Corps. On a shelf rest a Congressional Staff Directory and a Federal Staff Directory. He taught physical education in San Jose; now he's president of the Yosemite Park and Curry Company, as MCA calls this largest concession in the entire system of national parks.

"I think that to eliminate the automobile is a fine goal," Hardy says. "The thing to recognize is the timing. Until we figure out alternatives to the automobile, I don't feel the valley should be exclusively used by the backpacker." I don't recall anyone proposing to stop all motorized access, but we move on.

"One thing we can do is manage the automobile so it's tied up while it's here. Leave it at Camp 4 or wherever. As we accept more and more distance from the automobile, we can eventually leave it out of the park."

What is his company doing to encourage buses? "We're running the bus line. We pay 50 percent of the cost of the newspaper that you get at the park entrance, and it encourages people to ride the bus."

Working half-time as Hardy's environmental advisor, Garrett DeBell was editor of *The Environmental Handbook*, popular in the era of Earth Day. An updated edition still sells well. Through DeBell's efforts, the company has run a recycling program for seven years and supports the protection of Mono Lake, west of the park, through congressional testimony and money given to the Mono Lake Committee. DeBell drafts policy positions for the company, such as one supporting the development of a staging area at the Wawona entrance, where people could park and board buses. MCA would also build a new gift shop at the bus stop.

Hardy proposes no expansion of commercial facilities in the valley, but neither does he think the place is overcrowded. "My wife and I like to read to each other, and even on the busiest days, we can find an isolated place without people.

"If Yosemite is harmed, this company certainly stands to lose a lot. There are many watchdogs over the environment up here, and I'm one of them."

Back at Sunnyside, I have a problem, an old one. My permit to camp on a ten-by-ten piece of ground has been given to someone else because I didn't renew in time. Nancy Mertz says, "Sorry, Tim, we're filled up."

I'll go to the ranger program because Len McKenzie is showing slides tonight, then I'll park at the orchard where hundreds of other people park while staying at the Curry Village cabins or in the backcountry. Who will notice? In ranger jargon, this is OB camping—out of bounds—but it will save me mileage. I'll keep the windows up and the candle out.

At 2:00 A.M., the ranger sneaks up behind the van and places the palm of his hand on the back door. With the other hand he makes a fist, and with the heel of it, he strikes a staccato rap on the door. Bang! Awakened rudely, I jump, he feels the van rock, and it's all over for me.

A curt voice announces, "This is the ranger, I need to talk to you, step outside please." He waits at a safe distance behind, the lights on me. I pull on my jeans and T-shirt. Humbly I step into the beams, and my name, gleaned from a computer that was fed my license number, squelches over the ranger's radio: "Timothy Palmer."

"You know you're parked illegally."

"Well, you see, I—"

"Let me have your driver's license please."

He is one of a thousand rangers, McKinley-to-Everglades, with a furrowed brow, an occupational squint and, most saliently, a mustache and a gun.

To find my license, I return to the shelter of my van, which makes the ranger nervous, and I don't blame him. At Crater Lake last summer a ranger pursued a man who was exceeding the speed limit. The speeder prepared to throw a hand grenade at her, even pulled the pin, but had apparently forgotten to roll his window down. The chase ended abruptly when the speeder's car blew up. The incident is widely used as evidence that rangers can't trust anybody. I reemerge, and the officer again steps out of the darkness to share the glare with me.

I don't want him to read the fine print. I must divert his attention. "You know, I was camping in Sunnyside but forgot—"

"Just a minute please." Clearly in the cop mode, not the ranger mode, he's beaming his five-cell flashlight on my license.

"Do you know that this license is *expired?*"

"Yes, sir, ah, a woman in the grocery store told me that just the other day when I was cashing a traveler's check. Before that I didn't even—"

"You're driving without a license!"

"Well, no, sir. I mean, yes, sir, I'm driving, but that's my license right there. I haven't been to Pennsylvania for a year and a half, and it's one of those picture things, you know, I have to get my picture taken."

I ask, "Where's the closest site I can camp for the rest of the night?" He is uninterested in my evasion, and I could swear that behind the squint, his eyes are gleaming at the possibility that he has a real, live offender here.

"I could cite you for not having a current driver's license!"

"Yes, sure, but look, what would *you* do in my position? Go to Pennsylvania just for a snapshot?"

It's clear that he would not get into my position. He says, "What do you do, just ride around the country for years at a time?" This gunslinger is one of the few men I've met in years who is critical of my traveling. More troubling, his curiosity is unusual for cops. I'm suspicious of the direction he's heading.

"Is there an FTA on you?"

"A what?"

"A failure to appear."

I have failed to appear in many places. Curious, I ask, "Appear where?"

"In court."

"No! God, no. Court? You must be kidding!"

I can't believe how badly my situation is deteriorating. If I don't move the van, he's going to arrest me for OB camping, but when I move the van, he's going to arrest me for driving without a license.

"Here's my story," I offer. He takes one step back. "I'm writing a book about the Sierra Nevada." I understand his skepticism. "I interviewed Steve Hickman today, and in the morning I talk to Bob Binnewies again, and I didn't want to drive all the way to El Portal when I could sleep here without bothering anyone."

He considers this, then says, "You realize that it wouldn't be fair to let you stay here and no one else?" Of course I realize that.

Fighting to stay awake, I drive down the canyon, cross the park boundary, and pull over in El Portal.

Other than talk to people and try to find a place to sleep at night, what did I see and do in Yosemite Valley?

One morning at 3 A.M. I heard someone yell from the cliffs along the Yosemite Falls trail, far above the campground. They yelled again, and again. A climber from the rescue site shouted back, "Do—you—need—help?" A garbled answer came down: "No." The climber yelled, "If—you—do—not—need—help—*shut up!*" The yelling continued. At 4:30 Grant Hiskes and ranger Jim Lee walked up the trail, and in ten minutes they returned with two Curry Company employees.

On some mornings I worked in my van, at Camp 4, surrounded by dozens of rock climbers talking in their own language. Three radios played in the parking lot while hackysack games ran by the hour. Climbers spread rainbow colored ropes and slings with glittering pitons and carabiners on the ground. When the Doors' "Touch Me Baby" came on the radio, the volume went up, and in the bright morning sun, beneath those bright granite cliffs, the whole place seethed with energy.

"Hey, been boating?" asked a curly-haired, soft-spoken man with a powerful upper body. He looked at the scars on my Mad River canoe.

"Not much. A raft trip on the Tuolumne." Lars Holbek and I became friends. He cowrote *A Guide to the Best Whitewater in the State of California.* Lars's Grand Canyon of the Tuolumne trip required six miles of portage; his upper Mokelumne trip, thirty carries and several runnable falls. The Clavey and the Golden Gate run on the South Fork of the American may be his favorites.

In the cafeteria I met the Nortons, about fifty, and Paul and I walked to Yosemite Falls together. In the Indian museum I watched Julia Parker, an Indian, weave a basket with centuries-old care. I bought four books at the Visitor Center, washed my laundry amid a mob, and rode my bicycle all over. I was by myself but enjoyed few redeeming qualities of solitude, so I felt lonely. Couples and small groups everywhere reminded me that most people were with friends or partners or family.

It's not until my final evening in the valley that I go for the Walk. When I leave the van, I have no idea that I will see anything special. I pass the gas station, the tent city behind Yosemite Lodge, and the fresh asphalt of the bike trail. Here I leave my sneakers. In a quarter mile the trail bridges the Merced, but I enter Leidig Meadow.

Within ten steps I stop. Something has changed. The grass underfoot is the first signal, soft and wild. The touch of grass resets my senses so that I once again see a landscape that is almost unbelievable. The smell of the sweet evening air imparadises me. I hear the swish of water against the shore.

My narrow path bends to the river, where I walk in coarse sand that long ago crumbled from granite. I see three deer. Across the river stands a dark, silent forest. Downriver, the Cathedral Spires rise high. The day's final light shines on massive Sentinel Rock. The flat side of Half Dome, four miles away, is gold.

I think of what Robert Redford said about his first view of Yosemite Valley when he was seventeen: "It was the most magnificent thing I had ever seen. To some, the size and the space are overwhelming, but I didn't see it that way. I saw it as an opportunity, as a challenge. To me, that image of the valley meant unlimited opportunities, unlimited possibilities. Much of my concern for the environment relates to that first impression, and it helped to set a course for the rest of my life."

What with the campground, cafeteria, grocery store, laundry, reservations, bike riding, and cars, I haven't seen the unlimited possibilities very well.

Now the Merced is a silent mirror reflecting cottonwoods, a symbol of wet lowlands. It is not only the big scene that captures me; each detail is exquisite. Near the water, alders grow in a cluster of three, where wrens and sparrows feed. The sky is violet behind spires streaked with white and gray. I stand as an insignificant speck in a place that gives me prospect and refuge, unlimited opportunities. At this moment, this place makes me feel better than anyplace I have ever known. If this is not sacred, what is?

My sense of belonging lasts only minutes because the traffic noise converges from both sides of the wide meadow. Inbound traffic runs to my left, outbound to my right. I stand on the world's most beautiful median strip.

I dream of the Escape to places uncramped by traffic. But I want to escape to *here* because *here* is the best place on earth.

If people parked their cars and left them at their lodge or campsite, and if single-day users were shuttled in by bus, then one road through the valley might be enough. One side of this meadow—heaven if it exists anywhere—could be a refuge from cars. Yosemite Valley could be a world apart. I wonder, do people want to get away or simply to drive to another pretty place? Another Lake Tahoe. Is Yosemite just another stop on a road to monuments, curiosities, and accommodations? Like Ed Hardy, I can find isolation here. I can find a hiding place from the frenzy of Yosemite Valley, but I do not find that Yosemite Valley is a hiding place from the frenzy of the world.

Go higher. Somewhere up there beyond the canyon rim, maybe I can find a different side of this national park.

I'm driving toward the headwaters of the Tuolumne, and I cross the geographic center of the Sierra Nevada near the Tamarack Flat Campground. From here, 200 miles of the Sierra run north to Lake Almanor; 200 miles run south to Tehachapi Pass.

Yosemite covers 760,917 acres—about the size of Rhode Island. If the California Wilderness Bill passes, 90 percent of the park will be protected as wilderness, bisected by this road, built for the Tioga Mine, which yielded not one ton of ore. The road was neglected until 1915, when Stephen Mather, the first director of the Park Service, bought it for $15,000 and gave it to the government. Crossing Tioga Pass, 9,945 feet above sea level, Route 120 became the highest road over the Sierra, and Tuolumne Meadows—the largest meadow in the range, according to the Forest Service—was open for visitors.

When the road was being rebuilt in the 1950s, Sierra Club leaders, including Ansel Adams, Harold Bradley, and David Brower, unsuccessfully opposed a plan to blast a seventy-foot-wide cut around the shore of the granite-rimmed gem, Tenaya Lake. They fought the road as a way to save the scenery, while the Park Service justified the road as a way to show off the scenery. At the highway's dedication in 1961, former Park Service director Conrad Wirth said, "Now anyone who can get in a car, no matter how old or feeble, may share this magnificent treasure." They could before—they just had to drive a little more slowly. The new interior secretary, Stewart Udall, later called the road location a "mistake" and an "egregious error."

David Brower still regrets the blasting at Tenaya Lake and the interstate scale of road cuts in Lee Vining Canyon, where the highway descends the Sierra's east slope: "Those are two of the worst things we've done to the High Sierra in my lifetime. Now we have rapidly passing scenery instead of a unique experience."

In other conservation battles in the Sierra, south of here, Brower won. His involvement with the range began in 1918, at age six, on a family trip to Lake Tahoe, when they pushed the car up the steep grades of the Lincoln Highway, later replaced by Route 40, later replaced by Interstate 80. In 1931, on a backpack trip in the southern Sierra, Brower was "marked"; the Sierra's effect on him was "total," leading him to his career in environmental protection. He joined the Sierra Club in 1933, when Richard Leonard signed his application.

From 1935 to 1938, Brower worked in the publicity department of the Yosemite Park and Curry Company, and to promote the valley, he used photographs by Ansel Adams. Brower spent hours helping the photographer in his darkroom, where they talked about the mountains and what should be done to save them. Brower made thirty first ascents of Sierra peaks, and in 1935 he made the first ski ascent of Mount Lyell, the park's highest summit. In 1955, he became the Sierra Club's first full-time director. For fifteen years he built the organization into a major national force for conservation. After taking a stand against the Diablo Canyon nuclear power plant, he was voted out of office, and he started a new organization, Friends of the Earth.

Brower calls Yosemite and the Sierra "a principal source of inspiration and recreation that led to the national park idea and to conservation advancements all over America." Yet he looks ahead more than back. The park is threatened on all sides: dams are proposed on the Merced to the southwest and the Tuolumne to the west. Eastward, Mono Lake waters are being diverted. Even wilderness designation under the California Wilderness Bill would exempt hydroelectric dams on the nearby North Fork of the San Joaquin. Brower calls for a "Greater Yosemite National Park" that would include the entire Yosemite ecosystem. His idea is not for Park Service acquisition but for a "green-line concept" of protection that would stop harmful projects, encourage county zoning, and lead to protective management by the Forest Service, Park Service, and other agencies.

I drive past granite domes where layers of rock peel like layers of onion. Half Dome, Polly Dome, Fairview Dome, and others rise as rounded caps of granite from the vast block that underlies most of the Sierra, that unifies it as one place.

Crossing the divide from the Merced to the Tuolumne, I roll on to Tuolumne Meadows, elevation 8,600 feet, fifty-five road miles from Yosemite Valley. Each summer, 250,000 people visit here, but after the valley, this place does not seem crowded. The land is high and vast, ringed by peaks such as Unicorn, Cathedral, Conness, and Dana, with a feeling of openness. The Tuolumne curves through grassy fields before cutting into granite and plunging headlong through its grand canyon, then into the flooded valley of Hetch Hetchy.

I find a campsite, and after supper I walk across the campground for one more ranger's slide show about black bears or the water cycle or something. The themes are getting old, but slides are fun, and the ranger programs are a social life for me.

"Do you wonder *why* people climb the peaks?" Ginger Burley asks. She says that most people, except the climbers, do wonder about this. "I led a group on a week-long trip this summer, and after we reached the pass above Merced Lake, I asked if anyone wanted to go on, to climb to the top of Vogelsang Peak. We hid our packs in the rocks and started up. "Behind us, the views opened as we climbed, and we hurried in order to get back down before dark. It was steep and all rocks, and I said to myself, 'Why are you doing this?'

"Then we reached the top, and there was no more question. All the way up, the other side was hidden from view, and then it stretched out before us, ridge after ridge, and beautiful. The Cathedral Range was spread out below us. The view was something that could not be imagined from below. At the end of the backpacking trip, people talked about what they liked, and you know, the people who enjoyed the trip the most were the ones who went to the top of the mountain."

Ginger stands straight. Her ranger pants, shirt, and jacket are pressed and perfect. The brim of her hat runs straight across her forehead. "When I first came here, I watched the climbers. I was impressed. Technical climbing is different from going to the top of Vogelsang, and I didn't understand it. I asked them, 'Why do you do this?' The usual answers, 'Because it's there.' 'Because I'm a climber.' One day Chuck Pratt said, 'Ginger, I can't *tell* you why, but I can *show* you.' " [Chuck Pratt! He is renowned among climbers.]

"I didn't sleep much the night before. At 8 A.M. Chuck knocked on my door. His rope was coiled over one shoulder, his climbing boots hung over the other. A dozen carabiners jangled from his waist. He said, 'Let's go.'

" 'Where?'

" 'Cathedral Peak.'

"We hiked up to the base of the peak. It was straight up. I couldn't possibly do it. Chuck said, 'I'll show you.' I strapped a nylon harness around my waist and he tied the end of the rope to me.

"He reached for a knob of granite here, a crack there, and stepped up. 'See this Ginger? You can hold on here.' I couldn't see what he was holding. Pretty soon he was fifty feet up and said, 'Okay.'

"I made it one step. 'Just keep coming,' he said. In fifteen minutes I sat on the ledge with him. Not until then did I look down.

" 'Chuck, I can't go any farther. I'm terrified.'

" 'You can do it,' he said.

" 'How?' "

"I'll teach you.' "

"I got to a place where I couldn't go up or down. I yelled, 'I can't go any higher.'

"Chuck answered, 'Yes, you can, because it doesn't get any harder.'

"Twice I cried. My fingers bled. I have no idea how long it took. And then I was on the top.

"What made it so special? Now I *knew* that I could do it. I had trusted a friend. I was on top of the mountain. It was the best day of my life."

Ginger has inspired me, and I decide to try it. At "Rescue 1," a campsite with a four-burner cookstove, bicycles, kayaks, and a jungle gym of ropes, I find Steve Schneider. As at Camp 4, the Park Service gives Steve and a few other climbers an outdoor home in return for rescue services.

Sharing the site are a young, blond woman, a small man who Steve says is one of the most gifted climbers he knows, and curly-haired Bill Meyers.

The three men cook breakfasts, each on separate camp stoves. I ask Steve if he will take me on a climb. "Oh, yeah, sure. We could go most any time. If I'm not climbing, you can find me here or down at the beach." The beach is the north shore of Tenaya Lake. "Want to go now?"

He borrows a guidebook from the woman. "Here's one." The diagram shows two moves rated 5.9.

"Hey, Steve, you know, I don't even have climbing *shoes*. I just want to see what climbing is *like*."

"Oh, yeah, okay."

The kid says, "How about the Golfer's Route?" It's 5.7. No problem. We get in my van and drive to Low Profile Dome. Steve points to where we will go, where I will try to go. "See the big black streak where water runs down in the springtime? That's the route. The water wears away soft stuff and leaves the harder rock. It's tilted back more than it looks, covered with granite knobs." This puts me in mind of doorknobs. Fine.

He adds, "Once in a while a knob breaks off." Not so fine.

We walk to the base. "Okay, put this harness on." It is nylon webbing running around my waist and between my legs. "Make it real tight." This is the belt to which my leash will be tied, one that will save me from dying if I slip or if a knob breaks. "A little tighter. It should hold you if you turn upside down." Steve ties one end of the red climbing rope to my harness and gives me a chalk bag for clammy hands, of which I have two.

I've been waiting for firm advice, for a lesson. Steve finally says, "Take your time. Make good solid moves." He quietly looks up at the rock.

"I'll go up to that bolt." A piece of metal sticks out of the cliff thirty feet up. "You don't need to belay me until the second pitch." To do that, I'll stand up where the bolt is, clipped by carabiners into it. I'll hold the rope that's tied to Steve, and I'll release enough slack for him to advance. If he falls, I'll catch him by holding the rope, which will pass through a brake—a metal ring tied to my waist and causing friction on the rope, making it easier to arrest a falling person, theoretically.

I stare up at the route. Steve is distracted by the climbers next to us who attempt Darth Vader's Revenge. "Poor style," he says. At the crux move, a man grabs hold of his rope and fishes for a toehold. This is called "direct aid," meaning that the climber depends on his "protection"—his rope and hardware—in order to hold on or ascend. Most climbers now consider this cheating. "Free" climbing is when protection is used only to save the climber if he falls.

Steve moves smoothly, secure on his holds, though they are too small for me to see. He reaches the ledge, clips himself to the bolt, and pulls up the slack rope. "You're on belay. That means it's safe to climb now."

I respond to this opportunity by tightening my shoe laces. Steve had old climbing shoes, but they didn't fit, so I'm wearing my hiking sneakers, which are not made for this. I put my left foot on a knob, reach with my left hand, and find nothing. I put my foot back down and look around.

"You're on belay," Steve reminds me. "You can climb now."

All right already. "Climbing," I yell back up.

Suddenly the sun is oppressively hot. I draw in a breath, put pressure on my left foot, reach, clutch a knob with my right hand, and lean forward. I step up.

The thrill is tactile, muscular, visual, and immediate. My fingers feel for roughness and lumps on the rock. My palms tell me important information about what is now the most important piece of the world. My arms and legs stiffen, tense as I hold on; holding on is everything. Holding on is life, it's that simple. Life is simple. Move, rest. Move, rest. Then I look around. I've found a new view of the earth. I'm headed up and feeling strong.

With one hand low and one high, I push-pull to a higher knob. I stand up into the air instead of hunkering into the rock, which feels more secure but puts dangerous outward pressure on my feet. I stretch high and hang much of my weight from a straight-arm while stepping to the left.

The fright is overcome by the thrill. This has something to do with empty space around me. I have holds that are big and secure but exposed—I'm hanging out in space. On lazier days, I lie in the grass and feel good looking at the sky, at all that emptiness above me. Now, the empty space is alongside me and even below me, and this unexpected turn almost makes me laugh out of some odd, sensational glee. Here I have all the prospect I could hope for, but my only refuge is a one-inch granite knob. I reach the ledge, and Steve says, "All right. Pretty nice up here, huh?"

His blond hair, neck-length, blows in the wind that gains afternoon strength. I sit on the ledge with this man, and I remember a rule I usually follow: never trust my life to a person I don't know. For the difficult pitch to come, I hope I know Steve well enough. I know he has lived at Yosemite for nine months a year, three years, and he's still alive. He has climbed El Capitan ten times, and part of one route had not been scaled. He's twenty-four.

Steve didn't say much down below, but on the ledge he talks. "Why climb? I like the life-style around it. And definitely the freedom." I am literally tied to the mountain—this is more fettered than a ball and chain—yet the feeling is one of freedom. I think it's that space below me. Is freedom a matter of empty space? There are many freedoms, and I think I would forgo most of them before I would relinquish the freedom of empty space.

"When you're climbing, you're concentrating," Steve says. "There's only one thing on my mind. I'm not thinking about car payments." I saw Steve's van, and I think he means repair bills. Not to miss the point: within this world of hopeless complexity, the focus is on one thing. Some climbers call this "total engagement."

Doug Robinson wrote that climbing is an activity requiring full attention: "To climb with intense concentration is to shut out the world, which, when it reappears, will be a fresh experience, strange and wonderful in its newness. . . . By contrast, the disadvantage of the low-level activity is that it cannot shut out the world, which then never ceases being familiar and is thus ignored."

It strikes me that being on this cliff is an escape, but the quality of the place is only part of what makes the escape possible. The other part is my putting the rest of the world away, out of mind.

Steve says, "When you're climbing, you're getting to know your body real well. It's addictive. I have to do it. You'd love a long climb. The bivouac sites on ledges are great. You get up there 1,000 feet, pull up your bags, and tie in a hammock or porta ledge. Always you're tied in by your harness. It's pretty casual. You have a beer, fix dinner. It's not so scary, especially after dark. After dark you can't see the ground anyway."

Steve went to college for two years, until "it got to be a prison." He thinks he will climb full-time for another ten years. For three months each winter he works for his older brother, Bob Schneider, also a noted climber, who builds houses in Davis.

"Now and then I see friends from high school. Almost all of them stayed in the Bay Area. They don't do much, you know, they get up and go to work, then they go to bed, then they go to work. Friday after work is a big deal. It's hard to see what they're accomplishing. Me, I feel real successful."

It's time to go up. "It's harder up above," Steve says. He takes off, clips his rope into another bolt fifteen feet up, disappears over a bulge in the cliff, and reappears far above. "On belay," he yells.

Not only do the holds shrink in size but also the cliff leans out more steeply. I advance slowly, taking time between moves until I realize that I must get on with it or fall from fatigue. I cling to a knob, my sneakers bending at their edges. In ten seconds they will be bent too much to hold me. My arms shake from unrelieved tension. For the first time I feel as if I could fall. Of course, Steve would catch me. But I don't want to fall. I don't think of this until later, but sure enough, I'm totally engaged. The rest of the world has disappeared. If I had a car payment to make, it would be the last thing on my mind. If it were on my mind, it would be of trivial importance. I step up and reach, not knowing if there's a good hold. There isn't. I cannot trust my mushy foothold one second longer, so I settle for a tiny handhold. My fingertips pull, feeling vaguely separate from me. I step on another knob—I would call it a welt—and gain added friction by pressing my hands against the rock. I'm amazed that I stay here, and realize that I need less security than I thought. My fingers are now a part of me requiring no orders at all. And my fingers are a part of the rock; they are my connection. Finally, I reach a resting place. I breathe hard. Something inside has changed. The world is bright. I feel air filling my lungs. I feel incredibly good.

Is the feeling in the accomplishment or the relief? Both. And in the view: Fairview Dome rises across the canyon. Tenaya Lake lies below. Tuolumne Meadows stretches out of sight, and the Sierra crest rises to snowfields on Mount Dana—a place that hardened John Muir's attachment to the Sierra when he climbed to the summit. I've struggled with tenuous holds on this side of a mountain, and those peaks rise far above me like lures. I think, "Keep going. Go higher."

The next day Ginger leads a nature walk, and I go along. I never fail to learn something on these outings, if only that beavers are the largest rodent, that deer mice are the most abundant mammal in North America, and that rainbow trout are the only native game-fish up here. In one night, bats eat several times their weight in insects! Holding bubbles on its feet, the water shrew walks on water! Mainly I want to see how Ginger does her job.

A group of fifteen, ages twelve to seventy, gather at the eastern end of the meadows. Ginger is again topped with the flat-brimmed hat.

"Let's get away from the road," she says. While walking, she carries her hat. Her hair is dark and streaked with gray; bangs cover the top half of her forehead. Her eyes are blue. She smiles often, but a serious quality predominates. Her attractiveness is equaled by her professionalism. She was chosen to be Prince Charles's guide when he and Queen Elizabeth visited Yosemite in 1983. She is forty-one.

To show us the first thing about Tuolumne Meadows, she says, "Close your eyes. Now, imagine you were here five months ago." I see the place where I *was* five months ago, in my van, parked along the Ebbetts Pass road, buried in white. Ginger's story begins like mine did, in the snow, in March. A few people think that the snow was ten feet deep, and they are right.

Next we try to imagine being here 10,000 years ago. The Tuolumne Glacier, sixty miles long, covered everything but a few summits. It was the largest glacier in the Sierra, flowing down the Tuolumne Canyon, which is 5,000 feet deep, as deep as the Grand Canyon though half its width. Ginger points to Unicorn and Cathedral peaks, their tops craggy, unsmoothed by the flowing ice that was 2,000 feet thick.

It's easier to imagine the Sierra before the glaciers, and before the uplift that preceded them. These mountains were rolling hills, something like the Appalachians. As the eastern side rose by earthquakes, streams cut into the hills, then glaciers scraped out troughs and left U-shaped canyons in place of the V-shaped ones that water had worn. The reddish plateaus on mountains such as Dana, which Ginger points to, are roof pendants—remnants of that ancient, gentle topography, lifted intact to extreme heights.

Without winter storms, snowfall, and glaciers, the Sierra would look a lot more like the White Mountains, the next range east of the Sierra, almost as high but with nearly uniform ridge lines and with slopes of steady gradient instead of the Sierra's erratic, ice-carved topography.

The Sierra's Ice Age glaciers completely melted during a 2,300-year warm spell. The sixty or more small glaciers seen today are remnants from the Little Ice Age, a cold snap of two centuries that ended in the mid-1800s.

We come to what other rangers call Ginger's Pond. Her schooling was in aquatic ecology, and she shows us freshwater sponges, whirligig beetles, and dragonflies. "What is filling the pond?" I say silt. No. "Organic debris: leaves, twigs, algae, and grass." Other ponds along the Tuolumne were filled long ago because the river deposited silt in them, but this one is landlocked and fills much slower. It has been here 10,000 years—since the last large glacier.

Give me the rocky shores of rivers instead of the muck-rims of ponds, but I'm in a minority if all creatures are counted. "Ponds teem with life. Organic debris that settles to the bottom is full of nutrients and more productive than the river." Here is a mountain paradox: a stagnant pond without mosquitoes. Because there are no fish in this isolated water, insects such as dragonflies thrive and eat the mosquitoes. To kill mosquitoes in the 1940s, the government poured oil on the ponds, which killed the insect predators, allowing mosquitoes to multiply. The Park Service sprayed DDT on Tuolumne Meadows in 1953, and it later sprayed malathion to kill needle miner larvae that hollow out lodgepole pine needles. Today, nature takes its course. When lodgepoles are killed, others grow back in. One dissected mountain chickadee had 250 needle miner caterpillars in its stomach. Ginger says, "We need more chickadees."

We follow the river downstream and eat lunch at the cascades. We find shards of obsidian, and Ginger tells us how Indians made arrowheads from them, but it's difficult to picture unless you see someone performing this nearly lost art.

Anything we want to know, Ginger can tell us, except that I want to know about Ginger herself. When the others have lagged behind, I say, "Hey Ginger." She turns to field another question. "Would you like to have dinner tonight, at my van?" She accepts. Then she thinks about it.

"Why don't we just meet at my cabin. There's more room there. Except I'll warn you, I turn in early."

With one hand I hold a squash, a pound of cheese, and a bottle of California chablis, and with the other hand I knock on the door. Ginger wears jeans, a sweater, and no ranger hat.

Her cabin is twenty by fifteen feet, two rooms. Dominating the kitchen is a wood-burning Wedgewood stove. A colorful collection of Celestial Seasonings teas is shelved above a small table. Most of this is covered with papers bearing Ginger's handwriting, quick and hieroglyphic. The other room houses a single bed, more like a cot, and a table large enough for two diners. Books include Sierra guides, Steinbeck novels, and essays by that most rooted author, Wendell Berry. Her music: Dan Fogelberg, The Doors, the Grateful Dead, and so forth. In my van, the table seats only one, but this home and mine have much in common.

We put her vegetables and mine on the table and decide to use them all. I wash them and Ginger peels and chops—but slowly, with long pauses, vegetable in my hand, knife in her hand, both of us listening, both talking. As a third-grader in Yorkville, Illinois, Ginger collected butterflies and caterpillars when the other kids, not so interested in life cycles, collected only butterflies. "I recognized that I was a little different."

Until the family traveled to Colorado when she was seventeen, Ginger had never seen a mountain. "I thought it was weird—the Rockies always looked purple on the calendars, but then I saw them, and they really were purple.

"Girls weren't supposed to take sciences back then, but I majored in zoology, then went on for a master's degree."

She got married, but not for very long. "I didn't know what to do, or where to go, but California had a certain allure." That was 1968, the year my pack was stolen in Yosemite.

"I worked as a substitute teacher in Merced. I don't like alcohol, but every day I went home and poured a good stiff drink. It was the only time in my life I watched daytime television. I didn't have many friends because I'm shy. I think I was unhappy then."

On her first trip to the Sierra, Ginger walked into the Mariposa sequoia grove. "I was afraid. All that wilderness. It was sort of dark. I started hearing things. I turned around and went back."

That old mountain specialty—the seasons—lured Ginger up again. "In the Central Valley I missed winter, so I drove to Yosemite and met some people who worked for the Curry Company. I started spending weekends there while subbing at the Merced schools." She met a ranger and fell in love.

"It was 1972, and because of the riot, the park had money for new programs. They decided that they should reach more than the usual middle class, so I was hired to lead raft trips on the Merced. Four days a week I got into my bathing suit and guided hordes of people—sometimes a hundred—down the river. I took collecting nets and talked about freshwater biology.

"Yosemite Valley was the best place to learn my trade. There are big crowds, and you deal with all kinds of people. Up here it's easier, more of a national park experience."

The Sierra is now Ginger's home. "For a long time, I wouldn't say I was a Californian. Then I went back to Illinois for a funeral, a dreary, ugly day. On the plane, coming back, we crossed Nevada, and then I saw Mono Lake on the right and Lake Crowley to the left. Then Mammoth Mountain. When we went north of Banner and Ritter, I knew we'd be crossing Yosemite. There we were, over Nevada Falls. I cried. I knew that this was my home."

The vegetables sizzle in olive oil. I pour wine, and the stories continue. What's it like, living at 8,600 feet every summer?

"Wonderful. Let's see, what is it? I can step out at night and see so many stars. I'm not afraid. Part of it is knowing an area so well. I don't worry about walking cross-country and breaking a leg, though it took me years to feel comfortable. The people have a lot to do with it, too. I'm gregarious, but choosy. People are different here. There's a freedom here. People are not completely indoctrinated into the system.

"Sometimes I wish I could have a dog, and I've always had the urge to do gardening, but I don't miss the nice clothes or fancy cars. Doing environmental things, you don't get paid very well. But I suppose if I stayed at my winter house below Mariposa with a dog and a garden and a job down there, I'd be bored to death.

"I don't get lonely up here. I really love my staff. They're wonderful people."

Ginger wonders how I cope with time alone. Part of my happiness depends on a shield of isolation. But tonight—this is a lot of fun. I miss friends the most when I get close. Then, I don't know what I want, except more. Damn this life-style of mine. I don't want to talk about the range of feelings, one extreme to another, that I get from living alone, all the time on the road. I don't want to tell Ginger that what I really miss is a girlfriend. We return to her job. Why does she do this work?

"In the normal two-hour nature walk, you can't change anybody's life. After a while you feel like an entertainer. Still, you try to get across the message: these places are very important to us as a society and as a species. We need mountain reserves not only for water and timber but for people—so people can know themselves better. We're lucky Yosemite is protected, but it's only protected as long as people know it's valuable." She stands quietly for a minute while the noodles boil. She looks at me, leans against the doorway, and smiles.

"I taught a fifteen-credit college class from Santa Cruz—for two months we were in the Sierra following the snowmelt uphill through April and May. But you know what? Last year not enough students signed up for the course. Isn't that sad? Kids today—it's changed. The big thing is to get an MBA and a job selling something."

I ask, "Ginger, why don't they want to live the simple life?" and I wave a hand at her cabin, her wood stove, and her supply of essentials. Ginger doesn't have much that I can point to, but I think she has most of what the world needs.

We sit at the table and eat and talk, and we laugh, and then we wash the dishes, and as I drive away into the cool, dark night, Ginger waves good-bye from the warm yellow light of her window.

6

The Sunrise Mountains

IT MAY HAVE BEEN ONLY A SMALL READJUSTMENT. It may have been a humbling reminder or a warning or just a settling of the earth, unsettling in many ways. No one knew what was really happening on May 25, 1980, one month after Mount Saint Helens erupted, when the ground shook violently on the east side of the Sierra. Along the Hilton Creek Fault, the earth buckled and lurched in a surge of power.

One quarter of a mile from the epicenter, Grant Hiskes ran out of his house as fast as he could. "It sounded like a truck hit the place. Everything was shaking. The top of the house shifted from the bottom, like it was leaning, and then it shifted back again. It was made of wood and wasn't damaged much. The ground shook for one and a half hours."

Geologists watched with tense caution, knowing that more—much more—could follow. Someday the earthquake may not be the main event but only a precursor to an eruption.

Three geysers spouted at Hot Creek, eight miles from the town of Mammoth Lakes, where water mains broke, a few chimneys fell, and roads were cracked open. The Safeway grocery store reported $50,000 worth of damage; restaurants and a drugstore also claimed losses. A new elementary school, unoccupied, was wrecked. In high-priced condominiums, foundations cracked, and beams were pushed off center. Windows broke. "The whole place shook a lot," said Jack Lintott, owner of a Timber Ridge condominium. "There were hundreds of tremors, and you could hear the big ones; kind of a roar. The neighbors left with the breakfast dishes right on the table." Damage at Mammoth Lakes was $2 million, not great considering that a couple of large homes in that community cost that much. On the other side of the range, in Yosemite National Park, hikers were injured by earthquake-triggered slides. The Richter scale registered magnitude 6 (the San Francisco earthquake in 1906 was 8.3). For three days following May 25, 8 earthquakes were rated at 5 to 6, and 500 lesser tremors were recorded, from not one fault but many.

Shaking, grinding, heaving, and venting heat from a pocket of molten rock that lies only two miles underground, the eastern Sierra attracts geologists, who study the making of mountains and who will do their best to predict the big eruption. All agree on the high probability of a volcanic eruption near Mammoth someday. But on the topic of natural disasters, "someday" stirs little but yawns from Californians, who live on faults from Mexico to Oregon as surely as they live on dirt.

Earthquakes and volcanoes may be the most fundamental of all mountain events, making mountains mountains. While the topography rises, it is also worn down by gravity plus water, which causes erosion. The San Joaquin River, for example, carries its landscape away at a basin-wide rate of 1 inch per 1,000 years, according to *Geology of the Sierra Nevada*. For the person whose thinking tends toward the long-term, the east side raises fascinating questions: Is it rising faster than it is eroding? Is the Sierra Nevada getting higher?

"Yes, we think it is," said N. King Huber, a geologist with the U.S. Geological Survey. "I estimate the uplift to be one-third of a millimeter per year." This is slower than my imagination, impatient for a high peak, can grasp, but the millimeters—25.4 of them per inch—add up. "The present uplift began about 25 million years ago and has accelerated through time. The Sierra Nevada is probably rising faster now than ever." One-fourth of the range's rise occurred in the last 3 million years.

In the larger picture, the Sierra fits within the Rim of Fire—a circle of mountains that, counterclockwise, encompasses Antarctica, the 4,500-mile-long Andes (the world's longest range), the Sierra, the Alaska Range, and the mountains of Japan, the South Pacific islands, and New Zealand. All of them shake and erupt with the movement of continental and oceanic plates—huge masses of the earth's crust that float on the molten innards of the planet. Geologists theorize that the action at Mammoth may be linked to the slippage of the Pacific plate against the North American plate.

How high will the Sierra go? "We have no idea," Huber answered. Will this range be another Himalayas? "No. That is a different situation. They are the direct result of a collision between continental plates, a very rare situation on the present-day globe. We don't understand the mechanics of the Sierra uplift, but there is no plate subduction zone south of Mendocino, on the coast."

On the Sierra's east side, even if you don't feel the earth shake, it's easy to believe that these mountains are still becoming. This is the steep side. In six miles you walk through plant zones that span sixty miles on the west side. The east slope rises at twenty-five to thirty degrees; the west slope, at two to three degrees, a configuration that led the eminent geologist François Matthes to write, "The Sierra Nevada may be likened to a gigantic ocean wave rolling landward from the west." On the east side, the mountains are growing up toward the sky as if hinged to the ground on the west side. It is by measuring changes in the tilt of this block that Huber estimated the Sierra's rate of growth.

Many facts stem from the fundamental fact of earthquake-induced gradient. The east side is the dry side. Soggy Pacific clouds drop their load on the west slope when the wind pushes them up to the crest. Then the air descends the east side, warms, and holds most of the remaining vapor.

Pointing to views that rival the Tetons, many people say that the east side is the Sierra's more scenic side. Although 90 percent of the range's acreage lies west of the crest, those mountains are often hidden by trees. Not in the east; there peaks soar from flat desert to jagged crest.

For California's vast population living west of the Sierra, the east side is the world beyond the mountains, the unknown side, the lonely side, farther from cities—with two exceptions. Reno sprawls within ten miles of the range, and Los Angeles lies due south (its longitude is east of Reno's).

The influence of the southern megalopolis, where one out of twenty Americans live, is felt in more than the crowds of fishermen and skiers. To gain water rights, Los Angeles bought most of the land at the base of the range from Lee Vining south, involving half of the eastern Sierra frontage. Los Angeles even controls the water flowing in Lee Vining Creek, at the edge of Yosemite National Park, by manipulating flows in dams and aqueducts. The city controls much that nature and people do, but not everything and not everybody.

The west side of the mountains is California, and the east side is the West. Here the land is divided not into farms but into ranches, with cowboys who still do not wear sneakers even around the house, and who I can't even imagine in shorts. Mobile homes shine at the edge of irrigated pastures, and towns emphasize gas, motels, and sporting goods.

The east is the side of the water war; of trout fishing in streams endangered by hydroelectric proposals; of Mono Lake, unique in the world; of warm days at Lone Pine in January and skiing at Mammoth in July; of two of the Sierra's larger towns; of Mount Whitney, the highest peak in the range. Here also is a refuge for animals. The tule elk, native to the Central Valley, was saved from extinction in the 1930s, when game officials brought it to the Owens Valley of the eastern Sierra. Bighorn sheep survive in small pockets on the east side. Biologist Verna Johnston wrote that the eastern Sierra has the largest belt of Jeffrey pine in the world.

I had been to Yosemite before, but traveling through the eastern Sierra is new. Pushing this edge of my personal experience, I have the feeling that I'll be on the edge of something more. Of course I'll straddle the edge where the mountains meet the Great Basin desert, but I mean something more. Edges are those thin lines filled with change, conflict, diversity, innovation, and potential.

The east side has its own character, a certain feeling caused by topography and light. This is the land of the sunrise through desert air clear enough to bathe the lungs. The sun rises brilliantly as it shines against the escarpment of white and gray rock—the longest barrier to roads in forty-nine states, and the highest mountain front. At the other end of the day, when the earth has turned, when the dry desert heat radiates back out into twilight's space, the east side lies in the shadow of the mountains. Then this extreme land—this hot earth whose magma may erupt in front of my eyes, this dry land that is dazzlingly washed by rivers of snowmelt—this east side of the mountains lies gold and purple, mysterious and strange, dark and exotic, a place I am ready to explore.

Lake Tahoe lies on the east side of the Sierra crest, but Tahoe is Tahoe and not a part of the rest of the east. If I had traveled southward from the lake, down the eastern Sierra on Route 89, I would have crossed Luther Pass over the Carson Range, an arm of the Sierra separating the Truckee River basin from that of the Carson, the smallest in watershed area of the fifteen major Sierra rivers. The West Fork of the Carson drains Carson Pass, 8,573 feet. From north to south, this is the fifth of ten major highway passes over the Sierra crest. In my opinion, Carson has the range's finest road-accessible cross-country skiing, and it has Kirkwood, my favorite downhill resort. At the eastern foot of Carson Pass lies idyllic Hope

Valley, where the Mormons named the place but did not stay, where Snowshoe Thompson crossed with the mail, where the Bureau of Reclamation proposed a dam, and where others propose subdivisions.

Along Highway 89, thirty-six miles south of Tahoe (twenty miles by air) sits Markleeville, a town with frame buildings from the days of silver mining, and with a courthouse that must be the state's most diminutive. Alpine County is California's lowest in population and highest in average elevation. Two ski areas—Kirkwood and Mount Reba—provide 47 percent of the tax revenue of this county, which is traversed by 3.2 million people a year. The East Fork of the Carson River is a popular rafting and canoeing run when the early summer snowmelt washes from Ebbetts Pass, 8,731 feet, where Highway 4 crosses the range. (Sierra trivia: This pass was the highway of one of the oddest groups to cross the mountains—nine camels in 1861.) Moving southeast, Highway 89 crosses Monitor Pass over the Pine Nut Range—an eastern extension from the Sierra—and then the road meets Route 395, the north-south artery that can carry me along the foot of the Sierra to the southern limit of the range.

The Walker River is the smallest in volume of the Sierra's major rivers, and Route 395 climbs the valley of its West Fork. To the west rises Sonora Pass, 9,624 feet, where Route 108 crosses the Sierra.

Four miles up 108 from 395 is the Mountain Warfare Training Center, where 1,500 camouflage-clad marines are trained for one month to fight wars in the mountains. About 15 percent of the combat force attends the school, located here in 1950 because of its similarities to Korea. Marines say that the site's current value is in its similarities to Norway. The trainees, none of whom volunteer for this mountain vacation, camp out on twenty-six of thirty nights during winter. None of the trainees is screened for previous mountain experience. (As a marine once told me, "The Marine Corps believes all men are the same, and if you don't have the skills, you can learn them." Attempts to teach skiers telemark turns lead to "many casualties.")

South on Route 395 is Bridgeport, population 500, elevation 6,465, with a historic courthouse and views of the craggiest Sierra this far north—Sawtooth Ridge in northern Yosemite National Park. Farther south is Lee Vining, population 317, elevation 6,780 feet, overlooking Mono Lake, directly east of Yosemite, and exactly halfway down the Sierra Nevada from north to south.

When I left Ginger's cabin in Tuolumne Meadows on that cool night in late July, my destination was the eastern Sierra, six miles away.

At Tioga Pass, Route 120 is the last road over the Sierra for 145 miles southward. I cross from west to east and begin the steep descent of the sunrise mountains. Below the ghost town of Bennettville (one building) and just below the rustic Tioga Pass Resort, I turn left and camp near Saddlebag Lake, which is dammed.

The next day I hike in some of the Sierra's finest high country within a few miles of a road. I eat dinner, wash the dishes, and set them on the hood to dry. After dark I put the dishes away and go to bed.

In the first light of dawn, I think I hear mice. They search for holes to the inside and to my food boxes. But the scratching is slower than a mouse's, and the unknown creature does not scurry but steps. When the entire van rocks, I decide to look. I see a darkness in motion, barely visible but filling most of the windshield. A bear stands on the hood.

In pursuit of food, bears have changed the shapes of cars. Probably vans also. I jump into the driver's seat and start the engine. The large black bear jumps off the hood, leaving muddy prints, and disappears around the right side. A cool breeze dropping from Mount Conness reminds me that my window is down. I roll it up as my visitor reappears. Like begging bears at Yellowstone used to do, he stands, paws at the window, and peers inside, weaving right and left, trying to see. I sit eye to eye with 300 pounds of wildlife, so to speak. I knock on the window and startle him, but he returns. I knock again and he leaves. After cautiously eating breakfast, I leave bear country and drive down to coyote land.

At the bottom of the pass I reach Lee Vining, stretched along Highway 395 for half a mile. I park and walk.

"Nice day," a man says from a seat on a makeshift bench in front of a building that probably dates to mining days. He would stand maybe five foot five, has a broad forehead and broad shoulders, and wears a faded flannel shirt, faded jeans, and hiking boots worn to the nubs. He smiles, and his teeth are crooked, his face as rough as the Mono Craters landscape to the south. He fits in well, indigenous. His hair, black streaked with gray, is tied in a ponytail.

"Yeah, real nice day," I say.

"Don't make 'em like this any more, ah ha ha ha." I sit next to him.

"You been around here long?" I ask.

"Born here. Yeah, us Indians, we've been here longer'n anybody. How about you?"

"Ten minutes."

"There're things you'd never know. It's nice here now, but nothing like it used to be."

There are not many jobs on the east side, so this man does what his ancestors did. He makes arrowheads.

"How do you do it?"

He picks up a piece of a broken bottle, and a stone, and chips off a few flakes of glass. Not satisfied, he drops the stone and glass. "You got a car?"

"Do tourists walk?"

"Give me a ride home?"

We head south and turn onto a dirt road, yellow dust streaming behind. I drive straight toward the escarpment of the Sierra, an exotic view to me but not to him. "Right there," and he points ahead, "Bloody Canyon." John Muir met a band of Indians in this canyon during his first summer in the Sierra.

"Not too many Indians around here any more," my guide says. "About three families in Lee Vining. There's no reservation; this used to be kind of an Indian colony, but just one family of us now. There're more at Bridgeport."

At a cluster of trailers and old cars, we pass this man's sister's place, then arrive at a fifteen-foot-square, tar-paper-covered home. The grounds remain landscaped as they always were, with sage-brush and pinyon pine. Tools and a number of things are stored outdoors: a spool of barbed wire, a wooden door, a thirty-year-old car, a tire, and near the door, thousands of fragments of glittering black rock.

Obsidian, the coal-black volcanic glass, is so plentiful near here that you can climb on Glass Mountain, yet so rare in most of the country that it was coveted in trade among the Indians. Archae-ologists found Central American obsidian in the Ohio River Valley. This rock is the opposite of granite: while granite is coarsely tex-tured with large crystals resulting from slow cooling beneath the surface, obsidian has no crystalline structure—it's as smooth as glass—because it cooled rapidly on the skin of the lava flow.

"Come on in."

The house holds a bed and a wood-burning stove. Recent mail addressed to Donald Rambeux lies on a table. He picks up a coffee can heavy with obsidian, and we go outside, where Donald sits at a small table in the shade of an elm.

"I'll show you." He holds a one-by-one-half-inch shard of obsi-dian against a piece of leather on a block of wood, and with the end of a nail, he presses against the glassy black edge, chipping off a flake. He holds up the nail: "They used to use an antler." As fast as I might flick a potato peeler, Donald chips at the glass, up one side, then up the other until the rock resembles a triangle. Like a view coming slowly into focus through binoculars, what was a rock becomes a Stone Age weapon. Its crudeness is now addressed by

Donald's hands. The flakes falling to the ground are smaller, now pulverized glass like powdered sugar.

"Hey, take a look back by that sagebrush." He points with the nail. Behind the waist-high clump of sage I see a stone slab the size of a card table. The rock contains two bowllike depressions, eight inches deep. Here, kneeling in the sun, the Paiute grandmothers, mothers, and daughters ground acorns and pine nuts, mortar-and-pestle fashion. I stare into the holes, created by the subtraction of one grain at a time through the unexpected abrasion of acorns on rock. I look at Donald, chipping a stone in the morning sun. He waves.

I kneel and reach into the rock and feel the wholeness of the circle. Only two lifetimes could take me back to the Indian women who knelt here and to an earlier Donald. I try to imagine going back, erasing the contrail in the sky. The breeze from the canyon is cool; it's midsummer, but time to prepare for the long season by storing firewood and acorn meal. The breeze whispers through scented sage. Talk to me.

Donald's ancestors' civilization in the Sierra lasted about 10,000 years. Ours, about 150 years old, has included the Gold Rush and nuclear bomb tests in Nevada, which made flashes visible in Tuolumne Meadows.

Today Donald is at home making Stone Age weapons in the way of his grandfather and great-grandfather, and so forth. It is inconceivable to me that we can last as long as the Indians lasted. My white liberal guilt says that it is too bad we have dragged them along to wherever we are headed. Slowly, I walk back, each step crunching on the soil and on dry leaves of sage. The Sierra rises in morning light, brilliant. Then a sonic boom echoes against the mountains.

"Lot of pine nuts smashed back there," Donald says. "Up there are my pine nuts." He points to a burlap sack on the roof. Donald gathers pinyon cones when they are closed and sticky, roasts them on a fire, then dries them in the sack until the nuts—pea-size but oblong—fall out of the cones. He shells them and eats them raw, fries them in a pan, or grinds them with an oval stone against a flat rock, precisely as his ancestors ground pine nuts for soup.

"Did they grind acorns, too?"

"Yeah—ones they got by trading." He points up Bloody Canyon. From the west side, Miwok Indians brought acorns, berries, baskets, seashells, and arrows. From the east, Paiute and Washoe (from the Tahoe area) brought pine nuts, salt, rabbit skins, buffalo robes, caterpillars, dried Mono Lake fly pupae that were good to eat, and obsidian.

Donald has finished the arrowhead, complete with notches where it can be tied to the shaft of a dogwood arrow if I get one in trade from the Miwok. "Here," Donald says, handing his work to me. He should be supplying the Smithsonian or Fred Bear's archery company. In my palm, the arrowhead is translucently sharp.

Donald disappears inside and returns with a paper bag. "Look." He retrieves an oval stone from the bag. "They used it like this." He holds it and smacks it into his grainy palm. It's a grinding stone, used by the women out back. "Here, you can have it."

The stone does not belong in my van, rolling all over America. It belongs here. "No, you should keep it."

"Go ahead."

I smack it into my palm the way Donald did. He smiles. "Look," I point to my van. "I have no bedrock to go with it. I have no place for it."

"Neither do I."

I return the stone anyway. Donald shrugs his shoulders. "Well, whatever."

"But I want to buy the arrowhead from you." Foolish, I cannot think of anything to trade. "How much do you sell them for?"

"Ah, $1.50 to $3.25, it depends." I have a five so I give it to him.

"I'll make you another one."

He picks out a thin piece of obsidian. "See—it's an old arrowhead." The front third has been broken off, perhaps by an Indian who shot an arrow and hit a rock instead of a deer. "I'll see what I can do." He chips one edge and then the other, leaving the flat end intact but tapering the point to make a smaller arrowhead. The sun shines on my face; the blue Sierra sky meets the reddish summits of Dana and Gibbs. The Mono Craters rise to our east. Some of them were formed by eruptions only hundreds of years ago, so perhaps they are newer than the arrowhead Donald is refurbishing. A red-tailed hawk soars high.

Donald gives me the second arrowhead.

"Hey, you want something to eat?" I ask.

"Sure."

I dig into my food boxes and return with crackers, cheese, an orange, and peanuts. "Nothing like pine nuts," I say as I set the Planter's jar down. "White people's nuts."

Donald looks up with an impish grin. "You said it, not me, ha ha."

"Time to gather firewood," Donald says. "Yeah, winter'll be coming. Winter's kind of slow; you have to keep busy."

"What do you do?"

"Me, I walk into town and back." We finish eating. "Could you give me a ride back into town?"

Rolling down the dirt road, we face Mono Lake, big and round, blue water in volcanic desert. The lake is lined by a ring of white, a ring around a bathtub. Donald says, "It's low. Too low. Los Angeles takes all the water. They ruin it. When I was a kid, we had a diving board, way out there. Now it's dry land. The lake, it looks nice, but it's nothing like it used to be."

No ordinary lake, this nine-by-thirteen-mile oval of water is three times as saline as the oceans and eighty times as alkaline, not because anything unusual flows in but because of what flows out: nothing. Through its life of perhaps 700,000 years, Mono's level had been determined by Sierra runoff from five streams, countered only by evaporation.

Lake Tahoe is the only lake in California that is larger or older than the improbable Mono, and like Tahoe, Mono offers more than the statistics of the extreme. A weird visual feast surrounds the shores, decorated by eerie towers of tufa, which look something like stalagmites in caves. White calcium carbonate from bubbling aquifers created the towers when the lake was higher. Tufa is found elsewhere, but the only towers of tufa in the known world are here. As John Muir understated in 1869, this is "a country of wonderful contrasts." Muir wanted Mono Lake included in Yosemite National Park.

The southern background shows the youngest mountain chain in North America. The Mono Craters resulted from eruptions 640 years ago, a blink in geologic time. A quicker blink is Paoha Island, an upwelling of magma that appeared about when the Declaration of Independence was signed. To the west is the Sierra escarpment.

Mark Twain, entertaining but inaccurate, called Mono Lake a "lifeless, hideous, treeless desert" and a "dead sea." It lacks fish, yes, but because of that, an invertebrate population thrives in unique simplicity. Emphatically, the lake does not lack life. Biologists counted 50,000 tiny brine shrimp in a cubic yard of Mono Lake. Brine flies congregate in black masses, and birds live on the flies and shrimp.

Ninety-five percent of the state's California gulls—one-quarter of the world's population—nested here. One-third of the world's Wilson's phalaropes stop here during migration, and seventy-seven other species of birds depend on the lake. Because of Sierra runoff, more than 800,000 waterfowl and 150,000 shorebirds flock here.

Also because of Sierra runoff, Los Angeles enjoys an inexpensive source of water. In 1913, the city's aqueduct tapped the Owens River south of here, and in 1941, the LA Department of Water and Power extended its reach, by tunnel, into the Mono basin. In 1970, the DWP completed a second aqueduct, diverting the flow of four streams that had fed the lake. Water was shunted 338 miles south; flows to the lake were cut by 60 percent. As a result, Mono Lake dropped an average of a foot a year from 1941 to 1982, lost 45 percent of its volume, and shrunk from 55,000 to 40,000 acres (about 63 square miles). Salinity doubled. At that rate, the lake will shrink to one-third its 1941 size in fifty to a hundred years. It will be three times as salty and will probably support little of the life now found.

This is done to meet human needs and human whims, to provide one-sixth of the water used by 3 million people (though only one-five-hundredth of the water used in California), to drink, to fill swimming pools, but mainly to water lawns and shrubbery that account for 75 percent of the water used at Los Angeles homes.

Isolated from its lifelines, Mono Lake dropped enough to expose a land bridge to Negit Island, where most of the gulls had nested. Coyotes decimated the rookery. Changes in water chemistry have upset a delicate ecological balance by which algae is eaten by brine flies and brine shrimp, which in turn are eaten by birds. More than 18,000 acres of dry lake bed form the bathtub ring of alkali powder that blows in the wind and can cut downwind visibility to that of the Oklahoma dust bowl.

Water development in California was the story of one group getting the water out before other people knew they wanted it. Today it's the story of getting the water out in spite of others wanting it, and Mono Lake is emblematic of the conflict.

The lake's story is one of plentiful life but impending death, of regional struggles, pipelines, power, deception, court victories, legislative losses, and big money against a young and ingenious band of opponents. The story is told at Lee Vining in an unlikely corrugated metal building marked by an official-looking blue and white sign built to interstate highway specifications that says, "Tourist Information."

Biologists David and Sally Gaines started the Mono Lake Committee after a summer of ecological studies for the National Science Foundation in 1976. They worked without pay until 1980. Since then, bearded David, an outstanding biologist, ornithologist, political strategist, and publicist, has received the salary of a clerk-typist for the LA Department of Water and Power. He does his own typing.

The committee's goal is to restore and stabilize the lake ten feet above its 1976 level so that Negit Island will be an island instead of a peninsula. With data provided by a variety of academic, government, and private groups, an Interagency Task Force chaired by the state Department of Water Resources under Governor Jerry Brown shared this goal. With unanimity except for LA's vote, the task force called for the city to reduce Mono basin withdrawals by

85,000 acre-feet per year, still allowing it to take 15,000 acre-feet. Los Angeles can do this by storing and exporting more Sierra runoff during wet years and by conserving water. A 15 percent reduction in water use—easily achieved by other cities with water conservation programs—would save 93,300 acre-feet a year. Even LA cut use by 16 percent during the 1976–77 drought. The task force reported that the cost to Los Angeles of saving Mono Lake, per year per resident, including losses in hydroelectric power, would be 54 cents. Resources secretary Huey Johnson called for national monument status for the lake.

DWP officials in LA called the Interagency Task Force report unrealistic and biased and in 1980 testified to the legislature that "there is no scientific evidence whatsoever that the use by the City of Los Angeles of Mono Lake water is highly detrimental to Mono Lake." A DWP report stated that 159 gallons of water are used per person per day in Los Angeles, compared to 285 in Sacramento (but only 132 in Marin County), and that adequate conservation of water to meet the task force goal is possible only by mandatory rationing. DWP calculations showed that to save Mono Lake by buying other water would cost $10.20 per resident per year. Richard Verble, of DWP in Bishop, said, "We feel that the issues should be adequately studied by the scientific community in a cooperative way to see what the effects of our withdrawals in the basin will be." A DWP color brochure features beautiful pictures of the eastern Sierra but ignores the streams below the diversion dams, which leave nothing but scum, and assures, "The lake will stop receding . . . in about 100 years, and the lake will still have an area of nearly 40 square miles."

So far unsuccessful in the legislature (I am reminded of John Muir's comment, "The love of Nature among Californians is desperately moderate"), the Mono Lake Committee, with help from the National Audubon Society and other groups, uses existing laws. The California Supreme Court ruled that the Public Trust Doctrine must be applied to Mono Lake: even though Los Angeles bought water rights, it did not buy the right to ruin the lake, which is irreplaceable public property. The court mandated a "better balance" between diversions and the "public interest." Tediously, further litigation will tell if the city will do anything to maintain or restore the level of the lake.

When high runoff in 1982 overflowed diversion dams above the lake and sent water down Rush Creek, rated the seventh best American trout stream in 1930 but then dried up by LA, the fish wasted no time moving in. Two groups, the Mammoth Flyrodders and California Trout, invoked a law requiring flows to maintain fisheries below dams, and a court injunction now requires the city to release a small amount of water (19 cubic feet per second) to the creek and lake. Under an old agreement with the Department of Fish and Game, DWP does not release any flows for fish at the three other Mono basin streams. Was the agreement legal? Further litigation may tell.

Congressman Richard Lehman, who represents the area, said, "Though the long struggle for Mono Lake continues, we are now in a position to win that battle. Apart from past legal rights, there are moral rights to that water, and today, that makes a difference. The parochial interests of Los Angeles will be overcome by the doctrine of public trust."

The Committee to Save Mono Lake has attracted a remarkable amount of media exposure, including the cover of *Life* magazine in July 1981. Gaines explains, "The lake has a strange kind of beauty. Also, we're seen as a small group struggling against this enormous thing—Los Angeles."

The committee consists of eight full-time staff and three interns, who receive free lodging and $250 a month. The Gaineses and the others have won a war of public information and a court victory. To do this, they must work hard, both on the political end and on the survival end, and to talk to David, I must help.

We unload firewood. From the pickup bed, the biologist tosses me two-foot-long pieces of cordwood. I stack it at the Gaineses' tin-roof home in Lee Vining. I'm glad for the job because David was up all night writing the Mono Lake newsletter and will now stay awake to throw the logs accurately. I hope.

"The importance is much greater than the lake. If the water continues to drop, this would be an alkaline dust bowl seen from many parts of the Sierra crest. Also, the gulls up there come from down here.

"We think Mono Lake is symbolic of how we're treating the earth. The Public Trust Doctrine will be of tremendous value in other places. This is just a vanguard of public interest in water. We need a new ethic to apply to all of the land, and Mono Lake is dramatic enough for a focus of attention. The only reason Mono Lake is being destroyed is because no economic value is placed on the resource. I would argue that it is a priceless, sacred place. You may as well quarry granite from Half Dome as dry up Mono Lake." Toss, catch. "Any splinters yet?"

Good news: after a low ebb in 1982, heavy snows raised the lake nine vertical feet to match its level in 1974. Negit Island again became an island, barely. Even though Los Angeles had ample water from other sources during 1983, the DWP continued to divert Mono

Lake tributaries and later dumped the water into the dried-up bed
of Owens Lake for evaporation. Why did DWP divert the water if
they were not going to use it in Los Angeles? Because the water
provided a small amount of hydroelectric power.

The California Wilderness Bill would designate Mono Lake as a
national scenic area administered by the Forest Service. Compro-
mised for passage, the bill would protect scenic shorelines, but LA's
diversions would probably go unaffected.

Sally invites us to a lunch of burritos. While he eats, David plays
with their two-year-old daughter, Vireo. He came from Southern
California and Sally came from the San Francisco Bay Area, but
they will stay on the east side of the mountains. "This is home now,"
David says. "I think there will be enough to do here for a long time."

It may not be long until the next earthquake shakes on the east
side of the Sierra. After the 1980 earthquake at Mammoth, twenty-
five miles south of Mono Lake, major tremors shook the east side
in October 1981, May 1982, and January 1983. After the 1980 event,
the U.S. Geological Survey issued a stage II hazard watch for dam-
aging earthquakes, stage III being the most imminent. In 1982, the
Survey issued a hazard notice for potential volcanic activity—a
stage I alert—the least hazardous situation for which the government officially warned people about volcanoes. Both statements
remained in effect until the Geological Survey decided to change
the warning procedure because of criticism from Mammoth Lakes
businessmen and others. The three-tiered notices were eliminated.
The current policy is to wait until an eruption appears imminent,
and then to issue a hazard warning.

To understand even a small part of what is happening, I try to
look back 700,000 years. Near today's Mammoth Lakes, a magma
(lava) chamber erupted with about 2,400 times the magma of Mount
Saint Helens. Long Valley was among the largest volcanic eruptions
known in North America. Ash and pumice covered 600 square miles,
some of which were buried 1,000 feet deep. Then the roof over the
magma chamber collapsed, leaving a depression—the Long Valley
Caldera, ten by eighteen miles. Mammoth Mountain rises at the
side of the caldera, a literal hot spot of geologic activity.

The geologists say that many aspects of earthquakes, volcanoes,
hot springs, and bulging magma are related. Since 1975, this part
of the Sierra has had more earthquakes than during the previous
100 years, the most activity occurring 1.2 miles east of Mammoth
Lakes, population 5,000, the second largest urban area in the Sierra
Nevada.

In most places around the globe, the earth's crust is twenty to
thirty miles thick, but here, magma is within two miles and rising.

A section of Highway 395 rose ten inches between 1975 and 1980. The magma is rhyolite—the tan rock seen at the Mono Craters—rich in silica and gas, the most explosive ingredient in lava.

Dan Miller, of the Geological Survey's Volcanic Hazards Project, said, "To be frank, we are concerned about the possibility of an eruption."

Local officials emphasize that a volcano may not erupt for a long time, possibly thousands of years. Mammoth's earthquake hazard rating is no worse than Southern California's, though volcanos are not predicted in the south. People who live here say that it all comes down to this: to be here is worth the risk.

The cultural eruption has occurred. With the exception of South Lake Tahoe, Mammoth Lakes is the most intensively commercialized place in the Sierra Nevada. The town grew on the model pioneered and idealized by its parent city of Los Angeles: commerce by car. The two main streets are three or four lanes wide, and the frontage is commercial, with an emphasis on shopping centers, where parking lots are bordered on three sides by attractive wooden facades of restaurants, banks, ski shops, and boutiques.

Here is the place to witness changes that come when 25,000 people converge on the mountains at once. In one of the most spectacular town settings in the Sierra, I find a restaurant with outdoor tables, but the view shows cars, asphalt, and the four-lane street.

People come by car. Once a day a bus goes to Reno and to Los Angeles. Rental cars are available from Avis; however, if you drive to San Francisco, you pay $100 extra because that city is not in Mammoth's service area. The service area is south, where 15 million people live at the other end of Route 395. County planner Kitty Hitchcock said, "Mammoth is like a transplanted suburb of Los Angeles. Planning tends to be for short-term economic development. They need to look at a pedestrian system and establish some pattern to the development of the town."

I find a place I like, at least on the inside. The Stove serves the best breakfasts this side of the Squeeze In at Truckee, and along with the all-Sierra great—Morning Thunder in Quincy—the Stove makes my top three list.

In the Safeway, normally known for food, the liquor is stacked four shelves high in six rows that run a total of 192 feet, according to my calculations made by pacing the distance, for a total of 768 running shelf-feet of alcoholic treats stacked five bottles deep. I buy a bottle of wine.

Mostly I see young people. "A lot come and stay for two or three years," one acquaintance told me. "Then they get their lives together and move on." Or perhaps they don't get their lives together and move on. And I suppose that some whose lives were together come here, fall apart, and also move on. A few stay.

Mammoth Lakes is an odd sight, considering that it's in the mountains. It is unlike Quincy, unlike Yosemite. It has Tahoe's urban intensity but is different. Of course, there are many kinds of people here, even the occasional elderly, blue-collar worker, intellectual, and longhair, but I'm impressed with the homogeneity of what appears to be the fast life that has driven 350 miles up the road and brought its trappings along.

In 1901, John Muir noticed the "artificial" appearance of tourists, "arrayed more gorgeously than scarlet tanagers." But about people in the mountains he reasoned, "This is encouraging, and may well be regarded as a hopeful sign of the times." He reasoned that once people experienced the mountains, no matter how trivially, they would be willing to save the mountains. Here, in fact, is an excellent place for the residents of one of America's largest urban areas to become familiar with the Sierra, with mountain life, and the value of it. For Mammoth Lakes, however, the chamber of commerce lists twenty-seven organizations, including a yachting club at 7,860 feet above sea level, but not one environmental protection group. Even so, I still see the Old Man's name: bulldozed into a volcanic hillside, climbing through complexes of condominiums, is John Muir Drive.

The condominiums start at $138,000, but the mortgage is only one bill. At Timber Ridge, the highest and snowiest condo cluster, fees for services such as snow removal and the Jacuzzi cost each owner $3,600, not once, but once a year. This does not count a 1984 assessment of $3,000 to each owner for repairs to damaged foundations. This does not count utilities, one being electric heat at $500 a month in winter.

The early 1970s were the golden age not only of environmentalism, the peace movement, and organic gardening but also of condos. People couldn't get enough, so the builders kept building. The market is now flooded. Banks, by default, are becoming barons of hard-to-sell real estate.

The community's veneer of wealth, seen in the many new buildings, resulted from the boom in the mid-seventies. Mono County growth during the 1970s was 114 percent, nearly all at Mammoth, but in 1983 the population fell by seventy-five people, an indicator that the boom is over and the recession, deep. One of Mammoth Lake's major shopping centers recently went bankrupt. Vacant windows abound. About 150,000 square feet of commercial space is empty (a small store is 1,000 square feet). If you believe in the economic rebound, now is the time to buy at Mammoth. Mimi Lyster at the chamber of commerce blames the slump on the general economy and on the nonexistent volcano. "All over, California is a geologically active area. You can pick your disaster and go anywhere. I think people up here now recognize there's nothing to worry about."

I've encountered the cart before the horse. Why does this unexpected community exist on a volcanic landscape otherwise shaded by Jeffrey and lodgepole pines? The most fundamental reason is a mountain that receives twenty-five feet of snow per winter, and the most remarkable reason is Dave McCoy.

If McCoy had not been hired by the Los Angeles Department of Water and Power to measure snow depth, or if he had not collected $15 in small change from friends who used his private rope tow one day in the 1930s, there might not be a single condominium, shopping center, or Bon Appetit T-shirt in Mammoth Lakes today. The town is here because of a ski resort built by McCoy, still being built by McCoy, and no doubt remaining to be built by McCoy until he dies, something that people agree will be done in ski boots. Starting with a rope tow powered by a Model A Ford, McCoy transformed Mammoth Mountain into the nation's most used winter resort. Born in 1916, McCoy is a motocross racer, a bicycler, an extraordinary skier who holds the national downhill racing title for his age class, and the employer of 1,400 or more people.

Why does McCoy do it? "It's fun. It's fun seeing people having fun. We're serving a need; we've made the mountain beautiful and improved it, made it usable." What does he think of development in the Mammoth area? "Every day it's getting better and better." McCoy's plans are to expand northward to the smaller June Mountain ski area and increase Mammoth's skiing area to five times its current size. "We'll need it. This is the only major ski area for Southern California. The earthquakes don't bother us. We don't stop for anything."

On a busy day, 20,000 skiers come here; in a peak year, 1.5 million ride the twenty-three chair lifts and two gondolas. One man I met skis ninety days a year. "It's within commuting distance," he says of the 700-mile round trip from Los Angeles. "What do you do on Friday night anyway? Drink and spend money. May as well drive."

Because it receives so much snow, Mammoth was passed over by other ski developers. The bases of the lifts are at an elevation above the summits of Tahoe's ski areas. Mammoth's summit is 11,053 feet.

Five miles beyond town, I enter a sea of asphalt bordered by lodges and support buildings rambling out into the hills. I try to look over all this, and up above I see the mountain, vast, open in spacious, sunny bowls, steep enough at the top for a free-fall of thrills, so extensive it defies a skier to track it all in a week. The mountain, leased by McCoy from the Forest Service, is literally mammoth.

Still steaming in places, it's a volcano rising from a low gap in the Sierra, and here is the reason for Mammoth's snow: the mountain catches the full brunt of winter storms that arrive unspent because of the unusually low elevation of the mountains due west.

One look shows that here is an excellent mountain for skiing. Consider the season: November to July, with entire months when you might see skiers in bathing suits. Dave McCoy's resort is a weekend destination from Southern California, but the mountain is world class and offers the whole range of skiing experiences.

"It's not the quick experience that counts, but the full experience," Andrea says. "My bravery lesson for the year is to go, without poles, up to a run called the Paranoids at the top of Mammoth Mountain. You feel safe and supported, even though it's as steep as can be. But it depends on the mood you're in. There's this transition in yourself. You ride to the top of the lift, but you're not yet there. You climb farther up, and that personal involvement is the key. All the time while you're walking up, you're looking down, and psyching yourself up.

"The edge is the thing. You have to put your mind out there over the edge. You can dare yourself, and question yourself, but somewhere inside, you have to make a commitment. Then you're physically out there, and when you jump off, you've made the commitment. You've done it. There's a proposal to build a ski lift so you could ride straight up there, but if you don't walk to it, if you don't follow that ridge slowly, on your own, with lots of time to look and think before you jump off, you won't have the full experience."

Andrea Mead Lawrence of Mammoth Lakes has had the full experience. She was raised in Vermont, and at fifteen she raced in the 1948 Olympics. In 1952, she was the first skier in history to win two gold medals in one Olympics. No other American and no other woman has won two. Yet racing was only part of the experience.

After meeting on the ski circuit, marrying, and ranching in Colorado, Andrea and her husband separated when her oldest child was twelve. In 1968, with all five children, she moved from Malibu to Mammoth. For a summer she rented a cabin on a bluff above town. "It was idyllic. No electricity. There was a stillness to it. In that house there was no motion taking place except for our own. As soon as you put electricity in a place, the character changes. We had a swing hanging from a tree, facing the Sierra crest. It was wonderful."

We are in Andrea's Snow Creek condominium at the edge of Mammoth Lakes, with a view of the Sierra. "The development here is not as random as it is in other neighborhoods. Here, at least there is a sense of place, of where you are. The parking is out of the way, and you can see the mountains. Would you like some tea?"

While Andrea heats water, I soak up the view and glance at her magazines: *Smithsonian, Wilderness, Vermont Life,* and *Atlantic.* "I wish I had more time to read," she says. "I'd like to have a cabin so that I could leave all of this behind." She sweeps an arm at a table covered with paperwork. "I should have the self-discipline to step away from that, but when it's here, I work on it." We sit on the outdoor balcony, soon to be stacked with firewood.

Andrea's hair is dark and mixed with gray, her body is straight and fit and stronger looking than the pictures I have seen from her racing days. Her look and manner are a rare blend: self-confident and receptive. Absolutely direct, she speaks fast. She asks where I'm from.

"I'm a nomad, and right now the Sierra is my home."

"Really? Tell me more about yourself," she encourages. This woman is always learning things. She wants to know if anyplace in the Sierra is like Mammoth.

"Definitely not."

Besides being the greatest woman skier of her era and raising a family, Andrea won the last race for county supervisor on the platform of land-use planning for Mammoth Lakes.

"It all started with Friends of Mammoth. A high-rise was planned— a bad project—and it galvanized people who had not paid attention to the future of Mammoth Lakes. People asked if I would lead the group, and so I was pitched right into the controversy. We said the California Environmental Quality Act required an impact statement for developments. The state supreme court granted an injunction in 1972, and our case set a precedent for requirements on large private developments. We finally won by attrition; the developer went bankrupt.

"I began thinking about this place. If anyplace needs planning, it's here. Good planning is our obligation to the future, to keep this part of the Sierra so that people can come here and enjoy it. I don't think the art of planning is here yet, but we have to move toward it. People say, 'It's my land and I'll do what I please,' but when that starts affecting me, I have a problem with that outlook.

"People can see great beauty here, but it's difficult to plan for great beauty. In my heart of hearts, I would turn back the clock many years, but we can't do that. I'm not against development, it's *how* we develop that counts. I think recreation is great. The more recreation we get, the healthier we are, and the healthier the society is going to be.

"Places are incredibly important to me. I'll remember a place before I remember people. There's a real contact that can be made between a person and a place. For me it's here, this part of the eastern Sierra. It has to do with light, and space, and electromagnetic fields, and who knows what all. We've barely begun to understand it.

"There's something I'd like to show you. Would you like to go for a walk?"

Andrea Lawrence, fifty-two, does not just walk. She jumps across streams, kicks pine cones and then races her dog to them, cuts cross-country through the woods, and leads me up grades that are this afternoon's version of the Paranoids. We are on our way to the bluff, beyond the developed part of town.

"It wasn't the winning, but the extension, putting yourself out there on the edge. . . . You gather energy, then release it and go as far as you can. . . . Having to deal with success and failure—that's something you use for the rest of your life. . . . I never said, 'Good luck.' I always said, 'Have fun.' . . . Competition is very destructive to many, but it can be good.

"In competition, everything was focused on one place; many parts, but one place. Then came the family, and the energy went in many directions. It had depth and was a very enriching experience, but the energy is pulled out when the attention goes in many ways. Now the cycle has turned; I'm focused again on single things."

When a view opens up, Andrea asks where the Sierra begins and ends. I tell her, "Almanor to Tehachapi," and I elaborate.

"So," she says, "it is also many parts, but one place. There's a wholeness here in the mountains, and people are drawn to that. I believe that is why the environmental movement gained such strength.

"Politics is new to me, but the goal is the same—to be effective. At first I was the only woman on the county board of supervisors. Some people thought they were going to manipulate me, but no way. Some see my intensity as aggressive. I just get involved, that's all. Last winter I skied six hours, an all-time low. This year I'm going to cross-country ski a lot more. Tell me, how do *you* mix in the fun with what you do?"

We reach the bluff, with its view of the Long Valley Caldera, the town of Mammoth Lakes, and the Sierra crest. Above the volcanic

edge that drops in cliffs toward Sherwin Creek, the bluff is blan-
keted with Jeffrey pine and fir the way the town used to be. "The
bluff was subdivided but never developed. It was laid out on a grid,
but it should be divided according to the topography, leaving the
trees, and with narrow country lanes instead of sixty-foot-wide
roads."

We come to the cabin of stones, logs, and cedar shakes where
Andrea and her children lived during the great transition of their
summer in the Sierra. "There's the tree where we tied the swing.
Look, a piece of rope is still there." The swing faced a view of Mammoth Crest above Lake Mary. The site has prospect, and the site
has refuge, and that's the way Andrea's summer was, with five children in a new mountain world. We sit on a volcanic rock where
prospect exceeds refuge by a lot and enjoy what Andrea calls "that
luxury of letting your eyes go out across the earth.

"As human beings, we're attracted to natural elements. Me, I'm
tied to the mountains. I think it goes back to being raised in Vermont. I couldn't go back, though. My first backpack trip was to
Thousand Island Lake, and I felt something very strong. A lot of it
has to do with space, geometry, gradient. The Sierra Nevada really
has it: edges, movement, views, light, thousands of things constantly changing. The changes—that's why the fall is my favorite
time. In this kind of place you can rise to meet the demands of life,
and more than that. There's a spiritual quality here."

Andrea flew to Washington in 1979 to testify for one of the first
drafts of the California Wilderness Bill and to stop the proposed
Minaret Summit road that would have crossed near here. She flew
back recently to testify for the new Wilderness Bill and protection
of Mono Lake. As a county supervisor, she started a water resources
committee that could influence the entire future of the east side.
"I've drawn a lot from the Sierra, and from many mountains, and
now I'm trying to put something back into the system."

In the evening, in my van, I return to the bluff, and I camp, facing
east. A full moon, enormous, rises over the White Mountains. I stare
at the white light, and at the Long Valley Caldera, itself looking like
the moon. I cannot go to sleep: I'm not tired up here.

The sun rises. I sit and bask on the edge of the Sierra, and my
eyes go out across the volcanic landscape, silent but strung in seismic
tension, a land being created, and I think, this land is alive!

In the south, the Sierra began rising earlier than in the north.
The mountains reach higher, and the rocks come from deeper in
the earth. While the peaks climb in elevation, I drop in elevation

as I roll down 395 toward the Owens Valley. Convict Lake, nine miles from Mammoth, is nearly enclosed by the cupped hand of striped, metamorphic walls, the oldest exposed rocks in the Sierra. Norman Clyde considered this the most beautiful lake at the base of the eastern Sierra. He knew the area well; between 1914 and 1970, he made 200 first ascents of peaks. He carried four cameras and hardback classics in Greek, and David Brower called him "the pack that walks like a man."

South of Convict Lake, Rock Creek—exquisite, lined with water-loving willows, cottonwood, and aspen—plunges clear and cold from the crest. Like many east-slope streams, this one is excellent for trout. I can see Laurel Mountain, Mount Morrison, McGee Mountain, and others, many of them unnamed, and I'm glad. Enough mountains have been named.

At an intersection called Tom's Place, a road used to loop into the mountains, but the Forest Service abandoned the route, and it it now grown over. "It shows that wilderness can be reclaimed," David Brower said. About other eastern Sierra roads he said, "I'd like to see the Onion Valley road stopped at Independence and the Cottonwood Lakes road stopped at Lone Pine."

East of Route 395 is Lake Crowley, built by the Los Angeles Department of Water and Power to store Owens River water. On the first weekend of trout season, I might be able to walk across the two-mile-wide lake by stepping from boat to boat. Part of this 15,000-fisherman extravaganza is the result of two tagged trout worth prizes of $1,000.

After a long grade of four-lane highway paralleling the Owens Gorge, mostly dry because of the aqueduct, I roll into Bishop. Hundreds of miles from a major city, surrounded by desert owned by Los Angeles, between two of the highest mountain ranges in forty-nine states, basking in summer sun, Bishop is one of the largest towns of the Sierra—3,680 people at elevation 4,140, about half as high as Mammoth and thirty airline miles south of it.

Here is where anglers and hunters flock during their seasons, where tackle shops open at 6 A.M., where campers sleep overnight in city parking lots, and where you can see snow on the peaks if you catch the skinny views between buildings.

Beyond the three-block-long downtown, one of few in the Sierra with a real-town character, I find generic highway restaurants and drive-ins. Bishop and the other east-side towns were born of agricultural needs but have lost that purpose and now provide for transient needs: gas, coffee, beds, burgers, ice, tires, and bait. Behind the sunny main street are shady streets and friendly people.

I suppose there are residents who only tolerate the place, but I did not meet them. Everyone I met loved living in Bishop. "What could be better?" asked Mignon Shumway, who collects data on streams for the Department of Fish and Game. "It's the great weather, and *that!*" She points to the mountains.

Only in Bishop: on Memorial Day weekend 500 mules parade through town during "Mule Days." Jack's Waffle House, open all night, fills with fishermen before dawn. Climber Galen Rowell spoke in an auditorium packed full of more young and fit people than I've ever seen in an auditorium. Also old and fit people. At dusk I camp in a city park near a stream, under a cottonwood—that scented symbol of the lowlands and the western riverfront.

When I cross the street at 7 A.M., the Umetco Minerals bus rolls up 395, taking men to Pine Creek canyon, the world's largest tungsten mine, which opens and closes, depending on the world economy.

My breakfast spot is the Bishop Grill, downtown. A man sits on the stool next to me. "Hot, it's hot already." He was an electrician working in CCC camps during the Depression, and one day while traveling from Los Angeles to his job near Reno, he passed through Bishop. "I said, 'I like it here. I could stay here the rest of my life.' So I did." Another man came to work in a mine, and when the mine closed, he stayed.

Phil Pister came and stayed, and it's time to see if he's in his office. I leave a tip for the woman who calls me "honey" and walk to the California Fish and Game office.

The east side is the territory of Phil Pister. Everybody who is much involved in the region knows of him. He's the caretaker of the streams and lakes on the east slope; he's the steward we speak of when we say "stewardship of the land."

"He's exceptionally clever," one Fish and Game official said.

"That Inyo and Mono country has been a love affair of his since day 1," a long-time acquaintance told me. Day 1 was when Pister began research at Convict Creek in 1950.

"He has his own thing going on over there."

"He's always scheming for the department."

"He's an imp."

"He is popular, colorful, dedicated, and sometimes controversial," said Richard May, president of California Trout.

"The Fish and Game biologists were the activists in the fifties and sixties, and a few like Pister have never stopped," said ex-biologist Bill Kier. "Pister is the archetypal Fish and Game biologist who doesn't know where vocation leaves off and avocation begins." Pister says that his wife would agree with this.

"Just because this area is not a national park doesn't mean that it's any less valuable." That is Pister's opening thesis. He is fifty-five, bald, energetic, and emphatic, the intensity liberally mixed with humor. He does not hesitate, not in anything I see. For example, to answer the phone in the next office, he runs. On the way, he says that I may look through a shoe box to my right. It's full of Gary Larson animal cartoons. He returns and says, "Let me run through these slides with you."

His show proves his point. He alternates pictures of Yellowstone or Grand Teton national parks with the eastern Sierra. The escarpment near Bishop could be a Teton. Hot springs along Hot Creek ("one of the very best trout fisheries per acre of water in California") resemble those along the Firehole River, except that here in California the springs are full of people. "No one would drill for geothermal power on the Firehole. But near Mammoth, they're turning an area into a big piece of Swiss cheese. They don't know what the effects on the water will be. Developers think that our area is wide open. I find that difficult to accept.

"Here, you tell me the difference," Pister challenges, and a new slide shows bighorn sheep. "More people come to the east side for recreation than go to Yellowstone." The Inyo National Forest alone records 5.8 million visitor-days a year, the most in the Sierra and the fourth highest in the nation. Pister says that the eastern Sierra will soon become one of the most important and heavily used recreation areas in the world.

He grew up in Stockton on land settled by his great-grandparents in 1850, just before California became a state. The Department of Fish and Game stationed him on the South Fork of the Eel River in Northern California, but this man had visions of granite, sunlight, snowmelt, and the diamond spray of trout streams. He negotiated a transfer and has been in Bishop working on nettlesome problems for twenty-seven years. A sign on his desk says, "Press on. Nothing in the world can take the place of persistence."

His job, of course, involves fish, but what he does has changed. "Catch per hour was the approach in the old days, but it was all through stocking—a disturbingly artificial thing. The trout you catch here are not even native.

"Eventually I came to the important question: what about the entire fishery resource? I was astonished to find that of four fishes endemic to the Owens River system, two were virtually extinct and one was marginally secure." Only one fish excelled: the Owens sucker.

"I often reflect on my activities of the past thirty years and ask myself if I have done anything really important. Angling is fine, but you know, you only pass this way once, and you like to leave more than dead fish heads laying around on the ground. We should leave the earth in an equal or better condition than what we found here. *That* should be the criterion for success, for progress, for a good economy.

"Well, here is something important: from the West Fork of the Walker south to Cottonwood Creek, there are some ninety applications for hydroelectric developments. For each stream there are from one to six applications. Many dams are proposed by developers who would reap the economic benefits in places such as Texas. The most desirable portion of the stream mileage between the wilderness boundaries and the Owens aqueduct could be affected, and already, 88 percent of our stream mileage outside the wilderness has been impacted by diversions. The heart of the stream recreation resource could be destroyed."

Pister and his two colleagues are responsible for 10 million acres in the eastern Sierra. Pister alone is responsible for 1,000 lakes, streams, and desert springs, and he spends one-fourth of his time on hydroelectric proposals. "You have to enjoy this work and know you're doing something worthwhile or you'll go out of your gourd."

One hydroelectric plan by Joseph Keating is on Lee Vining Creek just outside Yosemite. Six other proposals would wire Rock Creek. Additional dams would go up on Bishop Creek, the largest in the southeastern Sierra, a turbine-spinner's dream, dropping 5,500 feet in fourteen miles, where in the late 1800s power was produced and sent to mines near Tonopah, Nevada, 113 miles away, through the longest transmission line in the world. The new dams may be small, but they would divert the water in pipes, sometimes for miles.

I first heard of Phil Pister through this *Los Angeles Times* quote about the impacts of small hydroelectric development: "It comes down to the logic that it's awfully hard to go fishing or grow trees in a pipe."

"Our Sierra resources are serving us well today, but you've heard about the goose that laid the golden egg. The moral: he who wants more often loses all."

Switching from fables to the future, Pister says, "The time is going to come, almost tomorrow, when people will say, 'Why did we let this happen?' Water is very critical here. There's not much of it—five inches a year in the valley. The riparian growth is like a line drawn with a felt-tip pen on a basketball court, but that habitat supports 90 percent of the wildlife. To ruin a stream for the wealth of one man is not in the public interest. Technology will no doubt bring improved ways to produce power, but no one has shown us how to build a trout stream."

State regulations demand that hydroelectric developers leave enough water for fish, and there is Pister's grip. He reviews plans and makes recommendations to his bosses in Sacramento. Pister finds that the developers rarely plan to leave enough water, and he presses them to conduct proper studies. He's trying to require the preparation of an environmental impact statement on the cumulative effects of power developments in the eastern Sierra. He wants the Federal Energy Regulatory Commission to look at all the proposals and to require the sponsors to gather scientific data needed for decisions on stream flow. So far, none of the dams and diversions to which Pister objects have been approved by his superiors. He says, "I'm putting my neck way out there." But he does not hesitate.

He glances at his watch and says, "I have to photograph a Department of Water and Power project. Want to come?" We head north in his car.

Pister's tactical war amounts to slugging it out in the mail with the developers, but the strategic war is educational. "People must understand what's at stake over here." He looks to his left at the Sierra crest. "I give slide shows, and talk, and talk. To change the thinking is like building the Great Wall of China, one stone at a time. The goal is for the destruction of this environment to become ethically unacceptable.

"Look at the effects of the Horseshoe Meadows Road on the golden trout in the Cottonwood basin." In the 1920s, a dirt road was built from Lone Pine, up the escarpment to the 7,000-foot level. Anticipating the Horseshoe Meadows ski area, which was later stopped, the Forest Service upgraded the road until it became the worst bulldozed scar in the entire mountain range—worse than Interstate 80. Cottonwood Lakes, near the end of the road, is where fishery biologists collect eggs of the rare golden trout for stocking in other streams. With the new road, use soared from 5,000 to 50,000 recreation-days a year, requiring the Fish and Game Department to close some of the lakes to public fishing altogether.

The Tahoe syndrome struck again: a road, built at enormous public expense, entices public overuse of an area, requiring regulations against public use, but even these are inadequate, and the resource fades toward oblivion. The Forest Service pays a lot of money, people are unhappy about the rules, and the golden trout are in deep trouble.

We arrive at the Owens River, where a crane operator tries to lift one end of a pipe, eight feet in diameter, thirty feet long, half full of mud and half full of water. It's too heavy. A bulldozer also lifts on the pipe's end. The pipe rises, inch by inch. Water runs from one end. The machines roar in a new crescendo. With the sound of a high-powered rifle, the cable snaps, and hard-hatted men flinch. The operators regroup and string two cables. "I'm glad they're on our side," Pister says. Once the pipe is gone, brown trout will migrate into several miles of the Owens River above here.

"The Department of Fish and Game should never have let DWP dry up seventy miles of the Owens. We traded one of the finest brown trout fisheries in the United States for $25,000 and a lease on a hatchery, like the Indians selling Manhattan for trinkets. But there are several good aspects to the DWP. The Owens Valley is undeveloped because LA owns the land. If they hadn't bought out the farmers, this place would look like the San Joaquin Valley, full of irrigated fields and steel pole barns and polluted runoff." In Mono and Inyo counties, DWP owns 308,000 acres. "One of my fears is that Los Angeles will run into a budget crunch and start selling this land."

In many ways, the future of the valley is up to Los Angeles. This deepest valley is a colony of America's third largest city.

In 1905, Los Angeles agents posed as ranchers and bought water rights from Owens Valley farmers. Eventually, the city controlled the Owens River, the Sierra's second in basin acreage but twelfth in volume of water. The federal government cooperated when a Bureau of Reclamation agent, secretly paid by DWP, talked ranchers into signing away their rights to future reservoirs with the promise that they would receive irrigation water. The Bureau then gave the water rights to Los Angeles. To aid the city, chief forester Gifford Pinchot banned homesteading on many acres of sagebrush by designating them a forest preserve. The city eventually bought most of Owens Valley, paying two times market value for some of it.

Not only did the eastern Sierra farmers have to be fooled; the power brokers of Los Angeles had to fool their own people. Just before the vote on bonds for the aqueduct, officials fabricated a water shortage by dumping supplies down storm drains. When the 233-mile-long aqueduct was finished, the water was delivered not to Los Angeles but to the outlying San Fernando Valley, where many of the same rich businessmen who had devised the Owens Valley plan had bought farmland for $5 an acre. After the water arrived, they sold it for $1,000 an acre.

When Los Angeles pumped Owens Valley groundwater and ranchers' wells went dry, the ranchers diverted water into ditches from the city's supply. DWP workers were ordered to dynamite the ditches, and the ranchers responded by blowing up the aqueduct, four miles north of Lone Pine, in 1924. In 1927, they dynamited the aqueduct seventeen times. It was nearly a sporting event; local residents held a barbecue attended by 1,500 people during one of the aqueduct takeovers. Public sympathy was mostly on the farmers' side. The California Senate called LA's taking of the water "one of the darkest pages in our history." The DWP responded by mounting machine guns at strategic points above the aqueduct. More money was paid to remaining landowners, resulting in a cease-fire in the late 1920s that lasted fifty years.

Another casualty: 120 miles south of Mono Lake, the DWP cut off the water supply to Owens Lake, once big enough for steamboats hauling ore. The lake dried up, and winds now blow dust from the alkaline lake bed—nine-foot-thick crystallized brine—causing air pollution twenty times the regulatory limit. Is this the fate of Mono Lake?

A new chapter in the Owens Valley tale of engineering genius and associated strife began in 1972 with a court case regarding groundwater. In 1977, residents again dynamited the LA lifeline. The problem was that the city had announced it would double the amount of groundwater to be pumped. The valley soil is Sierra alluvium, where water often lies less than ten feet deep and nourishes native plants. With the pumping, vegetation may die, and dust storms may envelop the valley.

Los Angeles wants the groundwater and the Mono Lake water because it costs less than half the price of alternate supplies. In 1984, the Inyo County supervisors and DWP reached an agreement that calls for groundwater studies and "mitigation" while DWP pumps three times the amount that the county had recommended.

The Owens Valley Committee says that the county gave up too much. "DWP gets everything it could not get from twelve years of litigation," said Mary DeDecker, an authority on native plants and a member of the committee.

LA's thirst raises the question that perhaps so many people should not be living in an arid basin where they are dependent on the Feather River of the northern Sierra, the Owens River of the eastern Sierra, and the Colorado River of the Rocky Mountains. But Phil Pister has a point: "I would rather see the people down there than up here."

Big Pine, population 1,500, elevation 3,985, lies fifteen miles south of Bishop and is built on the same model of roadside business. South of town I see Mount Baxter, home of the largest herd of bighorn sheep. The bighorn, who once populated the Sierra above timberline from Sonora Pass south, were reduced to two herds on Mount Williamson and Mount Baxter. Diseases brought up by domestic sheep are probably the reason for the Sierra bighorn's near extinction. Cattle also host diseases, and until 1962, they competed for forage on national forest land that was the bighorn's winter range. By trapping and moving the sheep from the prolific Baxter herd, new herds have been tenuously established in the eastern Sierra at Wheeler Crest near Bishop and Mount Langley near Lone Pine.

The best site for the next reintroduction is Lee Vining Canyon, except that the Forest Service has leased it to a domestic sheep rancher for several generations. Because an individual was once allowed the privilege of running sheep on public land at almost no cost (currently less than a penny per sheep per day), Forest Service officials insist that they must renew the lease. The only alternative is to pay a great amount of money to the herder so that he will return the public lands to public use. A nongovernment group, the Yosemite Association, is hoping to do this.

The eastern Sierra is a refuge for the rock-loving bighorn, and it's a refuge for the man who knows the most about them—John Wehausen. After receiving his Ph.D. in wildlife management, Wehausen decided that he wanted to live on the east side and save the bighorn. He has tracked the sheep, lived in their habitat, counted them, diagnosed their diseases, determined where herds should be reestablished, trapped the sheep, moved them, and monitored their success. Sometimes he does this work as a consultant for federal and state agencies; sometimes he does it because it's his life.

South of Baxter, the mountains rise higher. About 360 peaks are between 12,000 and 13,000 feet in the Sierra; about 140 are between 13,000 and 14,000. Eleven are over 14,000. One of the most spectacular from the Owens Valley is Mount Williamson, south of Independence. At 14,375, it is the sixth highest mountain in forty-nine states, the second highest in the Sierra. In 1870, the state approved plans for a road over the Sierra at Kearsage Pass, but the highway was never built.

I pass Independence, home of 1,000 people. Near here, 900 American Indians were forced from their homes and required to go to the other side of the Sierra for confinement in 1862. Many escaped, and I see their ancestors here today. South of Independence I pass Manzanar. Ten thousand Japanese-Americans were forced from their homes on the other side of the Sierra and were required to come here for confinement during World War II.

At a long desert straightaway I turn east onto a dirt road and camp. Sagebrush runs for miles in this immense, treeless valley. Maligned as a weed, some sage lives 200 years. The Sierra rises purple to the west; the Inyo Mountains to the east are an extension of the White Mountains. For supper I sauté vegetables that will otherwise spoil in another afternoon of 110-degree heat in a locked van.

The quiet is penetrating. There is no motion except for my own. To the east and west, the valley meets no limits until it reaches the mountains; to the north and south, it encounters no visible limits at all.

After dinner I unhook the lawn chair and watch for the first star, not a star but Jupiter. The mountains are nearly black against a navy blue sky. A coyote yips, then another, and now they howl and sing. I have company.

The last light fades, and I go to bed. Through the windshield I see the dipper and the north star, pointing back the way I've come. I'm 280 miles from that northern tip of the range. Nearly four months have flown past, and they've been full, but something is missing. A certain intensity, beyond the planned and the expected and the comfortable, escapes me. Fading away, I think that there is something I must grab hold of. Or is it something that I must let go of? I began by taking a trip; now I'm the one who is being taken, but where? A coyote yowls again, and with my company, in dreams of loping effortlessly across this landscape, I'm gone.

At last I reach Lone Pine, population 2,060, 3,700 feet above the sea, nearly due east of the Central Valley city of Visalia and only seventy miles from it, though by road it is 250 miles. The Owens Valley continues south to the dust flats of old Owens Lake and to the Kennedy Meadows Road—the first, frail, trans-Sierra road in 145 miles—and on to Walker Pass. Farther south are the Joshua-tree-studded slopes at Tehachapi Pass—the southern end of the range.

The eastern Sierra runs down to those places, but south of here the mountains drop lower, and the Mojave Desert begins. I'm not ready for the southern end of the Sierra. I cannot face the end of the mountains. I'm going to change my plans.

Lone Pine sits more than two vertical miles beneath the summit of Mount Whitney, the seventeenth highest mountain in the United States. The seventeenth longest river is the vague Pecos. The seventeenth largest metropolitan area is nobody's favorite—Newark. But among mountains, the top sixteen are in Alaska.

The town is pleasant, with a business district about three blocks long. One red light—a hidden cost of tourism—was installed so that locals can cross the street during the Mammoth-to-LA rush hour that runs nonstop for three days on all winter weekends and on many in the summer. Horses graze in backyards; homes are small and frame, all have shade trees, and all are near a view of Whitney.

Here was the center of the severest earthquake in California history (the severest in the United States was in Missouri). In 1872, the land near Lone Pine dropped thirteen or more feet and slipped sideways twenty feet. At 8.3 on the Richter scale, the earthquake destroyed fifty-two buildings, leaving seven.

Between Lone Pine and the escarpment are the Alabama Hills, a cowboy-ambush landscape where Hopalong Cassidy adventures and later westerns were filmed. Among giant rocks I search for a campsite. I pass a blue van and stop a hundred yards beyond, where I stare at Whitney through the window above my table. In half an hour the owner of the blue van and his dog cautiously approach.

He needs a battery jump. "No problem," I say. Jerry worked as a ranger-naturalist for the National Park Service and taught school on Arizona Indian reservations, in Alaska, and in Southern California, which he wanted to leave. The east side of the Sierra is where he wants to live. "Out here, you remember what you had forgotten back in the city. Space is such an important thing—I need lots of it, and here it is."

For three months he looked for work from Lee Vining to Lone Pine. Then he ran out of money. "When you're fifty years old, this kind of thing shouldn't be happening." He must return to Orange County.

We connect my jumper cables, but his van will not start. I tow it to town. Jerry and his dog are out of groceries. Three days ago Dusty began sharing her food with her master.

I give him a bag of groceries that he says he does not need. The mechanic later tells Jerry that it will cost $55 to rebuild the distributor. I give him $70. He gives it back. I give it back. Perhaps he planned poorly, but all he wanted to do was to find something better on this side of the mountains. As Wayne Dakan said of life on the road, "We were always looking for something better. We never found it, but we kept looking anyway."

At the Sportsman Cafe I'm drinking black coffee, but not much; mainly I'm trolling for the local view of things. The man to my left has quietly eaten breakfast and stares sullenly while sipping coffee. He's maybe forty. I ask, "How were the pancakes?"

"It was French toast. Good." Moments pass. "Traveling?"

"Yes," I say.

"Where?"

"I was headed south, but I'm changing my plans."

"Yeah. Well, stick around for a while. That's what I did. Been here three years now."

"Why'd you stay?"

"I came to climb that mountain. You know. Whitney. I was thinking about getting married and wanted some insight, you know what I mean? So I went up there, then got married. Me, I'm from Massachusetts, but my wife was from Louisiana. We came here, a big adjustment. It didn't work out.

"Out here, I like the clean water, clean air, and the mountains. Back east I like the morals. You from back east? . . . You think it's different?"

I say, "In small towns, not so much. In cities, yes."

"You got something there. This is a small town, you know, but there are ten churches here."

"Which is the biggest?"

"In size, the Catholic. In numbers of people, hard to say, Mormon, Catholic, Nazarene, or Episcopal."

"What do you do for work?" I ask.

"Cut lawns, odd jobs, remodeling. I trade work for rent."

"What do other people do?"

"The tourist industry's the big thing. Some raise cattle or do a little mining. Some work for DWP. Some don't care for DWP. It's like, 'Remember the Alamo.' But most don't have any opinion. Most don't care what goes on."

Some people in Lone Pine do care about what goes on. I have a scrap of paper that says so: "Mike Prather—Russ Shay says see him."

Mike is thirty-eight, with a dark beard of medium length, a direct look in his hazel eyes, and a welcoming smile. He is fit and handsome, about five foot nine. He grew up in Santa Rosa, and his wife, Nancy, in Redding. After college in Chico, Mike and Nancy decided to seek a new life on the other side of the mountains.

At Death Valley, the lowest, hottest place in America but only eighty airline miles from Mount Whitney, Mike and Nancy found teaching jobs and stayed eight years. In 1981, they moved to Lone Pine. "We came here to raise a family. The school is larger, and our daughters get to have more friends. What could be better: a small town at the edge of the desert and at the edge of the mountains."

This year Mike will teach twenty-three students in the fourth and fifth grades. "Larger classes would be good for the kids; as it is, the selection of friends is small. But teaching here is not much different from other places.

"On the street, I recently saw one of the students from 1977, and she remembered two things: she asked if I still play my guitar and sing Jambalaya, and she said that she quit squashing ants just for fun. Jambalaya—well, so what? But the ants—that's something. The thing we have to deal with is looking at life fresh; we have to change behavior. The point is not ants; the point is life. I'd like every student to look at a flower and see the universe, to see life and its importance, to have a reverence for life.

"So much of it is a matter of getting kids into the right situations. Get them out in the mountains. You go out there, and I don't know about you, but I feel good. You don't need Zen. You don't need a catechism. You don't need to think. People out there start talking softer, and talking less. They look and see, and they take the feeling home.

"If we make the connection between those good mountain feelings and our everyday lives in the places where we live, we'll take better care of those places. Kids who learn to see and feel, they're like ripples in a pond, and once we have enough ripples, they'll all begin to touch each other.

"In the last four years, environmentalism has come out of the closet in the eastern Sierra. People used to be intimidated by bumper stickers saying, 'Fight World Hunger, Eat a Sierra Clubber.' I looked around and said, 'Hey, this is 1981.' I started calling meetings, and a lot of people showed up. We went to local government meetings and nobody threw tomatoes at us. If you say, 'Hey, listen for a minute, we just want to be a part of the process,' and if you're reasonable, then people listen.

"With five active people you can do something, but activism can really get out of hand. I might go to two or three night meetings a week—the Sierra Club, a new Audubon group that we're starting, and the Native Plant Society. Then I go to regional meetings in Los Angeles and Reno. When you live way out here, you have to be tied into other people in order to be effective."

Where does the motivation come from? Wayne Dakan's motivation came from seeing his old homeland fall toward ruin; Andrea Lawrence's, from Friends of Mammoth and a commitment to the future; Phil Pister's, from a desire to do something worthwhile with his career. Jim Hildinger at Tahoe, Bill Center on the American, Jerry Meral on the Tuolumne, Ginger Burley at Yosemite, David Gaines at Mono Lake—they were all motivated by something. Now Mike Prather answers, "It came from the sixties and early seventies.

"I guess I'm a child of the sixties, and I'm really glad I grew up then. Those years gave you a zest for life." Mike Prather searches for words and stares me in the eye. "That was an extraordinary era, so full of life." He smiles.

"There were causes then—of course, opposition to the Vietnam War. I remember marching in San Francisco when a hundred thousand people walked through the city. One hundred thousand people who believed in life. Somebody like Robert Kennedy or Eugene McCarthy came along, and they were going to do something about the pride and the politics that were killing so many. I worked for McCarthy, and there was a feeling that you *could* do something about the problems. I was studying biology, and all of this came together into some wholeness: learning about life and having life itself as the big social cause.

"Now I see a lot of apathy. People are into material wealth, not into cooperation or righting things that are wrong. Back then, I think there was more real enjoyment of life. People talked about ideas. Life is so short, why waste it in idle talk? Why waste it in idle goals?

"Those people are in their thirties now, but they still sparkle with enthusiasm. The empathy is still there for the earth and for social causes. We have to keep that spirit going, because in my lifetime, it's the only thing that I've seen that can make a difference."

I walk toward my van. Coming my direction is a young woman. I slow down. Her hair, reaching to her waist, is light brown with sun-bleached blond on top, tied back. We approach each other, she smiles, and I say, "Hi."

"Hi."

I stop.

"Looking for somebody's house?" she asks.

"No. I'm just looking around. I mean, I was just visiting with Mike Prather."

"Oh, Mike. I'm a teacher too. I teach in the room next to his."

Who is this with the bright blue eyes? She has traveled a long road from somewhere. Everybody has a story locked up as a mystery to nearly everybody else, and our lives go by, one never knowing the other.

"Do you want to sit down?" she asks and invites me onto her porch. She walks and sits confidently. She wears a long skirt and an embroidered vest.

Christy Lynch and I talk easily. She is twenty-eight and single. "When I was young, the sea was my wilderness, my playground and spiritual source. That's where I looked out. When I graduated from college, I wanted to teach in a beach town, but it was hard to find jobs." Lone Pine has no beach, unless you count the caustic alkali flats of LA's dust-plagued, desiccated Owens Lake, a few miles south, but this was the district that called Christy. "The job was not even here. It was in Olancha." Christy looks at me blankly. Olancha is twenty miles down the desert from here. "There were forty-eight kids in six grades. I had first through third. The first night I called Mom and Dad and cried, 'I can't do it.' Dad's a teacher also, and said, 'You can too.' "

When a teacher left Lone Pine, Christy got the job. "It's great working here. The school's good, the pay is the best I know of, and the kids are nice. But then there's the other side.

"If I were married and raising a family, this would be fine. But I'm the only woman in my position in the area. Single, working, and kind of young. Women here don't go hiking in the mountains like I do.

"I've had chances to get married, but I'd have to leave the Sierra. Why should I leave? I like it in Lone Pine. But here I am in the 'best years' of my life. I ought to be looking around, seeing who I do want to marry, but I'm here on the east side of the Sierra.

"I talked to my sister about this, and she said, 'Get *out* of there.' I think I will eventually. There's just no way around the social problem. Trouble is, I don't know where to go. I can't picture myself in LA. I don't want a city man. What do you do there? Go to parties and drink? The mountains have taken over for me. They're my horizon now. You know what I mean? Cedar Grove in Kings Canyon was a family vacation spot, but now the mountains aren't a vacation. Now I belong here."

Christy is a gem at the edge of the Sierra. I hate to leave, so I don't. It is a mystery: what allows two people to interact so well when they first meet? A greater mystery: why is this so rare? Suddenly it's 6:00. Christy has a dinner date with a man who wants to marry her. For me, it's time to move on, but where?

In the desert, now in the shadow of the mountains near the Owens River, I camp. This is the final night of my east-side tour, and I must plan ahead. At least for tomorrow.

Whitney stands jagged and purple, high in the twilight. It's hard to imagine the trail that winds up to its summit. The entire crest is high, but in the center, Whitney grows in a vertical cleavage of granite, in long, sky-pointing needles, as clean and sharp as if they had just sprouted from the ground and pushed the rest of the continent aside. It is the perfection of gradient, the climax of many earthquakes, the climax of the range.

Three men from Lone Pine were the first to climb Whitney in 1873. They named it Fisherman's Peak, after themselves, and were miffed that bureaucrats called it Whitney, after Josiah Whitney, head of the state Geological Survey. One of the anglers wrote,

"Whitney's agent . . . finds fault with the people here for their lack of romance in calling it Fisherman's Peak. Ain't it as romantic as Whitney?"

In the early 1970s, up to 800 people at once could be seen on the mountain. How large would crowds grow? In Japan, up to 25,000 people climb Fujiyama. *Per day!* I prefer the regulatory approach to the anthill approach; the Forest Service now limits overnight campers to seventy-five. Five times a year, a helicopter flies a new outhouse up and an old one down, so if you think you see toilets flying over, you do. The limit on camping tends to limit the number of people going to the top, because the 10.7-mile trail, which rises 6,000 vertical feet, is difficult to do in a day. Up to 200 people at once still populate the summit. I'm sidetracked, and I don't decide what to do tomorrow.

In the morning, with the sunrise on Whitney, it is beguiling— lower slopes a mass of rocks and trees, then more rocks and fewer trees, finally more rocks, snow, and no trees. I stare as the light on the peak increases from faint and colorless to pale blue, to yellow. No sound breaks the spell.

A change—I'm in need of a change. Even I—in my van, always ready to go and always going—even I am in need of escape. Van life is fine, but maybe my Coleman stove, six-gallon water jug, and library of a hundred books are too much. My technology has removed me from real contact with life. "Let's get back to it," Bill Kier said. Escape!

For too long now I've been at the edge but not beyond. It's time to make the commitment, to plunge or to climb, to somehow get the full experience.

Where can adventure be found? So many people have been all over the Sierra and especially up Mount Whitney. But I will forget that others have gone before me. Let's go.

Why stop at Whitney? All of the summits excite me. To search for places I've never seen, built by forces I cannot imagine, at a scale I cannot comprehend—I'm ready. What does the world look like from Whitney, and what lies beyond it? I cannot just climb Whitney; it's not enough. What's up there on that windy crest that's been a silhouette every evening since I rolled down from Tioga Pass? I want to see more, more. Get out and *go!*

From the northern end of the Sierra I've come 300 miles out of 400, but while the mountains have risen to their highest, I sit on my lawn chair down at 3,700 feet, beyond reach of whatever is up there. The mountains remain unknown. Here is what I will do: I'll return north, maybe halfway back to the northern beginning of the Sierra, and I'll start a different kind of journey, higher in the mountains, a new journey in search of all that I've missed.

Winter in the Sierra at Basin Peak   Spring skiing, Hope Valley

Northern Sierra from the Sierra Buttes

Logging with cables, Plumas
National Forest

Indian Creek Falls

Middle Fork of the Feather
below Milsap Bar

Quincy

Wayne Dakan at Butterfly
Valley

Lake Tahoe

Stateline, Nevada

Tahoe Keys subdivision

Land development in Tuolumne County near Groveland

Desolation Wilderness, Pyramid Peak on the left

Bill Kier at the Strawberry Lodge   Bill Center at Lotus

South Fork of the American
above Coloma

Auburn Dam foundation

Silver Fork of the American

Merced River below El Portal

Tuolumne River below Clavey
Falls

Pinball Rapid on the
Tuolumne River, normally
flooded by New Don Pedro
Reservoir

River recreation near the
Kings

Reservoir recreation at New Don Pedro

Yosemite Valley from Half Dome

Merced River, Yosemite Falls

Climbers, Camp 4, Yosemite

Armand Quartini at
Yosemite

Steve Schneider at Tuolumne Meadows

Ginger Burley at Tuolumne Cascades

Donald Rambeux making an arrowhead

Mono Lake, with David Gaines facing camera

The town of Mammoth Lakes, Mammoth Mountain

Andrea Mead Lawrence at
Mammoth

Downtown Bishop

Phil Pister at the Owens River

Lone Pine, with Mount Whitney at the right

Mike Prather, Lone Pine   Christy Lynch

Cattle fences in the Carson-Iceberg Wilderness

Cattle, Toiyabe National Forest

Carl Sharsmith at Tuolumne Meadows

Banner and Ritter peaks; Lake Catherine

Mammoth Mountain from the northwest

Alexander Gaguine on Mather Pass

The southern Sierra from Mount Whitney

Kings River a half mile above
Pine Flat Reservoir

South Fork of the Kings

Tehipite Valley and Dome

Sequoia trees, Sequoia
National Park

Middle Fork of the Kaweah

North Fork, Kern River canyon

Folks of the Kern rafting trip, North Fork of the Kern River

North Fork of the Kern above Johnsondale

Dry Meadow Creek, Sequoia National Forest

Ardis Walker, Kernville

Windmills, Tehachapi Pass

7

Escape

IT'S TIME TO LOOK CLOSER. I've camped in the van, talked to people, hiked, climbed rocks, and run rivers, but still I don't know the mountains. Old Wayne Dakan said I'll never know them, but I can do better than this. I need to make a different kind of Sierra journey. This time I'll stay high, away from the road, and follow the crest south.

DAY 1

For the first quarter mile, the no-return reality of my journey sinks in, and with it, a feeling that I forgot something. The second quarter mile and the weight of my pack tells me that if I didn't forget some things, I should have.

At a cliff that falls away in front of volcanic peaks, I stop, beyond earshot of Ebbetts Pass and Highway 4—the same road where I sat snowbound five months ago in March. This morning I left the van at Ronnie James's cabin, where it will be safe. My reason for starting at Ebbetts: if I hike south ten miles a day, I'll climb to the summit of Mount Whitney in five weeks, and because my goal is to finish the journey to the southernmost Sierra by winter, five weeks for this hike is the limit. Counting day hikes, I'll walk 400 miles. From San Francisco to Los Angeles on the interstate, the distance is the same, but the scenery is not. The view here is of wilderness. My progress so far is half of one mile.

John Muir wrote, "Only by going alone in silence, without baggage, can one truly get into the heart of the wilderness." I have silence, but I have baggage. In the big Kelty pack I carry a sleeping bag, pad, tent, clothes, food, and odds and ends. The weight that sets me apart is in the two cameras, two lenses, tripod, 200 pages of manuscript, and several books. I drew the line at half my weight and nearly reached it. At seventy pounds, my pack—"It" for short— is a load.

On the sunny side of a basalt boulder, I abandon It, shoes, and shirt, and I think: high country for thirty-some days. Of fifteen major river basins in the Sierra, I'll walk through parts of nine. Hundreds of uphill grades will make me pant, hundreds of windy ridge tops will cool me. On this breathless mountainside, I stop at the idea of wind.

After deciding to make this trek with a calculated notion about knowledge of the mountains, I must admit that a simple sense of adventure is what lured me here. Lazy and safe, I say, "Adventure, yes." If this is it, count me in. But adventure involves risk and danger. The dictionary also says, "an exciting or remarkable experience." I seek the remarkable part but would sooner leave danger down below where I last saw it, where it runs rampant in civilized places.

In *The Adventurer*, Paul Zweig quotes people and stacks up the footnotes on this unlikely subject for Princeton University Press. He says that adventurers are people who bring back stories of unknown places, "enlarging the boundary of what men know." A high order now when everyplace is known. Zweig says the adventurer is one who escapes: he "pokes holes in the walled city." Adventurers go for themselves and the sake of going, not for some notion about their country or corporation or whatever (people who do that are heroes, an entirely different cut of individual). Zweig wrote a whole chapter on adventurers' flights from domestic lives with women. Of course, not all women fit Zweig's stereotype, and maybe not all adventurers do, either.

Adventurers experience life for the sake of the experience and do not bog down in introspection or the endopsychic neuroses that crowd out the physical. Because the physical is all I really hope to know, everything else being a can of worms when I get right down to it, I enjoy this part of the book.

The element of challenge—to the body and the mind—brings people on long hikes like this. I'm not as interested in being challenged as in living the Good Life, close to the ground, free of the drudgery and the killing boredom of my nine-to-five experiences, free of past regrets and future ambitions, facing each day as a whole life. The Good Life is the escape from much of what I see down below.

The Escape—to get away—reappears as a theme in success stories of many kinds: escape from the Old World, the ghetto, the Indians, the white people, prison, the establishment. Then escape from conformity, authority, tradition, mediocrity, stress, and fear. The list is endless, which must say something about our situation. Yet to fill the heart, I must also arrive someplace, and that is more difficult. Let's shoulder that pack and see how it goes. Watching where I put my feet now, I think that I just want to enjoy the mountains, though I admit to curiosity. What makes the mountains so enjoyable? And I would be a fool to think that episodes down the trail will not lead me to encounters running off tangent from fun.

My reasons for coming here are more complicated than I thought. I seek knowledge of the mountains, adventure, the Good Life, the Escape, and something more elusive: I want to be part of these mountains, to belong here. Can I belong here in a month? A year? A lifetime? I don't know what will happen to make me a part of the mountains, and I won't push it. All I'll try to do is survive and have a good time, and the rest will take care of itself.

Out ahead lies my route, which I picture from someone else's perch in the clouds. I'm a tiny speck, and southward lies a jumble of forest, rock, and snow. Whitney, remarkably distant, is beyond a substantial curve in the earth; to get there looks impossible. But the trail winds as a thread up the canyons and over the passes between the summits. My repeated obstacle is gradient. It's my love, giving me views, and it's my enemy, pitting me against gravity.

I could leave this wildness by backtracking or by hiking for a day or two east or west. It's not a boundless wilderness, just large enough for the feeling of wildness. If I tried to avoid people, I could wander back here for a week and not see a soul. If a person were lost, the same thing could happen.

Sunlight and mountains—I can't get enough. I want to shout, to climb on a rock and scream, but something stops me. Through the next month, I'll surely get enough of wildness and mountains. I cross the Mokelumne headwaters.

My body has been straining, so in a meadow along the stream I stop, splendidly exhausted, physically and emotionally. I lie in the late sunlight where I'm engulfed by the meadow's grass. I feel like I'm floating on it. Slowly, mysteriously, it grows, long at my sides, up between my legs, and as it gets longer by the minute, it bends over me, shading my eyes, burying me like it does a branch that fell to the ground years ago. Green and warm, leaves of grass touch my face. I'm protected, but then a coolness creeps in from above. The sun has set, and I awake and make my camp.

DAY 2

At dawn the tent sparkles with frost, and I slide deeper into my bag. It is abnormally cold. I wonder if the clothes I brought will do. And my boots? I don't wear boots, but hiking sneakers that I've already worn for a year. They say that one pound on your feet equals five on your back. What about snow? Accumulations are rare before mid-September; snow usually melts until November. I'll be okay if the weather is normal.

I rejoin the Pacific Crest Trail, the ultimate route for long-distance hikers. In 1968, Congress passed the National Trails System Act, authorizing this trail from Mexico to Canada, 2,578 miles. Through the Sierra, it runs 735 miles.

I cannot say that day 2 is all fun. It hurts. After three uphill grades, the score is Palmer 3, gravity 0, though the rounds have taken their toll. Careless once, I slid on gravel, my left leg shot forward, and I buckled under the load of cameras, peanuts, and adzuki beans. Blisters have been born on each foot, my pack rubs my back so that I must wear a shirt, and the load knots muscles in that home of tension, the neck. I visualize my problem this way: underneath is the ground of the Sierra, rising and forcing me to climb. On top of me is It—my possessions. While the ground pushes up, It pushes down, and my muscles strain to keep the two separate. My inspiration is posted in Phil Pister's office: "Press on. Nothing in the world can take the place of persistence."

Today I see one person. He started in Bishop and will finish at Mount Shasta.

At the head of Golden Canyon, I camp and cook: lentils, barley, a package of Knorr's dried soup, and Parmesan cheese. I will rotate seven meals. For breakfast: shredded wheat, granola, and wheat germ with dried milk, raisins, and dried fruit. Lunch: leftovers, crackers, peanut butter and jelly, fruit, peanuts, walnuts, and sunflower seeds. I will restock three times. Cooking gear consists of a spoon, a knife, a small grill for campfires, a backpacking stove, and two aluminum pots.

Now that supper is eaten, I wonder: should I hang my food above the reach of bears? These bears live off the land, without the junk-food addictions so common in Yosemite, but bears are bears, big and hungry. This morning I eyed a pile of fresh, black dung. Ten days of food is a lot to lose, not to mention the need to hike out and restock.

To one end of my fifty-foot nylon cord I tie a stone and pitch it over a limb. The limb must be small enough that a bear won't walk on it and high enough that a bear can't stand up and snag the food. Now the line passes over the limb, both ends dangling. I tie a stuff sack full of food to one end of the cord and try to hoist it by pulling on the other end. Instead of my line crossing a single limb, it crosses the limb and several branches growing from it, tripling friction. I must pull hard while balancing on a skinny fallen log, five feet off the ground, directly under the limb.

In spite of my efforts, excess rope has onerously wrapped itself around my left foot, and I trip. I list to the right, and slowly, but no less hopelessly, begin my plunge to the ground. This time gravity is my enemy for sure. I land on a bed of fir branches, and roll belly up in time to see the food bag's rapid descent that began the instant I let go of the rope. Bam! The bag hits me in the belly. The next try works, and once I have a food sack pulled up, I tie a second sack to the rope and push it up with a stick so that both bags sway in the breeze, maybe beyond a bear's reach.

Day 3

To my right lies the Stanislaus National Forest and to my left the Toiyabe National Forest, only I call it the Toiyabe National Pasture. In one three-acre meadow that I know God meant a small stream to run through undisturbed, thirty cows and calves graze. I name the place Manure Meadow, representative of many. The stream and boggy areas are pockmarked with six-inch-deep hoofprints, nurseries for mosquitoes. Plants are trampled or bit off. Cow droppings are three feet apart except in the stream, where water has washed them away. For a half mile I tramp on cow manure at every step, every one. At a ridge top, my panoramic view is preceded by a broken barbed wire fence that reminds me of European battlefront photographs.

Let me say that I have milked cows and have not minded shoveling out stalls any more than the next hand. I do not shun the barnyard experience, though I did not come *here* for one. I take care not to track the ever-present roughage lodged in my Vibram soles into my tent, but I am not repulsed by the droppings of cattle. I prefer their odor over that of car exhaust and maybe even my wet sneakers. But cattle bring their ecosystem with them.

Undigested seeds are sown by defecating cows with the thoroughness of Johnny Appleseed, and the seeds grow into alien plants that crowd out native grasses and flowers. A cast of flies enjoy their favorite sticky habitat, alternately breeding on it and landing on me. Where I see cattle, I see no deer or bighorn sheep, and no marmots. I see cowbirds.

Before the 1930s, brown-headed cowbirds did not live in the Sierra. Now they are common where cows graze and where horses and mules are used. Delighting in once-digested food, the cowbirds follow the beef, and the impacts include death to mountain birds, including vireos, warblers, flycatchers, and grosbeaks—researchers have counted twenty-two species. Cowbirds do not tend nests but rather lay eggs in the nests of smaller birds. After baby cowbirds hatch, they kill or outcompete their fellow nestlings. The warbling vireo is nearly extinct in the Sierra for this reason. A study by the Forest Service and the University of California found that 22.4 percent of the nests of vireos and similar species contained a big baby cowbird, causing an 80 percent loss of reproductive potential in the nests surveyed. In defense of the cowbirds, they have always been dung eaters that could not stop long enough to tend nests of their own because they followed buffalo herds on the plains. We, of course, eliminated their buffalo as part of our attempted genocide of the Indians. However, I remain prejudiced in favor of the smaller native birds because they were here first.

Maybe the worst thing about cattle is Giardia. These microscopic protozoans infest water supplies, and if they are swallowed, they may attach themselves to the small intestine and cause loss of appetite, weakness, nausea, diarrhea, and severe cramps. At least thirty mammals, including beavers and dogs, carry Giardia. This fact has recently become better known, and the attitude borders on paranoia.

A stock description of paradise includes people drinking from streams: "You can even drink the water." To cup my hands and drink that icy runoff is a reason to backpack. Drinking while I swim in green pools is an unmatched pleasure. But because of Giardia, those days are supposedly over. Rangers say to boil water for a minute (three to five minutes at high altitudes), treat with chlorine or iodine, or filter, which I often do. This amounts to one more barrier between me and the wilderness. Warned or not, I drink a lot of raw water at high elevations. Some backcountry rangers do also. One said, "I don't drink from the heavily used lakes, but the side drainages are as good as ever." Steve Sorenson, a Giardia researcher for the U.S. Geological Survey said, "We frequently find small amounts of Giardia in the high country. It may not be different than in earlier years, but it's valid to worry about it." In 1984, the Geological Survey sampled for Giardia cysts at sixty-nine Sierra streams, including forty-two that were high-use recreation sites and twenty-seven that were low-use sites. Twenty-two of the sites had Giardia, though only two of these sites had more than half a dozen cysts in 100 gallons of water.

Cows carry Giardia. Cowboys are quick to say that deer and marmots carry the protozoan, so why pick on cows? I pick on them because this is not their home any more than it is mine. They are trucked up in the summer and trucked down in the fall. Down below, they drink dirty water, then bring their diseases up here and dump them in clean streams. The Forest Service and other agencies make much of the fact that people carry Giardia; we must relieve ourselves a hundred feet from streams and bury our droppings eight inches deep. I agree. I just think that cows should be restricted the same way.

The cattle are here, of course, because people eat beef. But only 3 percent of the nation's beef is produced on 361 million acres of public land. (Much of it administered by the Bureau of Land Management.) Florida—that sunny retirement community— produces about the same amount of beef as all of the public lands in the West, the fabled land of ranching.

In the national forests of the Sierra, more than 4,406,382 acres are in grazing allotments, 1,100,152 of them classified "suitable." In 1984, 32,019 cattle and 21,808 sheep grazed here for a total of 162,056 animal unit months (one AUM is one month of grazing by one cow, one horse, or five sheep over six months of age). Cattle have the run of the forest. The Plumas Forest plan, for example, calls for the "grazing of domestic livestock . . . unless restricted in an individual management unit." Among the national forests in the Sierra Nevada, the Sequoia and Sierra forests receive the most use—36,783 AUMs each. In the Stanislaus Forest, 733,441 of 898,322 acres are open to grazing. No other activity in the mountains, or for that matter in the United States, uses as much land.

Forest Service range managers were reducing the numbers of livestock in wilderness areas, but in the late 1970s, the cattle industry lobbied successfully to tie the managers' hands and prohibit cutbacks. Since then grazing has increased.

Mike Gravle is a mountain cowboy in a tradition set in 1863, when ranchers drove their herds to the Sierra to escape summer drought. I met him at the Strawberry Lodge, where he wore a flannel shirt, jeans, old boots, and a tall cowboy hat. Forget the squinting cowboy in Marlboro ads; if you've seen pictures of the honest-to-God, old-time cowboys, you might recognize Mike Gravle as the real thing.

He stays with his 150 head for the summer. "You have to live with

'em to know what they're doing and where they are." In September
he rounds them up. In two days he found 130, plus many calves.
For the next twenty days he searched for the rest, which are worth
$800 each.

To keep one cow for the summer on leased land down below
would cost Gravle $12, including purchased clover. Up here he spends
$6, including trucking. "Still, it doesn't pay that well. I'm here because
I like being here. Most of the ranchers on Forest Service allotments
have small outfits—one man or maybe two brothers. Over on the
east side, some are bigger.

"The cattle don't do damage. You keep the numbers down, and
they have lots of feed. You can drink the water twenty feet below
where the cows are in it, and it won't hurt you. The Forest Service
men, some are reasonable and some aren't. Here the guy's pretty
good. You say, 'Let's try putting ten more on,' and he says, 'Okay,
we'll see how it goes.' Four years ago the Forest Service didn't want
to have cows up here. Now the attitude's a lot better. The idea is to
use what they have, to get something out of our natural resources."

Steve Brougher, wildlife biologist on the Stanislaus National
Forest, said, "There's only so much forage available. When you put
cattle out there, food for wildlife is less available. Grazing alters
the ecosystem and makes it harder for some species to survive. For
instance, gophers may thrive but meadow mice decline where heavy
grazing occurs. Meadow mice are the preferred food of the great
gray owl, a species we're concerned about. Grazing may be extremely
detrimental to the continued survival of the owl in this area."

Because funds are short, much of the Forest Service's range work
is done by biologists. Brougher determines where livestock should
graze, and when the ground is dry enough to let them on. This is
done within significant "political constraints." If Brougher has time,
he may inspect the area to see if extra cows were released, and at
the end of the season he may do a utilization study to see how much
forage they ate. He rarely has time.

The fees from ranchers do not cover this work. Cattlemen pay $4
to $8 per AUM for comparable private grazing privileges, but $1.30
to $1.80 for Forest Service land. Try feeding a house cat for $1.80
a month. The grazing costs are not determined by competitive bid.
Nationwide, federal agencies received $24.9 million for grazing in
1981 but spent $58.5 million on the program. Taxpayers subsidize
the western ranching industry, as they subsidize water development. Even if fees are raised (this has been proposed since the
1940s), much of the money would likely be spent for backcountry
water supplies to benefit cattle, fencing to benefit cattle, and the
spraying of herbicides to benefit cattle.

Brougher said, "What we're talking about are enormous impacts for a minuscule amount of beef. I'd like to see no cattle on national forests, especially not in wilderness areas. It would probably not affect the price of beef in the store. But the directive is to have more grazing. Streamside areas are unprotected now. All I can see is a continual deterioration of the range, and it's a mess already."

Zane Smith, regional forester for California, said, "In all of California, we allocate 500,000 animal unit months, which is only one-third the capacity. We're not financed to manage grazing because we don't get fair market value for the range. Once the government receives a higher price for forage, and once streamside areas are better protected, the numbers of cattle will go up."

At camp 3 I'm above the cattle for the first time. At the head of White Canyon, Sonora Peak rises above me. From here to Canada, no other site on the Pacific Crest Trail reaches 10,000 feet. The sun sets behind Stanislaus Peak, part of the 160,000-acre Carson-Iceberg Wilderness that will be the Sierra's largest new protected area if the California Wilderness Bill passes.

Straight above, the sky is the deep blue of infinite space. Its color fades westward to robin's-egg blue, baby blue, yellow, orange, and red. On the ground, chunks of granite are like a torn-apart puzzle—pieces that have taken their first step toward the sea by breaking from the Sierra batholith. The light is soft, indirect, reflected from the mountains with no shadows, no shading. The air is stone still. It is darker now; sharp-edged rocks fade to a gray mass. Lightless, the land is a silhouette when an owl flies over, soundless. The owl circles again. Above White Mountain I see a star, bright and clear, and I laugh out loud, I don't know why. They say you can see 6,000 stars with the naked eye.

Three times I turn from my rock to go to bed, but don't. The last light reflects from Pyramid Peak, fifty miles north. I will see that landmark no more. The Dipper appears above it, showing the way north, the way back to all that I've seen. I go to bed without the tent and try not to sleep, the sky is so good, but I fade away. Not for long. Mosquitoes—John Muir called them "the small insect people"—bite me, and a cold-footed mouse runs over me.

DAY 4

People along Highway 108 are dots from where I eat breakfast overlooking Sonora Pass. On the trail, I traverse a landslide with gritty rocks that roll when I step on them. Horseback riders wind up the mountain while I wind down; we meet halfway.

"How's the trail up ahead?" the first rider asks.

"Rough in spots. Where are you headed?"

"Canada. Yeah, I know we're kind of late, but we had to wait for the snow to melt on Forester Pass. Maybe winter won't come till late."

They started at Mexico. They ride loose-jointedly and wear cowboy hats, cowboy boots, and cowboy chaps, but they don't chew and don't have that bony, bowlegged look of cowboys. One wears her long hair in a braid; the other wears her hair down.

South of the road, I begin a 1,200-foot climb where a man and woman slog through mud below a snowfield. He carries his pack across and returns for hers. She's in tears. "Oh no. No. Don't let go. I'm going to fall. *No!*" He says, "It's only rocks and mud, now come on."

At Latopie Lake a man camps behind rocks, a hundred yards from me. We act as if the other does not exist.

DAY 5

For five miles the trail clings near the top of broad volcanic ridges, not just above the timber but 2,000 feet above it. Clouds block the sun and remind me: mountain weather is erratic. Snow could come any week now, and the difference between sun and shade can be the difference between no shirt and a down parka, if I had one. I leave my pack near the trail and walk a mile to a fifty-acre field of alpine lupine as blue as the sky.

At the rim of the canyon above Kennedy Lake, I rock-sit in a dream of open space, mountains everywhere. One-quarter of the earth's land is above 3,000 feet, mostly mountainous, and some of the lower land, such as the Appalachians and the California Coast Ranges, is also mountainous. Ten percent of the earth's land is above timberline, harsh. In the mountains, life is an uphill struggle half the time, but would I trade it for the flats? Never.

The comfort of this rock imprisons me and glues me to the view. With the rest of me, my mind wanders further afield each day. Here is the Escape and here is the Arrival. John Muir said, "Going to the mountains is going home." Here with my view, I reflect on the past and feel good, but there's a longing to be closer, to let go, to feel the raw power and to thrill in the extravagance of this country.

Today marks a turning point. The fatigue, aches, and blisters do not bother me. I feel strong under It, which loses two pounds of food a day. Down toward the West Fork of the Walker, the smell of fir pulls me along, as it has done so often since Lake Almanor. I walk through God's plenty of unspoiled earth, new earth, untrampled. I've had to go far and high to escape, but I've done it.

There's another cowbell. In a mile I see thirty head and two cowboys, a young one in a ball cap and an old one in a cowboy hat. He yells, "Hey, haaa, heahh," like they did on "Rawhide."

From my camp along the headwaters of the Walker River, I wander into the Emigrant Wilderness, which scored highest in a Forest Service rating of Northern California wilderness areas.

DAY 6

Forsyth Peak, sharp and snowy, rises at the entrance to Yosemite, due east of Santa Rosa (don't be confused by California road maps, which are not oriented to the north). Yosemite is a Sierra dividing line: north of here the mountains are mostly volcanic; south of here they are granitic.

At Dorothy Lake I veer right and become lost. I don't realize this until I'm deeply mired in strange topography. The first clue is that the map is all wrong. Evidence accumulates: the trail signs are wrong, the compass has gone haywire, and for the first time ever, the sun sets in the north. It is not information I lack but humility, and when it sets in, I see that I've hiked to the Emigrant Primitive Area—a wedge between the Emigrant Wilderness and Yosemite, unprotected because of tungsten mining. Nothing profitable remains, so the California Wilderness Bill would add my unplanned campsite to the wilderness area.

DAY 7

Life is a rigorous matter of zigzagging east against the grain of the Tuolumne River's tributaries, which zigzag south through 2,000-foot-deep canyons. As I drop toward Rancheria Creek, I spot a huge man, carrying a huge pack, and climbing slowly without the momentum that makes walking a continuous movement. With his every step he must lift 350 pounds. He breathes hard, stares at the ground, and doesn't see me. When my foot skids and scrapes, he jerks his head up. It is on a thick wrestler's neck. His eyes flash wide and stop me.

"Scared me," the giant says. This formidable creature is John Gallagher, a teacher of survival and emergency preparedness at Quincy's Feather River College. "I teach all year, then come out here and survive." He left Tuolumne Meadows with 110 pounds— thirty days of food. I carry twelve at most. Gallagher will walk to the Feather River without restocking.

At my island campsite along Rancheria Creek, I must bag my food and hang it expertly because this place crawls with bears. I've seen tracks and I've seen scat. Underneath the ideal tree I score the perfect throw over a dead limb, thirty feet above the ground, reaching far from the trunk.

No sooner do I crawl into my dark tent than I hear the crash of a breaking branch and the thud of my food bags hitting earth. I advance cowardly, armed with my penlight—the kind the doctor uses to look into your throat. A throat is not what I hope to find. The darkness is quiet. I take another step. Another. There lies my food and a lot of rope. The branch broke under the weight of my red beans and rice. In the dark I gather my provisions and seek another limb. I hoist the bags, then sleep occasionally.

Day 8

At Benson Lake I stand on the expansive beach as though I had reached my final goal. I could stay here. Other hikers camp nearby, all of us far from town, self-powered, sitting out the same storms, sleeping through the same cool nights, filtering Giardia, hanging food in trees. We are each destined for empty canyons and desolate peaks, but now we gather at the Benson Lake crossroads. The people nearest me are Alan Raymond, his daughter, and friends. He grew up in Hawaii but prefers the Sierra. "I'm a pine tree person." He invites me over for fresh fish.

At dusk we watch an otter. It dives with a porpoise's roll of the back, hangs buoylike, looks at us, hisses, and dives. It's the only otter I've seen in the Sierra. Maybe other lakes do not contain enough fish.

Day 9

At dawn I'm walking and soon watching the sunrise. After a few hours I find a stream with a tree to lean against and a view, and I take my break, not for ten minutes but for four hours. In a microclimate of cool air, I think about what I've seen, and I write. When the break is over, I'm fresh. I hike ten miles and have enough daylight for an evening walk without the backpack.

Today is different, a fourteen-miler. I race darkness to Miller Lake. Coming the other way, Jerry Butler, sixty-seven, is headed for the Feather River. Although our meeting lasts only minutes, he stays on my mind. He sees what I see, but is it different for him? How would age change this experience? Smiling and putting on the miles, Jerry is what I want to be in thirty years. But I won't count on his luck. Right now I'll get in my miles and see what there is to see.

There's no way to predict when special things will happen. In the twilight I round a switchback, then stop suddenly in a whoosh of air. From the thick forest a great bird flies out, so close that it's a blur. The hawk's wings fan cool air on my face. I could have touched that extraordinary creature, normally so distant.

DAY 10

Here are the crowds: twenty scouts, two families at Return Creek, a string of horses and mules transporting six people and supplies. I could avoid people by hiking in September, staying off trails, or skirting the parks, but I want to see who is here. A young woman wrangler rides a horse with two mules tied behind. Her eyes are glued to a paperback novel. "What are you reading?"

"Smut. Well, its a *long* trail."

A group of adults sit on rocks, and one face is familiar. "Ginger!" We talk, happy to see each other. She and wilderness ranger Laurel Munson are leading a group for the Yosemite Association.

"Watch out for the bears," Ginger says.

Cold Canyon leads me toward Glen Aulin and the Tuolumne River Canyon, where I had my first good look at the Sierra Nevada sixteen years ago.

A dozen canvas tents mounted on wooden platforms, a corral for twenty horses or mules, a restaurant, a shower house, and more await me. This is the Glen Aulin High Sierra Camp, one of five in the Yosemite backcountry. Should the National Park Service support motels and restaurants in the wilderness? Each day, forty-eight people's sewage runs into an artificial mound of sand. Park scientist Jan Van Wagtendonk said, "For Yosemite backcountry, one of the biggest problems is the High Sierra camps. When you provide hot showers, fresh food, and linen in the wilderness, you're going to have impacts." Generators pump water. Pack trains of ten mules import everything from canned pineapple to clean sheets twice a week and sometimes more. But dinner smells good, and I follow my nose. I pay for tonight's lemon chicken, prepared by Jean Deluca. She and her husband, Bob, manage the camp. Jean says, "All of us spend a lot of time marveling at the unique experience."

An assistant says, "Yeah, you could write a sitcom about it: 'Life in a Linen Tent.'"

"We get a specialized clientele," Jean continues, "people who love the outdoors but want to take it easy, people who have some money, though this place is a good deal at $46.50 a day."

Patrons do not pay all the expenses, however, even at $13.75 for great chicken. Under the National Park Service's contract with the Music Corporation of America—the owner and operator of the camps—the government subsidizes heavily by paying for utilities. This included about $30,000 for a new sewage system here and

$80,000 for one at Merced Lake. The complaint I heard from employees from two of the camps was that raw sewage overflows on the ground.

When I asked Garrett DeBell of MCA why the government pays for MCA's treatment systems, he said, "People pay taxes, and this is a common thing to get for your tax money." Wayne Schulz, in charge of concessions for the Park Service said, "It's in legislation and in the contract."

Bill Matteson, a Park Service engineer, said, "It takes a lot of technology to serve those camps. They have sophisticated water and sewer systems. You don't send your average cowboy back there with a wrench to fix things."

Park planner Don Fox said, "If it takes that much technology to support a facility in the backcountry, then maybe it's time to take the facility out."

Free of my pack, I walk to one of the largest rivers of the hike. A thirty-foot fall foams into a green pool before speeding down a remarkable cascade and into the Tuolumne's Grand Canyon.

A woman in a lawn chair reads an issue of *Parabola* dealing appropriately with the "pilgrimage." We make eye contact. Doris Nelson is about fifty, soft-spoken, with eyes that are strong and direct. All her life she has lived in America's largest cities: first New York, then for twenty-five years Los Angeles, where she is president of the League of Women Voters. To get to Glen Aulin, she and her ten-year-old son, Christopher, rode mules from Tuolumne Meadows. "It really is a re-creation, a renewal. You leave other things behind. Back home, you never stop. It isn't meaningless—so many things are important to do. But here it's different. You see the world fresh."

When the mess tent triangle clangs, guests swarm from tents. Doris, Christopher, and I sit with a family of three. Dave is a particle physicist at the Stanford Linear Accelerator. Dee is a chairwoman of the San Francisco Youth Symphony. Their child is about Christopher's age. Jim, who I met in Cold Canyon this afternoon, sits at the next table. He says, "I didn't go very far. Just being out here again is the thing." He lives near Oakland and has come to Tuolumne Meadows since 1932. "There's something special about returning to a place that doesn't change."

Servers bring dinner in four courses, and it's better than my lentils and bulger wheat. When we're done, Bob Deluca presents what is essentially a comedy act. He introduces the staff. One guest tells a joke. For being the rowdiest, one table accepts an extra dessert. "Just don't throw it," Bob cautions. The sun is setting, and to see it, people walk a quarter mile. It's a thronging affair, but I scramble down to the river.

The sun shines up from the horizon and strikes the bottom of a washboard of clouds, now firelight red. The Tuolumne, crashing down a staircase, is not white but red from the sky. Granite walls glow in the deepening canyon.

It was 1968 when I first came here, but while I stare, it seems like yesterday—the curve of granite, cluster of fir, scent of pine. Down there I hiked for miles and days. I feel like a different person. Between then and now have come many miles, but the place remains the same, and that is a reason for wilderness. Here is something stable, a ruler to mark my movement: growth, regression, or doldrums. John Muir pounded sticks in the glacier on Mount McClure then other sticks off to the side so that he could measure the downhill movement of ice. Tonight's view is like one of those sticks that are placed off to the side. It has stood still, and it enables me to measure the flow of my ice. Maybe I'll return here when I'm Jerry Butler's age or, if I'm lucky, to Quincy when I'm Wayne Dakan's age.

"Isn't it something?" Doris says, with thoughts of her own while she holds Christopher's hand.

DAY 11

The trail to Tuolumne Meadows crosses one of the most scenic landscapes of the Sierra. When the Tuolumne River is not in rapids it is in waterfalls. Swept by the broom of the river, wide granite slabs lie clean and white.

There is no problem finding the way: just follow the brown manure road. As the particle physicist said at Glen Aulin, "The stink on the trail is enough for a blind man to follow." I'm not the only visitor who is unenthusiastic about an overdose of horses and mules. A ranger working in backcountry management said, "We get fifteen or twenty-five letters of complaint each year in the mail, but rangers get complaints left and right, hundreds of them."

When the trail enters the meadows and woods, it is worn forty feet wide; in other places there are six separate trails, two feet apart and parallel. Stock put more pounds on each square inch of earth and cause damage perhaps many times that of a comparable number of people because horses step anywhere, whereas people aim their feet at rocks when crossing streams or boggy places. Researchers Frissell and Duncan found that vegetation and soil at horse camps are impacted ten times as much as at people's camps in the Rocky Mountains. At streams, my trail is temporarily free of dung because the water has washed it down to Hetch Hetchy Reservoir, the inlet to everyone's tap in San Francisco, to nearly 10 percent of the drinking water in California.

Today's use of horses and mules is one-sixth that of 1930, according to the Kings Canyon National Park Stock Use Plan. There and in Yosemite, packers led 150 head at once. Throughout the Sierra, more than 3,000 horses and mules operated out of more than fifty pack stations. Meadows were grazed into mud. In 1935, David Brower wrote, "What Muir had objected to in the impact of commercial sheep is now being accomplished by animals hired for pleasure." The limit in Yosemite is now thirty-five head for day trips and twenty-five for overnights.

One point convincingly favors horses and mules: you don't have to walk. The Sierra Club still sponsors trips with stock. "These outings are suitable even for people who have little or no experience with burros or camping, and also for experienced campers who want to explore without a backpack."

Charlie Morgan of the High Sierra Stock Users Association encourages riders to rake droppings from campsites and to tie stock beyond sight of the trail. Once a commercial packer, he recognizes that impacts are too heavy in some areas, but he says, "It's not fair to cut back on this form of wilderness travel that accounts for only a small percentage of the use."

Except for ranger-naturalists who dislike stock use, officials at Yosemite saw no need for tighter management. Steve Hickman, chairman of a stock use committee, said, "There's an ideological rift resulting from people's feelings, not from facts."

Hickman is right; other than what I see on the trail, facts are hard to come by. The U.S. Geological Survey and the California Department of Health Services have not tested horses for Giardia, though they have tested thirty other mammals, including ones as small as pocket gophers. Some people say horses do not carry the protozoan, but Steve Sorenson, head of the Geological Survey study, calls this "wishful thinking," and a paper from the University of Pennsylvania's School of Veterinary Medicine reported on a horse with Giardia.

Even assuming that stock carry Giardia, managers saw no need to ban pack animals from even the most remote, unspoiled watersheds. Superintendent Bob Binnewies said, "We tell people to filter or boil the water. Giardia is going to be in the streams anyway. Unless you eliminate all of the causes, you won't eliminate the problem."

Garrett DeBell of MCA said, "When I walk along a trail and see a bit of horse manure, it doesn't bother me. People who are bothered by droppings can get a map that shows the trails that are used by stock the most, and they can choose other trails." The Park Service titles this the "Expectations Map," and more than fifty miles of prime scenic trail are coded for stock use equivalent to or greater than the amount going to Glen Aulin.

Why, I ask, should the most scenic and popular trails, like this one along the Tuolumne, be written off to ungulate dung when only 2 percent of Yosemite backcountry users travel by horse or mule? Perhaps the riders, being such a minority, should get a map and avoid hiking routes.

A major source of roughage on the Glen Aulin trail is mule trains supplying the High Sierra camp. Ed Hardy, director of MCA's operations, said, "I think you'll see some changes, so less stock will be needed to supply the High Sierra camps. But you may still see more riders. Equestrian activity in California is growing rapidly." MCA's horse stable operation is the largest in the United States and accounts for 73 percent of stock use in Yosemite (the Park Service accounts for 20 percent). Most of MCA's clients go for rides lasting only a few hours, which presents fewer problems because riders stay on bridle paths.

At Tuolumne Meadows, hundreds of cars speed along the first road I've seen in a week. Here is Steve Schneider. He and Lars Holbek have been climbing, as usual.

Unexpected news at the post office: a letter from Boyd Murray, my brother-in-law, says he's coming to join me. Confident that we will connect, he's on a plane to San Francisco at this moment. Later I phone him and we arrange to meet in two days. Meanwhile, I schedule an interview recommended by Ginger Burley.

Wood smoke swirls around the roof of Carl Sharsmith's tent cabin when I tap on the door. "Ho. Yes. Come on in." I drop my pack and hold my hands over a cook stove, hot and popping on this cold, rainy night. "Ah, yes," Carl says, "nothing like a wood stove now, is there?"

Carl may have worked for the Park Service longer than anybody. At eighty-one, he is, of course, wrinkled, slightly stooped, and thin on hair. He wears glasses, an old shirt, and pants with suspenders. Ginger, who walks or runs six miles a day, said that Carl could outwalk her until this year. Last winter he had a heart attack. He debated about returning to lead hikes at 8,600 feet above sea level, but Tuolumne Meadows is a hard habit to break.

How was Carl's day? "It's good to see people enjoying Yosemite. Gosh, yes. People like to walk on Mother Earth. Tuolumne Meadows is an island of happiness."

He stirs a pot of bean soup, nursing it for ten minutes. As soon as I say that I have crackers, cheese, and an apple for supper, Carl serves himself, and the serious story telling begins.

"I came across the writings of John Muir in 1914 and never got over them. When I first saw the Sierra, it was more than I could stand. We were on the train, me and the boys, we called ourselves the Trail Finders, going up the Owens Valley. We got out near Army Pass, south of Whitney. No sooner than we started across the desert toward the mountains than three men with guns held us up. They thought we were surveyors for Los Angeles—the Owens Valley water war was going on then, you see; it was in the twenties."

Harold Bryant and Loye Miller had developed a prototypal nature guide program for the University of California at Lake Tahoe, and in 1925, Park Service director Stephen Mather persuaded them to establish the Yosemite Field School. Carl says, "Yes, right here is where the parks' naturalists' programs began." In 1930, at age twenty-seven, Carl applied. That season set a lifelong pattern of summers in the Sierra.

Carl became the first ranger-naturalist at Tuolumne Meadows. "They called us nature guides. It was a groping thing, kind of factual at first: what flower is that? It was a long time before we indicated the relationships between things. I was lucky. Here I was in this wonderful place, and I was going to get every person to love Tuolumne Meadows."

Since 1931, Carl has spent nearly every summer here, "but there was the meadow survey in 1957." What he did then helped change the course of land management in the High Sierra. For the Department of the Interior, Carl surveyed meadows from Sequoia National Park north through Yosemite. "I had a sack of flour and of course a big sack of beans, and worked my way slowly north, looking at the effects of horses, mules, and cattle. Many of the meadows were in terrible condition and getting worse. The upshot was that many were closed to grazing. Oh, we still have problems. The horse outfits have a lot of influence. For a hundred years they've soft-soaped the superintendents and done pretty much what they damned well pleased."

From Berkeley, this seventh-grade dropout had received a Ph.D., then he taught at San Jose State from 1950 to 1972 and became the eminent botanist of the High Sierra. A forget-me-not that he discovered is called *Hackelia sharsmithii*, a "sensitive plant species of unique distributional occurrence" in Sequoia National Park.

Carl guided Eleanor Roosevelt at Glacier Point above Yosemite Valley and hiked with the noted geologist François Matthes. "When he talked about the rocks, we were entranced. He had eyes to see beyond the bald facts." Carl knew acquaintances of John Muir: "They were either enthusiastically sentimental or they couldn't stand him."

Someone knocks on the door. It's Betty O'Neill, who wrote the Tuolumne Meadows history, *Meadow in the Sky*. A retired teacher, she's writing a biography of Carl.

"Oh, it was different in the old days," he reflects. "Till '38 people drove up and camped anywhere in the meadows, even a mile back off the road. You can still see those tracks.

"If someone was on a trail without a fishing pole, people said, 'What are you doing in Yosemite if you're not fishing?' Now the tide is reversed, and I say to fishermen, 'You mean that all you came to Yosemite for is to catch a fish?'

"The people have changed, and the duties have changed. We patrolled the backcountry, fought fires, and planted fish. Now we plant fewer fish because it's an artificial thing. Now we let a lot of the fires burn. The idea is to let nature have its way, and it's about time.

"Rescues have changed, too. Now, many are made by helicopter." In 1935, Carl fell from Mount McClure and nearly died before he was carried down and driven to a hospital, where he stayed for two months.

"The big change to Tuolumne Meadows came with the road. Used to be it took all day to come up from Yosemite Valley. There were never more than sixty people here. Then the road was widened in '61. The road builders said, 'You'll get used to it.' Yeah, cut my arm off and I'll get used to that, too. It's a vicious circle. More people came, and so we built more buildings. Over the years there were other proposals, some to make your hair stand on end. During the war they looked for tungsten in the park."

Another knock on the door. It's Elaine, also a ranger-naturalist, here to borrow a book. Carl says, "Ah, now there's a change. Used to be all men. Gradually girls came on the scene in the late seventies, and it's a good thing."

A memory hits Carl suddenly, and he says, "Oh, I'll tell you what was different in the old days. Ha, yes. The superintendent believed that if you fed the bears garbage, they wouldn't pilfer from campers, and Horace Albright, bless his soul, was head of the Park Service and wanted to 'bring the wildlife to the people.' You see, environmental awareness was something that came later. So every night in the valley we had a bear-feeding show. We spread the garbage out very nicely and got the floodlights ready, but wait! You couldn't turn them on until the big open bus from the Ahwahnee Hotel arrived. Maybe there'd be twenty bears, maybe just an old skunk. But when the lights went on, the whole crowd went, 'ahhh.' "

For years Carl was the only naturalist at Tuolumne Meadows. "Now I'm supervised." I say the old ranger has little complaint: his boss is Ginger Burley.

Here in a warm cabin I've heard some stories, but to know someone, I have to see him in his element, especially Carl—a personality type that I call element-intensive.

"May I join you on your walk tomorrow?"
"Gosh, yes. Come along. Come along."

DAY 12

Some of the twenty-five people are gray-haired and have known Carl since they were kids. He begins, "I'm just an ordinary guy in boots, walking around. Maybe a little luckier than most."

He explains the meadow: "Trees can't grow because there's too much water. You see, granite ledges block the river at the Tuolumne cascades and form an underground lake that makes the soil too wet for trees, but not for grasses or sedges." Grasses have hollow, rounded stems; sedges grow in wet areas and have solid, triangular stems. Each time Carl stops, we see a new form of life, a new set of relationships between plant and water, water and soil, soil and rock, rock and weather. Carl says, "Whenever you look into one aspect of nature, it opens up more, and you know what? The story never ends."

Our route has appeared to be aimless but has led to some large rocks. "Here's a picture of everything that is Tuolumne. I call it my shrine." Two glacier-delivered boulders frame Cathedral Peak, named by the other old man, John Muir. Carl places a hand on a rock. "Wouldn't it be something," he says, looking across at all the faces, "if we could change ourselves into rocks? Wouldn't it be nice to live 300 years—to stay in one place for a long time, to see the changes here?"

The other old man said, "For my part, I should like to stay here all winter or all my life or even all eternity."

Carl picks up two stones, one with sharp edges, one round. The first broke from a larger rock nearby. The second was rolled many miles by glaciers. "It's like old age; the sharp corners wear off."

Carl belongs here in these mountains, like Wayne Dakan, Jim Hildinger, Ginger Burley, Phil Pister, and Andrea Lawrence. He's starting his second half of a century here, and now, with not many years left, he thinks that to know this place better, to be a part of it, he would like to become a rock, to become the earth itself. Maybe that's what it takes to be a part of the mountains. Maybe that is my answer.

DAY 13

Boyd steps off the bus at the tent town of Tuolumne Meadows Lodge. We shake hands and slap each other on the shoulder. He recovers his pack from the underbelly of the bus and says, "Here we go."

Not yet. Before we walk far from a trash can, we must eat and drink the lunch that Boyd carries in a bag and bottle. We sit by the Dana Fork of the Tuolumne, eat cheese, crackers, and pepperoni, and drink wine. "Here's to the Sierra," Boyd says.

"Here's to your escape from the fourteenth floor of your sky-scraper," I say.

"Here's to my new boots and $40 worth of freeze-dried food."

"Here's to the bears who would love to eat it."

For years, our visits have been limited to holiday dinners. Now we will have a chance to talk as we have never talked and to argue once a day about politics. Up ahead is Donohue Pass—a barrier and a challenge—exciting enough to me, more so to my brother-in-law. The question is whether to camp at Ireland Creek or go on, and the consequences could be great. The problem here is bears, worse than anywhere else on the Pacific Crest Trail. Because rangers tied a cable between two trees for hanging food, we stay.

The largest animal in the mountains is on our minds. For bedtime stories, Boyd tells bear tales from canoe trips in Canada, and I tell a few from Alaska. But no place has as contemptible a reputation as Yosemite for nuisance bears. With their teeth they have punctured propane containers. Who knows why. In one sitting, a bear will eat a five-day supply of food for four backpackers. A bear will spend an hour chewing through a three-inch-diameter limb to eat food tied on the end. From higher limbs, cubs jump and dive-bomb food bags tied beyond reach. They lose their fear of people and smash into cars where they see coolers. The most troublesome of these junk-food-addict psychopaths are drugged, trapped, and trucked out of Yosemite Valley to lowland habitat in the park, often to Hetch Hetchy, twenty-eight airline miles away. Within twenty days most return. One with a poor sense of direction appeared in South Lake Tahoe, and its behavior had not changed.

Most bears that acquire a taste for people's food cannot be rehabilitated. Dick Riegelhuth, chief of resource protection in Yosemite, said, "We keep a dossier on each animal. We have a hearing for each problem bear and sometimes capture them seven times before killing them. Doing that is one of the hardest things I have to ask my employees to do." Each year about seven are killed. For all this trouble, Riegelhuth couldn't recall one serious injury to a person in the park. Black bears very rarely hurt people unless directly provoked, such as by punching one. Due to bear-proofing of garbage cans and people's hiding their food, the campground problems are reduced from the 1968–76 era, but in the backcountry, it's worse—one in seven groups suffers property damage.

Boyd and I know that once it's dark, the bears will enjoy open season on everything that we laboriously lugged up here, so we hang our food on the cable, wash dishes spotlessly, and leave our packs opened and unzipped so that the bear doesn't have to rip them to sniff inside. I pile the gear two steps from the tent. If a bear comes, I'll know it.

Late in the night I awaken, wide-eyed. I hear heavy breathing, and it is not Boyd. Now I hear snorts and grunts. Now the clank of the cook pot overturning, and still, the heavy breathing. I unzip the mosquito net and look into the face of a bear.

What do you do when confronted by 400 pounds of animal that's wild but not wild enough to stay out of your pack? Don't get close. The bear is five feet away. I yell, "Hey." He backs off; he seems to have an unreasonable fear of an unarmed human. I crawl out of the tent and see him milling around in the dark, black on black.

DAY 14

The threat now, as we climb most of the day toward Donohue Pass, is altitude sickness. At Tuolumne Meadows the air pressure is two-thirds that of sea level, and rare oxygen and low pressure can cause shortness of breath, headaches, and nausea if people do not sit back and acclimatize for a few days. At higher elevations the hazard is pulmonary edema, a complex danger involving lack of oxygen, alkalinity in the blood, fluid in the lungs, and retention of water that can lead to incoherency, unconsciousness, and death.

Boyd's home overlooks the Ohio River from 800 feet above sea level, and now we will climb to 11,056. He weighs 230 pounds and is as strong as last night's visitor. We trek steadily, and in a brisk wind we step onto the rounded top of Donohue. Boyd points down the canyon. "Where's all this go?"

I describe Glen Aulin, the Grand Canyon of the Tuolumne, Hetch Hetchy, Meral's Pool, Clavey Falls, and the muddy edge of New Don Pedro Reservoir. After rafting on the Tuolumne, hiking through its canyon, and wandering in its meadows, I've reached the headwaters, almost. The Mount Lyell glacier, one of the Sierra's largest, is higher, but there's no time. We drop east of the crest and camp where the stream braids around tufts of grass the size of beds, and where the wind blows hard.

DAY 15

At two o'clock in the afternoon Boyd and I pitch camp at Thousand Island Lake, where we face one of the most striking lake and mountain views in the United States. The water stretches nearly two miles, broken by about a hundred islands, some too small to stand on. The metamorphic and volcanic rock of Banner Peak rises 3,000 feet to its dark summit, overpowering and sharp like the craggy home of the devil in Walt Disney's *Fantasia*. Dante said mountains were the gates of hell. Norse mythology said that Mountain Giants were the enemies of all that was good.

But mountains have also been holy places. The Greek gods lived on Olympus and Parnassus. Moses received the Ten Commandments on Mount Sinai, now called Gebel Mûsa. Mount Zion was David's choice for a city, and Jesus' sermon was on the "Mount." A Chinese center of the universe is the mountain Sun Chan, and Buddhists and Hindus have various mountains as the centers of everything. All over North America, the Indians regarded mountains as holy places. Four sacred peaks surround the Navajo's center of the universe, Mount El Huerfano. Evil or holy, loved or hated, hot in the sun or cold in storms, nothing about mountains is neutral. Maybe that's part of the appeal.

Where we camp, the eye is led outward by the lake to the water's end, where Banner Peak's snowfields are as distinct as in a paint-by-numbers canvas. Adjoining Banner is Mount Ritter, about 200 feet higher but invisible from here, the two of them creating a double-crested island in the sky. The scene is perfect, irresistible.

Cumulus clouds threaten, so I pack rain gear and matches, though where I'm going there will be nothing to burn. It's too late to climb Banner or Ritter—the snowfields would be icy by the time I return after sunset, and I carry no ice axe. Besides, I'm alone. But I'll go up for a look.

Without the heavy pack, I speed past a thousand details that deserve a long stare. Saxifrage colors cool pockets. I jump across the inlet streams and climb toward the skyline, where a saddle dips north of Banner, then rises to Mount Davis.

From meadows speckled red, blue, and white, I climb to rocks the size of desks that fell when buttresses of Banner and Davis smashed to lower ground. Rocks bury the stream up ahead, so I drink one last time. Where the snowfield begins, I step far out from the last rock because its warmth melts a hollow space around it. The top two inches of snow are soft and my shoes grip as I hustle up, drawn excitedly by the ridge and by the mystery: what's on the other side? The snowfield ends at a rocky headwall.

Western mountains rise into view as I slowly step up. Now I stand on an arête—nothing but a knife-edge after back-to-back glaciers plucked rocks from both sides. Lake Catherine, a blue black gem, lies below. Banner and Ritter rise in walls of rock and snow, and granite waves of canyons cut by the San Joaquin's North Fork fill the background. At the boundary of Yosemite, the Clark Range juts into my horizon. I look down thousands of feet to canyons that drop thousands more. The world rests in a different perspective—constantly changing perspectives—the ultimate in three-dimensional space, richer by far than the two-dimensional lowlands. Up here I know where I am, and I can see beyond where I am.

John Muir also scrambled to this ridge and wrote, "Arriving on the summit of this dividing crest, one of the most exciting pieces of pure wilderness was disclosed that I ever discovered in all my mountaineering." One hundred and twelve years later, the view is the same. Even though I had decided not to go, I wonder about climbing up there. Muir wrote, "I could not distinctly hope to reach the summit from this side, yet I moved on across the glacier as if driven by fate. . . . We little know until tried how much of the uncontrollable there is in us, urging across glaciers and torrents, and up dangerous heights, let the judgment forbid as it may."

He climbed halfway before running into trouble. "I was suddenly brought to a dead stop, with arms outspread, clinging close to the face of the rock, unable to move hand or foot either up or down. My doom appeared fixed. I *must* fall. There would be a moment of bewilderment, and then a lifeless rumble down the one general precipice to the glacier below.

"When this final danger flashed upon me, I became nerve-shaken for the first time since setting foot on the mountains, and my mind seemed to fill with a stifling smoke. But this terrible eclipse lasted only a moment, when life blazed forth again with preternatural clearness. I seemed suddenly to become possessed of a new sense. The other self, bygone experiences, Instinct, or Guardian Angel— call it what you will—came forward and assumed control. Then my trembling muscles became firm again, every rift and flaw in the rock was seen as through a microscope, and my limbs moved with a positiveness and precision with which I seemed to have nothing at all to do. Had I been borne aloft upon wings, my deliverance could not have been more complete."

Now that would be something, to be saved by preternatural clearness. Even better, by an angel. I turn away from Banner and Ritter and traverse up the boulder field to the easy summit of Mount Davis.

Here I picture my Sierra journey from Lake Almanor to Tehachapi Pass. Not the usual map view from above, but the profile. Almanor was 4,482 feet above sea level. The hike in Desolation reached 8,500. The high country south of Sonora Pass was 11,000, and Donohue, 11,056. Now 12,311. South of here, 14,494.

The world lies below me. Thousand Island Lake is a puddle, and Mono Lake, amoeba shaped, survives in shrunken form to the east. The Owens Valley drops toward Bishop. Banner and Ritter—the tallest mountains of the central and northern Sierra—loom point-blank, south of me.

Here on the summit, the overbearing, inescapable impression is that of the wind, a continental blast of it, unchecked since Fuji-yama. The wind blows me off course when I walk. It is threatening but thrilling, disabling but energizing. The sky is enormous because it extends even below me for thousands of feet. I realize something that is always true but finally obvious: I'm a creature of the air, with only my feet on the ground.

The sun is low; an evening wind chills me through a sweaty shirt. What would the night wind be like? A dark shiver replaces my euphoric sigh of only minutes ago. The wind is growing and the weather intensifying as my journey continues.

The evening grows cool and dark as I walk into camp. Coyotes across the lake sound like they are a hundred yards away, the chorus of howls, yips, barks, and falsetto barks could come from two or twenty animals—I cannot tell. We hang our food from a tree that grows on a shelf of rock above the tent. Boyd says, "This is good. We'll know if the bear tries to get our food; when he lunges for it, he'll fall off this rock and land on the tent."

DAY 16

Perfect days are what we have come to expect. The lake lies glassy, the air invisible even to mountains miles away. Sunlight shines golden on Banner.

We see an old German couple, a black man and his son, twelve scouts trailed by an exhausted leader, a young couple obviously in love, and a lone woman about forty.

We pass the falls of Shadow Creek, east of the jagged Minarets, an area that Richard Leonard called "one of the most beautiful places in the Sierra." This land, along with Banner and Ritter, 325,000 acres running twelve miles back to Yosemite, was in the original Yosemite National Park in 1890 but was deleted in 1905 because the pared-off property included minerals that miners wanted to haul away. In the 1950s, a mining road was proposed up Shadow Creek, but it was stopped.

Many switchbacks ascend through a conifer forest that could be New England—evergreens and rocks. We camp along Rosalie Lake near a group of young people led by John Thompson, a geology and environmental education teacher at San Jose State University. They will hike twenty miles cross-country by compass.

Trying to hang our food, I hook the first bag on a jagged limb and cannot get it down. My stick won't reach and the limb is too weak to climb on. I jerk the rope. The bag flies loose and descends as if hurled at Boyd. He catches it and says, "Strike."

DAY 17

Down from the high country, we walk miles on pumice—a tan, bubble-filled cinder, the rock that floats. As in sand, our feet slide forward half an inch each step, and the knees are better for the slippage.

"Aaahhchk. You sonofabitch!" It's another mustached, denim-jacketed packer encouraging his stock. The hikers multiply and look different since we left Tuolumne Meadows. Three teenage girls with wide-necked sweatshirts sit along the trail, a young man smokes and coughs, and a lot of dudes ride north on horseback.

Boyd and I camp along the Middle Fork of the San Joaquin, the only Sierra river that used to flow from the other side of the ridge that is now the Sierra crest. The ancient headwaters were cut off 3.2 million years ago near Mammoth when the eastern Sierra rose by earthquakes.

DAY 18

Since Donohue Pass, the sky toward Mammoth has looked stormy, and now that we're under it, we know it's stormy. We read, and in two hours, when the rain stops, we walk toward the town of Mammoth Lakes, where Boyd will catch the bus to Reno and San Francisco. At the road we hitch a ride in the back of a pickup.

If Tuolumne Meadows was a change of pace on this hike, Mammoth is culture shock. I see women in skintight designer jeans and high, pointed heels. Boyd and I walk from shopping center to shopping center down the four-lane street. I get my mail—a box of food from Tim Palmer. Unimaginative, he sent me the same old stuff, and my pack grows to sixty-five pounds. Boyd buys a bus ticket, then calls my sister Brenda.

We eat at the Stove, where the waitresses are all blond and shaped exactly like women. I've been in the woods a long time. My waitress says, "Readydaorderyet?" I ask for huevos rancheros.

"Yawantoasterbiscuitswithet?"

Smokers sit next to us. I eat huevos with toast and breathe smoke. I'm satisfied with an excellent breakfast but relieved to step back outside.

Walking down the street, Boyd stops suddenly and grits his teeth.

"What's the matter?"

"My knee." He tore ligaments when skiing fifteen years ago. After forty miles on the trail, Boyd is brought down on the four-lane in

Mammoth. He sits on the ground. "How about a good bar where I can prop my leg until the bus comes?" We inch toward a restaurant-bar near the gas station where the bus stops on its LA-Reno run.

We've had a fine trip, and I hesitate to abandon my friend and relative, but I've tended to the first priorities of wilderness survival: he is under adequate shelter and will not dehydrate. As for the first priority of survival in Mammoth, Boyd has money. We say good-bye, and I set off for the country again. I hitch a ride to the ski area and catch the Devils Postpile bus. Two young women step on behind me.

The road curves sharply, drops steeply toward a dead-end in Devils Postpile National Monument, and offers a rare example of limiting cars in a park. I sit four rows back, and the young women sit behind the driver.

He grinds in second gear toward Minaret Summit, a landmark in Sierra Nevada conservation. Highway planners proposed a trans-Sierra road that would cut from the western foothills, up the Middle Fork of the San Joaquin, and over this pass to Mammoth, ultimately linking San Francisco and Denver. The road had support: chambers of commerce, congressmen, the California Department of Transportation, and the Forest Service. In 1955, the California Assembly passed a resolution calling the road a " defense" highway. It would chop in two the wilderness running from Tuolumne Meadows south—the longest de facto wilderness in forty-nine states.

Up in the front seat, one of the women wears shorts that hide not much. In the rear-view mirror, the driver's eyebrows rise. "Hi," he says.

"Oh, hi."

"Going hiking?" He takes off his sunglasses.

"Yeah, but only for a little while. We're coming back this evening."

The other woman says, "We thought it'd be kind of fun to spend the evening in town."

The driver smiles tentatively, and when he sees them smile he says, "It can be a hell of a good time."

First gear brings us to the summit, where between the trees, I see strobelike glimpses of the view: Banner, Ritter, the Minarets, and the San Joaquin canyon of domes and forests. The road was designed for sixty miles per hour, cutting thirty-two miles of wilderness.

Today it may sound easy to stop a project that would accomplish so little and destroy so much so expensively—$1.3 million would be needed per year just for snow removal at 1966 prices. But that was the era of building roads, the era of building anything. The interstate highway system was under construction, fleets of bulldozers carved I-80 along the South Fork of the Yuba, and the Tioga Pass road was relocated at Tenaya Lake. Highways and automobiles were symbols of progress. Environmental awareness, as Carl Sharsmith said, was something that came later.

Our bus rolls over the summit, 9,175 feet, and starts down the west side. "You know," the driver says, these ski towns, there are never enough women to go around. You two will probably like it here. Me, I haven't had a girlfriend in four years. There are a lot of guys, and the women don't stay."

"Umm," one woman says, and leans against the bar that separates the driver from the passengers.

The road proposal encountered serious trouble in Norman (Ike) Livermore, the state resources secretary who had owned and operated a horse packing station in the southern Sierra. As early as the 1930s, Livermore—a student at Stanford University—gave a speech to San Francisco's Commonwealth Club opposing the Minaret Summit road. Bob Tanner, owner of the Reds Meadow pack station, hosted the governor on a horseback trip to see what was at stake.

"Ah, where's the action at night?" the other woman asks.

"Let's see, you got a band playing at Whiskey Creek. What night's this? Tuesday? Kinda slow. I'll tell you what, there's a great hot tub place."

One woman just happens to be looking at a brochure. "Yeah, it says here to bring your bathing suit for the hot tubs. Well, *I* brought my bathing suit *bottoms*."

The driver looks in the mirror. "All right!"

Governor Ronald Reagan agreed with Livermore, the Sierra Club, and others that the road should not be built. However, the corridor was bypassed when wilderness areas were designated. Protection could be granted this year in the California Wilderness Bill, though President Reagan does not support the measure and may veto it if it passes Congress. The women get off, and the driver says, "See you tonight."

Devils Postpile is a textbook case—one of the world's geometrically finest—of vertical basalt columns, which are usually six-sided. They look like sixty-foot-high corduroy, formed when lava cooled and crystallized slowly. Like Minaret Summit, this place is important in the history of American land protection.

In 1910, a Forest Service engineer, Walter Huber, received an application from miners to dam the San Joaquin's Middle Fork and destroy the Postpile in the process. Huber waged a personal campaign to save the place, and in 1911, President William Howard Taft designated the national monument, protecting it like a national park. This little-known victory came in the midst of the Hetch Hetchy furor. The Middle Fork of the San Joaquin was one of the first American rivers saved because of natural values.

The California Wilderness Bill allows exemptions on the North Fork of the San Joaquin for other hydroelectric dams. Even if the bill is passed, the dam fights will continue.

Leaving the Pacific Crest Trail for the evening, I hike to Rainbow Falls, 140 feet high, and beyond. The San Joaquin—the Sierra's fifth largest river in volume—is alluring. I want to walk down there but can't because I must go south. My days are good and full, but I'm sorry they are not the lingering days the Old Man enjoyed. Muir wrote, "Life seems neither long nor short, and we take no more heed to save time or make haste than do the trees and stars. This is true freedom. . . ." The problem with limiting my trip to thirty-some days is that I'm too rushed.

Day 19

In two miles I reach the last civilization for fourteen days. The Reds Meadow pack station is one of the most popular in the Sierra, according to evidence on the trail. It's a paradox: the outdoors has drawn me here, yet the Reds Meadow cafe is irresistible. I step in and sit at the counter.

The cafe is called the Mule House, but it's a mule deer that is mounted on the wall and sporting a sailor's cap. Other people are here for a mule trip. In 1935, one of David Brower's first stories about the Sierra was called, "Far From the Madding Mules," about backpacking without stock support, which was unusual fifty years ago. I drink a cup of coffee and leave.

I'm hurrying and realize that I see nothing but the ground at my feet. On the trail I gain speed, safety, convenience, and order, but something is lost, so every day I walk off trail, if only for a hundred yards. Otherwise, I get the idea that this experience is on a line instead of through a space. I wander down Boundary Creek, to be protected if the Wilderness Bill passes. My trail has run through five areas that would be designated, but the whole is larger than the parts. The bill would link these and other new areas with nine existing wilderness areas in the Sierra. The longest designated wilderness outside Alaska would result—145 miles.

I walk past a spring, but its size—twenty feet in diameter—impresses me. I go back. Is it hot? I reach to feel and then notice the bottom, one of the eeriest things I've seen. It seems to boil, yet the water is ice cold. The gray bed of the spring vibrates and bubbles up in miniature explosions, then settles while another spot bubbles up, the whole thing alive. Patterns like cream poured into coffee appear, writhe, then disappear. The water looks three feet deep. Curiosity has the best of me.

I cannot wade in; it's all or nothing, so I let go. The flash of cold shocks me, and my breath is gone. Then the knowledge shocks me: this is deeper than I thought, maybe deeper than I can imagine. My feet reach for a bottom that isn't there, and I see that I'm immersed in the bottom itself. The gray suspension is so light I hardly feel it, and I'm faced with a new reality—what I thought would support me will not. It's like reaching out to touch the wall, but instead, my hand disappears into the wall. What I thought was earth is a hole in the ground. The upper three feet of clear water is underlain by volcanic ash saturated with water, and this runs like a well into the earth, where it may connect to underground rivers, who knows? Water lies in the mountain where thousands of years ago earth spewed from the volcano's core. Could I go there by diving?

I want out right now. I kick against the illusionary bottom and clutch a handful of grass, but like a lunker being landed without a net, I break my line. Gravity pulls me back into the spring—I feel like I'm sucked back in—this time over my head in the bottomless gray hole. I surface, and by the friction of my body against the bank, drag myself out of the mouth of the earth, wondrous but frightening.

I enter the John Muir Wilderness. In the 1940s, at hearings on Kings Canyon National Park, Ansel Adams spoke in favor of a John Muir National Park from Yosemite to Whitney, but the wilderness area perhaps serves as well. It borders Kings Canyon and Sequoia national parks, extends south of Whitney, and receives about twice the use of any other national forest wilderness in California.

Never before have I seen more than several bucks together, but here on the north side of Cascade Canyon, I spot seven.

I'm hungry, tired, and cold after sixteen miles. At Purple Lake, people fill the campsites, twenty-four horses and mules are corralled on the hill, and three couples laugh and yell. When I pitch my tent on a flat spot, I almost push a stake into horseshit. No, it's a person's. I can't move now, it's dark. I put a big rock on the dry turd. The packer's sheepdog barks. In the middle of the night, mice run in and out of my pack, where by mistake I left a baseball-sized bag of nuts. I hide them in the tent. The mice scratch on the tent. There are mice fights over who gets to scratch. I take what is left of the nuts and throw them into the woods.

DAY 20

Last night was the worst, but the morning is bright and promising. The climb up Mount Davis, the dip in the spring, and the day-to-day wonders have brought me close to the mountains. As the Old

Man said, I have been "steeping in the mountain influences." What will happen today?

As I drop into Tully Hole on Fish Creek, stones rattle, too loud for a deer. A bear? "Clink." It's the trail crew.

One man—Izzy—works under Forest Service contract on six miles of switchbacks. With David Beck, he teaches cross-country skiing in the winter at Mammoth. He clears trail with a McLeod—a rake on one side with a hoe on the other, and a Pulaski—an axe on one side with a hoe opposite. "I just like being out here," Izzy says. He will work until October 20 or until his trail is snowbound, but he hikes out each weekend. "I used to stay back here, but I got married and like to go out now."

During my break, I discover that I don't have enough food. The wilderness is instantly wilder. John Muir fasted in the mountains; some people think this gave him part of his "high" in the Sierra Nevada. I am unconvinced and would not go hungry by choice.

Some wonders are large and some are small. A rock the size of a paperback book has been tipped on edge by a mushroom emerging from the ground. Sounding like rattlesnakes in a meadow, hundreds of grasshoppers fly. The Indians ate them—they are said to taste something like shrimp. When I run out of food, maybe I'll see. Ladybugs crawl on rocks. At lower elevations I've seen them by the thousands covering stones and logs. They taste so bitter that even a starving bird won't eat one. Gardeners love them because they eat aphids.

A calliope hummingbird hovers for an eyeball-to-eyeball look at me. It darts off and returns. Their diet of flower nectar maintains a nervous energy level, but on cold nights they enter a state of torpor.

From a rock pile, an adult yellow-bellied marmot and five puppy-sized ones stare with their left eyes on me, then disappear when the mother says, "Chuck." They reappear one by one from the same spots. They are the largest North American member of the squirrel family and the largest true hibernator.

After a good trip, a few scenes play on my mind, adding to my view of the world. One of these is from Silver Pass, 10,900 feet. Banner and Ritter rise as distant landmarks above the rock and snow. To the south I see ridge beyond ridge, and I will go beyond even what I see. I'm in the heart of the Sierra. Was this the goal? So many mountainsides I have crossed, so many I have to go, each with its own demands, its own gifts. Here at the pass, before sunset, I have the world to myself. I cannot get enough, but I'm coming close.

Eight lakes glimmer, and the wind roughens their surfaces. Eastern ridges catch the evening light, as I do. This is late summer, but the air is cold, exciting, sharp. Tonight, the earth's heat will radiate into space, unblocked by clouds. It grows darker. I sit quietly and do nothing. It has been a good evening, though it is only the beginning of the most remarkable mountain night I have ever known.

The sun disappears below the western crest and burns an iridescent yellow line along the horizon. The wind rises to concert pitch. Two hundred feet beneath me, pines whistle; 600 feet below, whitecaps break on Chief Lake.

Through the weeks I've been gaining an awareness of things, physical and otherwise: gradient, wind, air, light, depth, solitude, adventure, escape, arrival, old age. All of these pieces of mountain wonder are coming together like the many speeds of a river—slow along the shore, fast in the middle, but ultimately moving together to the sea. I'm beginning to understand why I like the mountains, but the feeling goes beyond understanding, and I don't know when it will stop. I don't know where—exhausted and full—I'll take shelter from yet more sensations.

The wind causes sheet-ripping sounds during powerful gusts. This is the strongest wind yet. Somewhere else, say on the plains, this wind would be nerve-racking; in the Central Valley it would carry a veil of dust and grit. But up here it sweeps the land invisibly, not a blower of trash but one of earth's great media, lifelike. It's a wind that I zip my jacket to, lean into, squint into, one that would in time wrinkle me and wear me down. It wears down rocks.

Like the coldwater spring that ran deep into the earth, so this wind comes from a distance, maybe thousands of miles across the sea, and it flows like a river, an Amazon of the sky. It is not the breeze that rustles leaves but the continental wind, not a playful thing but a global one, one that warms the poles, cools the tropics, and makes the temperate zone just right. It is intoxicating. The wind's source of air is a finite supply made infinite by recirculation, by cycles. I think of Carl Sharsmith's dream of becoming a rock, Wayne Dakan's dream of being buried at the roots of a tree.

The sky turns from red to navy blue to purple. Stars fall into it. For a few minutes I see both the deep infinity of the night sky and the textured world of daylight. Then the rocks congeal to an aphotic mass. Other places and other lives of mine seem so distant. This moment is all that exists. How will I go back? How will I go down?

Stronger now, the wind blows in my face, not just freshness, not just coolness, but a fierce energy, a raw mountain wildness, piercing and strange. The night is cold but something heats my blood. The rock is cold, but each grain feels distinct and good where I touch it.

Lakes shine like mercury, bright in my eyes though it is almost dark. The silhouetted ridge to the west is the top of the world, and I, too, am on a ridge like that one. But I'm not on the top.

To reach the top, I clutch knoblike handholds and wedge my feet in cracks, and I climb up. Now I plant my feet firmly where the wind plasters my clothes against me, blows my hair straight back, roars around me, and my insides are knotted in the excitement, my muscles, tense and ready.

Between gusts a coyote howls in a piercing pitch from the basin below, and before it's done, I scream into the wind and into the emptiness. I scream again, "Rahaaa," and heat rushes to my head, and my heart beats like a drum, but the wind roars again. My voice doesn't echo from cliffs and canyons. It's lost at the instant I stop, making the wind seem even stronger, the mountains larger.

I know that I am nothing, absolutely nothing out here. Yet I am everything, because I am a life made of earth itself, like the rest of life, like the rest of earth. I stand until the wind feels cold, and then, like the pikas and marmots and mice, who are the only other animals who stay up here tonight, I hunt for shelter among the rocks.

Day 21

It's freezing, and I want to get down. My Sierra journey has run through spring and summer, and last night the season changed again.

At this elevation it is fall. The aspen will turn yellow, and the mornings will be slippery with ice. The fall means an end to easy days and a beginning of the struggle to survive. Nothing reminds me so much of the grip of time, unless it might be the age of my knees aching on the downhill.

Before this morning, a cotton shirt, wool shirt, and sweat pants were the most I wore while hiking. Walking down to Silver Pass Creek I add a sweater, rain parka, rain pants, and cap—everything but the tent, usable as a wraparound. The edges of small lakes are brittle with ice. These peaks are 12,000 feet; next week the peaks around me will be 13,000, then 14,000, and each 1,000 feet in elevation means a five-degree drop in temperature.

Along the North Fork of Mono Creek, a blue grouse says, "Ruk ruk ruk ruk," softer than a chicken's cluck. Junipers' cinnamon trunks grow on bald granite, roots in cracks. One juniper in the Sierra is 3,000 years old. Near Sonora Pass, the Bennett Juniper, thirteen and a half feet in diameter, is the largest in the world. Unbending limbs and brute strength set the juniper apart from the other fifteen or so common Sierra trees.

At lower elevations, the ponderosa pine wears bark cracked like burnt brownies. The Jeffrey pine is similar, but it grows above 6,000 feet and on the east side. The Douglas fir has furrowed bark, and its wood is prized for lumber because it is stronger, per weight, than pine. The incense cedar, at low elevations on the west side, is the best conifer for firewood. Three-quarters of all pencils are made from this tree. White fir, with needles that I break and sniff, grow cones that sit upright on the branches. Red fir thrive at high elevations. The plentiful lodgepole pine is the second best firewood. Sugar pine is the largest pine, 220 feet tall with foot-long cones. Among Sierra trees, only the sequoia grows larger. The aspen, one of the few deciduous trees at high elevations, have nearly white trunks that brighten the conifer scene, leaves that turn to autumn brilliant, and branches that are a beaver's favorite meal. The silver pine, also called mountain pine and western white pine, is my favorite Sierra tree and Muir's "king of the alpine woods." Mountain hemlock was Muir's favorite. Its durability is due not to mean strength but to bending and swaying. The whitebark pine is often the only tree near timberline. Muir called the foxtail pine of the southern Sierra "extravagantly picturesque." I've not seen one, but I'm looking. Finally, the cottonwood smells sweet and is an indicator of streams and low places. To me it means comfort; it must be warm and watered. When I come down from the high country, cottonwoods are a sign that the mountains are behind me, that the excitement is over.

I cross Mono Creek one mile above Thomas Edison Reservoir. Sierra Club leader Edgar Wayburn called this flooding of Mono Creek and Vermilion Valley "one of the major losses in the Sierra. No one opposed the dam. People didn't realize the effects of those early reservoirs. It took a generation to realize what was happening."

The trail leads me up Bear Creek, a smaller twin of the Tuolumne. I pitch the tent and hide from a sleet storm. Will tomorrow be winter or Indian summer?

My stove burns not at all or in two-foot-high flames. I dump a pot of water on the torch. Good riddance. Camp stoves are heavy, hissing, stinking, temperamental. True, high country does not have wood to go around. Campers light forest fires and leave scars of ashes blended with pop-tops, twisties, and tinfoil. Wood fires are built too large, too often, and in the wrong places. But I've been using fires since I was ten, and they don't have to be so bad.

I gather a few dead sticks, break them just right so they split, and create a fire no bigger than a fist. I do this on an existing pile of ashes, and if I will be above timberline or in lean woods at supper time, I'll cook early and carry leftovers up. Lodgepole twigs are popping, resin burning bright, water boiling, and supper smelling good.

Day 22

Today my break is at Marie Lake—my favorite, with granite peninsulas, soft meadows, and the shoreline of a miniature Maine. Juncos, the commonest bird of the trip, play in the willows. Also along the trail are ravens, red-tailed hawks, Steller's jays, flickers, the killer cowbirds, and gray-crowned rosy finches—the only bird to nest in the Sierra's alpine zone. South of Selden Pass, the trail drops to the South Fork of the San Joaquin.

Something rare: two women camp along the river. One wears a large necklace. "Tibetan healing charms," she says. The other is Maggie, a physical education teacher who gives me extra granola and an extra freeze-dried meal, resolving my food shortage. She directs me to the hot springs, which are only warm.

I camp in another tract that may be protected by the California Wilderness Bill.

Day 23

The name alone is magic to me: Kings Canyon National Park. Here is what I consider the most spectacular backcountry in America. Even the park entrance is sublime; Piute Creek flows lucidly, with a white bottom like lumpy ice. Behind a juniper that was probably born before the time of Christ are rustling aspens, granite domes, and peaks that climb a vertical mile.

Since Purple Lake I've seen fewer people—about fifteen a day. Now at Goddard Canyon, three boys on one side of the creek and three on the other splash each other. I ask a man if it's crowded up in Evolution Valley. "Well, it's not like *this*." The trail is busy enough that I no longer practice bird calls out loud.

The median age of the hikers rises: forty "Sierra seniors," age sixty and up, descend past the Evolution Creek waterfalls. Their gear is on mules. At the ford—a high-water hazard in early summer—two young women cross ahead of me. Amanda and Allison will hike from Mammoth to Whitney. They are from Santa Barbara. Five days on the trail, they crave health food. "Just think of it: spinach salad, fruit and yogurt, tofu." I must admit that what I crave is fat. If I had butter, I'd spread an opaque layer on my bread, if I had bread.

My campsite is on the shore of Evolution Lake beneath a fairyland of 13,000-foot peaks, pinnacles, and knife-edges flaming in sunset gold.

Day 24

Here in Evolution Basin the glaciers seem to have melted yesterday. Puffy clouds cruise by in fast motion. A little man with a trimmed beard scurries north. He will hike until October 15, when his wife will pick him up somewhere. I say, "Have fun," and he says, "God bless you."

At Muir Pass, frosted with snow eleven months a year, I stop at a shelter in the style of southern Italy's trulli houses, something like a stone igloo, built in 1931 by Sierra Club members. Way up here a mayfly hatch is on; twenty of the buttery mothlike flies hover over me. The trail leads to an azure lake, past waterfalls, and around peaks that could be used in fables. The afternoon takes me through sunshine, across blue shadows, and into a hailstorm.

A young German couple warn me about bears in French Pete Meadow, where Alexander Gaguine is due tomorrow with my fifteen final pounds of food. We know each other from the fight to save the Stanislaus and from trips on other rivers, and our friendship survives in spite of my wandering life.

DAY 25

Silently, at dawn, I sneak up to Alexander's tent. I have not seen it before, but it fits his description. I growl. No movement. I growl louder and pull on one of the tent lines. Nothing. When I sneak around to the front, he explodes from the door with a growl of his own.

"It's a nice place to have a reunion," my old friend says. We lower his food bags from a tree, fix breakfast, and sit on a rock by the Middle Fork of the Kings. "It's good to be home," Alexander says. This year he quit guiding raft trips through the Grand Canyon, the Salmon in Idaho, and the Tuolumne. Instead, he works in the Tassajara Bakery, a Buddhist enterprise in San Francisco. He says, "There are good people there, and what's more important than healthy food?"

For two months he is on leave from the bakery to work on the California Wilderness Bill, and for six days he is on leave from that work to see the wilderness itself. All of this Kings Canyon backcountry would be designated if the bill passes.

Alexander brings me up to date on the politics of the places I've been seeing. The bill passed by the Senate excludes 700,000 acres of wilderness that had been approved in 1983 by the House. Some Sierra acreage was pared back, but the big reductions were in the Coast Ranges of Northern California. Representative Tony Coelho from Merced still fights to keep the Tuolumne out of the bill and allow the dams to be built, but he has been isolated by a landslide of wild river support.

Along the Middle Fork of the Kings, it's a unanimous vote of two that we have come to paradise. Indian summer heats LeConte Canyon with a vengeance; today is one of the hottest of the trip. The weight of the canyon walls is heavy above us as we drop deeper and they loom higher. At noon we begin the ascent of Palisade Creek. Thunderstorms brew; the atmosphere we breathe turns close and sultry.

The choice is to climb a 2,000-foot staircase to Palisade Lakes or camp. Up there, peaks ring a wet basin with no shelter. The cumulus clouds may lead to lightning, and lightning strikes the highest ground, but when the rocks are wet, the charge can carry through the mineralized film of water, especially on unbroken sheets of granite. Lightning has killed people camped on soggy ground far beneath the peaks. We stay low.

DAY 26

The air is clear and the earth is scented as only after a storm. Before breakfast we climb to the lakes, then loaf for three hours. Thunderheads pile up again, unusually early in the day, so we pack for the 1,000-foot ascent to Mather Pass. Clouds squeeze out the blue. We climb and the wind increases; moisture swirls around the western peaks. I want to cross the 12,100-foot pass. Alexander is less concerned.

We walk fast, push hard for half an hour, breathe deeply, step up, step higher, switch back, stride out on the level, hold pace on the grade, sweat, pant, and tighten all over for one final burst of energy to the summit.

The mind makes the body go, then the body rewards the mind. I'm dazzled and euphoric with a runner's high on the top. Colors, textures, and sounds are brighter, sharper, and clearer. Although Alexander may not be acclimatized, he doesn't show it. He's in excellent condition.

There is not much to say in this swirl of cloud in a universe of peaks. We see the snow of the North Palisade, 14,242 feet, the third highest Sierra mountain, the one Norman Clyde called the most striking of the 14,000-foot peaks. The Palisade Glacier is the Sierra's largest.

We drop to Upper Basin, where Alexander is as happy as I've ever seen him. Desertlike in simplicity, it runs four miles south, lined by ridges. Alexander says, "I wouldn't say I like it better than Yosemite Valley, but I'll take this, in its present condition, over Yosemite Valley in *its* present condition."

A man walks north, headed for the pass even though it will turn dark. Bob Kenan, a wilderness ranger for ten years, is packing out for the winter. About this country he says, "It fills your cup." He will attend college. "If I don't like it, I'll come back here." He says to talk to Dario Melango, the ranger near Whitney, a "forty-year-old boy wonder who climbs peaks before breakfast."

Alexander and I camp in the first miniature grove of whitebark pine. Clouds batter the summits, swirl circles around us, and make me wonder what we are in for. A gap shows blue sky, but it disappears like the slow motion of water reclaiming the hole in a lake where a rock has been thrown.

A strange phenomenon appears over the crest. Paralleling the crest, a cloud is rolling like a horizontal tube, thousands of feet in diameter, miles long, hanging for hours while other clouds come and go. The top and bottom edges—the sides of the tube—are not fuzzy like other clouds but razor sharp. It is a "Sierra wave," with air currents that have pushed planes erratically down and up.

Alexander studies his topo map for an hour, reading the lay of the land. We don't talk much. At other times, we've said what runs through our minds. He hitchhiked from Washington, D.C., and stayed in California, working for six years trying to save the Stanislaus River. He wrote brilliantly to involve people in the river and saw through events to the meaning of them. He craved roots in the land, worked odd jobs, wandered, returned, fell in love with women he could not stay with, looked toward the future with few answers and many questions, but was always brightened by places like this, always pulled along by a powerful sense of wonder that has him studying the map right now. He looks up and says, "Let's stay a month."

Day 27

We hike over Pinchot Pass and down Woods Creek. Alexander will hike out to Cedar Grove, where Patrick Carr, a newsletter editor for the Sierra Club and Friends of the River, will pick him up.

Day 28

Day 28? Everything is running together. My knees hurt, partly because the heels of my hiking shoes are breaking down toward the inside. I'm almost nauseated—something I drank? Through the lengthening nights of autumn, I do not sleep well; my bed makes me stiff. Something is wrong. Maybe this dry diet is getting to me. Maybe I need more protein. I crave restaurant food. Old songs play in my head, though all I want to hear are birds and wind and water. I remind myself, "*See!* Look at this with the eyes you had when you were twenty." This country is 2,000 feet higher than the country down north; maybe the altitude is affecting me.

DAY 29

An icy crust hardens the soil. At Rae Lakes, renowned for beauty and notorious for crowds of backpackers, I eat breakfast and stay warm in a sun pocket though frost glazes the grass.

Glen Pass is the steepest yet; it seems impossible that the trail would go where it goes. A wiry man with a small pack trots down. Another speeds by. A third one tells me they are running the John Muir Trail in eight days, "a marathon a day." They are 48, 52, and 55.

Never has the trail been so crowded. Southern Californians flock to the Kearsarge Pass–Rae Lakes loop. T-shirts say "Hard Rock Cafe," and running shorts say "UCLA." I break for peanuts and raisins; three groups pass me. Twenty people sit on the summit. Six boys, fighting over lunch, yell to friends down below.

On the entire hike I saw about 800 people, not counting those at Tuolumne Meadows or Mammoth but including 100 at Mount Whitney. Less than one-fourth were women (surveys in Yosemite found that 40 percent of backcountry hikers were women). About 50 of the people I saw were single hikers; 4 of them women. I know that 22 planned to hike a hundred miles or more (the average number of nights spent in Yosemite backcountry is 2.7). For all of the evidence of horses on the trail, I saw only about 150 head, including pack mules without riders, which accounted for more than half the animals. I've seen a lot of people, but off the trail I see few signs of use. In as little as ten minutes I can hike to unknown places and see not one person in this populated range. And perhaps that's as it should be. Dick Riegelhuth of Yosemite calls off-trail use the "curse of the backcountry" because of its impacts on wildlife such as the easily disturbed wolverine and fisher.

Glen Pass is a transition. South of here, the land seems drier, with fewer plants. I wonder if grasses and wildflowers grew more thickly before sheep grazed on granite soils that never recovered.

Foxtail pine, which grow in small stands, are different from anything I've seen except for the smaller bristlecone pine in Utah and in the White Mountains. Foxtail bark is orange or rusty brown; needles make short bottle brushes at the ends of branches. I camp in a grove of familiar lodgepole pine.

DAY 30

Forester Pass requires a head-to-the-ground climb of nearly 3,000 feet, up to 13,108, the highest point on the Pacific Crest Trail (a side trail leads to Mount Whitney). Here is the crux for early summer travelers; they must wait for snow to melt or mount the pass with ice axes and courage. On top, I lie on the trail, fall asleep, then awaken, amazed at where I am.

The view west shows the Kings-Kern Divide—a jaw full of molars, canines, buck teeth, and fangs. Southward lies a different world: the Kern Plateau, vast, much of it gently rolling. Also in view are hanging valleys and chaotic ranges, Alaskan in scale, full of space, and space, and space.

Right where you are, picture the scene outside your window without one person, building, or shred of civilization. Then picture yourself looking out for thirty miles around, probably including the place where you work, maybe the places where millions work. Picture this with no sign of humanity. In the wilderness of the Sierra that exists.

Nearly. From the south, a thick haze looks like the smog and agricultural dust of the Central Valley blowing up the Kern Canyon from Bakersfield. Also, beyond my wilderness view, loggers are clearcutting pines of the Sequoia National Forest, where stands may never recover on hot, dusty soils.

Quickly I zigzag down the south side of the pass. Looking back, the route is no pass at all but a gunsight notch in the wall of the divide.

Foxtail pine are scattered in sunlit groves down to the 9,000-foot elevation. Ancient trees point downwind with branches contorted by centuries of storms. Some trees are "double piggybacks"—exposed to severe winds, the top died, and a downwind branch took over as the new leader, but then it died, and another branch even farther downwind took the lead. Skeletons of trees stand in ranch-sized graveyards—places that seem somehow sacred, where I do not want to leave a track.

Some live trees are 2,000 years old; dead ones, with stark trunks curving against blue sky, are like monuments to entire climates. I feel like I'm walking through a prehistoric age. René Dubos wrote that wilderness "invites us to escape from daily life into the realms of eternity and infinity."

In this strange environment, surrounded by these incredibly weathered lives, I feel old. What does Wayne Dakan feel when he hikes in the Sierra, wishing for the ponderosa and the steelhead that he knew? What does Carl Sharsmith wonder about in his Tuolumne Meadows home? Will I ever see this again? Will I ever again be this wild and free? I guess that I've decided I want to stay this wild and free.

Except for a fire circle and damage by sheep that I cannot assess, my campsite could be in any year between 6,000 B.C. and today, or

30 years from now, or, I hope, 6,000 years from now. I've escaped time; it's all the same.

DAY 31

The landscape is utterly immense. My world is made of vast rolling slopes with views far out to the Great Western Divide and to the Whitney group of 14,000-foot peaks. I'm awe-struck and small as an ant among all of this earth, golden light on rocks, golden trunks of foxtails, golden reflections on lakes.

The Kern River is the interior river of the Sierra—instead of running from the crest and west like other west-slope rivers (except San Joaquin headwaters), the Kern runs south, splitting the range. The canyon is straight for thirty miles, with an inner gorge 2,000 feet deep. Jet pilots from the Air Force and Navy scream through, a hundred feet above the trees. Sequoia and Kings Canyon National Parks are an official "military operating area." At Crabtree Meadow, backcountry ranger Dario Malengo says that the jets come almost every day; sometimes fifteen or twenty of them break the sound barrier. "I begin to feel like I'm under attack."

Dario is muscular but trim, with dark curly hair and bright eyes, quick to laugh and share stories. "I took a backpacking trip in Kings Canyon eleven years ago and then applied for ranger jobs." This is his tenth season. "It's a good place to work. The parks and wilderness areas are really about all we have left. The rest of the country has been pretty much maxed out.

"Up here, it's better now than it was—less trash and fewer horses. Packers have cut back, but still, you go south of here, and between the horses and the cows, it's mowed over. The stockmen have a lot of influence down at the end of the road, and they got meadows opened up that had been closed. They say, 'It's our livelihood.' Sure, we all have livelihoods; guys who cut trees have livelihoods. Guys who dig for tungsten have livelihoods. But what's a national park all about?"

Twelve other backcountry rangers and Dario cover a million acres in Sequoia and Kings Canyon. Dario has rescued five people with broken ankles. He found a man with pulmonary edema at Glen Pass and radioed a helicopter. "They're usually there in twenty minutes, but it took an hour. The man was unconscious the whole time."

This time of year hurricanes blow up from the south, and it can turn cold and rain for days. In the fall of 1978, seventeen people at once dried out in Dario's one-room cabin. "Up toward Whitney two people just lay down on the trail and died of hypothermia." This lowering of body temperature can cause shivering, incoherency, shock, and death, usually at temperatures between 30 and 50 degrees when people are wet. The best thing to do is to put the cold person under sleeping bags, between two other undressed people. Dario says, "The main point is to stay dry in the first place."

The sky threatens this evening, but I'll stay with my plan: climb as high on Whitney as I can so that I can cover the two-mile-long side trail to the summit at sunrise. When I reload my pack, I realize that I may climb into a storm. Clouds grow dark and ominous, but not awful or black. I hope that the Sierra weather will stay normal: after sunset, the sky will clear.

To predict mountain weather is risky; to depend on it is asking for trouble. Half a mile above timberline, a wind-driven rain pelts me on the back. Then I'm stung by sleet, but I continue. These freak showers don't last long.

It rains harder. Even though this should not be happening, I cannot deny that my situation is deteriorating. I'm getting wet. I squat like a sherpa under my tent fly. Thunder rumbles from the peaks near Whitney. Now two miles above timberline, I don't want to be a foot higher.

Abandoning my plan, I pitch the tent. Whitney lies straight ahead, looking fat from this western view, nothing like its elegant vertical face on the east. Granite peaks encircle me. The basin is a wet one, and I wonder about lightning hazards more than I reflect on this being the final night of my journey. I fall asleep.

Not for long. I'm inside a bass drum. It's midnight and the thunder is higher pitched than normal, a strangely artificial sound reverberating for ten seconds. Faint flashes illuminate my yellow tent; wind rustles the fly. I look outside. The flashes are alarmingly brighter, due west. Through thin clouds, half a moon lights the rocky landscape, but to the west the sky is opaque, the black clouds devouring stars at a rapid clip and cruising bloblike straight toward me. A flash makes me blink and see spots, then thunder begins not with a rumble but a clap. The peaks of 14,000 feet will draw the lightning. But the granite runs down to where I am, on shallow soil that is already wet and soon to be soaking when the blob arrives. I see that I'm essentially sitting in water at the end of the wire that grounds those peaks—lightning rods of a continent. Suddenly I'm feeling raw fear.

I could really be in trouble, the Big Consequence. I have to get out of here. Am I paranoid? Maybe. People camp up here often. But from Tuolumne Meadows, I remember Ginger Burley's description of a wet mountain struck by lightning: "The whole thing lit up like Saint Elmo's Fire." Drops like a volley of BBs spit on the tent. I have to get out of here fast. I'll leave my tent and pack here.

It's going to be wet and cold; wear all your clothes. Rain suit on top. Flashlight. Matches. Take the ensolite pad to put over your head in the rain.

I burst out of the tent, throw my pack inside, and wonder, how will I find the tent in the dark? One time twenty years ago I lost my camp at night. I run straight to the trail and barricade it with my tripod.

I begin my flight down the mountain. The trail is typical Sierra—rocky. I jog. The penlight with its month-old batteries is weak. I cannot see enough to say, "There's a rock," yet my feet somehow know where to go. During lightning flashes, maybe every ten seconds, I adjust my course. I stumble and recover. Down, faster! Rain stings my face. Get off this slab of granite. This sort of monologue goes on for ten breath-stealing, heart-pounding minutes.

Now the black cloud is over me, around me, I'm breathing it. I'm strangely lightheaded. Fear? Adrenaline? Negative ions from the lightning? I think that the clouds' updraft, caused by the peaks, has sucked in clouds from the fringe of the storm to concentrate the storm on me. After flashes I count five seconds between lightning and thunder. Now four. The flashes, brilliant, leave me blinded.

Three seconds. Now I must settle in, abandon this rivulet of a trail that could be like a copper wire. During a flash I see a slope of loose rocks. I scramble up, and at a flat bench I pile small rocks on large ones to create air space underneath me. I think that air will not carry the electricity if lightning strikes above me and runs down through the water that coats the granite like a glazed donut.

Two seconds.

Thunder explodes like dynamite. Two claps are reverberating when a third one strikes. I'm drowning in the noise. I crouch with my feet close together. I pull my hood up and hold the pad overhead, then decide to shove it underneath for added insulation from lightning. I clutch my legs below the knees and do not touch the ground with my hands.

One second. The lightning is about 1,000 feet away. My world is bright, loud, and wet.

The flashes are spectacular beyond anything I can imagine. I look into blackness that for a split second seems as bright as a dozen noons. All of it is white—peaks, boulders, millions of rocks—blindingly white, yet so quickly gone that I can't grasp it. During one flash, the craggy profile of Mount Hitchcock is burned into my brain. Then I see a grotesque boulder with many heads. I've seen how a flashbulb, outdoors in the dark, overexposes a person's face while the background stays black. Now I see billions of flashbulbs going off at once and whitening the country for miles, a satin-black sky beyond.

The flashes are too bright to look at but I look anyway. In between, I don't see black. I see solid blood-red for full seconds. Then spots, then black, then before my eyes can adjust, lightning blinds me again. I picture what I look like, for an instant exposed on a pile of rocks that looks like a grave protected from buzzards. What a place to end up after all those miles.

I guess this is adventure. For whatever a book on the subject is worth, Paul Zweig says, "In the midst of action, each moment is dense with the weight of a lifetime, and is a lifetime, blazing with momentary intensity."

The rain beats harder. It's important that I stay dry, because the storm could mark the advance of a cold front—a wedge of heavy northern air with its sharp edge to the ground, pushing the warm air up, causing it to cool rapidly and rain.

The thunder subsides. I look for stars. Lightning illuminates Whitney. Under the storm it looks capable of withstanding anything. I count seven seconds before thunder. The rain comes hard, easy, hard, easy. My shoulders are beginning to get wet, and my legs ache, but then I see a star.

Day 32

Storm clouds surround the cirque, so I pack my tent and hike down toward Crabtree Meadow and watch the weather on Whitney through the only layover day of the trip.

Day 33

Light reflects from only the largest, smoothest rocks, but I'm walking fast. My goal is to reach the summit early. Panting hard, I cover six miles and climb 2,000 feet by 8:30. Overheated, I shed both sweater and shirt, but at Whitney Pass I put on all my clothes.

The cold air that forced the warm air violently upward now rules the sky: clear, frigid, blasting with wind. The wind causes me to grip my jacket and harden my resolve. Maybe I've worn myself out or maybe the altitude is getting the best of me even after thirty-two days. Whatever, I face heavy fatigue for the final two miles to the top of the Sierra.

The last steps take me across the mountain's bald crown, nearly flat, to the summit, directly above the sheer eastern face. Finally, I'm there, on Whitney, 14,494 feet.

To the west I see the Kings-Kern Divide. Mount Brewer stands alone. Far north I spot a Palisades snowfield above the camp that Alexander and I made on Day 25. Below Whitney's 2,000-foot face are rock-rimmed lakes. Tulainyo is the continent's highest lake, not counting glacial tarns. Beyond lie the Owens Valley desert and Lone Pine, its grid of streets lined with shade trees reduced by distance to a green tint, where Mike Prather and Christy Lynch are teaching school, where meals are being served at the Sportsman Cafe.

To the south, peaks are impressive, but for the first time since my journey began at Lake Almanor, the southern mountains are not higher than me. They drop toward their end, something I want to deny, something I'm glad I cannot see from here.

To the southwest, the Kern Plateau fades in yellow haze, discordant to the longest wilderness, and in the haze the Kern canyon is unseen from here, dropping to places that I try to imagine but can't because I know they are different from anything I've seen. The southern Sierra is next—my final exploration to the end of the range.

After 400 miles of walking in the high country, the hike down the east side is my descent to lower earth. I feel like I'm dropping in a slow-motion free-fall, returning to a world that, to me, may always lie in the shadow of the Sierra.

Rapidly I drop, lower and lower, down hundreds of switchbacks, through entire zones of climate. I shed clothes as I go. The trail enters the trees: foxtail pine, lodgepole pine, white fir, and Jeffrey pine, each at home in a lower place. Then, only a hundred yards ahead, beside Lone Pine Creek, the smell of the cottonwoods is rich.

8

The South

THE SEASON IS FALL. With crisp air, showers of leaves, and brittle frost, this is surely the most vivid season, though many of its ways sneak only subtly into the days of September. Sunshine grows leaner, and I seek it more. Darkness comes early and daylight late, so I compensate by burning candles at my table in the van. Near cabins, the air is mixed with wood smoke's scent. The quiet is greater than that of summer, and so there's a hushed feel in the prospect of the mountains and the refuge of the woods, where life will slow down and ease into a moratorium. The long season looms ahead. Provisional snow paints the high peaks, though here on the west side, where I camp in my van, I see few summits above the coniferous foreground. Afternoons are nearly as blue as Tahoe, and warm, and—best of all—sweet with the scent of rotting alder, willow, and cottonwood leaves along streams.

Evenings are cool, ominous in an exciting way. Nights are dark with new intensity. With life in transition, this is a season of reflection. What have I learned about the Sierra? What will I do when I finish the journey?

On dirt roads leading from the mountains, hunters return, their headlights bobbing in the distance, while I cook supper by candlelight (eating by candlelight is one thing; cooking by it, another). Today I have little in common with the riflemen in their four-wheel-drive pickups, but hunting fills an inordinately large spot in my autumn reverie. Even though I have not hunted in eighteen years, I breathe this autumn air and say, "It's time to hunt." I no longer kill animals, not even ants, but I'm always hunting. I'm infected with my own gold fever, and that nugget, out there somewhere, out there everywhere, keeps me hunting, traveling, living. What will I find today?

Now that I've seen a lot of the mountains, I want to see the rest in an almost urgent way. My wish is to see everything, and my opponent is time—I aim to beat the winter in a race to the southernmost Sierra. I want to see the end, yet I dread it. No more mountains? My universe, now so vast because I don't know its limits, will have shrunk to a numbered and pictured piece, and so at times I do not want to reach the end of the Sierra, not tomorrow, not next month, not ever. Now that I'm almost there, I know I've fooled myself. I had goals, but the Going was the real goal. Soon my success will be my defeat. Paul Zweig wrote that the adventurer is "a man gifted for wandering, . . . condemned to a life of endless mobility.

"Because he is at home everywhere, he will be at home nowhere.

"His existence will be humanly pointless.

"The idle adventurer is less than no man."

As if on a rubber band, any of my thoughts at this time of year snap back to thoughts of the season. The coyote howls lonelier now— it sounds that way to me—and I answer, and I'm lonelier without the carefree embrace in summer's orgy, when it's so easy to be close to the earth, to lie there sleeping in its grass.

The fall always reminds me that, beyond the season, the times are changing, and the big change that I see is the coming Technological Dark Age. Awhile back it looked as though the counterculture kicked some of the mechanized, industrialized dominance that had grown at a cancerous rate since Eli Whitney and interchangeable parts. Now technology has come back with a vengeance of high-tech gadgetry and space-age style. Maybe my problem with the civilization down below stems from being raised in the Appalachian foothills, where the outdoors captured me but the destruction surrounded me. My wilderness was the ripped-apart Ohio River Valley, and I dreamed of its past or I pretended that the crumbs that had been left for me were whole loaves, when in fact they were crumbs. The system served me well, but at the same time it was killing me, so I've come to the mountains with curiosity and adventure in mind. I am not one to escape to my inner self, so I've escaped to the here-and-now mountains, and they've filled me and become my Eden.

Good news! Jim Eaton of the California Wilderness Coalition, John Amodio of the Tuolumne Trust, Russ Shay of the Sierra Club, and others prevailed in the political morass of Washington. In the House, action on the Wilderness Bill was renewed, and a bandwagon of support for saving the Tuolumne River rolled through Congress. Seeing the writing on the wall, Tony Coelho voted for the bill, which passed 368 to 41.

This is the most recent evidence that a new concept of the world has arrived. The Bible lists *wilderness* 300 times, each use derogatory, most of them affiliated with evil or hopelessness. An attitude was established and was adapted to the Sierra when people heard news of the Donner Party eating each other near Lake Tahoe. Wilderness was a place in which to starve. With a different view, people now spend 2.4 million days a year having fun in the wilderness areas of California; the mountains are now sacred, and hell-on-earth is found down below in traffic jams.

Except for Alaska, the California Wilderness Act will be the largest addition to the wilderness system since the original Wilderness Act of 1964. Why California? Russ Shay says, "Except for Alaska, this is the largest state with wilderness. Phillip Burton was in the House and Alan Cranston in the Senate. We have a powerful environmental community, and for eight years we had Governor Jerry Brown and resources secretary Huey Johnson. No other states had those advantages." Jerry Brown was the only governor who supported more wilderness than the Forest Service, which isn't saying a lot. In half of the national forests in the Sierra, no areas with commercially harvestable timber were recommended by the Forest Service for wilderness protection. In the Sierra National Forest, 30,900 acres were recommended out of 156,800 acres of roadless area. In the Sequoia, 0 acres were recommended out of 130,000 roadless acres.

Some reasons for the successful bill are intricate with scheming, leverage, and gambles. A 1979 lawsuit by California—Huey Johnson's work—had blocked Forest Service timber sales in roadless areas that qualified as wilderness. To release most of the roadless acreage for logging, Congress had to act on the wilderness issue. In addition to Johnson's fly in the timber industry's ointment, the Forest Service couldn't finish required land management plans until the wilderness issue was resolved. Also, in the late seventies, big timber corporations had bought logging rights to huge tracts of national forest land at high prices, squeezing out small timber companies (which blamed environmentalists for their problems). When the housing market collapsed, the big companies' speculative buying resulted in little cutting. The Forest Service could not easily sell the timber again, yet government foresters wanted to cut timber in roadless areas to meet board-foot quotas, by which the performance of the foresters is evaluated—rangers must sell timber if they want to be promoted. All of these factors meant that a wilderness act was needed to get on with logging in the unprotected areas.

Included in the House bill are 3.2 million acres of wilderness statewide, 1.4 million of it in Yosemite, Kings Canyon, and Sequoia national parks. Congress added fourteen new Sierra wilderness areas to nine areas already in the system. Nine areas now adjoin each other for an unbroken chain of 145 miles—the longest wilderness in forty-nine states. An adjoining 80 miles of Sierra crest wilderness are interrupted only by narrow corridors for the Ebbetts, Sonora, and Tioga pass roads in the north and the Kennedy Meadows road in the south. The most important addition in the Sierra: the Ansel Adams Wilderness prohibits the Minaret Summit Road near Mammoth.

The industry carped about greedy environmentalists, but the industry did well. More than three acres of California roadless areas were opened up for logging for each acre protected as wilderness. Statewide, 6 million acres in national forests qualified for wilderness protection, the Forest Service recommended 0.9 million, and Congress designated 1.8 million, down from the 2.3 million that the House had approved in 1983 in the respectful wake of Phillip Burton's death. In his first press release about the Wilderness Act, forest supervisor Gene Murphy stressed that 319,390 acres on the Inyo Forest were released from wilderness consideration. Only 50,000 acres were protected in that forest.

Once politicians had agreed on the acreage, the Tuolumne River became the pivotal point in the bill. National river status for eighty-three miles from the headwaters to New Don Pedro Reservoir bans the proposed hydroelectric dams and ensures that an outstanding trout river and whitewater run will be left the way it is. The act also establishes the Mono Basin National Forest Scenic Area but apparently does not restrain the export of water to Los Angeles.

None of this is law yet; President Reagan must sign the bill, and he might not do it. His assistant secretary of agriculture for natural resources and the environment, including the Forest Service, is the former general counsel for Louisiana Pacific Lumber Company; his head of the Bureau of Land Management was a rancher; and his secretary of the interior was James Watt. Yet somehow a few ideals have survived. Attitudes drawn from Thoreau, Muir, Marshall, Leopold, and Brower have resulted in the laws protecting the mountain wilderness, and those very civilized ideals are what make my escape from civilization possible.

My escape from civilization is getting colder. Both ends of these autumn days call for wool socks, wool sweaters, and a wool cap. The fall forces thoughts about the future—winter—when some fish survive frozen in ice for twenty-nine days, some longer. Unlike my neighbors, I cannot grow fur, fly south, or hibernate, though I can do variations of these.

The end is nearly in sight for both the year and my journey. Squirrels hurry to bury pine cones. Deer browse down into the canyons; a thousand of them will congregate on the east side near Bishop, migrating through a proposed Sherwin Bowl ski area from as far as Dinkey Creek on the west slope. The pikas stash sun-dried grass. Marmots are already hibernating. A foggy haze caused by temperature inversions—common in fall and winter—envelopes the Central Valley and creeps up the hills, reaching my current level of 6,000 feet in the sequoia forest by two o'clock in the afternoon. At night, downdrafts from the Sierra push the haze back into the valley.

I've poured my journey into a glass that is now three-quarters full—300 miles from north to south. Is the Sierra Nevada one place or many? Do I understand the kinds of things I came looking for in that Ebbetts Pass snowstorm so long ago? After today's equinox, September 22, what remains of my Sierra journey? After the hike from Ebbetts Pass to Whitney, what remains must surely be a letdown.

For this section of the Sierra, the first thing in my notes is the largest living organism on earth.

The tallest tree in the world (though not the largest in volume) is a redwood near the California coast. To see it, I once forded a large creek and hiked several miles. The journey prepared me for what I saw and protected the site's integrity. When I wanted to see the oldest trees on earth—the bristlecone pine in the White Mountains across Owens Valley from the Sierra—I walked two miles, and by the time I arrived, I was slightly humbled and ready.

Not here in Sequoia National Park. The largest living thing on earth is 150 feet from the road that leads to the parking lot, where I'm careful to lock the van. I must look both ways before crossing the road, then I walk on the ten-foot-wide asphalt trail. Log fences channel the millions and reduce dust bowl effects. Straight ahead, at the end of the pavement, I see it, the label leaving no doubt as to identity. A sign, front and center at the tree, does not call this a tree. The sign simply says, "General Sherman." A garbage can in the left foreground helps to keep the litter problem under control.

The tree was named in 1879 for the Union general who burned the South during a pioneering model of taking military problems out on the civilians. To Sherman's credit, he helped stop slavery, and in 1880 he said, "There's many a boy here today who look on war as all glory, but boys, it is all hell." Another one of the large trees is named for General Grant, whose wartime experience prepared him to be perhaps our worst president. The road that takes me to some of the earth's finest examples of the triumph of life is called "The Generals Highway."

Beyond the pavement and the name stands the real thing. The largest living thing on earth: Taller than a sixteen-story building! Thirty-six-and-a-half feet in diameter at its base! One hundred and thirty feet up to the first large branch! A tree that is my senior by fifty human generations! Here is the tree, drawing minerals from soil, making food from dirt and air and water, weathering storms that repeatedly knock its top off, bearing snows of thousands of winters, whistling in winds since Rome was founded. The bristlecone pine is the only tree that lives longer.

I try to imagine those years. If living long is the goal, and an impressive sampling of our culture indicates that it is, then I'm staring at success. As a symbol of life, wouldn't this be an excellent choice? This should be a sacred place.

It is not. The tree is another quick stop in a hectic trip by car. Park, get out, go look. It's worse than Yosemite Falls. There, the water fights back with noise that overpowers impatient voices. Here it's like "Scenic View, See 5 Counties." People take pictures, but they will be disappointed. John Steinbeck wrote, "No one has ever successfully painted or photographed a redwood tree. The feeling they produce is not transferable."

"It's not the quick experience that counts, but the full experience," Andrea Lawrence said, and here by this giant tree, I remember her story about skiing the Paranoids—how the slow walk up is what made the steep run down an exceptional experience. The average length of a visit at Giant Forest is 3.5 hours, and for many people, that includes a lot of time inside the cafeteria and gift shop. I think of Bill Kier: "Technology has removed us from real contact with life."

Here at this tree, it's impossible for some people to be reverent, but it might be easier if we left the cars farther away and walked through the forest on a path—allowing a separation from the road, allowing an awareness of the setting—so that when we finally arrive, there's a hush, a long stare, a wonderment at how incredibly special this example of life is.

The park master plan includes an objective: "To encourage visitors to absorb the inspiring atmosphere of the sequoia groves and to relate the survival of the sequoias . . . with our own survival and welfare." The plan considers it "essential" that people have the opportunity of "walking in a quiet and unspoiled grove of sequoias to experience the magnificence of the trees in an atmosphere of tranquility." The plan also calls for "motor nature trails" in phrasing that is unclear about what will be motorized: nature, the trail, or the visitor.

Although the pavement crowding General Sherman will remain, progress is being made. The cafeteria and lodge complex that sleeps 1,240 within the Giant Forest grove, where pavement even surrounds a giant tree, are being relocated to a less important site called Lodgepole.

The first white man's lodging up here was probably that of Hale Tharp, who visited in 1858 and returned for many summers. His home is an unusual registered historic landmark: a log. Tharp invited John Muir to visit, and he described the accommodations as "a spacious log-house of one log, carbon-lined, centuries old, yet sweet and fresh, weather proof, earthquake proof, likely to outlast the most durable stone castle, and commanding views of a garden and grove grander far than the richest king ever enjoyed."

After walking about a mile, I come to the log. Tharp built a fireplace, and in front of it he has a bench and table, where he and Muir probably sat and told stories. The ceiling is black from the fires that hollowed out the log; the floor is dirt. The place is a womb for a full-grown man. Here, deep in the sequoia forest, the charms of the woods twist my arm, and I go farther, though the sun is low and the autumn darkness will come earlier tonight than on any night so far.

The ecology of the giant sequoia is, of course, unique. After a youth of several centuries, the sequoia begins to reproduce. Two thousand cones may grow in a season, but many would remain on branches for as long as twenty years if Douglas squirrels didn't cut them down and bury them. At one tree, 1,242 cones were found in underground storage. These do not open on their own; fire is normally needed to open the cones, release the seeds, and burn the white fir that would otherwise shade the sequoia seedlings.

If anything was designed to last forever, the giant sequoia is it. A mature sequoia's bark is six to thirty-one inches thick and fire-resistant because it lacks resin. Tannin is so repellent to insects and fungi that juncos bathe in the dust of the fallen bark—insect powder for birds. Another secret to living forever: the wood fractures in chunks rather than splitting, so when lightning strikes—often on these lightning rods of the forest—it blasts away the top but does not split down through the heart of the tree. The Grizzly Giant in the Wawona Grove at Yosemite was hit by lightning six times in one storm. The trees top out in height after only 800 years because lightning prunes them back, but they keep growing in girth.

Now it's dark enough that the ravens quit croaking and the robins sing a twilight song. The day is too short; I must turn back. The woods grow dark, then very dark, and I must use more than sight to find my way. Although I can't really see the trail, I sense a vague openness above the path. The concave cross section of the trail tells my feet where to go. Now and then I stop short with a feeling that I call "dead air." From where I stop, I can touch a tree two feet in front of me.

Even a step or two off the trail, at night, reminds me how untracked and unknown this country once was. The first report of a giant sequoia was by Zenas Leonard of the Walker expedition in 1833. He wrote, "Incredibly large."

The settlers came and the logging began, but the same brittleness that curbs lightning's effect on the sequoia causes the wood to shatter when a sawed-off tree falls to the ground. The sequoia's only commercial value was for shingles and for stakes to support grape vines, yet big trees were felled anyway. To move the sequoia corpses, as problematic as beached whales, loggers dynamited them to smithereens.

In 1878, George W. Stewart, editor of the *Visalia Delta*, organized a movement to protect the best remaining trees, and in 1890, with the rationale that the trees were economically worthless, Congress designated Sequoia as America's second national park. In 1926, Sequoia was expanded to include the summit of Mount Whitney and 385,000 acres in all. Public agencies now protect all of the 36,000 acres of giant sequoia groves, found as far north as the Middle Fork of the American River.

Saving one of North America's deepest canyons was not as easy. Kings Canyon, the deepest canyon in the United States, drops 8,240 feet beneath Spanish Mountain. Among all rivers in America, the Kings has the greatest vertical drop unchecked by dams. In an 1891 issue of *Century* magazine, John Muir called for a Kings Canyon National Park to extend from the headwaters to Mill Flat Creek, but Los Angeles proposed dams. In a rare example of environmental concern, the federal Power Commission denied the city's request in 1923.

Without park protection, the dam proposals resurfaced, yet even the Sierra Club opposed park status. "The Forest Service had been handling the area well," said Dick Leonard, honorary president of the club in the 1980s. "We were afraid that the Park Service would overdevelop the canyon." Leonard changed his mind after he met with Franklin Roosevelt's interior secretary, Harold Ickes. "He persuaded me that we should make a park out of it—if we would have a bad secretary of agriculture, the wilderness protection could be wiped out." Dick Leonard and Dave Brower led the Kings Canyon fight, Ansel Adams carried photographs to Washington and showed them to congressmen, and in 1940 Kings Canyon was one of the first parks to be created for protection of its "wilderness character" rather than for natural monuments and curiosities. Leonard said, "In other areas we had been trying to correct a hundred years of mistakes, but here we had a brand new canyon to work with. We thought, 'Here's one we can save.'" Yet this goal was strangely incongruous with other club positions.

The Sierra Club had supported the construction of a Kings Canyon road above Cedar Grove. An Ahwahnee-sized hotel and a duplication of Yosemite Valley's development would be built. The club's charter, written before the use of the automobile, included "to render the mountains accessible." Dick Leonard said, "The club also supported roads over Piute Pass, and up the Merced and Tenaya canyons. By an eight to seven vote we opposed the road up the Kings. Then Dave Brower and I rewrote the charter, and the club eliminated the access provision in 1952." The Park Service still built a road to Zumwalt Meadows, above Cedar Grove, but plans for a major development were dropped.

In the name of political expediency, three critical dam sites had been excluded from the park, and even park status did not dissuade Los Angeles from proposing additional sites. In 1952, the city applied for hydroelectric dams inside the park at Simpson Meadow, Paradise Valley, and Grand Sentinel, and outside the park at Tehipite Valley, Cedar Grove, and the Middle and South Fork confluence. To reach the remarkable Tehipite—where a granite dome rises as a monolith over the Kings' Middle Fork—normally requires two or more days of walking. Cedar Grove is reached by road, but it, too, is a low-elevation riverine paradise. The Sierra Club, the National Parks and Conservation Association, and other groups fought the proposals. The Federal Power Commission again denied LA's request, and in 1965, after a seventy-year struggle for a complete Kings Canyon Park, Congress added Tehipite Valley and Cedar Grove.

The park, now 454,000 acres, remains incomplete. Another proposal to dam the Kings has heated up. At Rogers Crossing, downriver from the park, the Kings River Conservation District, gov-
erned by seven wealthy farmers in the San Joaquin Valley, hopes
to build a dam that would flood the state's largest designated wild
trout fishery, a whitewater rafting run used by 13,000 people a year,
and one of the Sierra's finest advanced canoeing runs. The Army
Corps of Engineers and the district studied the site in the 1960s
and found it uneconomical, but with increased hydroelectric values,
the district now hopes for a profitable project. George Whitmore,
of the Sierra Club in Fresno, said that the Kings may become "one
of the biggest environmental issues" facing the Sierra in the coming
decade. Donn Furman, Chairman of the Committee to Save the
Kings River, said, "We're preparing to fight for years or for however
long it takes to save the river." The committee and Friends of the
River are leading a campaign to add the Kings to the national wild
and scenic rivers system. Representative Richard Lehman, who
grew up near the river, said, "I regard my decision to save the Kings
River as irreversible."

The year of victory for Tehipite Valley and Kings Canyon was a
year of threats in neighboring Sequoia National Park. In 1965, Walt
Disney personally presented his plans for a ski resort. A miners'
road, clinging to canyon walls for twenty-five miles, penetrated the
high southern Sierra farther than any other road, yet traffic was
limited by remoteness. Three hundred acres of meadow along the
East Fork of the Kaweah River in Mineral King Valley remained in
snowy splendor. Nearly surrounded by the park, the valley was a
peninsula of national forest land designated as a game refuge.

Many Sierra Club leaders skied, so skiing was not the problem.
Disney was not the problem either; the club had honored him with
a life membership in 1955 for excellence in wildlife films. But now
Disney proposed that 2.5 million visitor-days per year would be
spent in Mineral King—more people than visited Yosemite Valley,
though on one-seventh the acreage—and that 16 restaurants, a coffee shop at 11,000 feet, 22 lifts, 1,200 cabins, and a 3,600-car parking
garage would be built. The planned visitation was later cut to about
a million, but the problem remained one of a large resort deep in
wild mountains. John Harper, a Bakersfield resident, enjoyed Mineral King as it was—a primitive stepping-off place of the high country—and when he discovered Disney's plans, he sought Sierra Club
opposition.

Some club directors took the approach that a resort was inevitable and should simply be designed well, but not Martin Litton.

He flatly moved that "the Sierra Club oppose any recreational development in the Mineral King area."

The Sequoia National Forest supervisor boasted that his forest would have "the finest winter recreation area in the United States." Mineral King would become a place of business and importance. The Disney enterprise would serve many more people than the primitive Mineral King, and to serve the greatest number of people had been Gifford Pinchot's goal for American forestry and resource management since it began.

Governor Reagan signed a bill not only endorsing the development but also paying for part of it—committing the state to a subsidy of $20 million for road work that would later be estimated to cost $42 million. Interior Secretary Stewart Udall opposed the road because it would cross Sequoia National Park. He favored a monorail but yielded to President Lyndon Johnson's Office of Management and Budget, which was bargaining to gain Governor Reagan's support of Redwood National Park on California's north coast.

Disney Enterprises scheduled construction for 1969, but the Sierra Club sued. In 1972, the United States Supreme Court ruled that the club did not have standing—it had not shown that its members were affected. In a historic dissent, Justice William O. Douglas argued that it should be possible to litigate environmental issues "in the name of the inanimate object about to be despoiled. . . . Those people who have so frequented the place as to know its values and wonders will be able to speak for the entire ecological community." The court invited the club to amend its complaint.

The National Environmental Policy Act now required the Forest Service to prepare an environmental impact statement. California legislator Edwin Z'berg, who had led efforts to save Lake Tahoe, led passage of a bill rescinding state funding for the road, and Fresno congressman John Krebs backed federal protection for Mineral King. Facing dismal economics, Disney officials in 1975 announced a suspension of planning that was in fact the end of planning. In a masterly bill engineered by Congressman Phillip Burton, Mineral King was added to Sequoia National Park in 1978. This was the fifth major success in building the two national parks of the southern Sierra.

When asked to name the greatest modern accomplishment for conservation in the Sierra Nevada, David Brower said, "The additions to Sequoia and Kings Canyon national parks." Always looking forward more than back, Brower added, "We still need protection for the Kern Plateau south of Sequoia, and there should be a green line around the parks—additional protection for a greater national park that includes all of that ecosystem."

The big trees draw most of Kings Canyon and Sequoia national parks' 2 million annual visitors, but the majority of the two adjoining parks' acreage is a wilderness, with some of America's remotest backcountry, regarded by many people as America's most spectacular. Jointly managed, Sequoia and Kings Canyon include 878,758 acres, 46 percent of California's coldwater lakes, the South and Middle forks of the Kings River, the top of Mount Whitney, the toothy Sierra subrange known as the Kings-Kern Divide, the 6,000-foot-deep trench of the North Fork of the Kern, and the Kaweah River, with canyons 7,000 feet deep. If the president signs the California Wilderness Act, 87 percent of the two national parks will be protected as wilderness. Within a half-day drive is a population of 15 million—more than the population of any state in the nation except three.

Chief ranger Bob Smith was the chief ranger at Yosemite from 1965 to 1968, and he says, "Our problems are not much different, though Yosemite has more of them. Down here, the pay's the same but the headaches are fewer. Our trend is in the direction of Yosemite's problems, but we won't arrive at them. Our use is not concentrated like it is there. Our limit on overnight lodging will be 2,000 people; there are now accommodations for 1,700."

In the national parks and forests of the Sierra, I've had first-hand or second-hand experience with crowds, crime, traffic, livestock, Giardia, dams, development, and other problems that rangers may be able to solve at their green-map refuges. But at Sequoia I hear about a problem that spreads from beyond reach. David Parsons, research scientist at Sequoia, says, "I personally believe that the biggest threat to the parks is acid rain and ozone." For many years, air pollution has killed trees in the San Bernardino National Forest, south of the Sierra. Ozone, which consists of oxides of nitrogen that result from the sun's effects on pollution, has turned ponderosa pine needles brown in Sequoia National Park since 1965. In Los Angeles, a smog alert is declared when ozone reaches 20 parts per 100 million, but ponderosa are damaged at only 7 parts per 100 million, and 14 parts per 100 million are found in Sequoia. Minor damage occurs as far north as the Tioga Pass road in Yosemite. The ozone and acid rain originate from cars, smokestacks, and even agricultural herbicides that are exposed to sunshine. "The pollution is everywhere," Parsons said. "We're beginning studies now because the potential for long-term impacts is very real."

Because of acid rain, hundreds of lakes in the northeast are devoid of fish, thousands more are endangered, and crops and forests suffer critical damage. The Environmental Defense Fund reported that damage to structures, forests, wildlife, and recreation areas in the United States exceeds $10 billion a year.

In Southern California, where most of the acid rain and ozone infecting the Sierra originates, more than 2 million tons of carbon monoxide, 500,000 tons of particulates, and 365,000 tons of nitrogen oxides were dumped into the sky in 1983 alone. The Los Angeles air basin violates federal ozone standards more than 150 times a year.

Seven states and the Environmental Defense Fund have advanced a lawsuit demanding that the federal Environmental Protection Agency enforce Clean Air Act regulations on sulfur pollution. Canada has also objected to the U.S. pollution that falls as acid rain after crossing the border.

After years of delay and pressure by Canadian Prime Minister Brian Mulroney, President Reagan admitted that acid rain is a serious environmental problem, but he calls for nothing but five years and $5 billion of study.

The southern San Joaquin Valley, downhill but upwind from the park, is potentially one of the worst air basins in the United States, and pollution already affects agricultural production. Representative Richard Lehman said that "very stringent steps will be needed" for pollution control, essential to the parks, to public health, and to the entire agricultural industry, which involves the region's economy and the nation's security. "A nation that does not protect its farmland is not going to be secure no matter how many MX missiles it has."

For most people, Kings Canyon and Sequoia are the highlights of the southern Sierra, but there's much more. North of the Kings River, Bass and Huntington lakes are reservoirs ringed by cabins, buzzing with motorboats, drawing throngs from the hot valley. The Sierra National Forest fills most of the mountainous area between Yosemite and Kings Canyon. In one year, 4.5 million visitor-days were recorded, placing Sierra in the top ten most used national forests in America. Throughout the range, only the Inyo and Tahoe national forests are used more. Combined, the national forests of the Sierra Nevada account for about 25 million visitor-days out of 52 million for all national forests in the state—about one-eighth of the recreation on all national forests in the nation.

Surprisingly, recreation in much of the Sierra peaked in 1978, when the baby boom generation was spending a lot of time outdoors. Use of the John Muir Wilderness dropped from 602,200 visitor-days in 1982 to 449,000 in 1984 (some of the statistical decline could be a result of less enforcement of permit regulations). Backpacking in Yosemite dropped to 84 percent of its peak in 1975. In some areas, however, use is increasing; the Emigrant Wilderness recorded 195,400 visitor-days in 1982 and 224,700 in 1984. And the lull, wherever it is found, probably will not last.

The nearness of Southern California's population—one out of twenty Americans—and the growth of the statewide population are inescapable facts. Projections call for an increase to 5.6 million visitor-days in the Sierra National Forest by the year 2000, when the state will have climbed from its teeming mid-1980s 26.4 million people to an anthill of 32.9 million, no doubt bringing aggravated neuroses and a prescription for more recreation. The state Department of Finance estimates the population in the year 2020 at 39.6 million. Statewide, the Forest Service projects a 63 percent increase in recreation by the year 2030.

South of Sequoia National Park, Sequoia National Forest records 3.1 million visitor-days a year. Part of the forest lies in the basin of the Kern's North Fork, whose upper reaches run headlong south, twenty-five miles through the national park in a ruler-straight canyon that parallels an earthquake fault. Continuing through the national forest, the North Fork is longer than any other free-flowing river in the Sierra.

At the Forks of the Kern, where the North Fork and Little Kern join, rafters and kayakers hike three miles, with gear on horseback, and embark on a seventeen-mile descent, including eighty major rapids, some of them Class V. The finale to this intense run, first explored in 1980, is the thirteen-foot plunge over Carson Falls.

West of the Kern, the Sierra Nevada has been the summer habitat of up to one-third of the California condors. With nine-foot wingspans, they are the continent's largest land bird and are perhaps irrevocably endangered. Less than twenty-seven individuals survive in 1984, most of them in captivity. Also west of the Kern is the proposed Peppermint ski area.

With curious enthusiasm for the chair lift, the Forest Service proposes up to 10,500 skiers a day. Julie Allen, Forest Service coordinator for the resort's environmental impact statement said, "The exposure to the sun and the low elevation would take Peppermint out of the world class category, but it could be a very good regional area for intermediate skiers. It would be the largest area this close to Los Angeles—about four and a half hours away."

Local citizens forming the Peppermint Alert say that the season is too short, the access road is too long and winding, the cabin-in-the-woods character of the area should be left alone, and adequate water cannot be found (33 million gallons would be needed per year on the site, plus 55 million gallons for snow making). One of the highways to Peppermint passes within a mile of an old condor nest where egg shells were found. Lodging and support facilities for guests and 2,375 employees would probably be built in habitat where condors have fed in the past. Linda Blum, of the Condor Research Center, stated, "The proposed Peppermint Ski Resort Project has the potential to produce substantial adverse impacts upon the condor, both directly and indirectly."

"History repeats itself in the funniest ways," Allen said. "Mineral King was suggested as an alternative to the San Gorgonio ski proposal. Then Horseshoe Meadows as an alternative to Mineral King. Then Peppermint as an alternative to Horseshoe Meadows. We feel there are no unacceptable environmental impacts. It comes down to financial feasibility. The county stands to gain $700,000 a year. The ski area would provide a 1 or 2 percent increase in employment. In diversifying the agricultural economic base, the ski area is complimentary." The Kern County Cattlemen and Springville Farm Bureau Center oppose the resort because of expected increases in development and traffic.

The Forest Service spent $250,000 on planning with no commitment from a developer. "We want it that way," explained Allen. "That way the studies are not biased." Why does the Forest Service spend so much to encourage development of the forest? "There's a large unmet demand for ski areas. They are part of multiple use, and we're in the business of planning for recreational areas for the public."

Steve Brougher, wildlife biologist for the Stanislaus National Forest, had a different opinion on the development of national forest lands in the 1980s: "The trend is to increase anything that can make money for private industry."

East of Peppermint and south of Sequoia National Park lies the Kern Plateau, high country with meadows running for miles. Here is one of the few wilderness enclaves in forty-nine states where a person can be more than ten miles from a road (northern Yosemite National Park, the upper Yellowstone region, and the Anaconda-Pintlar Wilderness in Montana are others).

In a four-volume Ph.D. thesis, John Harper stated, "The principal land use problem in the southern Sierra is the virtual absence of comprehensive planning on a regional basis." His statement echoes Bob Twiss at Lake Tahoe on the need for Sierra-wide planning. In the same way that conservationists' reform of timber management failed in the northern Sierra and led to the narrower focus on wilderness designation, regretted by Gordon Robinson, so in the south regional planning failed and led to the wilderness lobby.

"If the entire resource cannot be managed wisely, then at least we can try to protect the very best," explained Bob Barnes, a leader in efforts to pass the California Wilderness Act. If the president signs the act, wilderness will predominate in the high country of the southern Sierra. The Monarch and Jennie lakes areas will be designated at the western border of Kings Canyon National Park. South of Sequoia Park and next to the John Muir Wilderness, the Golden Trout Wilderness was named in 1978 to protect the habitat of a rare trout considered the most beautiful. Adjoining the Golden Trout area, the South Sierra Wilderness is in the new act, followed by a thin gap for the Kennedy Meadows (Sherman Pass) road. South of it is the new Dome Land Additions Wilderness. Farther south, the Dome Land Wilderness extends within half a mile of Highway 178, the first paved crossing of the Sierra since Tioga Pass, 165 airline miles north. The only longer chains of protected mountains in North America are in Alaska and in Banff and Jasper national parks in the Canadian Rockies, where 335 continuous miles have only three road crossings.

Combined, several of the wilderness areas will protect sixty-one miles of the Kern's South Fork as the longest reach of wilderness along any Sierra river. In this basin, ecoregions meet: provinces of the Intermountain Sagebrush, American Desert, Sierra Forest, California Chaparral, and California Grassland. Among basins of similar size, this amount of mixing may be unique in America. The result is a botanical museum of 1,200 plant species and probably others as yet undiscovered. As recently as 1978, zoologists discovered two new kinds of salamanders.

When I arrive at Camp Whitsett, near the North Fork of the Kern, several campers are pitching tents. Bob Barnes will be here for the Sierra Club's Kern-Kaweah Chapter meeting. So will Jim Eaton, director of the California Wilderness Coalition. Boyd Evison, superintendent of Sequoia and Kings Canyon national parks, will arrive tomorrow. His employees call him "the best superintendent in the national park system." Joe Fontaine will come; I've entered the territory of Joe Fontaine.

Good news! Barnes and Eaton have brought champagne because today, September 28, 1984, the California Wilderness Act was signed by a noncommenting President Reagan. The protection that Sierra conservationists have been working for—from Quincy to here, from the Tuolumne's western foothills to Mono Lake's eastern shore—is now law.

After dark, the meeting begins. Before celebrating one of the finest and hardest-earned conservation victories in the history of the Sierra, the chairman aims to rid the docket of procedural matters. I talk with Terry Winckler, a friend, fisherman, and journalist for the *Porterville Recorder.* He writes the news as he sees it, which is no small feat. His editor is "virulently antienvironmentalist." Winckler's time in Porterville—the closest large town to the southern Sierra—represents a flight from Los Angeles but also a trap. "It's one hour to nice country, but you need more than that. I should get out of here. Seven years is enough. It's a very conservative community. People think the Sierra Club is a Cesar Chavez type of thing or students at Berkeley or people from San Francisco."

At last Jim Eaton pops the cork. He has a bear's burly body and dark hair thick as sheep's wool with a beard to match. A field representative for the Wilderness Society until they "went for the corporate and mass-media image," he now directs the California Wilderness Coalition, which coordinated many groups backing the bill. He speaks of areas still unprotected. The Sierra National Forest, for example, calls for an increase in its road system of 1 percent a year for the next thirty-five years.

Operating one of the largest transportation systems in the United States, the Forest Service in the Sierra already has 3,566 miles of roads suitable for cars, and arterial and collector roads such as these average only one-fourth of the total Forest Service road mileage on a nationwide basis (the Sierra Nevada figure does not include many hundreds of miles of state-maintained roads). The Forest Service publication *Forest Roads: Help or Hindrance?* states: "Roads are needed for many reasons. They provide access to log timber, to fight wildfires, do wildlife habitat improvement projects, to visit campgrounds and just to get within walking distance of remote forest areas." More than 200 miles of new roads suitable for cars are built each year in Sierra Nevada national forests. But they will not be built in the new wilderness areas, so tonight we drink, we celebrate.

Bob Barnes toasts "what has been saved." He is relaxed in front of a group, and without talking down to us, he is explicit and entertaining in the way of a sixth-grade teacher, which he is. Later I learn that he migrated from Massachusetts to Porterville to teach school, and in the environmental movement of the early seventies, he joined the Audubon Society. In 1979, he took a leave of absence without pay to work for Audubon. Half of the areas he strove to protect are in the new Wilderness Act. Out of 8.1 million acres of national forest in the Sierra Nevada, 1,926,298 are protected as wilderness, more than 500,000 of them in the new act. Including parts of the three national parks, 3,340,878 acres are protected as wilderness throughout the Sierra.

The big celebration is yet to come. It will be a festive gathering of hundreds, requiring planning for food, music, guests, and overnight accommodations. It will be in Sonora in late October, and I will try to be there.

The talk runs to two things: areas "in" and areas "out." Bob Barnes says, "Yes, the Dome Land Additions is in, and almost connect with the South Sierra Wilderness, but Little Trout Creek is out. It has the best timber in the South Fork basin. The timber industry gave up nothing in the southern Sierra."

On Saturday morning I find Joe Fontaine rolling up his sleeping bag. He is another of many schoolteachers involved in the future of the Sierra: Mike Yost, Jim Hildinger, Ginger Burley, Carl Sharsmith, Mike Prather, Christy Lynch, Bob Barnes, and others. Joe and I agree to meet later at his home near Tehachapi, at the southern end of the Sierra.

Boyd Evison, who arrived at his Sequoia job by motorcycle from Washington, D.C., arrives by motorcycle again. When he takes his helmet off, he looks only middle-aged, though his career has taken him three times to Washington, to several parks, and to the Grand Canyon, where he directed the government's training program for rangers. He talks about the backcountry management plan for the parks. A stock users group says he wants to "virtually ban" horses in the high country. In fact, the plan allows increases in stock use, though it closes some meadows to grazing.

The discussion turns to future priorities of the Sierra Club now that the California Wilderness Act has been passed. "The Bureau of Land Management has areas that should be designated wilderness," says Bob Barnes. Other thoughts: national river status for the Kern, new timber management policies in the national forests, reform of cattle grazing on public lands, and hydroelectric diversions on the east side. Also, national forest land-use plans are due soon, and they will address the entire future of the Sierra Nevada.

When the meeting ends, I accept an invitation to meet Barnes and Eaton next week in Kernville for a plane ride over the southern Sierra. "The flight will let us see what needs saving next," Bob says. "Besides, you'll enjoy meeting the pilot." Terry Winckler and I hope to keep in touch, but he doesn't know where he will be—maybe Central America—and I don't know where I will be. He leaves for a fishing trip along the South Fork of the Kern, trailless and difficult.

I'm off to see a river myself, and I hope my journey will not be difficult. The Kern is the Sierra's longest river and the farthest south; it flows from the highest peak, through the straightest canyon; and it is closest to Los Angeles. But this waterway was unknown to me until now. I'll canoe three miles on the North Fork—not much, but canoeable rivers in the Sierra are rare, especially during the low flows of autumn, and so I'll take what I can get.

Near Johnsondale, a company logging town of a dozen buildings that closed in 1979, I drive across the North Fork and turn downstream. I pass quiet reaches where floating leaves of alder barely move. I pass rapids big enough to eat trucks. From the ponderosa belt I drop into the oak belt. Because of the low latitude and dryness, the chaparral in the southern Sierra runs 2,000 to 3,000 feet higher than in the north; on the peaks, timberline climbs 1,000 feet higher. As I drive downriver, the canyon deepens.

In early October, life is easy here, but on Labor Day, five weeks ago, it was pandemonium. On the Kern—the closest mountain river to half of all Californians—the scene is more crowded than on any other Sierra river. Three hundred thousand visitors come here in a year, and buses shuttle 30,000 rafters on three sections of the river. On Thursday before the weekend rush, Southern Californians rush to fill six campgrounds. Latecomers camp next to the road, pitch tents in parking lots, and sit in lawn chairs ten feet from the highway. Riding Harley Davidsons are bands of twenty with sunburned foreheads, tattoos, and sleeveless jackets or halter tops. The sheriff's deputy cruises in a Blazer with a shotgun on a rack and a dog in the back, but he addresses only the gravest offenses. Four-by-four drivers bash through chaparral to unlikely campsites. There is an insect quality without the order or random construction of insect life. Is this the future? How soon will the American River be infected? The Kings? The Merced? Is the Feather River immune?

Only shell fragments from this war to have a good time remain in October. Now the river runs alone and alluring in rapids, honed by the edges of low water. The presence of the place—its own character and not that of the people—has returned.

The Forest Service recommended seventy-eight miles of the North Fork as a national river, but the Reagan administration cut this to sixty-one, eliminating the Johnsondale-Kernville section that is most in need of better management. Friends of the River lobbies for reinstatement.

Below a small hydroelectric dam, I set my canoe into the river, step into the boat, and leave the land. I know that no killer rapids lie ahead, but otherwise I know so little about this river that I'm excited. I'd be excited anyway: I'm afloat; I'm on a river. I paddle to the center and drift. My journey southward through the Sierra is now effortless.

Unlike the raft, the canoe responds quickly to my paddle, also to the river, the rocks, and gravity. In rapids, I brace against the water with my paddle, I put weight on one knee or the other to tilt the boat downriver when I hit a crosscurrent, I pull for momentum to break through holes, and I catch eddies for refuge from which to look and think. This means of reaching Kernville is right; a waterborne trip belongs near the end of my Sierra journey. Down here toward the end of the range, I join the runoff from last winter's snowstorms like the one in which I began, seven months ago. The October sun shines on me.

I hit a wave and hole and ship a bucket of water over the bow. With new caution, I stop and scout the next drop, rated Class III— potentially difficult in an open canoe. In another rapid, I hit something hard that may have originated on Whitney, but it is a forgiving chunk of mountain. I slide over the rock and slip through a chute.

Soon I see homes cut into the hillsides, then the bridge. I've reached Kernville. I hitch back to the van with a man from Los Angeles. I return, park near the bridge, and settle into the town, a tempting place where I camp by the river, where I have access to fresh vegetables and to a post office where mail arrives general delivery.

The winter climate is easy here. With my kerosene heater I could survive. Darkness, however, grows around me and eats at my days from both ends. The long season closes in on me. Against winter, even in the warm south, two candle flames make a poor defense.

Kernville is unique in the Sierra. It's the only real river town, its halves bridged together, its rapids playing music heard by all. I believe it is unique in America: near here is outstanding white-water, Class I through VI (easy to murderous), in a climate that invites paddling all year. International racers train here in winter. I've seen only one place—Ohiopyle on the Youghiogheny River in Pennsylvania—that is more of a whitewater river-running town. In the center of Kernville, kayak instructor and designer Tom Johnson has built a rapid by arranging rocks that concentrate the flow and create eddies. The river provides fun, and it also bolsters the economy through new enterprises.

"I wandered into town five years ago," says Tom Moore, "and was offered a job guiding rafts on the Kern." He had grown up in flat Nebraska and flat, paved Houston, so the southern Sierra looked good. For two years he guided and managed a rafting business. In the winter he worked at ski resorts, and in between, he traveled. "In my wanderings, I passed through the Nantahala Outdoor Center in North Carolina and was impressed with what they did, teaching people. I realized that I wanted to do something different with my life."

The bread and butter of Moore's outdoor center is in guided raft trips and equipment sales, but the heart of it is in instruction. "The idea is to learn by doing. We want to give people the skills so that they can safely enjoy the outdoors.

"Our clientele is from Los Angeles. People are looking for something to counter the other life-style. We're all adrenaline junkies. With new skills, people can face new risks—not in the stress of the city but in the challenges of the mountains."

Risk-free, I spend the afternoons working and reading in the park along the Kern, where kids picnic during sixth-grade field trips, fishermen test popular holes, bums pass the day, and families do family things.

In the morning, at the Whitewater Cafe, two old men sit in the corner, both in cowboy hats, cowboy boots, and cowboy shirts. They eat a silent breakfast. I imagine that they are brothers, and that everything has been said, and that not much needed saying in the first place.

On the wall, on a poster, a woman aims a revolver between my eyes: "Vote for Pistol Packin' Mama, Frontier Marshall, early California Days." The waitress hustles with plates, menus, and customers. I hear the cowboys speak.

"Pretty soon it'll be dark by five."

"Five? Four thirty." They return to their bacon and eggs.

Next to me, Red sits down. I don't know if he is named for his hair or his even redder face. He is friendly without letup. "Looks like rain. Gonna' rain? You heard if it's gonna' rain?"

"No."

"You haven't heard. Looks like it might. Can't tell. Happens in the winter, you know. That's how you know winter's comin'."

Ten minutes elapse and the cowboys speak again.

"Mita got snow up there last night."

"'Bout time."

"How many head they got?"

"Four, five hundred."

"'Bout time to bring 'em down."

About time. I walk to the river and watch a wave. It's time to leave Kernville.

I'm running out of time. The earth at this latitude is cooling off, and winter will blow in from the west and down from the north. Over the Pacific Ocean, zones of high pressure will yield to low pressure, and October through April, the wet storms will bring 90 percent of the precipitation that falls on the Sierra Nevada. Half of the winter days will be cloudy. I could stay for the long season, but the mountains in winter are difficult, a whole other experience. Kernville lies low, protected from snow, but in the southern Sierra, at Giant Forest, one of the heaviest recorded one-day snowfalls in American history fell in 1933—sixty inches. With the first big snowfall, the Ebbetts Pass, Sonora Pass, Tioga Pass, and Kennedy Meadows roads will be closed, leaving a 235-mile-long winter wilderness. Last night's fresh snow in the high country is a reminder: the year is short. Worse yet: life is short. The days have passed, and soon the season will pass, and the journey, and the year. So much has passed, with so little to remember it by. Time has run away from me. It's a lucky man who has had as much time and life as Ardis Walker, whose name and address are on a scrap of paper in my pocket.

I knock on a solid wooden door. Thin, straight, leathery, elderly— Ardis answers. "Yes. Come in. Come in."

Ardis Walker has been living in the southern Sierra about as long as anybody. Through the entire Sierra, no one I know has worked for protection of the mountains longer than he has. While we talk, the morning sun lights a bright outline as it shines through Ardis's white hair. His face is long and lean, his nose slightly hooked, his hands wrinkled and folded. Entirely western, he wears Levis and a shirt with snaps. He hesitates often but never pauses once the thought begins. His voice is deep and gravelly, though he does not smoke. In 1861, his grandfather moved to Keyesville, where Ardis was born in 1901. "I wandered off barefoot and absorbed the natural scene. I was switched once or twice by my mother for wandering too far."

Ardis enrolled in the University of Southern California in electrical engineering. "I took that so I could afford to write poetry." To pay his way, he cleared roads in Yosemite in the summer. "I slept out at the foot of Yosemite Falls back when nobody stepped over you." Like Carl Sharsmith, Ardis spent summers on logging crews in the Northern California redwoods. "I was getting involved with the Save the Redwoods League, and the logging boss said, 'Ardis, if you want money for college, you'd better pipe down.'" In 1927, he graduated and worked for Bell Telephone on Manhattan Island. "They wanted me to go into research and development, but I didn't want to. I knew I'd lose myself. I enjoyed New York but was glad knowing that I wouldn't be there the rest of my life."

He returned to Keyesville during the Depression, wrote for the Bakersfield newspaper, married Gayle Mendelssohn, operated a mill at the Keyes mine, moved to Kernville when Isabella Reservoir flooded the Kern Valley, and owned a motel. For ten years he served as a judge, and for four years he was a county supervisor. "I pushed for land-use controls. People were buying small lots on the flood plain and on soils where sewage disposal won't work. I lasted one term. People moving up from Los Angeles to get away from smog will have the same problem here. The chamber of commerce cuts its own throat by getting more and more people to come."

Always Ardis wrote poetry about the Sierra—sonnets that reside at the University of Syracuse as examples of modern sonnet writing in America. "May I get you some tea?"

I look around. A potbellied stove forms the centerpiece of this richly interesting place. Southwestern Indian art, Navajo blankets, cowboy paintings, and prints cover every wall. One sketch, "The Trail Boss," is a Charles Russell original. A library of 1,000 books specializes in western America. I leaf through an elegant volume, *Sierra Nevada Sequence*, written by Ardis. He returns with my tea.

"You could see the forest being cut and not growing back, and I realized that too much would be gone if we didn't do something about it. If we had had today's appreciation of the unspoiled environment fifty years ago when I wanted a wilderness from Walker Pass to Whitney, we would have ended up with more than crumbs."

One of the substantial crumbs is the Golden Trout Wilderness, including 303,287 acres and twenty miles of the Kern's South Fork. "It was a long battle, and it often seemed that we had lost. I worked on that for forty years, but other people carried it out. Thank God we have people like Bob Barnes and Joe Fontaine.

"Outside the wilderness we see more clearcutting. It's total destruction. They're taking out toothpicks, scraping the bottom of the barrel. In the mountains I want to see timber, not a plowed field. Then they spread chemicals. The Forest Service forgets there's an ecosystem out there."

Unable to get attention from government officials two decades ago, Ardis began sponsoring workshops. "Because we got a lot of publicity, the Forest Service *had* to show up." His most recent workshop was a month ago.

"We need to work on a new level, teaching youngsters about the environment. By the time they get jobs, they're clamped into the system. There's so much to do. We need more time; life is so short. There's so much to learn. Education is a slow process, but life is a fast one."

In Kernville, one other man spends time at the river like I do—in fact, more time. He lives under the bridge.

"Whatta' *you* up to tonight?" he asks, an alert gleam in his eye. On a green bench, I sit next to Sam, age sixty. Two buttons remain on his shirt; his whiskers are pure hobo.

"How long have you lived under the bridge?"

"How long? I can't tell you how long. Too long." In winter, Sam finds another place.

"Where're ya' headed?" he asks.

"South."

"Don't do it. Don't go south 'a here. This town, I ain't got nottin' 'gainst this town. I like it here. People know me. Now if I partied up a storm, that'd be different. So I mind my own business."

"What business?"

"My business? I'm a drunk. An old man and a drunk. Oh, I flew airplanes once. I wasn't apeshit over it though. You go up, you come down. It's gonna' rain. Look up that canyon.

"Ya' see up that canyon? Another job I had—I took guys from the city up there, above Johnsondale, and you'd think they owed their life to me. I mean they liked it. Hey, you fish, you sleep anywhere, you say anything. How often do you just say what you wanna' say? You can't beat it. It's paradise up there."

It's time to fly, not that I'm "apeshit" over the idea, but it will be a chance to see from above what I've seen from the ground. Today I meet Bob Barnes and Jim Eaton at the airport. I splash my face with river water one last time from one last river of the Sierra. But before I leave Kernville on this cool autumn morning, I pack a bag of food and leave it under the bridge.

Even I can tell that the thirty-seven-year-old, radial-engine Cessna 195 is a classic. The pilot refuels and turns the propeller until it's vertical. He's in his late sixties, six feet or so, strongly built, springing when he walks, moving decisively. He has been weathered by California since childhood. Plentiful white hair includes a broad, pointed mustache and a full beard at Hemingway length. He wastes few words and none for welcome on this October morning. "Don't try to help. When people try to hold doors or do other things, they get in the way, so don't do anything to help me."

Bob Barnes set this trip up in order to see the Bureau of Land Management wilderness areas that ought to be protected, according to him. But of course we will see more. Jim Eaton has been up with this pilot before and inquires about a "crash" in his past.

The pilot denies that he has crashed. "Once the propeller came off and damaged the plane in the process." I want to know the circumstances of the inevitable landing, call it what you will, but I don't ask.

The white-haired man taxis to the end of the runway, turns the plane around, and squints, his elbow out the window, distinctly the image of old-time aviation. Expressionless as always, he throttles the plane into a roar. Martin Litton takes off.

No one, I suppose, can give a better airplane tour of the southern Sierra than Litton. Once airborne, he warms to the subject. Oblivious to maps, ignoring the compass, he will point out Woodpecker and Jackass meadows, Sky Parlor Meadow, Bald and Black mountains, and dozens of obscure landmarks below the heights of Whitney but above the depths of the Kern.

He has seen the changes all over California. Litton rode his bike to the beach by crossing "the nation's largest beanfield," now Los Angeles International Airport. He and a friend started a club in high school to fight a Porterville–Lone Pine road that would have cut the southern Sierra in two.

In 1934, the year Hetch Hetchy was flooded, they built packs out of canvas and trekked through the mountains. "We came up out of Olancha, hot and dry. We saw water on the trail and dug for a drink, then realized it was mule piss. When we reached Summit Meadow, it was paradise discovered. We drank from springs and lay in the grass. Forty years later I flew over the ridge and saw a dozen four-wheel-drive vehicles ripping the place apart. Now the meadows are in the new wilderness area."

This will be some ride. Eaton skipped breakfast. Like I said, he's been up with Litton before, who now tilts us on our wingtip. I look straight down to peaks.

During World War II, when not in combat, David Brower taught soldiers how to climb, and Martin Litton taught them how to fly gliders. After the war he took up river running, designed a white-water dory, and in the forties was one of the first people to regularly run the Grand Canyon.

Writing for the *Los Angeles Times*, Litton sounded the alarm about LA's plans to dam Kings Canyon in the 1950s. David Brower, then executive director of the Sierra Club, saw Litton's work, invited him to join the club, and quickly arranged his election to the board of directors.

Like Brower, Litton believed in fighting. After he led the club's defeat of the Mineral King ski area, the proposal was shifted to Horseshoe Meadows in the Inyo National Forest above Lone Pine. Some board members said that they had to compromise, but Litton applied characteristic zeal and buzz-saw impatience. "If it's wrong, it's wrong. Why save Mineral King if you're going to lose another important area?"

As travel editor for *Sunset* in the sixties, Litton wrote of the need for Redwood National Park. Lumber companies advertising in the magazine demanded that he be fired. He quit in 1969 and built Grand Canyon Dories into one of the more exceptional river companies in the world, running nonmotorized trips on the Colorado and other western rivers.

At 180 miles per hour, Litton cruises north over the green, gray, and yellow mosaic of fall. We must climb rapidly because the peaks climb rapidly. We fly at 12,000 feet, only 2,500 feet below Whitney. Outside it is zero degrees.

Monache Meadows, nine miles long with 10,000 acres, is one of the largest Sierra meadows and is "out" of the wilderness area, partly because ranchers objected, though designation would not prevent grazing. It would prevent geothermal development—a threat to both ranching and recreation. Lands around the meadows are "in," though at this moment they are aggressively crisscrossed by a dozen off-road-vehicle drivers, who from here look like they will collide and kill each other off. "After the Forest Service closes the roads down, that will be one of the first restored wildernesses," Barnes says. "Someday those roads will be grown over." Is this the beginning of wilderness reclamation? Edgar Wayburn and David Brower have greater ideas: they call for dismantling the dam at Hetch Hetchy. Dr. Wayburn said, "It's dreaming, I know, but I've seen dreams come true." Brower said, "It's not too early to start talking about it."

South of Olancha—the Sierra's southernmost 12,000-foot peak— Litton circles spectacularly. With little margin we clear the crest at Summit Meadows, "in," and fly into the Owens Valley void as the eastern escarpment instantly drops out from under us. In a matter of seconds we are 9,000 feet above the ground. Litton banks, returns to the west side, and flies north over Ardis Walker's Golden Trout Wilderness, mostly gentle terrain with meadows everywhere. Litton said we would not go to Whitney, but its lure is magnetic. Of course we will go to Whitney.

Now we are over Crabtree Meadow, home of the backcountry ranger Dario Malengo. I see Timberline Lake and the granite basin that I fled five weeks ago during the midnight lightning storm. When Litton circles to climb out of a cirque northwest of Whitney's summit, we passengers concentrate on feeling well.

We turn south down the Kern River canyon and cross the Great Western Divide highway near Camp Nelson. Jim says, "Roads, roads, roads."

Litton says, "Forget about this. Write it off."

Barnes has more of the hopefulness of middle-aged youth, or of a winner since the California Wilderness Act passed. "I'm not writing it off up there." He points to the Moses roadless area: "That is out but should be in."

We pass Kernville and continue south, probing ahead of my journey's progress on the ground. Isabella Reservoir, only 2,600 feet above sea level, is used for recreation more than any other Army

Corps of Engineers reservoir in California. The towns of Lake Isabella and Bodfish are full of mobile homes and cars.

Before entering the backwater of Isabella, the South Fork of the Kern flows through California's largest remaining cottonwood-willow riparian forest, preserved because of Bob Barnes, though action began with David and Sally Gaines from Mono Lake.

When David and Sally surveyed bird habitat for the Department of Fish and Game in 1977, they scanned maps and found a mass of riverside forest along the South Fork. They slept at Bob Barnes's home, and he went with them to see the promising woods. Armed with binoculars, they disappeared into the 14-mile-long, 3,000-acre tangle of Fremont cottonwood and willow underlain by shoulder-high weeds and ankle-deep mud in this Sierra Nevada gap, otherwise a desert. David played a tape of a yellow-billed cuckoo, and a real one answered. This caterpillar eater is written up as a "dedicated birdwatcher's dream bird." Barnes, Gaines, and Gaines found nine bird species listed as rare in California.

They waded out of the woods, and David said to Bob, "Sally and I have to save Mono Lake. You save the South Fork of the Kern." Bob called Steve McCormick at the Nature Conservancy in San Francisco, and he, Peter Seligmann, and Bill Burley came to look. Barnes says, "We stood on a bluff to the north, and they said this was the best riparian habitat they had ever seen." The Conservancy bought 1,500 acres along the South Fork. Downstream, the Army Corps of Engineers owns additional riparian land, so far dedicated to wildlife.

From our height, the Kern River Preserve is a sinew of green above Isabella Reservoir. The Army Corps is considering raising the reservoir fifteen feet, which would flood much of the finest habitat. Some local politicians want a more stable "recreational pool" for motorboating.

Across the reservoir I see the lower canyon of the Kern River, thirty-two miles long, the only Sierra canyon with palm trees. All but twelve miles is dammed or diverted for hydroelectricity. The excellent whitewater run that remains would be eliminated by the proposed Hobo Project, but Friends of the River is fighting.

Our uncharted flight takes us east to Walker Pass, 5,250 feet, the southernmost pass in the Sierra (Tehachapi lies to the south but marks the range's end). Only Beckwourth Pass—the northernmost—is lower than Walker. To the south are the Scodies, or Kiavah Mountains, covered with pinyon pine, dropped from the Wilderness Bill as a compromise in the "acreage game" between the California senators.

Litton crosses again to the western side of the crest. Through a yellow haze of dust, forest fire smoke, and pollution, I see jumbled ridges to the south. The Sierra fade in stature but remain a barrier separating the rest of California from the Mojave Desert.

Between the green Cascades and the brown Mojave, I've seen the Sierra Nevada. One place or many? From the Feather to the Kern, from Chester to Kernville, from the Ebbetts Pass snowstorm to the heat of the southern canyons, these are the mountains. The colors of the range are as varied as those of the Tuolumne River from dawn to dark, but they match and blend brightly like a rainbow or subtly like these fields in autumn. The earthquake in Mammoth loosened rocks in Yosemite. The storm that brings rain to Isabella brings snow to Quincy. Here at the southern end of the mountains, I feel at home—a home that runs back north to where the flood of Cascade lava starts a different mountain range. Andrea Lawrence said, "There's a wholeness here in the mountains, and people are drawn to that." Everything that I've seen is part of the great uplift, a part of earth rising into sky.

The common ground is more than a ridge 400 miles long. In few places on this island of gradient have I felt apart from the quality of light, the intensity of life, the chance for escape. Just by being here, the mountains show that a place—a piece of earth—can be an answer to some of the greatest needs. I feel good here, but the feeling goes further than that. It goes on to something undefinable, to something silently given to me without explanation.

My search in these mountains has led me to find the present and also pieces of the past. But what about the future? Because of winter storms and steep gradients, hydroelectric dams are proposed all over the range, yet I consider every river I've seen to be worth protecting. When I look at the saved Tuolumne, I think of the threatened American. I think of the high-voltage power line that could cross the range near Echo Summit and go down the South Fork of the American near Bill Kier's lodge, and then I wonder: in all the Sierra, where should that power line go? There is no place where I want to see a new power line cross the crest of the Sierra. If it must be built, put it in Donner Pass where there are wires already. The inescapable fact is that California houses a lot of people, and more are on the way. So we have clearcuts, herbicides, subdivisions, casinos, crowds, cows, Giardia, dams, diversions, highways, acid rain, ozone. It's all on the increase.

Do we really have any choice? Will the work by people trying to save the mountains make much difference in the long run? Will more compromises save what is left? David Brower said that by compromising at this late date we will end up halfway between a bad place and a horrible place.

With any group of people, there are certain things that we do, and certain things that we don't do because they are not accepted. Will the abuse of the mountains move from the accepted to the unaccepted? That Mono Lake is being killed should be an outrage, even to people in Los Angeles. It seems to me that to dam the very last section of the lower Kern's whitewater should be unthinkable—likewise the pollution of Lake Tahoe, the crowds of cars in Yosemite, the poison rain in Sequoia.

Can there be a greater Yosemite National Park as David Brower hopes? A greater Sequoia National Park? Can there be a mountain refuge throughout the Sierra Nevada? I don't mean a place locked up from people living there, but an identity and commitment. This place is too valuable to be destroyed. Can we use this place and live in it yet still prevent the loss of the irreplaceable?

Maybe the most we will see is some additional wilderness whose protection was postponed in the 1984 compromise. But maybe we'll also keep Tahoe blue, stop Auburn Dam, restore water to Mono Lake, designate national rivers on the Merced, Kings, and Kern. Maybe we'll protect pieces of the whole and buy time so that when other places have become dead to the touch, the mountains will still move the spirits of people. My hopes may be built only on illusions, but maybe there will be a mountain ethic for California. We can take good care of these mountains. The dream was born with John Muir, and it seems that good dreams, nourished by good earth, never die.

When I drive past Isabella Reservoir, people are winching motorboats onto trailers and locking hillside homes for the winter. The mud ring around the lake fattens daily as the Army Corps of Engineers lowers the reservoir for winter runoff.

Southward I climb into different country. People disagree about the boundary of the southern Sierra, as they disagree about the northern one. Some people call Walker Pass the limit—south of there the mountains are lower, rounder, warmer, drier. Sierra geology, however, runs on south.

Pines surround Walker Basin. Populated with cattle, it reminds me of Taylorsville in Plumas County. Down and up, down and up, the road twists in curves like a stream, never straight. At Caliente Creek, bulldozers pushed rocks out of the streambed following a flood and created a mess with the remains of a stream in the middle. At Highway 58, I turn left and drive up to the town of Tehachapi, where I dig in my files for a scrap of paper, the last of many.

On the paper are directions to the home of Joe Fontaine. He is past president of the Sierra Club. Bob Barnes said, "He's a scientific observer—he goes out and sees, and he respects the other side."

Ardis Walker said, "He's practical and dedicated."

A Sierra Club staff member said, "I wish we could clone Joe Fontaine and have fifteen of them constitute the board of directors."

Five miles outside Tehachapi I turn into a potholed road, pass tan fields and shady oaks, and in first gear roll up to a house where flowers grow wildly. Bugs Fontaine answers the door. "Come in." She is also involved in conservation, "mostly on local things."

Joe walks out from the living room, where he was reading in the morning light. "Hi. Come on in." He wears a T-shirt and old shorts. His hair is short and turning gray. Although his demeanor is entirely peaceful, he has a strong, forceful look about him. My first impression is that he would never fall over; my second impression is that he could never be knocked over. His forehead slopes slightly back and accentuates his eyes, blue and friendly.

In 1850, Joe's great-grandfather moved to the southern Sierra and drove freight wagons from Los Angeles to the mining camp of Havilah. The family has lived in the area ever since.

In 1955, Joe hiked up Mount Whitney and met Tom Jones, a backcountry ranger twenty-five years before Dario Malengo. "Tom was very discouraged. The wilderness was being lost. New roads were proposed across the range. Meeting him was one of the things that got me started. A year later I joined the Sierra Club."

Joe was a leader in the Mineral King fight and in the protracted battle for the Golden Trout Wilderness. In 1980, he was elected national president, then he gave the office his full time during a two-year leave from teaching high school science. He remains on the board and has booked club activities for every weekend until Christmas.

"While I was president, the national issues, such as Alaska, took most of my time. Now I get to work on local things again, and it's good. You always like to come home.

"We moved out here from Bakersfield to get away. Now a developer has built a shopping center down the road. That kind of land use should be in town. I'm not against development but against unplanned and irresponsible development. Too much of our planning caters to the fast-buck artist and not to the quality of life."

Regarding the California Wilderness Act, Joe says, "We've had an impact, made a difference. As California grows, not all of it will be turned into a Los Angeles–sized urban complex. You can't stop population growth, but we're saving some of the core areas of wilderness so people can see them.

"I've never found an area I like as much as the Sierra. The granite, the light, the high elevation, the good weather, the open aspect of views—I haven't seen that combination anywhere else. To many people, even in the East, the Sierra has a mystique.

"When I was a kid, I read about the mountains, and they seemed like a fairyland. Even now, they have that mystery to me. One of the problems is that so many people want to go there. Yet you can't expect to support protecting an area if they don't know it's there. If they've seen it, they know it's worth saving."

Past the small homes and shops of Tehachapi, I don't drive south, because I'm as far south in the Sierra as I can go. I drive east and up toward Tehachapi Pass, 4,064 feet. The land is dry, with scattered oaks. To my north is the railroad and a cement plant. Los Angeles built the first plant here to supply the Owens Valley Aqueduct.

On the tramp in 1933, Wayne Dakan passed through Tehachapi and was offered a job making cement. "We found out that people were getting sick working there." He turned the job down but made out all right. His needs are low enough that he always makes out all right.

Highway 58 is four-lane here at the end of the mountains. On the southern border of the range, pavement is plentiful and traffic, heavy.

It was in this pass, coming from east to west, that the Joad family in Steinbeck's *The Grapes of Wrath* first saw their land of hopes built on illusions. Looking west to a spinning windmill, Ruthie whispered to Winfield, "It's California."

It's late afternoon, and darkness is coming even earlier tonight than last night, so before reaching the pass, I turn at the Monolith exit and drive on a section of the old highway. Beyond dry pastures and run-down buildings, beyond three parked pickups and a rough huddle of six men and several six-packs, the road faces a 1,000-foot-high mountain, the very last one. I reach the dead end of my road, where a yellow sign is planted that says, "End."

I camp, parked so that the last, lean sun of this October day can shine through the windows and work on the enormous heat mass in my passive-solar van. The boating gear and skiing gear and books and ropes absorb heat and then radiate it back to me through the evening while I read. The van stays warm even when I go to bed.

After a night of awakenings, I'm reading to do something, so I roll out of bed before dawn. I dress warmly and light two candles. It's cold, and the wind rocks the van.

It's Saturday, but the days are all the same to me. They all have that good Saturday feel. I don't have to go anyplace, and I'm glad.

Yet something inside of me says I must go everyplace. Today, especially, a voice says to go to a special place, the last of the Sierra. I'll walk up to the summit that rises north of Tehachapi Pass; one last climb remains in my brief passage through the mountains.

Yet I resist seeing the end. For hours I delay my trip. I putter in the van, I stall through lunchtime. Finally, the voice of the journey, with 400 miles and half a year of momentum, wins.

I walk up a road that is here for one reason: the building of windmills. Not a single one, such as Steinbeck's Ruthie and Winfield saw, but hundreds, for the generation of electricity.

Once again, I'm happy to be a slow-moving creature of the land. The road is dirt, zigzagging with bare-soil cut-banks up the last mountain. It's not what I hoped to find at the end of the Sierra, but then, a dam at Lake Almanor for the generation of electricity was not what I hoped for at the beginning. I guess that some hopes are based on nothing but illusions, and that—rattlesnake!

It's only a foot and a half long, oddly gray, perhaps a Mojave rattlesnake, which is especially venomous. It coils, blocking my path to the summit. I walk far to the side.

The windmills, at once ancient and futuristic, stand closer now, on the ridge. Three metal blades, twenty feet long, rotate on a single pole, fifty feet high. The noise is a swish plus a drone. Many blades stand still, though not for lack of a westerly wind. As I climb, the wind increases, pushed from the ocean through a funnel-shaped gap formed by the Sierra to the north and the Tehachapi Mountains to the south. I guess the wind speed at forty miles per hour. On the ridge now, as on Mount Davis, I have trouble walking in a straight line.

Thirty windmills are in this wind farm; five other farms cover nearby hills. Tehachapi Pass is one of California's three prime sites for harvesting the wind. Here are the strongest winds, so erratic that they damage the equipment. The farms were constructed quickly in response to tax incentives; wind generation was seen by the Carter administration as a means to cut dependence on oil and nonrenewable fuels. During Governor Brown's administration, state incentives were also offered.

My journey began with sawmills in the north; it ends with windmills in the south. I've come from logging cuts with roads and cables for exporting trees to road cuts and cables for exporting electricity. I've come from timber—a resource that is supposedly renewable though managed in ways that could make it as nonrenewable as the cedars of Lebanon—to a resource that is unquestionably renewable—the wind.

Here, making electricity, is the same wind that I felt on the Sierra Buttes in the spring, at Tahoe in the canoe, at Silver Pass on a raw and euphoric night, and on Whitney in a cold continental blast. To be in the mountains is to be in the wind, and while it often energizes me, as it does these machines, it can also relax me if it is not too powerful. On nights when I'm unsettled, a gentle wind is a river, picking me up and floating me away in airy dreams.

Down below, the south-facing slope of the last of the Sierra Nevada lies rough, not with sweet cottonwood and soft willow, but with spiny Joshua trees and yucca. On the north side of the mountain, I find not the supple mountain hemlock but the stubby pinyon pine. I scare out a jackrabbit and six quail. Ravens, which have the run of the continent from the hottest desert to the Arctic, croak at me. Old Wayne said that I would never know the mountains, but at least I can identify the things I see—some of them.

Now I'm on the summit, higher than anything to my south, west, or east, but not high by the standards of the Sierra. Although my final destination was not a jagged crest but a rounded one, I still feel a part of the sky, as I did on my climb at Tuolumne Meadows or on Mount Davis. I stand and look: earth and sky, earth and sky.

Again I have the world below me, though right there, beyond the Sierra, it is not a world that I much want. To my west rise the smokestacks of the cement plant. To my south is Route 58, carrying a steady stream of trucks that grind on the uphill grade. Trains also strain to the pass. Eastward, the road and railroad disappear in the dusty distance after many straight miles in the desert. Southeast lies Mojave, a quaint community of many gas stations—a place to fuel up and keep moving through the geography of the furnace. Far off sits Barstow, and Saddleback Butte is a brown island of gradient in the desert.

My journey is over. How can I feel so full and so empty, both? Not only have I taken a journey through the Sierra Nevada; the Sierra Nevada has taken a journey through me.

I look north at mountains that climb higher, as the Sierra has always done except during my one morning on Whitney. Cache Peak rises to 6,708 feet. Here and there I see a jeep road as crooked as a string that has been stretched tight and then let go quickly.

Hopeful, wishing to back up my journey and start over again, I look farther north. I stare to the north. I cannot take my eyes away from the places where I've been, places beyond what I can see. Now I see something far away. It's white. Many miles away I see white against the gray green slopes. Is it a peak covered with snow? Or is it a cloud? I stare for long moments, north toward the highest reach of the Sierra, but I cannot tell if it's earth or sky.

9

The Celebration

IT IS LATE WHEN I ARRIVE, but exploring the Sierra was a lot to do, and it's a wonder that I have arrived at all.

Dozens of people are gathered outside, and in the darkness of October, at the fairgrounds in Sonora, elevation 1,796 in the foothills, halfway up the Sierra from south to north, I feel like I have returned to some extraordinary era.

People in small groups and large groups are talking and laughing, the sounds muffled in the evening's cool outdoors. Men and women nod and smile and welcome me with a word or two even though they don't know me.

We are all here for the same reason. The California Wilderness Bill was passed and signed. It is now the law of the land: new wilderness areas from Bucks Lake to the Dome Land will be protected, the Minaret Summit road can be forgotten forever, Mono Lake is recognized as a national scenic area, and the Tuolumne River will run wild and free as we all knew God meant it to do. We are here to celebrate.

The huge fairgrounds building is full of life, and I think its vibrations could move the Richter scale and shake Mammoth into erupting. I step inside, and the scene is more crowded than South Lake Tahoe or Yosemite Valley. But it is different. Hundreds of people are doing things and talking, and the gist of the conversation is, "Isn't this wonderful?"

In this building, in this crowd, there is an extraordinary potential. Call it electricity, call it chemistry, call it energy, though those words are for other things; what I see here is something different. I don't know what it is, but I could feel it from moment one.

Here in the light I see a few familiar faces. Catherine Fox, who guided me on my first Stanislaus raft trip in 1979. She is radiant about what has happened. Marty McDonnell says, "The thing that made a wild Tuolumne possible was the Stanislaus. It was there that people became involved." I have a reunion with Steve Brougher, a wildlife biologist who is exceptionally committed to a better caring for the earth. Now I see dozens of familiar faces. Doris Grimm is down from her archaeological studies on the east side, and we will dance together.

Here is Don Briggs. "Wait till you see the film," he says. Later in the evening, his movie of the Tuolumne, with scenes shot during our trip, will be shown nonstop, and people will watch it for hours at the opposite end of the building from Norton Buffalo and the Knockouts, who will play rock and roll while the people dance and dance—hundreds of people dancing in hundreds of styles, each one his own, her own.

Alexander! Gaguine and I bear hug. I last saw him disappearing down the trail toward the South Fork of the Kings River. He returned to San Francisco, and, revitalized by the country he saw with me, he led a blitz of grass-roots support to members of Congress. "Congratulations, Tim, you did it! Congratulations, Catherine, you did it! Everybody, you did it! You did it!"

Someone, no doubt a kayaker, screams "Eee-hah!" I don't know what his reasons are, but I'm sure they are good. Everyone is high on what has happened to the places that they love the most.

In my mind I see the others here also. Old Wayne Dakan, his voice faraway but right: "Hot damn, we're going to turn the corner yet!" Jim Hildinger, Ginger Burley, Bill Kier, Jerry Meral, David Brower, Andrea Lawrence, Phil Pister, Mike Prather, Christy Lynch, Carl Sharsmith, Bob Barnes, Martin Litton, Ardis Walker, Joe and Bugs Fontaine—they all come to mind, and while they are not all the partying type, they would enjoy this because here, tonight, the party is for the Sierra Nevada.

I look at this tribal gathering as one mass mutiny from civilization. Yet it may be the beginning of a real civilization. So far, since Donald Rambeux's ancestors' time, there has been little native character in the people of this land. I've seen individuals who reflect where they are, who are a part of their place, who are committed to the gentle use of their land, but I've seen few groups or communities with the elusive harmony of belonging. Now, tonight, it seems that the mountains and rivers have shaped a people who are determined not to misshape their place. Have I seen the future?

The food is great, and the beer quenches the thirst that comes with hot crowds.

Five hundred strong, we make the best of this indoor space. There is no smoking. In the tight spots, it's shoulder to shoulder, which to someone who has lived in the mountains, in a van, for months, alone, is just fine. After people have eaten, they sit in food groups and visit or they wander, as I do, seeing friends and seeing strangers who are also friends.

Now I detect a fertile calm in the air, a waiting, an anticipation that something will happen.

John Amodio stands on the platform and speaks into a microphone. He talks about Richard Lehman, whose congressional district includes 20 percent of the new wilderness, the Mono Lake Scenic Area, and the Tuolumne national river—the river of the Sierra. Amodio says that Lehman is our best friend in Congress; he has protected more wilderness than any freshman congressman in history. By the time John is done, the crowd, with rare respect for a politician, has quieted into a seemingly impossible hush, into a calm—one that is mysterious and patient, waiting.

Richard Lehman steps up on the platform, and he carries something odd: not one thing, but two, of cumbersome sizes. People strain to see what he holds. Richard Lehman stands straight, in the light, in front of the crowd, and he says not one word, but now, into the air he suddenly thrusts his hands, the right one clutching a two-foot-square, framed photograph of Mono Lake and the new wilderness of northern Yosemite, the left hand grasping a photograph of the brilliant Tuolumne River canyon. Triumphantly, Lehman holds the pictures high.

The roar is spontaneous, explosive. Then it grows and grows as people realize—truly realize—what we are celebrating, and it grows even more as the images of the photographs, so tiny but symbolic, are held high by this man who has returned from Washington. The place seems to shake with cheers, whistles, and shrieks, and the applause does not quit.

The moment is unique in my life. Perhaps it is unique to all. Where, in all the world, where else would people cheer their hearts out for the mountains and the rivers of their earth?

Maybe, just maybe, the things that have happened here will happen again and again. Maybe the Sierra Nevada will remain as it has been to me, so that it can take others, many others, for many generations, on journeys of wonder and of life, on journeys that will never end. If my journey through the Sierra would never end, I think I would say, fine.

The night flies by, and I work up a sweat dancing. Too soon the people are gone, except for some who camp at the fairgrounds in vans and trucks and tents. I look up. The sky is brewing; only a few stars are out. A woman strums a guitar and sings softly with her boyfriend on the grass.

The day has ended. Even at this low elevation, the late October air is sharp. Cold gusts whisper across the ground, and even the last two singers crawl into their sleeping bags. Another season has ended, and for me, the year has ended.

Where am I? I know exactly where I am: only a few miles south of Highway 4, which leads up the western slope of the Sierra, up the green highway, back to Ebbetts Pass, back to the storm, the beginning. I didn't think it would come to this, but I'm prepared. I've stocked up on food and kerosene, and the warm clothes are out.

I've enjoyed three seasons and learned much about them, but I do not really know the fourth season, the long season. Eight months ago I saw only the end of it. Now, a new beginning is near. Winter in the mountains. What would I see? How would I survive?

They say that by daybreak it will snow, maybe down to 5,000 feet. If I leave now, I can beat the storm; I can reach the high country without chains. There is a place waiting for me. I'm climbing up to meet the winter, to invite the silent white crystals of the storm to bury my van and to cover my tracks.

Epilogue and Update

WHEN THE EARTH BEGAN TO SHAKE on July 20, 1986, I was sitting on the ground along Bubbs Creek, above the South Fork of the Kings River. Rocks clattered down from cliffs, branches of pines quivered, then shook, and a rumble came from deep underneath me. When I later dipped a cup of water from the river, it was silty; like everything else, the streambed had moved, loosening sand and dirt. With its epicenter near Bishop, the earthquake was felt as far away as Los Angeles, San Francisco, and Salt Lake City. The Sierra Nevada continues to rise higher into the sky.

What else has happened since my journey of 1984?

The clearcutting increases, supported by new forest plans written under Reagan administration guidelines. In 1986, the Tahoe National Forest plan drew 12,000 letters of comment, 55 percent of them form letters, 97 percent of which expressed an "environmentally oriented" point of view compared with 3 percent that were "timber-oriented" (the Forest Service yielded no scores regarding the other 45 percent of the mail). The most concern was for clearcutting, maintaining roadless conditions, and protecting the backcountry for recreation.

In 1985 alone, 1,020 miles of new roads—enough to drive from San Francisco to Denver—were built on national forest lands in California (the rate of new road building has decreased since 1980, when 1,965 miles were constructed statewide, according to a government brochure). The Forest Service proposes that in the next ten years, 360,000 more acres will be affected by changes such as logging and road construction in national forests statewide.

Grazing on Sierra national forests increased from 162,096 animal unit months in 1984 to 221,670 in 1986, not counting the Plumas Forest, for which 1986 figures were not listed.

The ban on herbicide and pesticide spraying continued, and what had appeared to be simply a conservative judgment by regional forester Zane Smith to regard an Oregon lawsuit seriously has turned out to be a major policy change. But the Forest Service, perhaps hopeful about a new chemical age, printed the brochure *Herbicides: Friend or Foe?* which educates the public: "It's not easy being a tree seedling, where nature's 'survival of the fittest' rule can certainly hold true. In this competitive situation, herbicides are friends to those trees which make the best lumber." 2-4-D a friend?

Unequivocally a friend of trees, Wayne Dakan continued to cause trouble for those ruining his northern Sierra homeland, but he adjusted to old age: He quit drinking Stroh's. Michael Jackson lost his race for county supervisor, Rose quit waiting on Morning Thunder tables, the sawmills in the Quincy area are operating, and the population of Plumas County grew by an estimated 826—a 4.5 percent increase in only three years.

At Lake Tahoe, Harvey's high-rise expansion was completed without another bombing, and Harrah's planned another big hotel. The Forest Service continued to buy private lands to prevent development on some of the more erosive lots.

After thirteen years of litigation, the Dillingham Development Corporation, now called DilDev Co., was paid $4,313,500 of government money for 208 acres of marshland that the company had planned to develop.

Clarity of the lake has increased from 74.8 feet in 1984 to 79 feet in 1986, but carbon in the water (a measurement for algae) was up from about 108 grams per square meter of surface area in 1984 to 118 in 1986. A moratorium on nearly all development had been enacted but was lifted with an agreement that each year allows 300 new homes to be built and in the next decade allows 400,000 square feet of new commercial space and 200 lodging units. Remedial programs for existing damage are to be accelerated. The League to Save Lake Tahoe was pleased with the agreement because the Tahoe Regional Planning Agency's plan allowed 600 to 1,800 new housing units, 1.1 million square feet of new commercial space, and no limit on new rooms. "We have the lowest levels of development that we could negotiate," said negotiator Clement Shute, the league's lawyer. "Yes, if we didn't have this agreement, the injunction would have remained in effect, but the Nevada legislature would probably have tried to rescind the entire TRPA. It will take years, but we now have a chance through restoration efforts to see a reversal of Tahoe's decline."

Jim Bruner, ex-executive director of the league and now simply a member of the board, said, "Under the new agreement, there will be more traffic, more urbanization, more congestion, and a continued deterioration of water and air quality. They've institutionalized the casino brand of recreation and the South Lake Tahoe commercial syndrome; inherent in the plan is more of the same. I don't think there should have been a settlement. The TRPA allows a new hotel to be built and says that because bus stops are included, traffic will decrease. It doesn't. My position is that the lake should not get worse before it gets better. We now have a great portion of the basin in public ownership, but an increasingly smaller tail of private speculators continues to wag this very large dog. The fate of Lake Tahoe should be controlled by the people who own most of it, not by developers."

Above Highway 49, along the South Fork of the Yuba, a hydroelectric project by a wholly owned subsidiary of Électricité de France is opposed by American citizens and even by county supervisors. The state legislature has failed to protect the site, which includes state parklands.

On the upper South Fork of the American at Sayles Flat, a hydroelectric dam was built in spite of citizen protests and state action against the project. Nearby, the management of Strawberry Lodge turned over when Bill and Helen Kier moved back downhill to Marin County. Also along the American, a water project ("SOFAR") that would have dammed the South Fork near Kyburz and tributaries such as the splendid Silver Fork was stopped because of economic reasons.

In February 1986, more than a week of rainfall sent floodwaters down the American, Yuba, and other northern Sierra rivers. At the Auburn Dam site, the Bureau of Reclamation's 200-foot-high coffer dam was filled, then overtopped, then sliced like butter to its bottom. The breach released a torrent literally Mississippi-sized, which immediately filled the existing Folsom Reservoir, which spilled in excess of design capacities of Sacramento levees. The city's fortifications leaked a little but held. A flurry of support for Auburn Dam followed from the usual boosters, who claimed that for public safety,

Sacramento needed this project whose construction was halted in 1975 because of earthquake hazards.

Friends of the River and the Planning and Conservation League documented how Folsom Dam had been managed by the Bureau of Reclamation in ways that aggravated flood hazards, and the Army Corps of Engineers found that improvements to existing flood control projects could more than double Sacramento's protection. In 1987, the Corps suggested a dry dam that would be filled only during large floods. Representative Robert Matsui said, "Auburn Dam, as originally conceived, will never be built, and the endless debate on how to resurrect this dinosaur is keeping people from focusing on immediate solutions to Sacramento's flood control needs." The proposal seems dead, but the bickering goes on, most politicians preferring to prop up rather than bury the ripening corpse.

Following the storm of 1986 that caused the flood and included wet snowfall and some of history's most extreme avalanches was the low-water year of 1987 and the worst Sierra fire season since records have been kept. In the Sierra and its foothills, more than 214,758 acres burned, 146,000 in the Stanislaus National Forest, including the entire rafting run in the Tuolumne canyon. Nine thousand people in towns such as Groveland and Tuolumne were evacuated.

Also at the Stanislaus, Steve Brougher quit his wildlife biology job and reclaimed his prior position as a backcountry ranger in the Emigrant Wilderness. "It's good getting away from the politics of the Forest Service and from working on timber sales so much of the time. I love the backcountry, I'm interested in wilderness management, and I pursue my wildlife interests on my own time."

On the North Fork of the Stanislaus and its tributaries near Arnold, dam construction is on schedule. While performing part of the required "mitigation" for the new Spicer Meadow Dam, which will be one of the last large dams built in California for perhaps many years, archaeologists in 1986 uncovered what is apparently the oldest Indian structural remnant ever discovered in North America. Ann Peak, chief archaeologist of a mother-daughter consulting firm, said, "We're taking a quantum leap back into the past with this find, telling us that there was fairly intensive use of land in California by the Indians beyond 6,000 to 7,000 years ago, which is really the oldest most other California sites firmly indicated."

Historian Melinda Peak said, "We thought of the use in high mountain areas as transitory, but this shelter at 6,500 feet indicates people were staying for a while." The structure was at Gabbott Meadow, along Highland Creek, and was twelve feet long—the size of the inside of my van.

Although there isn't much antiquity to actually see at the 9,750-year-old site, Gabbott Meadow is to archaeology what El Capitan is to rocks, Sequoia to forests, and Kings to canyons. This meadow and Indian site on the Stanislaus National Forest will be buried under water by the 265-foot-high dam.

The dam is nearly completed; logging of the reservoir area is scheduled to begin at any time. I drop everything and drive down the freeway, turn east to Sonora, pass Pinecrest, cross the Middle Fork of the Stanislaus, and park at the end of a dirt road high on the western shoulder of the Dardanelles. Then I hike five miles through snow to Gabbott Meadow, brilliant in autumn sun, showcase of girthy cottonwoods, aspens chewed by beavers, aged ponderosa, and junipers probably 1,000 years old growing on granite boulders along Highland Creek. Iceberg and Airola peaks gleam snowy white in my view from the warmth of the mountain cove. In November 1987, I see Gabbott Meadow the way Indians saw it nearly 10,000 years ago. In 10,000 years, I suspect it will look this way again.

It's not taking that long on the Merced; a fifteen-foot-high hydroelectric dam at Yosemite will be removed—one of the more significant actions nationwide to eliminate a dam in order to return a river to its natural self. South of Yosemite, in the Ansel Adams Wilderness, plans for North Fork San Joaquin dams, allowed through a loophole in the 1984 Wilderness Act, were dropped by developers in 1987, though they will someday be back. The developers may also return on the lower South Fork of the American, which is guarded by Bill and Robin Center but reprieved by a lawmaker's moratorium for only a few more years.

Good news! After another intense, dramatic, classic struggle over the Kings River, Rick Lehman's legislation was passed in November 1987, banning the opprobrious Rogers Crossing Dam and designating eighty-three miles of the Kings River, with its South and Middle forks, as one of America's premier wild and scenic rivers. Bittersweet, the legislation allows the raising of Pine Flat Dam, where twenty more feet of head would destroy a superb mile of river on one of the Sierra's finest whitewater rafting and canoeing runs, already limited to nine miles because of the Army Corps of Engineers' edifice at Pine Flat. The future will hold one more fight at the Kings.

Lehman's legislation also calls for a trail to be built up the untouched Middle Fork to Tehipite Valley—the closest thing to another Yosemite. The new access would open that wilderness canyon to much more use by hikers than now enter on the two existing circuitous trails.

Another milestone in Sierra Nevada conservation: national wild and scenic river designation was won in 1987 for the Merced River, including its exquisite South Fork and its much-enjoyed main stem at El Portal, where Joseph Keating had planned a hydroelectric diversion just below Yosemite National Park. Representative Tony Coelho blocked Senate-passed protection for a lower section, where Mariposa County wants to dam the river, but he sponsored a wild and scenic river study instead.

Upstream at Yosemite Valley, a congressional hearing in 1985 became the stage for concerns, including those of congressmen, that the valley is overcrowded with cars, that air flights over the park should be restricted, and that law enforcement methods should be investigated. Little of note on these subjects has occurred, except that in 1987 Congress prohibited flights lower than 2,000 feet above the rim of the valley.

Many theories attempt to explain why superintendent Bob Binnewies was transferred from Yosemite to the San Francisco Regional Office of the Park Service. The agency refers to a mutual agreement between the superintendent and regional director. Many people in the valley say that anyone with even moderately liberal credentials fell victim to the administration's housecleaning. Binnewies retired in 1987 and moved back to Mariposa in the Sierra foothills. Jack Morehead, who worked at Yosemite in the early seventies, became superintendent.

Zane Smith was also reassigned from his regional forester's office in 1987, and Paul Barker took his place. "The chief of the Forest Service wanted Zane to lead the National Recreation Strategy Project" was the official word.

"I had been there nine years, which is almost unprecedented," Zane said. "Forest Service policy and tradition is to move people."

Were there disagreements between you and your superiors? (I knew, for example, that the Department of Agriculture's decision to rescind the wild and scenic river recommendation for the Tuolumne in 1983 was not Zane Smith's idea.)

"Well, I don't think I'm the favorite person of this administration."

Smith may leave an interesting legacy. His National Recreation Strategy Project could represent nothing less than the beginnings of a rebound from the Forest Service's bottoming-out in commercially exploitive timber policies of the 1980s. "The project is a response to public criticism of Forest Service applications of multiple use, particularly as it applies to recreation. If you ask people for their impressions of national forest management, they will say clearcutting, herbicides, and road building. Yet we are the principal recreation provider in the United States. We need to make some policy changes. Just because you cut timber doesn't mean that you can't think about recreation. If this works, recreation will become a higher priority, a part of every decision."

Although he was appointed in the Carter years, Smith ironically led the Forest Service in California during six Reagan years, when the timber-oriented policies he speaks of were instituted. Some people criticized him for going along; others think that he was as progressive a manager as could be found in the upper echelons of the Forest Service in the 1980s and that it's a wonder he lasted as long as he did.

What do you feel you accomplished during nine years of directing management of 63 percent of the Sierra Nevada?

"We've built an organization that reflects the modern world. I think I've opened up the agency, with more autonomy to younger people. They have a more intense interest in national forest amenity values. Not to say that older veterans didn't have that commitment, but they could almost manage amenities as a residual. Today, the residual is not enough.

"I think I helped turn the road-building program around. We don't build as many roads, and those that we build don't lie so harshly on the land.

"In suspending the use of herbicides, we set out to do a good environmental statement, and in that process we learned to not rely so heavily on herbicides. In the timber program [pause], we've instituted a good planning process." Smith retired in 1988.

In the eastern Sierra, the level of Mono Lake increased during the wet year of 1986, but in 1987 the lake dropped 18 inches, sacrificed to cheap water in LA. The city's obligations under the Public Trust Doctrine remain unresolved. A court ruled in 1987 that LA must release 4 to 5 cubic feet per second down Lee Vining Creek.

The efforts to protect the lake and all of its life will continue despite the death of David Gaines. In January 1988, he and Mono Lake Committee intern Don Oberlin were killed when they were hit by an oncoming vehicle during a snowstorm. The Sierra Nevada lost one of its finest supporters. If the lake is saved, Gaines's dedication will be perhaps the foremost reason. If saved, the lake may be "a symbol of a changing attitude about the earth," as David said in 1984. In 1987 he wrote, "The birds and animals, trees and grasses, rocks, water and wind are our allies. They waken our senses, rouse our passions, renew our spirits and fill us with vision, courage and joy."

In nearby Lee Vining Canyon, bighorn sheep, transplanted from the southern Sierra, sprinted for high country when they were turned loose in 1986. They now repopulate this long-vacant but historic homeland. Domestic sheep had finally been removed when the Yosemite Association, a nongovernment organization, acquired grazing rights from a private rancher who had preempted the national forest land essential to the native sheep.

Other wildlife does not do as well as the bighorns. Seeing radically declining deer herds, the state Fish and Game Department in 1987 scheduled a hunting season on mountain lions, which had been protected since 1972. The Mountain Lion Preservation Foundation won a delay through court action requiring that an adequate environmental statement be produced. The foundation documented that habitat loss is the deer herds' main problem, not lion predation. The Department of Forestry, for example, determined that since 1945, more than 590,584 acres of deer and lion habitat statewide were lost to urbanization and agriculture. In the Sierra, Nevada County is the fastest growing county, with a phenomenal population increase of 37.6 percent between 1980 and 1986. The county's general plan dryly states, "Larger mammals will become virtually nonexistent."

The state Department of Finance estimated that the statewide population will increase from 26,365,000 in 1987 to 32,853,000 in the year 2000 and to an anthill of 39,619,000 by 2020—a 1.4 percent average annual increase. Counties where the Sierra constitute 50 percent or more of the land area will grow from 418,600 people in 1987 to an estimated 655,577 in 2000 and 939,677 in 2020. The issue of crowding will affect more than wildlife. Those people who enjoy the mountains today may be more than tempted to move to Alaska, Idaho, or at least the east side of the Sierra.

At Mammoth, Dave McCoy, seventy-two, is aware of population trends and plans to expand his web of chair lifts to his newly acquired June Lake ski area and increase his snowy empire—which is already quite large relative to other ski areas worldwide—by a factor of five. "Nothing stops us." Eight miles of wildland frontage along the eastern Sierra would be Mammothed, not to mention a runaway multiplication of urban facilities catering to consumer appetites of Southern Californians and built in or near the seething Long Valley Caldera. The ski runs would be sensational, as anyone who has telemarked off San Joaquin Ridge knows. However, something may stop McCoy. His supply line of skiers is 350 miles long, the price of gas will go up again, a recession may cut discretionary spending, and opposition from those who enjoy the east side the way it is will surely surface. Another developer's plans for a Sherwin Bowl ski area are being refined just south of town.

The east side's economy, however, is chronically poor. In modern-day California, that means the place will not be suburbanized to the hilt, and the number of new K-Marts will be limited. This wondrous region may be one of few remaining refuges from the urban madness that engulfs so much of California and promises to engulf so much more.

Speaking of madness, fisheries biologist Phil Pister was again honored by a professional organization, but he opened a public talk by singing, "I'm nothing but a hound dog." Perhaps no one but Pister could have persuaded the Federal Energy Regulatory Commission to study cumulative environmental effects of east-side hydroelectric projects, but then he and the Department of Fish and Game boycotted the study because inadequate data were being used. Pister is winning; most projects are at a stalemate, and the state Energy Commission says that California does not need the power.

From Lone Pine, Christy Lynch moved to another teaching job in a small town on the California coast, where she lives within sight of the ocean, but she misses the mountains and visits when she can.

In the southern Sierra, acid rain and ozone worsen and threaten to be a chief plague of developed nations worldwide. Mountain biosystems are paying the price of noxious air elsewhere. Forests of the Alps could be lost to acid rain in no more than a few decades. Are New England and the Sierra next?

Also in the southern Sierra, Bob Barnes loaned $10,000 of his own money to hold the 1985 California Wilderness Conference—a fabulous celebration, reunion, and political plotting extravaganza attended by 500, who listened to Senator Alan Cranston address national forest management: "It's time to stop a timber-first policy and to start a conservation-first policy." After a standing ovation, the senior senator, so often reflecting a serious lifetime of political hardball, said, "I've made you feel good, now you've made me feel good, and isn't that the way it ought to be?"

On another occasion, Senator Pete Wilson, who was pushed tenaciously by Friends of the River and wilderness advocates until he yielded, said, "The push to build and develop . . . is being replaced by the push to conserve."

It might be apparent from this epilogue that I can't really tell if we are taking one step forward and two back or two forward and one back, but on good days it seems that the times may in fact be changing. Perhaps the most astonishing indicator is Interior Secretary Donald Hodel's proposal to pull the plug in Hetch Hetchy Reservoir, tear down O'Shaughnessy Dam, and return the Tuolumne River in Yosemite National Park to the way it was in John Muir's time. With this idea, Hodel on August 5, 1987, probably became the first high government official to propose the elimination of a major dam—the dam that ignited America's seminal controversy in river, wildland, and park protection. "What a thrilling project that would be," Hodel wrote. As much as $500 million may be needed to remove 674,000 cubic yards of concrete and 760 tons of steel, plus unknown millions to replace the water and power.

San Francisco Mayor Dianne Feinstein, who to her credit had supported protection for the remaining undammed Tuolumne, called O'Shaughnessy a "birthright left by our forefathers."

Hodel countered, "Yosemite National Park is America's birthright," and he stated, "I believe this is a good idea. The question is, can we make it feasible?" No proposal would be pursued, he stressed, without replacement of municipal water supplies.

Two million people in the Bay Area depend on San Francisco's plumbing grid; however, the elimination of the reservoir at Hetch Hetchy may reduce less than half of the municipal supplies because of nearby reservoirs at Lake Eleanor, Cherry Creek, and New Don Pedro. Hetch Hetchy contains only 13 percent of the total storage in the Tuolumne basin. From the massive New Don Pedro Reservoir, half financed by San Francisco, urban residents pay $220 for an acre-foot of water, while irrigating farmers, who still account for 85 percent of the water used in California, pay $4 for an identical amount. Do those prices encourage wise use? Elimination of Hetch Hetchy may cut in half San Francisco's hydroelectric power, 60 percent of which is sold to cover 3 percent of the city's budget.

Many people feared that the secretary's proposal was leverage for a horrible alternative. He wrote, "San Francisco might be willing to fund a portion of Auburn Dam in order to obtain as much or more water than it currently gets from Hetch Hetchy." Pressed immediately on this, Hodel stated that his idea was not to justify Auburn, and that his department was looking comprehensively at the California water system to see if efficiencies can be found to save water and avoid building another dam.

David Brower, seventy-five, took pleasure in seeing one of his more extreme lifelong visions suddenly embraced by a conservative secretary and said, "Conservation of water supplies is the answer."

Congressman Rick Lehman called Hodel "sincere" in his proposal to restore the Tuolumne, but the motivation of this stranger to environmentalism lingered mysteriously in the shadows of the debate. Making about as much sense as anyone, Representative Vic Fasio said, "Maybe he was visited by the ghost of John Muir."

Who knows? Sometimes—especially on these frosty winter nights when stars decorate the Sierra sky behind the granite landmarks I've grown to know in all seasons—sometimes it seems that the Old Man is with us still.

After a remarkable winter in the Sierra Nevada following my journey through the range, I wrote political and public information materials for the Committee to Save the Kings River, led by Donn Furman until the heated battle for that extraordinary canyon was won.

For eight of ten days in mid-October, I saw not a single person as I backpacked to Tehipite Valley and the upper Middle Fork of the Kings (Jerry Meral joined me for the first two days). In case of a snowstorm, I packed an extra three-day supply of food, but I lingered and ate it because I simply did not want to leave. Then I got lost on Spanish Mountain when it finally did snow during my hike out.

Now, after the summer and fall of 1987 in western Canada, which in many ways is what the Sierra used to be, I've returned for another winter in these incomparable mountains, where the rise of land and the quality of light say that I've come home, if only for one more season, if only for one more journey.

Acknowledgments

I offer thanks to all the people in this book for sharing information and stories with me. Additional dozens of people provided help ranging from volumes of government data to driveways where I slept in my van.

Barbara Dean, executive editor of Island Press, offered invaluable support. Her insight, skill, and hard work made the book a reality.

For reading drafts of the entire manuscript, I'd like to thank Jerry Meral, of the Planning and Conservation League, Ronnie James, and Mary Anne Davis. I know of no one else with Jerry's knowledge of the environmental issues facing all of California, including the Sierra. Ronnie and Mary Anne provided excellent suggestions.

Ernest Callenbach offered suggestions about the book's focus. Kathy Garrett was helpful in reading early chapters. Separate chapters were read and improved by Greg Bettencourt, Jack Lynch, Denee Stevenson, Wayne Dakan, Jim Bruner, Ginger Burley, Lars Holbek, Nancy Mertz, Jane Palmer May, Jim Palmer, Mike Prather, Bob Barnes, Jim Eaton, and Linda Brown. Portions of chapters were reviewed by many other people.

Librarians Barbara Lekisch, formerly of the Sierra Club in San Francisco, and Mary Vocelka and Linda Eade in Yosemite helped me with historical sources. Matt Mathes provided information from the Forest Service. Tom Lovering of Alpine West in Sacramento helped with equipment that I needed, Ed Grady provided photocopies at a reasonable cost, and Mark Anderman did his usual superb printing of black and white photos.

My special thanks go to Sharon Negri and Mark Dubois for sharing their Sacramento home, where I worked on parts of the manuscript, to Ronnie James for the use of her cabin on the Ebbetts Pass road, where I started the work, and to Gary Palmer (no relation to me) for the use of his cabin near Donner Pass, where I finished the book.

A Sierra Nevada Almanac

General Statistics of the Sierra Nevada
Selected Historic Events
Historic Environmental Events
Current Environmental Issues
National Parks
National Forests
Wilderness Areas
Counties, Population, and Projected Growth
Towns in the Sierra Nevada Region
Major Reservoirs in the Sierra Nevada and Foothills
Highway Passes
Rivers
Congressional Members and Districts in 1988
Government Agencies
Conservation Organizations

Information in the following lists is usually given from north to south.

General Statistics of the Sierra Nevada

Length	400 miles
Width	50 miles, discounting lower foothills (usually under the 3,000-foot elevation)
Width including foothills	70 miles
Area	20,000 square miles 12.8 million acres
Area counting foothills	28,000 square miles 17.9 million acres
Highest peak	Mount Whitney, 14,494 feet (highest in the U.S. outside Alaska)
Largest glacier	Palisade
Most used national forest	Inyo
Most used national park	Yosemite
Most used national forest wilderness area	John Muir
Number of major highway passes	10
Number of major rivers	15
Population (1987) of counties that include any amount of Sierra Nevada acreage	2,377,286
Population in counties with 50 percent or more of the acreage in the Sierra	418,600
Population estimated in the Sierra Nevada alone, excluding foothills	about 120,000
Recreation visitor-days annually in national forests and national parks	37,085,900 (one visitor-day is when one person spends twelve hours)

Selected Historic Events[a]

About 9734 B.C.   Indian artifacts were left at Clark Flat, Stanislaus River.

About 7764 B.C.   An Indian structure was used at Gabbott Meadow.

1772   First description of the Sierra was written by Fray Juan Crespi.

1776   The name Sierra Nevada was first used.

1827   Jedediah Smith crossed the Sierra at Ebbetts Pass.

1833   Joseph Walker crossed north of Tioga Pass and saw Yosemite Valley.

1834   Walker crossed west-to-east at Walker Pass.

1838   John Muir was born in Scotland.

1841   The Bidwell party crossed at Ebbetts Pass.

1844   John C. Frémont crossed at Carson Pass and saw Lake Tahoe.

1846   The Donner party attempted to cross at Donner Pass; California became a U.S. territory.

1848   Gold was discovered at Sutter's Mill.

1850   California became a state.

1851   James Beckwourth discovered Beckwourth Pass; the Mariposa Battalion entered Yosemite Valley.

1856   Snowshoe Thompson carried mail over the Sierra (until 1869).

1861   Mark Twain visited Lake Tahoe.

1863   Whitney Survey's work on the geography of the Sierra was begun.

1868   John Muir arrived in the Sierra Nevada and Yosemite; Central Pacific Railroad was completed over Donner Pass.

1873   Mount Whitney was climbed.

1874   A wagon road was built to Yosemite Valley.

1875   John Muir traveled through sequoia groves and the southern Sierra.

[a]For more information, see the list of historic environmental events.

Selected Historic Events (Continued)

1892 Hydroelectricity from Green Creek, near Bridgeport, was sent to Bodie.

1895 Hydroelectric power was generated at Folsom on the American River.

1900 The first automobile arrived in Yosemite Valley.

1901 The first Sierra Club outing took place in the Sierra.

1903 The Western Pacific Railroad was built along the North Fork of the Feather.

1911 Ishi left his Indian home near the northern Sierra.

1913 The dam at Lake Almanor was begun; automobiles were officially allowed in Yosemite Valley.

1914 John Muir died.

1917 The first cars crossed Donner Pass.

1925 The dam on the South Fork of the San Joaquin River formed Florence Lake.

1927 The Owens Valley Aqueduct was blown up by ranchers seventeen times.

1931 The first roped climb took place in the Sierra; the John Muir Trail was completed.

1935 The Badger Pass ski area opened.

1949 The Squaw Valley ski area was started.

1957 The first ascent of the northwest face of Half Dome occurred.

1958 The first ascent of El Capitan was made.

1960 The Winter Olympics were held at Squaw Valley; Interstate 80 was completed over Donner Pass.

1962 Commercial rafting began on the Stanislaus River.

1968 The Pacific Crest Trail was included in the National Trails System Act.

1986 February floods occurred in the northern Sierra; massive avalanches occurred.

1987 Forest fires were the worst in Sierra history.

Historic Environmental Events

1864 Yosemite was designated for protection, to be administered by California.

1884 Hydraulic mining was prohibited in California.

1890 Sequoia National Park was established; Yosemite National Park was established.

1892 The Sierra Club organized.

1893 Forest Reserves (national forests) were established.

1900 A Lake Tahoe National Park was first proposed.

1905 Tuolumne headwaters were added to Yosemite National Park; the Minarets and western areas were deleted.

1906 Yosemite Valley was ceded back to the federal government.

1910 Miners applied to dam the Middle Fork of the San Joaquin River at Devils Postpile.

1911 Devils Postpile National Monument was designated.

1913 The Raker Act authorized the damming of Hetch Hetchy Valley; the Owens Valley Aqueduct was finished.

1916 The National Park Service was formed; the Merced River hydroelectric dam was authorized in Yosemite.

1922 O'Shaughnessy dam was built at Hetch Hetchy Valley.

1923 Kings River dam proposals were rejected by the federal Power Commission.

1924 The last sighting of a grizzly bear occurred in the Sierra.

1926 Sequoia National Park was expanded to Mount Whitney.

1938 O'Shaughnessy Dam was raised 86 feet.

1940 Kings Canyon National Park was established.

1941 The Owens Valley Aqueduct was extended to the Mono basin.

1952 Los Angeles applied to dam the Kings River.

1955 A resolution for Minaret Summit Road passed the California legislature.

1957 The League to Save Lake Tahoe was organized; the Emerald Bay bridge was opposed.

1959 The Tahoe Area Council was organized.

1961 The new Tioga Pass Road was dedicated after opposition by David Brower and others.

1963 The first Tahoe Basin plan was written.

1964 The Wilderness Act was passed, including Sierra areas.

1965 Kings Canyon National Park was expanded; Disney Enterprises proposed a Mineral King ski area.

1968 The Feather River was designated a national wild and scenic river.

1970 The Tahoe Regional Planning Agency was organized; a second Owens Valley Aqueduct was finished.

1971 The first Yosemite Valley plan was written.

1972 The Supreme Court ruled on Mineral King; Friends of Mammoth won an injunction against high-rise development.

1973 Friends of the River was organized; a statewide initiative against New Melones Dam lost.

1975 Disney Enterprises suspended planning of Mineral King ski area; Auburn Dam construction was halted.

1976 Kings Canyon and Sequoia national parks were designated International Biosphere Reserves.

1977 Horseshoe Meadows ski area was stopped.

1978 Mineral King was added to Sequoia National Park; the North Fork of the American was added to the national rivers system; Giant Gap dam was stopped.

1980 The lower American River was added to the national rivers system; a Yosemite Valley plan was approved.

1982 The Stanislaus River Canyon was flooded by New Melones Dam; dams on the South Fork of the American were temporarily stopped.

1983 The California Supreme Court ruled on the Public Trust Doctrine in favor of Mono Lake; a biomass power plant was defeated near Quincy.

1984 The California Wilderness Act was passed; the Tuolumne River was added to the national rivers system; a Mono Lake Scenic Area was designated.

1985 Yosemite National Park was designated a World Heritage Site.

1986 Bighorn sheep were reintroduced in Lee Vining Canyon.

1987 The upper South Fork American hydroelectric dam was built at Sayles Flat; Kings River was added to the national rivers system; the Rogers Crossing Dam was stopped; the Merced River was added to the national rivers system; the North and South Forks of the Kern were added to the national rivers system; forest resource plans were completed; increased clearcutting was allowed; the interior secretary ordered a study of the elimination of O'Shaughnessy Dam.

1988 The campaign to stop Auburn Dam intensified.

Issue	Conservation Organization Involved[a]
Clearcutting	Sierra Club, Audubon Society, others
Pesticide and herbicide spraying	Local groups
National forest planning	Sierra Club, others
Weather modification (cloud seeding)	None
Grazing	Sierra Club
Stock use	None
Land development	Local groups
Off-road vehicles	Sierra Club chapters
Wilderness designation	California Wilderness Coalition
Mountain lion hunting	Mountain Lion Preservation Foundation
Acid rain and ozone	Sierra Club
Regional Issues, from North to South	
Indian Creek dam	Friends of Indian Creek
Fall River hydroelectric project	Friends of the River
Lake Tahoe water quality	League to Save Lake Tahoe
Yuba River dams	South Yuba Citizens League
Auburn Dam	Protect American River Canyons, Friends of the River
Power line across northern Sierra	Sierra Transmission Opposition Party
Mono Lake diversions	Mono Lake Committee
Caples Creek dam	Friends of the River
Mokelumne River dams	Friends of the River
Merced River dam at Bagby	Merced Canyon Committee
Mammoth ski area expansion	Sierra Club, Toiyabe Chapter
Sherwin Bowl ski proposal	Sierra, Toiyabe Chapter
Geothermal development	Sierra Club, Toiyabe Chapter
Crowley Reservoir expansion	Owens Valley Committee
Owens Valley groundwater	Owens Valley Committee
Peppermint ski area	Peppermint Alert
Bureau of Land Management wilderness	Sierra Club
Kern River dam (Hobo Project)	Friends of the River

[a]Sierra Club chapters are involved in nearly all land-based issues; Friends of the River, in nearly all river issues. Various groups are active on locally important issues not in this list. The addresses of conservation organizations appear in a separate list.

National Parks

Park	Acreage	Year Established	Selected Highlights	Address	Visits in 1986	Visitor-Days[a]
Yosemite	762,567	1890 1906	Yosemite Valley, Tuolumne Meadows, Half Dome, Mariposa Grove	Yosemite National Park, CA 95389	2,876,700	6,379,900
Kings Canyon	461,901	1940	Kings River, Palisades, Cedar Grove, Grant Grove, Tehipite Valley	Three Rivers, CA 93271	1,028,800	2,796,100
Sequoia	402,579	1890 1926 1978	Sequoia trees, Mount Whitney, Mineral King, Kaweah River	Three Rivers, CA 93271	1,056,500	2,879,100
Devils Postpile National Monument	798	1911	Basalt columns, Middle Fork of San Joaquin River	% Sequoia National Park, Three Rivers, CA 93271	89,500	30,800
Total:	1,627,845; 12.7 percent of the Sierra Nevada				5,051,500	12,085,900

[a]One visitor-day is when one person spends twelve hours. This corresponds to data used by the Forest Service.

National Forests

Forest and Address	Acres	Selected Highlights	Board Feet Cut in 1984 (millions)	Visitor-Days in 1986
Plumas 159 Lawrence Street Quincy, CA 95971 (916) 283-2050	1,161,724	Feather River, Bucks Lake, Grizzly Peak	182	2,034,400
Tahoe Highway 49 and Coyote Street Nevada City, CA 95959 (916) 265-4531	827,242	Lake Tahoe, ski areas, Yuba River, Castle Peak	143	5,101,000 Lake Tahoe management unit: 2,559,200
Eldorado 100 Forni Road Placerville, CA 95667 (916) 622-5061	674,286	Lake Tahoe, American River, Pyramid Peak, ski areas	93	3,377,100
Stanislaus 19777 Greenley Road Sonora, CA 95370 (209) 532-3671	898,616	Stanislaus River, Pinecrest Lake, Dardanelles, Tuolumne River	92	2,207,000
Toiyabe 1200 Franklin Way Sparks, NV 89431 (702) 784-5331	291,144 in Sierra 3,207,352 total	Carson River, Hope Valley, Walker River, east side of Sierra		

National Forests (Continued)

Forest and Address	Acres	Selected Highlights	Board Feet Cut in 1984 (millions)	Visitor-Days in 1986
Inyo 873 North Main Street Bishop, CA 93514 (619) 873-5841	1,800,884 in Sierra 1,886,736 total	Mammoth, Whitney Portal, Convict Lake, east side of Sierra	13	6,040,900
Sierra 1130 O Street Fresno, CA 93721 (209) 487-5155	1,303,201	Kings River, Bass Lake, Huntington Lake	110	3,862,400
Sequoia 900 West Grand Avenue Porterville, CA 93257 (209) 784-1500	1,124,185	Sequoia trees, Kern River, Kern Plateau	91	2,701,800
Total: 8 forests	8,081,282 in Sierra Nevada; 63.1 percent of the Sierra Nevada		724	27,883,800

Other addresses:

Lake Tahoe Basin Management Unit, 870 Emerald Bay Road, Box 8465, South Lake Tahoe, CA 95731 (916) 544-6420

Forest Service Regional Office, 630 Sansome Street, San Francisco, CA 94111 (415) 556-4310

Wilderness Areas

Area	National Forest or Park	Acres	Visitor-Days in 1986	Date Designated
Bucks Lake	Plumas	21,000	11,600	1984
Granite Chief	Tahoe	25,000	54,600	1984
Desolation	Eldorado	63,475	227,500	1969
Mokelumne	Eldorado, Stanislaus, Toiyabe	105,165	25,400	1964
Carson-Iceberg	Stanislaus, Toiyabe	160,000	33,900	1984
Emigrant	Stanislaus	117,596	59,900	1975; additions in 1984
Hoover	Toiyabe, Inyo	47,937	49,000	1964
Yosemite	Yosemite (park)	677,600	528,070[a] (105,614 people)	1984
Ansel Adams	Sierra, Inyo	221,000	159,800	1984, including former Minarets Wilderness of 1964
Kaiser	Sierra	22,700	14,400	1976
John Muir	Inyo, Sierra	584,000	451,400	1964
Dinkey Lakes	Sierra	30,000	24,700	1984

Wilderness Areas (Continued)

Area	National Forest or Park	Acres	Visitor-Days in 1986	Date Designated
Monarch	Sierra, Sequoia	56,952	1,300	1984
Jennie Lakes	Sequoia	10,500	30,800	1984
Kings Canyon	Kings Canyon (park)	456,552	370,160[a] (74,032 people)	1984
Sequoia	Sequoia (park)	280,428	406,090[a] (81,218 people)	1984
Golden Trout	Inyo, Sequoia	303,287	69,600	1978
South Sierra	Sequoia, Inyo	63,000	2,100	1984
Dome Land	Sequoia	94,686	4,300	1964; additions in 1984
Total: 19 areas		3,340,878; 26.1 percent of the Sierra Nevada		
		1,414,580 acres in national parks are 86.9 percent of national park acreage		
		1,926,298 acres in national forests are 23.8 percent of national forest acreage		

[a]The Park Service counts people, not visitor-days. The visitor-day figure is an estimate.

Counties, Population, and Projected Growth

County	Address of Planning Agency	Population in 1987 and Projected for 2000[a]	Area in Square Miles[b]	Percent and Square Miles of County in Sierra Nevada[c]
Plumas	P.O. Box 437 Quincy, CA 95971 (916) 283-2000	19,277 23,800	2,618	90% 2,356
Butte	7 County Center Drive Oroville, CA 95965 (916) 534-4601	164,002 221,900	1,670	10% 167
Yuba	938 14th Street Marysville, CA 95901 (916) 741-6418	54,052 63,200	640	10% 64
Sierra	P.O. Box 530 Downieville, CA 95936 (916) 289-3251	3,420 4,100	959	90% 863
Nevada	700 Zion Street Nevada City, CA 95959 (916) 265-1440	69,199 113,800	978	60% 587
Placer	11414 B Avenue Auburn, CA 95603 (916) 823-4721	139,948 203,700	1,500	50% 750
Washoe (Nevada)	P.O. Box 11130 Reno, NV 89520 (702) 785-4043	236,480 364,171	6,317	2% 126
Douglas (Nevada)	P.O. Box 218 Minden, NV 89423 (702) 782-9000	25,200 45,277	708	60% 425
El Dorado	360 Fair Lane Placerville, CA 95667 (916) 626-2438	105,666 158,500	1,708	70% 1,196
Alpine	Route 1, Box 37 Markleeville, CA 96120 (916) 694-2255	1,216 1,600	723	100% 723
Amador	108 Court Street Jackson, CA 95642 (209) 223-6380	23,452 36,800	601	40% 240
Calaveras	Government Center San Andreas, CA 95249 (209) 754-3841	27,214 42,800	1,100	50% 550

Counties, Population, and Projected Growth (Continued)

County	Address of Planning Agency	Population in 1987 and Projected for 2000[a]	Area in Square Miles[b]	Percent and Square Miles of County in Sierra Nevada[c]
Tuolumne	2 South Green Street Sonora, CA 95370 (209) 533-5611	41,713 64,600	2,217	80% 1,774
Mono	P.O. Box 8 Bridgeport, CA 93517 (619) 932-7911	9,146 10,600	3,000	40% 1,200
Mariposa	P.O. Box 2039 Mariposa, CA 95338 (209) 966-5151	13,407 20,300	1,463	60% 878
Madera	135 West Yosemite Avenue Madera, CA 93637 (209) 675-7821	77,434 115,500	2,147	30% 644
Fresno	4499 East Kings Canyon Road Fresno, CA 93702 (209) 488-2992	578,926 734,000	6,000	30% 1,800
Inyo	P.O. Drawer L Independence, CA 93526 (619) 878-2411	18,063 18,800	10,141	20% 2,028
Tulare	County Civic Center, Room 111 Visalia, CA 93291 (209) 733-6254	282,984 393,400	4,863	40% 1,945
Kern	1415 Truxtun Avenue Bakersfield, CA 93301 (805) 861-2615	486,487 662,600	8,490	20% 1,698
Total:	20 counties	2,377,286 3,299,448	57,843	20,014

Population data from California State Census Data Center, Department of Finance.

[a]Projections by the California Department of Finance, based on Bureau of Census data.

[b]One square mile equals 640 acres.

[c]Approximate acreage, excluding foothills that are generally below 3,000 feet.

Towns in the Sierra Nevada Region

Town	County	Population	Elevation	Incorpo-rated
*Chester	Plumas	1,756	4,525	No
*Susanville	Lassen	6,715	4,255	Yes
*Westwood	Lassen	2,081	5,113	No
Greenville	Plumas	1,537	3,570	No
Taylorsville	Plumas	357	3,545	No
Quincy	Plumas	4,451	3,423	No
Portola	Plumas	2,074	4,850	Yes
La Porte	Plumas	52	4,959	No
Downieville	Sierra	400	2,865	No
Loyalton	Sierra	1,181	4,955	Yes
Sierraville	Sierra	200	4,950	No
*Nevada City	Nevada	2,838	2,525	Yes
*Grass Valley	Nevada	8,742	2,420	Yes
*Colfax	Nevada	992	2,420	Yes
*Coloma	El Dorado	300	750	No
*Reno, NV	Washoe	118,520	4,400	Yes
*Sparks, NV	Washoe	51,700	4,400	Yes
Truckee	Nevada	2,389	5,820	No
Soda Springs	Nevada	336	6,768	No
*Auburn	Placer	8,519	1,255	Yes
Foresthill	Placer	1,304	3,225	No
Kings Beach	Placer	1,942	6,245	No
Tahoe City	Placer	1,836	6,240	No
South Lake Tahoe	El Dorado	21,858	6,260	Yes
Stateline, NV	Douglas	1,500	6,260	Yes
*Carson City, NV	(city)	36,650	4,687	Yes
*Minden/ Gardnerville, NV	Douglas	18,600	4,740	No
Pollock Pines	El Dorado	1,941	3,980	No
*Placerville	El Dorado	7,381	1,860	Yes
Woodfords	Alpine	150	5,630	No
Markleeville	Alpine	100	5,501	No
*Sutter Creek	Amador	1,995	1,198	Yes
*Jackson	Amador	3,277	1,200	Yes
*Mokelumne Hill	Calaveras	600	1,474	No

Towns in the Sierra Nevada Region (Continued)

Town	County	Population	Elevation	Incorpo-rated
*San Andreas	Calaveras	1,912	1,008	No
*Angels Camp	Calaveras	2,409	1,379	Yes
*Murphys	Calaveras	1,183	2,171	No
Arnold	Calaveras	2,385	4,000	No
Bear Valley	Alpine	250	7,030	No
Bridgeport	Mono	510	6,465	No
*Sonora	Tuolumne	4,165	1,796	Yes
Twain Harte	Tuolumne	1,369	3,650	No
Pinecrest	Tuolumne	500	5,600	No
Strawberry	Tuolumne	300	5,230	No
*Groveland	Tuolumne	350	2,844	No
Yosemite Valley	Mariposa	1,073	3,960	No
*El Portal	Mariposa	470	2,100	No
*Mariposa	Mariposa	1,150	1,953	No
Lee Vining	Mono	301	6,780	No
Mammoth Lakes	Mono	4,480	7,860	Yes
*Oakhurst	Madera	1,959	2,290	No
Bishop	Inyo	3,552	4,140	Yes
Big Pine	Inyo	1,510	3,985	No
Independence	Inyo	1,000	3,925	No
Lone Pine	Inyo	1,684	3,700	No
Shaver Lake	Fresno	1,000	5,530	No
Dinkey Creek	Fresno	420	5,920	No
*Three Rivers	Tulare	1,422	800	No
*Springville	Tulare	1,540	1,032	No
*Kernville	Kern	1,660	2,700	No
*Lake Isabella	Kern	3,428	2,512	No
*Tehachapi	Kern	4,645	3,969	Yes

Total: 360,901 (includes Reno/Sparks); about 63,942 in towns in Sierra Nevada, excluding foothills

Population data from California State Census Data Center (incorporated towns) and Department of Transportation (unincorporated towns, which often include population estimated from nearby areas).

* Towns in foothills (below 3,000-foot elevation) and in areas near the Sierra Nevada.

Major Reservoirs in the Sierra Nevada and Foothills[a]

River	Reservoir	Capacity in Acre-Feet
Feather	Almanor	1,308,000
	Oroville	3,625,000
	Bucks Lake	103,000
Yuba	New Bullards Bar	961,300
	Jackson Meadow	52,500
	Spaulding	74,773
	Englebright	70,000
American	French Meadows	134,000
	Hell Hole	270,000
	Loon Lake	76,500
	Union Valley	141,500
	Folsom	1,010,000
Truckee	Stampede	225,195
	Lake Tahoe	122,300,000 (745,000 used as a reservoir)
Carson	None[b]	
Walker	None[b]	
Mokelumne	Salt Springs	139,000
Stanislaus	New Spicer Meadow	189,000 (under construction)
	Relief	15,122
	Donnells	64,500
	Beardsley	97,500
	Pinecrest	18,600
	New Melones	2,420,000

Major Reservoirs in the Sierra Nevada and Foothills (Continued)

River	Reservoir	Capacity in Acre-Feet
Tuolumne	Cherry Creek (Lloyd)	268,000
	Eleanor	27,100
	O'Shaughnessy	360,360
	New Don Pedro	2,030,000
Merced	McClure	1,025,000
San Joaquin	Edison	125,000
	Mammoth	123,000
	Bass	45,410
	Huntington	88,834
	Shaver	135,000
	Millerton	520,000
	Friant	520,500
Kings	Courtright	123,000
	Wishon	128,000
	Pine Flat	1,000,000
Kaweah	Kaweah	150,000
Tule	Success	202,000
Kern	Isabella	570,000
Owens	Grant	47,525
	Crowley	184,000

[a]This list includes large reservoirs and others of special interest. Many reservoirs are not included; for example, there are eighteen in the Stanislaus basin.

[b]Diversion dams and reservoirs are found outside the Sierra Nevada.

Highway Passes

Pass	High-way	Elevation	River Seen from Road	National Forest or Park	Average Number of Vehicles per Day, 1986, and Average per Day in Peak Month
Major highway passes					
Beck-wourth	70	5,212	N. Fork Feather	Plumas	3,000
			M. Fork Feather		4,150
Highway 89	89	5,440	M. Fork Feather	Tahoe	900
			Little Truckee		1,450
Donner	I-80 40	7,239	S. Fork Yuba	Tahoe	20,400
			Truckee		28,500
Johnson (Echo Summit)	50	7,382	S. Fork American	Eldorado	11,000 15,700
Carson	88	8,573	Caples Creek	Eldorado	2,100
			W. Fork Carson		3,900
Ebbetts Closed in winter	4	8,731	N. Fork Stanislaus	Stanislaus	600[a]
			Mokelumne E. Fork Carson		1,050
Sonora Closed in winter	108	9,624	M. Fork Stanislaus	Stanislaus	670[a]
			W. Fork Walker		940
Tioga Closed in winter	120	9,945	Tuolumne Dana Fork Lee Vining Creek	Yosemite Inyo	1,250[a] 1,700

Highway Passes (Continued)

Pass	High-way	Elevation	River Seen from Road	National Forest or Park	Average Number of Vehicles per Day, 1986, and Average per Day in Peak Month
Sherman (Kennedy Meadows Road) Closed in winter, gravel road	22S05[b]	9,120	N. Fork Kern S. Fork Kern	Sequoia	
Walker	178	5,250	Kern S. Fork Kern	None	2,500 3,000
At northern border of the Sierra: Fredonyer	36	5,748	N. Fork Feather	Lassen	1,950 2,500
At southern border of the Sierra: Tehachapi	58	4,064	None	None	10,500 12,400

Minor highway passes

Forest Service (FS) Route 31, south of Beckwourth Pass

FS S860, south of Beckwourth Pass

FS 650, south of Beckwourth Pass

FS 07 (Henness Pass), south of Beckwourth Pass

FS 501, north of Tehachapi Pass

FS 29S02, north of Tehachapi Pass

---

[a]Average for months when the road is open, usually May through October.

[b]Forest Service road.

Rivers

River	Source	Avg. Vol. in Acre-Ft. per Year	Rank in Vol.	Area of Basin in Sq. Mi.[a]	Rank in Area	Recreational Uses[b]
*Feather	Lake Almanor Beckwourth Pass	4,430,000	1	3,626	1	f, k
Yuba	Yuba Pass Sierra Buttes	2,297,000	3	1,193	8	f, r, k, g, s
*American	Donner Pass Johnson Pass Desolation Wilderness	2,620,000	2	1,888	4	r, k, c, s, f, g
Truckee	Red Lake Peak Stevens Peak	609,000	11	970	11	f, r, k, c
Carson	Carson Pass Ebbetts Pass	338,000	14	471	15	f, r, c
Walker	Sonora Pass Hawksbeak Peak	295,000	15	910	12	f
Mokelumne	Ebbetts Pass	721,000	9	578	13	c, f
Stanislaus	Airola Peak Sonora Pass	1,116,000	7	986	10	f, k
*Tuolumne	Tioga Pass Mount Lyell	1,835,000	4	1,532	7	f, r, k, h
*Merced	Mount Lyell Yosemite Park	952,000	8	1,037	9	h, f, r, k, c
San Joaquin	Ritter Peak Mount Goddard	1,742,000	5	1,676	6	h, f, k
*Kings	North Palisade Kings Canyon Park	1,631,000	6	1,693	5	f, r, h, k, c
Kaweah	Kaweah-Kern Divide	431,000	13	561	14	f, k
*Kern	Mount Whitney Kings-Kern Divide Kaweah-Kern Divide	720,000	10	2,407	3	f, r, k, s
Owens	Deadman Summit Mammoth Mountain	500,000	12	3,197	2	f, c
Total:	15 rivers	20,237,000 (several small rivers not included)		22,725 (includes area outside the Sierra, but due to gauge locations, does not include all of the lands in each basin)		

*Rivers with sections designated as national wild and scenic rivers.
[a] Area above volume gauges, usually located at lower reaches of the river (California Department of Water Resources data).
[b] f: fishing; r: rafting; k: kayaking; c: canoeing; s: swimming; g: gold mining. (To some degree, nearly all rivers provide for most of these uses.)

Congressional Members and Districts in 1988

District	Member	Counties in Sierra	Address
2	Eugene Chappie (R)	Butte Yuba Nevada	270 East 4th Street Chico, CA 95926 (916) 893-8363
14	Eugene Shumway (R)	Plumas Sierra Nevada Placer El Dorado Alpine Amador	1150 West Robinhood Stockton, CA 95207 (209) 957-7773
15	Tony Coelho (D)	Mariposa	1130 O Street Fresno, CA 93721 (209) 487-5004
17	Charles Pashayan (R)	Fresno Tulare Kern	1702 East Bullard, #103 Fresno, CA 93710 (209) 487-5487
18	Richard Lehman (D)	Calaveras Tuolumne Mono Madera	1900 Mariposa Mall Fresno, CA 93721 (209) 487-5760
20	William Thomas (R)	Inyo Kern	1830 Truxtun Avenue Bakersfield, CA 93301 (805) 327-3611

Senators

Alan Cranston (D)

45 Polk Street
San Francisco, CA 94102
(415) 556-8440

5757 West Century Boulevard, #515
Los Angeles, CA 90045
(213) 215-2188

Pete Wilson (R)

880 Front Street, 6-S-9
San Diego, CA 92188
(619) 293-5257

450 Golden Gate Avenue
San Francisco, CA 94102
(415) 556-4307

Government Agencies

Agency	Address	Responsibilities
Federal		
Forest Service (Department of Agriculture)	630 Sansome Street San Francisco, CA 94111 (415) 556-4310 (See list of national forests for individual forest addresses.)	Administration of national forests
National Park Service (Department of the Interior)	450 Golden Gate Avenue San Francisco, CA 94102 (415) 556-8200	Administration of national parks
Geological Survey (Department of the Interior)	345 Middlefield Road Menlo Park, CA 94025 (415) 853-8300	Geological and related information
Army Corps of Engineers	650 Capitol Mall Sacramento, CA 95814 (916) 440-2292	Army corps dams; flood control
Bureau of Reclamation	2800 Cottage Way Sacramento, CA 95825 (916) 484-4678	Bureau of Reclamation dams; irrigation
State		
Department of Fish and Game (California Resources Agency)	1416 9th Street, 12th floor Sacramento, CA 95814 (916) 445-3531	Fish and wildlife protection and management

Government Agencies (Continued)

Agency	Address	Responsibilities
Department of Water Resources (California Resources Agency)	1416 9th Street Sacramento, CA 95814 (916) 445-9248	Water resource data; state water project water conservation
Department of Forestry (California Resources Agency)	1416 9th Street Sacramento, CA 95814 (916) 445-9920	Nonfederal forest resources
Department of Transportation	1120 N Street Sacramento, CA 95814 (916) 445-4616	State and federal roads
Air Resources Board	P.O. Box 2815 Sacramento, CA 95812 (916) 322-2990	Air quality
Office of Planning and Research	1400 10th Street Sacramento, CA 95814 (916) 322-2318	Land use and other data

Local

Counties: See list of counties

Los Angeles Department of Water and Power	111 North Hope Street Los Angeles, CA 90012 (213) 481-4211	Owens Valley Aqueduct and water system
Tahoe Regional Planning Agency	195 Highway 50 P.O. Box 1038 Zephyr Cove, NV 89448 (702) 588-4547	Planning and resource management in the Tahoe basin

Conservation Organizations

California Native Plant
Society
2380 Ellsworth, Suite D
Berkeley, CA 94720
(415) 841-5575

California Trout
870 Market Street, #859
San Francisco, CA 94102
(415) 392-8887

California Wilderness Coalition
2655 Portage Bay, #3
Davis, CA 95616
(916) 758-0380

Committee to Save the Kings
River
7591 North Angus Street
Fresno, CA 93710
(209) 436-1191

Friends of the River
909 12th Street
Sacramento, CA 95814
(916) 442-3155

League to Save Lake Tahoe
P.O. Box 10110
South Lake Tahoe, CA 95731
(916) 541-5388

Merced Canyon Committee
P.O. Box 152
El Portal, CA 95318

Mono Lake Committee
P.O. Box 29
Lee Vining, CA 93541
(619) 647-6360
or
1355 Westwood Boulevard, #6
Los Angeles, CA 90024
(213) 477-5754

Mountain Lion Preservation
Foundation
P.O. Box 1896
Sacramento, CA 95809
(916) 442-2666

National Audubon Society,
Western Regional Office
555 Audubon Place
Sacramento, CA 95825
(916) 481-5332

Owens Valley Committee
P.O. Box 330
Lone Pine, CA 93545

Conservation Organizations (Continued)

Peppermint Alert
P.O. Box 8332
Porterville, CA 93257
(209) 781-8445

Planning and Conservation
League
909 12th Street
Sacramento, CA 95814
(916) 444-8726

Protect American River
Canyons
P.O. Box 9312
Auburn, CA 95604

Sierra Club, National Office
730 Polk Street
San Francisco, CA 94109
(415) 776-2211

Sierra Club, Northern California Field Office
5428 College Avenue
Oakland, CA 94618
(415) 654-7847

Sierra Club, Southern California Field Office
3550 West 6th Street, #323
Los Angeles, CA 90020
(213) 387-6528

Sierra Club, Mother Lode
Chapter
P.O. Box 1335
Sacramento, CA 95806
(916) 444-2180

Sierra Club, Kern-Kaweah
Chapter
P.O. Box 3357
Bakersfield, CA 93385
(805) 323-3463

Sierra Club, Tehipite Chapter
P.O. Box 5396
Fresno, CA 93755
(209) 233-1820

Sierra Club, Toiyabe Chapter
P.O. Box 8096
Reno, NV 89507
(702) 323-3162

The Wilderness Society
1791 Pine Street
San Francisco, CA 94108
(415) 771-2020

Sources

A variety of sources were used in writing this book. Many of the important references follow. I relied heavily on interviews, while checking other sources for much of the material.

Also helpful but not listed were a complete set of *Headwaters* (Friends of the River's newsletter), the complete collections of the *Sierra Club Bulletin* and *Sierra* magazines at the club's library in San Francisco, and the newsletters of the Mono Lake Committee, the League to Save Lake Tahoe, and others. The *Sacramento Bee* was an excellent source of news articles, and articles by Gene Rose in the *Fresno Bee* were especially helpful. Dozens of government reports were consulted, including forestland management and resource plans (drafts), which are available for each national forest. Maps of national forests and topographic maps from the U.S. Geological Survey were used extensively.

GENERAL SOURCES

Browning, Peter. *Place Names of the Sierra Nevada.* Berkeley: Wilderness Press, 1986.

Farquhar, Francis P. *History of the Sierra Nevada*. Berkeley: University of California Press, 1965.

Farquhar, Francis P. *Place Names of the High Sierra*. San Francisco: Sierra Club, 1926.

Grater, Russell K. *Discovering Sierra Mammals*. El Portal, Calif.: Yosemite Natural History Association, 1978.

Hill, Mary, *Geology of the Sierra Nevada*. Berkeley: University of California Press, 1975.

Jerome, John. *On Mountains*. New York: McGraw-Hill, 1978.

Johnston, Verna R. *Sierra Nevada*. Boston: Houghton Mifflin Co., 1970. (natural history)

Lee, W. Storrs. *The Sierra*. New York: G. P. Putnam's Sons, 1962. (history)

Peattie, Roderick. *The Sierra Nevada: The Range of Light*. New York: Vanguard Press, 1947.

Price, Larry W. *Mountains and Man*. Berkeley: University of California Press, 1981. (mountain geography)

Reid, Robert Leonard, ed. *A Treasury of the Sierra Nevada*. Berkeley: Wilderness Press, 1983. (Sierra literature)

Storrer, Tracy I., and Usinger, Robert L. *Sierra Nevada Natural History*. Berkeley: University of California Press, 1963.

Webster, Paul, and the editors of the American West. *The Mighty Sierra*. New York: American West Publishing Co., 1972.

United States Department of Agriculture, Forest Service. *Facts about the National Forests in California*. (Brochure.) San Francisco: Forest Service, 1984.

Whitney, Stephen. *A Sierra Club Naturalist's Guide: The Sierra Nevada*. San Francisco: Sierra Club Books, 1979.

SOURCES ABOUT JOHN MUIR

Clark, James Mitchell. *The Life and Adventures of John Muir*. San Francisco: Sierra Club Books, 1980.

Cohen, Michael. *The Pathless Way*. Madison: University of Wisconsin Press, 1984.

Engberg, Robert, and Wesling, Donald, eds. *John Muir: To Yosemite and Beyond: Writings from the Years 1863 to 1875*. Madison: University of Wisconsin Press, 1980.

Fox, Stephen. *The American Conservation Movement: John Muir and His Legacy*. Madison: University of Wisconsin Press, 1985.

Muir, John. *The Mountains of California*. New York: Doubleday and Co., Inc., in cooperation with the American Museum of Natural History, 1961.

Muir, John. *My First Summer in the Sierra*. Boston: Houghton Mifflin Co., 1911.

Muir, John. *Our Yosemite National Park*. Golden, Colo.: Outbooks, 1980.

Turner, Frederick. *Rediscovering America: John Muir in His Time and Ours*. New York: Viking, 1985.

SOURCES BY CHAPTER

Chapter 2   The North

Biswell, H. H. "Man and Fire in Ponderosa Pine." *Sierra Club Bulletin*, October 1959.

Brower, David, ed. *Gentle Wilderness: The Sierra Nevada*. San Francisco: Sierra Club, 1967. (picture book)

California Department of Water Resources. *The California State Water Project, Bulletin No. 132*. Sacramento: Department of Water Resources.

Forrester, Steve. "Forest Service at a Loss." *Sierra*, November 1984.

Hanson, Dennis G. *Growth Stock: Trees for California*. Sacramento: California State Office of Appropriate Technology, 1982.

Muench, David, and Pike, Don. *Sierra Nevada*. Portland: Charles H. Belding, 1979. (picture book)

Plumas County Chamber of Commerce. *County Economic Profile*. Quincy: Plumas County Chamber of Commerce, 1984.

Raphael, Ray. *Tree Talk*. Covelo, Calif.: Island Press, 1981.

Wilderness Society. *National Forest Planning*. (Booklet.) Washington, D.C.: Wilderness Society, 1983.

United States Department of Agriculture, Forest Service. *Wildfire*. (Brochure.) Washington, D.C.: U.S. Government Printing Office, 1983.

United States Department of Agriculture, Forest Service. *Land Use Plan, Almanor Planning Unit, Lassen and Plumas National Forests*. Quincy, Calif.: Forest Service, 1977.

Interviews

Jerry Adams, Plumas National Forest, Quincy, timber sales

Steve Allen, planning staff, Plumas County Planning Commission

Michael Ayoob, merchant, Greenville

Bob Cermak, Deputy Regional Forester, Forest Service, San Francisco

Wayne Dakan, amateur botanist, Quincy

John Fiske, Forest Service, San Francisco, pesticides

Tom Gavin, National Park Service, San Francisco, prescribed burns

Jim Gossett, candidate and car salesman, Quincy

Michael Jackson, candidate and resident, Quincy

Bob Jesson, Plumas National Forest, Quincy, forest planning, clearcutting

Paula McMasters, Forest Service, San Francisco, forest planning

Guy McNett, Friends of Indian Creek, Taylorsville

Robert Moon, director, chamber of commerce, Quincy

Dick Nambo, Mount Lassen National Park

Ike Parker, Forest Service, San Francisco, forest planning

Lew Persons, resident and kayaker, Quincy

Gordon Robinson, forestry consultant, Tiburon
Russ Shay, Sierra Club, Oakland, forest planning, environmental issues
Zane Smith, regional forester, Forest Service, San Francisco
Bill Westmoreland, Lassen National Forest, Chester
Ralph Worbington, Forest Service, San Francisco, herbicides
Mike Yost, forestry teacher, Feather River College, Quincy

Chapter 3   The Deep Blue Lake

Bruner, James W., Jr. "What Will We Tell Our Kids about Lake Tahoe?" *National Parks and Conservation Magazine*, May 1980.

Calaveras County Citizens Advisory Committee. *Ebbetts Pass Scenic Highway Special Plan*. San Andreas, Calif.: Calaveras County, March 1984.

Goldman, Charles R., and Byron, Earl R. *Changing Water Quality at Lake Tahoe*. Davis, Calif.: University of California, Institute of Ecology, Tahoe Research Group, 1986.

Goldman, Charles R. *The Greening of Lake Tahoe*. Unpublished paper read at the annual meeting, League to Save Lake Tahoe, 1985.

Higgins, Eleanor, and Olmstead, John. *Adventures on and off Interstate 80*. Palo Alto, Calif.: Tioga Publishing Co., 1981.

McFarren, Jack. "New Hope for Lake Tahoe." *Nevada State Journal/Reno Evening Gazette*, September 9, 1981.

Peirce, Neal. *The Mountain States*. New York: W. W. Norton, 1972.

Rubin, Hal. "Lake Tahoe: A Tale of Two States." *Sierra*, November/December 1981, pp. 43–47.

Scott, Edward B. *Squaw Valley*. Crystal Bay, Lake Tahoe, Nev.: Sierra-Tahoe Publishing Co., 1960.

Stewart, George R. *Ordeal by Hunger*. New York: Pocket Books, 1960. (the Donner Party)

Strong, Douglas. *Tahoe: An Environmental History*. Lincoln: University of Nebraska Press, 1984.

Tahoe Regional Planning Agency. *Preserving Lake Tahoe's Water Quality: A Draft Plan for the Tahoe Basin*. South Lake Tahoe, Calif.: Tahoe Regional Planning Agency, January 1976.

Thomas, Graham. "Tahoe Regional Planning." *Sierra*, March 1975.

Twain, Mark. *Roughing It*. New York: Signet, 1962.

Wood, Robert S. "Desolation Wilderness." *Sierra Club Bulletin*, March 1971, pp. 4–7.

Zook, Martin. "Tahoe's Glitter Traps Those Fleeing Personal Problems." *Sacramento Bee*, July 9, 1984, p. B-1.

Interviews

Gordon Barrett, Tahoe Regional Planning Agency staff
Lauree Borup, Tuolumne County Planning Commission staff
James Bruner, Jr., League to Save Lake Tahoe
Brenda Bullard, realtor, Arnold

Don Clark, resident, Arnold

Wendy Corpening, resident, Avery

Shila Friedli, realtor, Arnold

Dr. Charles Goldman, professor of limnology, University of California at Davis

Bernard E. Frizzie, Dillingham Development Company, South Lake Tahoe

Joe Harn, Forest Service, San Francisco, wildlife, land use

James Hildinger, schoolteacher and resort owner, South Lake Tahoe

Richard Leonard, honorary president, Sierra Club, Berkeley

Wes Lewis, Stanislaus National Forest, Sonora, land use, dam proposals

John McArthur, Forest Service, San Francisco, land use

Tom Manning, Citizens Advisory Committee, County Planning Commission

Tom Martens, League to Save Lake Tahoe, South Lake Tahoe

John Mills, planning consultant, Sonora

William Morgan, executive director, Tahoe Regional Planning Agency, South Lake Tahoe

Paul Sabatier, University of California at Davis, Division of Environmental Studies

Gary Sinclair, Forest Service, San Francisco, recreation

Bob Twiss, chairman, Department of Landscape Architecture, University of California at Berkeley

Chapter 4   Rivers

Andrews, Betty, and Carr, Patrick. "Auburn Dam: Bad Dream or Living Nightmare?" *Headwaters*, May/June 1984.

Baker, George L., and DeVries, Tom. "Water: What We Don't Know and Why We Don't Know It." *New West*, June 16, 1980, p. 35.

California Department of Fish and Game. *North Fork American River Waterway Management Plan*. Sacramento: Department of Fish and Game, July 1977.

California Department of Water Resources. *Economic Analysis of Additional Hydropower Development on the Tuolumne River*. By Richard Norgaard. Sacramento: Department of Water Resources, 1982.

California Department of Water Resources. *Hydroelectric Energy Potential in California, Bulletin 194*. Sacramento: Department of Water Resources, 1974.

California Department of Water Resources. *Water Conservation in California, Bulletin No. 198*. By Glenn B. Sawyer et al. Sacramento: Department of Water Resources, 1976.

Environmental Defense Fund. *The Tuolumne River: Preservation or Development? An Economic Assessment*. Berkeley: Environmental Defense Fund, 1983.

Nash, Roderick. *Wilderness and the American Mind*. New Haven: Yale University Press, 1967.

Palmer, Tim. "The Auburn Dam Debate." *Sacramento*, April 1981, p. 46.

Palmer, Tim. *Endangered Rivers and the Conservation Movement*. Berkeley: University of California Press, 1986.

Palmer, Tim. *Stanislaus: The Struggle for a River*. Berkeley: University of California Press, 1982.

Planning and Conservation League Foundation. *Protecting Our Heritage: A Proposal for an Upper American River National Recreation Area*. Sacramento: Planning and Conservation League Foundation, 1984.

Rand Corporation. *Efficient Water Use in California*. 7 vols. Santa Monica, Calif.: Rand Corporation, 1978.

Reisner, Marc. *Cadillac Desert*. New York: Viking, 1986.

Seaborg, Eric. "The Battle for Hetch Hetchy." *Sierra*, November/December 1981, pp. 61–65.

Stoutenburg, Adrien, and Baker, Laura Nelson. *Snowshoe Thompson*. New York: Charles Scribner's Sons, 1957.

Tuolumne River Preservation Trust. *"Like Getting Another Yosemite for Free": The Case for Making the Tuolumne River Part of the Wild and Scenic Rivers System*. San Francisco: Tuolumne River Preservation Trust, 1982.

United States Department of Agriculture, Forest Service. *Tuolumne Wild and Scenic River Study*. San Francisco: Forest Service, 1979.

United States Department of the Interior, Office of Audit and Investigation. *Review of the Central Valley Project, Bureau of Reclamation*. [n.p.] Department of the Interior, January 1978.

"Water in California." *Fremontia* (entire issue, the California Native Plant Society), April 1982.

Watkins, T. H. *The Water Hustlers*. San Francisco: Sierra Club, 1971. (the state water project)

Interviews

John Amodio, Tuolumne River Preservation Trust, San Francisco

Laurel Anderson, Merced Canyon Committee, El Portal

Betty Andrews, Friends of the River, Sacramento

Arthur Baggett, Merced Canyon Committee, El Portal

Robert Broadbent, commissioner of reclamation, Bureau of Reclamation, Washington, D.C.

Chris Brown, American Rivers, Washington, D.C.

Michael Catino, regional director, Bureau of Reclamation, Sacramento

Bill Center, river outfitter and resident, Lotus

Robin Center, river outfitter and resident, Lotus

Bea Cooley, Friends of the River, Sacramento

Kevin Coyle, American Rivers, Washington, D.C.

Dale Crane, chief of staff, House Interior Subcommittee on National Parks and Recreation

Tony Diller, California Department of Water Resources

Mark Dubois, Friends of the River and International Rivers Network, Sacramento

Donn Furman, Committee to Save the Kings River, Fresno

John Haubert, National Park Service, Washington, D.C.

Roger Hicks, Nevada City, Yuba River

Huey Johnson, former secretary of the California Resources Agency

Bill Kier, lodge owner, Strawberry

Richard Lehman, U.S. House of Representatives, Sanger

Tom Lennon, Forest Service, Washington, D.C., nationwide rivers inventory

Susan Levitt, San Francisco, Yuba River

Tom Lewis, Stanislaus National Forest, Sonora, recreation

Dave McCauley, Forest Service, San Francisco, dams

Marty McDonnell, river outfitter, Sonora

Billy Martin, former regional director, Bureau of Reclamation, Sacramento

Jerry Meral, Planning and Conservation League, Sacramento

Jonas Minton, California Department of Water Resources, water conservation

Guy Phillips, California Assembly Office of Research

Bruce Rene, Stanislaus National Forest, Sonora, forest plans

Maurice Roos, California Department of Water Resources, hydrology

Jeff Schloss, Merced Canyon Committee, El Portal

Kim Schnorr, office of Representative Tony Coelho, Fresno

Jim Shiro, Forest Service, San Francisco, rivers specialist

Ron Stork, Merced Canyon Committee, Mariposa

Jeff Taylor, General Manager, Kings River Conservation District, Fresno

John Turner, Bureau of Reclamation, Sacramento, Auburn Dam

Kevin Wolfe, Friends of the River, Sacramento

Melinda Wright, river activist, Sonora

Chapter 5   Yosemite

Brooks, Paul. *Speaking for Nature.* San Francisco: Sierra Club Books, 1980.

Cameron, Robert. *Above Yosemite.* San Francisco: Cameron and Co., 1983.

Hope, Jack. "Hassles in the Park." *Natural History,* May 1971, p. 20.

Jones, Chris. *Climbing in North America.* Berkeley: University of California Press, 1976.

Jones, Holway R. *John Muir and the Sierra Club: The Battle for Yosemite.* San Francisco: Sierra Club, 1965.

Olmstead, Roger, "Yosemite Master Plan at Stake." *Sierra,* March 1975.

O'Neill, Elizabeth Stone. *Meadow in the Sky.* Fresno: Panorama West Books, 1983.

Robinson, Doug. "The Climber as Visionary." In *Voices for the Earth: A Treasury of the Sierra Club Bulletin,* edited by Ann Gilliam. San Francisco: Sierra Club Books, 1979.

Sanborn, Margaret. *Yosemite.* New York: Random House, 1981.

Strong, Douglas H. "The Sierra Club: A History." *Sierra,* October 1977 and November 1977.

United States Department of the Interior, National Park Service. *Backcountry Plan: Yosemite National Park.* Yosemite: National Park Service, 1976.

United States Department of the Interior, National Park Service. *Yosemite National Park: General Management Plan, Visitor Use/Park Operations/ Development.* El Portal, Calif.: National Park Service, September 1980.

Wyant, William K. *Westward in Eden.* Berkeley: University of California Press, 1982.

Interviews

Bob Binnewies, superintendent, Yosemite National Park

Richard Blair, photographer, Yosemite National Park

David Brower, Earth Island Institute, Berkeley

Ginger Burley, interpreter, Yosemite National Park

Howard Chapman, regional director, National Park Service, San Francisco

Garrett DeBell, Yosemite Park and Curry Company, Music Corporation of America

John Dill, Yosemite National Park, search and rescue

Becky Evans, Sierra Club, Yosemite master plan committee

Don Fox, landscape architect, Yosemite National Park

Ed Hardy, president, Yosemite Park and Curry Company, Music Corporation of America

Steve Hickman, assistant valley ranger, Yosemite National Park

Norman Hinson, criminal investigations, Yosemite National Park

Grant Hiskis, climber, Yosemite Valley and Mammoth

Lars Holbek, climber, Lotus and western North America

Vince Kehoe, Yosemite Institute

James Lee, ranger, Yosemite National Park

Richard Leonard, Sierra Club, Berkeley

Tim Luddington, Yosemite National Park, backcountry use

Len McKenzie, chief interpreter, Yosemite National Park

Nancy Mertz, campground ranger, Yosemite National Park

Laurel Munson, backcountry ranger, Yosemite National Park

Mike Murray, Yosemite National Park, search and rescue

Betty O'Neill, author, Groveland

Chuck Pratt, climber, Jackson, Wyoming

Armand Quartini, ranger, Yosemite National Park

Dick Riegelhuth, chief of resource protection, Yosemite National Park

Bob Roney, media specialist, Yosemite National Park

Steve Schneider, climber, Yosemite

Jim Snyder, trail crew foreman, Yosemite National Park
Lee Stetson, actor, El Portal
Jan Van Wagtendonk, research scientist, Yosemite National Park

Chapter 6   The Sunrise Mountains

Austin, Mary. *The Land of Little Rain.* Albuquerque: University of New Mexico Press, 1974.

California Supreme Court. *The Mono Lake 'Public Trust' Decision of the California Supreme Court.* Reprinted by the Mono Lake Committee, February 17, 1983.

Clyde, Norman. *Close Ups of the High Sierra.* Glendale, Calif.: La Siesta Press, 1976.

Dasmann, Raymond. *The Destruction of California.* New York: Collier Books, 1966. (Owens Valley water war)

Eriksen, Mary Ann. "Horseshoe Meadows: Another Mineral King?" *Sierra Club Bulletin*, November/December 1976.

Gaines, David, and the Mono Lake Committee. *Mono Lake Guidebook.* Lee Vining, Calif.: Kutsavi Books, 1981.

Gilbert, Bill. "Is This a Holy Place?" *Sports Illustrated*, May 30, 1983, pp. 77–90.

Johnson, William Oscar. "A Man and His Mountain." *Sports Illustrated*, February 25, 1985, pp. 60–70.

Los Angeles Department of Water and Power. *Mono Basin Water Supply Briefing Document.* Los Angeles: Department of Water and Power, June 1984.

Palmer, Mark J. "At Mono Lake." *Pacific Discovery*, July/September 1983.

Pister, E. P. *Information Supporting the Need for a Cumulative Impact Study of Proposed Small Hydroelectric Development in Inyo and Mono Counties.* Unpublished paper, California Department of Fish and Game, Bishop, 1982.

Mammoth Publishing Corporation. *Mono's Changing Geology.* Mammoth Lakes, Calif.: Mammoth Publishing Corporation, 1982.

The Mono Lake Committee. *Mono Lake: Endangered Oasis.* (Booklet.) Lee Vining, Calif.: Mono Lake Committee, 1983.

Reisner, Marc. *Cadillac Desert.* New York: Viking, 1986. (Owens Valley water war)

Smith, Genny. *Deepest Valley.* Los Altos, Calif.: William Kaufmann, Inc., 1978.

United States Department of the Interior, Geological Survey. *Amount and Timing of Late Cenozoic Uplift and Tilt of the Central Sierra Nevada, California.* By N. King Huber. Menlo Park, Calif.: Geological Survey, 1981.

Interviews

Tom Blankenship, wildlife biologist, California Department of Fish and Game, Bishop

Linda Brown, Mono Lake Committee

Mary DeDecker, amateur botanist, Independence

Grace Enfield, resident, Round Valley
Marjory Farquhar, Berkeley
David Gaines, Mono Lake Committee
Sally Gaines, Mono Lake Committee
Kitty Hitchcock, planner, Mono County Planning Commission, Bridgeport
N. King Huber, U.S. Geological Survey, Menlo Park
Larry Kuhl, sheriff, Alpine County
Andrea Mead Lawrence, county supervisor, Mono County
Jack Lintott, Mammoth
Vaughn Lintott, manager, Timber Ridge, Mammoth
Mimi Lyster, chamber of commerce, Mammoth
Christy Lynch, schoolteacher, Lone Pine
David McCoy, owner, Mammoth Mountain ski area
Ilene Mendelbaum, Mono Lake Committee
Kathy Noland, Inyo National Forest, Bishop, grazing
Jim Parker, Mono Lake Committee
Phil Pister, fisheries biologist, California Department of Fish and Game, Bishop
Mike Prather, schoolteacher, Lone Pine
Donald Rambeux, resident, Lee Vining
John Rupp, Inyo National Forest, Bishop, recreation
Richard Rynne, resident, Lone Pine
Mignon Shumway, resident, Bishop
Genny Smith, author, Mammoth Lakes
Richard Verble, Los Angeles Department of Water and Power, Bishop
John Wehausen, wildlife biologist, Bishop

Chapter 7   Escape

Arno, Stephen F., and Hammerly, Ramona P. *Timberline: Mountain and Arctic Forest Frontiers.* Seattle: Mountaineers, 1984.

Blake, Clifton G. *Outfitting and Guiding on the National Forests in the Western United States.* Unpublished report by Clifton Blake, recreation planner, Intermountain Region, U.S. Forest Service, Ogden, Utah, 1983. (stock use)

Ferguson, Denzel, and Ferguson, Nancy. *Sacred Cows at the Public Trough.* Bend, Ore.: Maverick Publications, 1983. (cattle grazing)

Fradkin, Philip L. "The Eating of the West." *Audubon*, January 1979, p. 94. (cattle grazing)

Knotts, David M. "Purifying Water in the Wild." *Sierra*, July/August 1983, pp. 57–59.

Leonard, Richard M. "The Clark Range and Adjacent Peaks." *Sierra Club Bulletin*, June 1951.

Lewis, Oscar. *High Sierra Country*. New York: Duell, Sloan and Pearce, 1955.

Mitchell, Richard G., Jr. *Mountain Experience: The Psychology and Sociology of Adventure*. Chicago: University of Chicago Press, 1983.

Peters, Ed, ed. *Mountaineering: The Freedom of the Hills*. Seattle, Mountaineers, 1982.

Rosetta, Noel. "Herds, Herds on the Range." *Sierra*, March/April, 1985, pp. 43–47.

Roth, Hal. *Pathway in the Sky: The Story of the John Muir Trail*. Berkeley: Howell-North Books, 1965.

Rothstein, Stephen; Verner, Jared; and Stevens, Ernest. "Range Expansion and Diurnal Changes in Dispersion of the Brown-Headed Cowbird in the Sierra Nevada." *The Auk* (U.S. Forest Service and University of California), May 5, 1980, p. 253.

Schaffer, Jeffrey P.; Schifrin, Ben; Winnett, Thomas; and Jenkins, J. C. *The Pacific Crest Trail. Volume 1: California*. Berkeley: Wilderness Press, 1982.

Schumacher, Genny and Sherwin, Raymond J. "Mammoth Pass Road: The Recurring Crisis." *Sierra Club Bulletin*, March 1967.

Sherwin, Judge Raymond J. "The Mammoth Pass Road." *Sierra Club Bulletin*, September 1966.

United States Department of Agriculture, Forest Service. *The Nation's Range Resources*. (Brochure.) Washington, D.C.: Forest Service, 1972.

United States Department of Agriculture, Forest Service. *Pacific Crest Trail*. (Brochure.) San Francisco: Forest Service, 1980.

United States Department of the Interior, Geological Survey. *Map Showing the Number of Giardia Cysts in Water Samples from 69 Streams in the Sierra Nevada, California*. By Thomas J. Suk, Stephen K. Sorenson, and Peter D. Dileanis. Menlo Park, Calif.: Geological Survey, 1986.

United States Department of Agriculture, Forest Service. *Proceedings—National Wilderness Research Conference: Current Research*. Ogden, Utah: Forest Service, Intermountain Research Station, 1986.

Van Wagtendonk, Jan W. "The Effect of Use Limits on Backcountry Visitation Trends in Yosemite National Park." *Leisure Sciences* 4, No. 3 (1981).

Zweig, Paul. *The Adventurer*. Princeton, N.J.: Princeton University Press.

Interviews

Dr. Norman Baker, University of California at Davis, School of Veterinary Medicine

Bob Binnewies, superintendent, Yosemite National Park

Steve Brougher, wildlife biologist, Stanislaus National Forest

Dr. George Cardinet, University of California at Davis, School of Veterinary Medicine

Trace De Sanders, Yosemite National Park, backcountry use

Jean Deluca, Glen Aulin High Sierra Camp

Alexander Gaguine, Tuolumne River Preservation Trust, San Francisco

Wayne Iseri, trail contractor and ski instructor, Mammoth

Verna Johnston, biologist, Camp Connell
Bob Kenan, backcountry ranger, Kings Canyon National Park
Richard Leonard, Sierra Club, Berkeley
Dario Malengo, backcountry ranger, Sequoia National Park
Bill Matteson, engineer, Yosemite National Park
Jack Miller, Forest Service, San Francisco, range and cattle
Charles Morgan, High Sierra Stock Users Association, Springville
Doris Nelson, League of Women Voters, Los Angeles
Dick Riegelhuth, chief of resource protection, Yosemite National Park
Wayne Schulz, concessions specialist, Yosemite National Park
Carl Sharsmith, interpreter, Yosemite National Park
Steve Sorenson, U.S. Geological Survey, Menlo Park, Giardia studies

Chapter 8   The South

Browning, Peter. "Mickey Mouse in the Mountains." *Harpers Magazine*, March 1972, p. 65.

Clark, Lew, and Clark, Ginny. *Kings Canyon Country*. San Luis Obispo, Calif.: Western Trails Publications, 1985.

Harper, John. *Mineral King: Public Concern with Governmental Policy*. Arcata, Calif.: Pacifica Publishing Co., 1982.

Harper, John L. *The Southern Sierra Nevada of California: A Regional Plan for Integrated Recreational Development*. Unpublished thesis, University of Colorado, Department of Geography, 1974.

Ise, John. *Our National Park Policy: A Critical History*. Washington, D.C.: Resources for the Future, Inc., 1961.

Palmer, Tim. *The Kings River*. Fresno: Committee to Save the Kings River, 1987.

Rapoport, Roger. "Disney's War Against the Wilderness." *Ramparts*, November 1971, p. 27.

Runte, Alfred. *National Parks: The American Experience*. Lincoln: University of Nebraska Press, 1979. (Kings Canyon)

Sax, Joseph L. *Mountains Without Handrails*. Ann Arbor: University of Michigan Press, 1980. (Mineral King)

Turner, Tom. "Mineral King: Did We Win or Lose?" *Not Man Apart*, June 1972.

United States Department of Agriculture, Forest Service. *Land Management and Resources Plan, Sequoia National Forest: Draft*. Porterville, Calif.: Forest Service, 1986.

United States Department of the Interior, National Park Service. *Backcountry Management Plan, Sequoia and Kings Canyon National Parks*. Three Rivers, Calif.: National Park Service, 1986.

Walker, Ardis M. *Sierra Nevada Sequence*. Sierra Trails Press, 1972.

White, John R. *Sequoia and Kings Canyon National Parks*. Stanford: Stanford University Press, 1949.

"The Wilderness Home of the Golden Trout." *Sunset*, June 1959, p. 60.

Interviews

Julie Allen, Sequoia National Forest, Porterville

Bob Barnes, Audubon Society, Porterville

Ron Bohigian, Committee to Save the Kings River, Fresno

Bob Brueggemann, wildlife biologist, California Department of Fish and Game, Fresno

Carla Cloer, Peppermint Alert, Porterville

Mark Dymkoski, Sequoia National Forest, Porterville, river recreation

Jim Eaton, California Wilderness Coalition, Davis

Dave Graber, Sequoia National Park, bear management

Boyd Evison, superintendent, Sequoia and Kings Canyon national parks

Bob Ferguson, river outfitter, Zephyr River Expeditions, Columbia

Joe Fontaine, past president, Sierra Club, Tehachapi

Donn Furman, Committee to Save the Kings River, Fresno

Rick Hewett, Kern River Preserve, The Nature Conservancy

Marvin Jensen, assistant to the superintendent, Sequoia and Kings Canyon national parks

Randy Kelly, fisheries biologist, California Department of Fish and Game, Fresno

Jan Knox, concession specialist, Sequoia and Kings Canyon national parks

Richard Lehman, U.S. House of Representatives, Sanger

Martin Litton, river outfitter, Palo Alto

Paula McMasters, Forest Service, San Francisco, forest planning

Tom Moore, river outfitter, Kernville

Larry Norris, botanist, Sequoia and Kings Canyon national parks

John Palmer, chief interpreter, Sequoia and Kings Canyon national parks

David Parsons, research scientist, Sequoia and Kings Canyon national parks

Gene Rose, journalist, *Fresno Bee*, Fresno

Dr. Jason Saleeby, professor of geology, California Institute of Technology, Pasadena

James Shevock, forest ecologist, Sequoia National Forest, Porterville

Bob Smith, chief ranger, Sequoia and Kings Canyon national parks

Ardis Walker, conservationist, Kernville

Jean Warner, fire lookout, Sequoia National Forest

Jim Warner, chief interpreter, Kings Canyon National Park

Dr. Edgar Wayburn, Sierra Club, Berkeley

Terry Winckler, journalist and editor, *Porterville Recorder*

Epilogue and Update

"Auburn Dam Controversy Rages—and a Friend Emerges!" *Headwaters*, April/May 1987.

Brazil, Eric. "Water Foes Split on Hetch Hetchy." *San Francisco Examiner*, August 11, 1987.

Calhoun, Fryar. "Restoring Hetch Hetchy Valley—Would It Really Work?" *Headwaters*, October/November 1987, p. 1.

Carr, Patrick. "American Fight Gets Hot." *Headwaters*, June/July 1987, p. 6.

Cartiere, Rich. "Sierra Find May Be Oldest Structure in North America." *San Francisco Examiner*, August 29, 1986, p. A-1.

Dolzani, M. "At Home in the Pleistocene?" *Mammoth Trumpet*, Center for the Study of Early Man, University of Maine, Orono, November 2, 1987, p. 1.

"French Connections to Yuba Dams Confirmed." *Headwaters*, June/July 1987.

Harrison, Sandy. "Fish and Game Cites Poor Data, Boycotts FERC." *Inyo Register*, September 22, 1985.

Johnson, John. "Giving Yosemite's Hetch Hetchy Back to Nature." *Sacramento Bee*, August 6, 1987, p. 1.

Johnson, John. "Hodel Tells SF: Hetch Hetchy Not a Birthright." *Sacramento Bee*, October 13, 1987, p. A-3.

Johnson, John. "'Visionary' Yosemite Plan Dims." *Sacramento Bee*, August 7, 1987.

Lafever, Susan. "Kings, Kern, Merced Bills Enter Home Stretch." *Headwaters*, August/September 1987, p. 3.

Ludlow, Lynn. "U.S. to Study Draining Hetch Hetchy." *San Francisco Examiner*, August 6, 1987, p. 1.

United States Department of Agriculture, Forest Service. "Public Response Analysis Summary." *The Tahoe Planner*, July 1987, p. 1.

United States Department of Agriculture, Forest Service. *Report of the Forest Service, Fiscal Year 1986*. Washington, D.C.: Forest Service, 1987.

Interviews

Jim Bruner, Davis

Peter Edwards, biologist, Mountain Lion Preservation Foundation

Susan Lafever, Friends of the River, Sacramento

Matt Mathes, Forest Service, San Francisco, public information

Melinda Peak, archaeologist, Sacramento

Ed Roman, Sacramento Municipal Utility District

Clement Shute, League to Save Lake Tahoe, attorney

Zane Smith, National Recreation Strategy Project, Forest Service, San Francisco

Dan Taylor, Western Regional Office, National Audubon Society

Frannie Waid, Sierra Club, Oakland

GUIDEBOOKS

Beck, David. *Ski Touring in California*. Berkeley: Wilderness Press, 1975.

Cassady, John. *A Guide to Three Rivers*. San Francisco: Friends of the River Foundation, 1981.

Cassady, Jim, and Calhoun, Fryar. *California White Water*. Cassady and Calhoun (available through Friends of the River), 1984.

Harris, Thomas. *Down the Wild Rivers*. San Francisco: Chronicle Books, 1973.

Holbec, Lars, and Stanley, Chuck. *A Guide to the Best Whitewater in the State of California*. San Francisco: Friends of the River Books, 1984.

Jenkins, J. C. *Self-Propelled in the Southern Sierra*. Berkeley: Wilderness Press, 1978.

Libkind, Marcus. *Ski Tours in the Sierra Nevada*. 4 vols. Livermore: Bittersweet Publishing Co., 1985.

Roper, Steve. *The Climber's Guide to the High Sierra*. San Francisco: Sierra Club Books, 1976.

Schaffer, Jeffrey P. *Yosemite National Park*. Berkeley: Wilderness Press, 1986.

Scharff, Robert, ed. *Yosemite National Park*. New York: David McKay Co., Inc., 1967.

Schumacher, Genny. *The Mammoth Lakes Sierra*. Berkeley: Wilderness Press, 1969.

Winnett, Thomas. *Guide to the John Muir Trail*. Berkeley: Wilderness Press, 1978.

Winnett, Thomas. *The Tahoe-Yosemite Trail*. Berkeley: Wilderness Press, 1979.

Winnett, Thomas, and Winnett, Jason. *Sierra North*. Berkeley: Wilderness Press, 1982.

Winnett, Thomas, and Winnett, Jason. *Sierra South*. Berkeley: Wilderness Press, 1980.

Wright, Terry. *Rocks and Rapids of the Tuolumne River*. Forestville, Calif.: Wilderness Interpretation Publications, 1983.

Many additional hiking guides for specific parts of the Sierra south of Lake Tahoe are available from Wilderness Press.

Index

Also Available from Island Press

Land and Resource Planning in the National Forests
By Charles F. Wilkinson and H. Michael Anderson
Foreword by Arnold W. Bolle

This comprehensive, in-depth review and analysis of planning, policy, and law in the National Forest system is the standard reference source on the National Forest Management Act of 1976 (NFMA). This clearly written, nontechnical book offers an insightful analysis of the Fifty Year Plans and how to participate in and influence them.

1987. xii, 396 pp., index.
Paper, ISBN 0-933280-38-6. **$19.95**

Reforming the Forest Service
By Randal O'Toole

Reforming the Forest Service contributes a completely new view to the current debate on the management of our national forests. O'Toole argues that poor management is an institutional problem; he shows that economic inefficiencies and environmental degradation are the inevitable result of the well-intentioned but poorly designed laws that govern the Forest Service. This book proposes sweeping reforms in the structure of the agency and new budgetary incentives as the best way to improve management.

1988. xii, 256 pp., graphs tables, notes.
Cloth, ISBN 0-933280-49-1. **$24.95**
Paper, ISBN 0-933280-45-9. **$16.95**

The Forest and the Trees: A Guide to Excellent Forestry
By Gordon Robinson
Foreword by Michael McCloskey

When is multiple use multiple abuse? In this detailed look at the management of our forests, Gordon Robinson provides specific information on the principles of true multiple-use forestry and on what is wrong with forestry as it is practiced today. He describes, in practical terms, "excellent forestry"—uneven-aged management for sustained yield, which safeguards the rich variety of life in the forest and protects all uses simultaneously. He offers the reader a short course in the mathematics of forestry and provides guidelines for commenting on forest plans. Includes nearly four hundred summaries of published research and expert opinions. Gordon Robinson is a well-known and respected forester with fifty years of experience in forest management.

1988. 288 pp., illustrations, tables.
Paper, ISBN 0-933280-40-8. **$19.95**
Cloth, ISBN 0-933280-41-6. **$34.95**

Last Stand of the Red Spruce
By Robert A. Mello
Published in cooperation with Natural Resources Defense Council

Acid rain—the debates rage between those who believe that the cause of the problem is clear and identifiable and those who believe that the evidence is inconclusive. In *Last Stand of the Red Spruce*, Robert A. Mello has written an ecological detective story that unravels this confusion and explains how air pollution is killing our nation's forests. Writing for a lay audience, the author traces the efforts of scientists trying to solve the mystery of the dying red spruce trees on Camels Hump in Vermont. Mello clearly and succinctly presents both sides of an issue on which even the scientific community is split and concludes that the scientific evidence uncovered on Camels Hump elevates the issues of air pollution and acid rain to new levels of national significance.

1987. xx, 205 pp., illus., references, bibliography.
Paper, ISBN 0-933280-37-8. **$14.95**

Western Water Made Simple, by the editors of **High Country News**
Edited by Ed Marston

Winner of the 1986 George Polk Award for environmental reporting, these four special issues of *High Country News* are here available for the first time in book form. Much has been written about the water crisis in the West, yet the issue remains confusing and difficult to understand. *Western Water Made Simple* by the editors of *High Country News*, lays out in clear language the complex issues of Western water. A survey of the West's three great rivers—the Colorado, the Columbia, and the Missouri—this work includes material that reaches to the heart of the West—its ways of life, its politics, and its aspirations. *Western Water Made Simple* approaches these three river basins in terms of overarching themes combined with case studies—the Columbia in an age of reform, the Colorado in the midst of a fight for control, and the Missouri in search of its destiny.

1987. 224 pp., maps, photographs, bibliography, index.
Paper, ISBN 0-933280-39-4. **$15.95**

The Report of the President's Commission on Americans Outdoors: The Legacy, the Challenge
With Case Studies
Preface by William K. Reilly

"If there is an example of pulling victory from the jaws of disaster, this report is it. The Commission did more than anyone expected, especially the administration. It gave Americans something serious to think about if we are to begin saving our natural resources."— Paul C. Pritchard, President, National Parks and Conservation Association.

This report is the first comprehensive attempt to examine the impact of a changing American society and its recreation habits since the work of the Outdoor Recreation Resource Review Commission, chaired by Laurance Rockefeller in 1962. The President's Commission took more than two years to complete its study; the Report contains over sixty recommendations, such as the preservation of a nationwide network of "greenways" for recreational purposes and the establishment of an annual $1 billion trust fund to finance the protection and preservation of our recreational resources. The Island Press edition provides the full text of the report, much of the additional material compiled by the Commission, and twelve selected case studies.

1987. xvi, 426 pp., illus., appendixes, case studies.
Paper, ISBN 0-933280-36-X. **$24.95**

Green Fields Forever: The Conservation Tillage Revolution in America
By Charles E. Little

"*Green Fields Forever* is a fascinating and lively account of one of the most important technological developments in American agriculture. . . . Be prepared to enjoy an exceptionally well-told tale, full of stubborn inventors, forgotten pioneers, enterprising farmers—and no small amount of controversy."—Ken Cook, World Wildlife Fund and The Conservation Foundation.

Here is the book that will change the way Americans think about agriculture. It is the story of "conservation tillage"—a new way to grow food that, for the first time, works *with*, rather than against, the soil. Farmers who are revolutionizing the course of American agriculture explain here how conservation tillage works. Some environmentalists think there are problems with the methods, however; author Charles E. Little demonstrates that on this issue both sides have a case, and the jury is still out.

1987. 189 pp., illus., appendixes, index, bibliography.
Cloth, ISBN 0-933280-35-1. **$24.95**
Paper, ISBN 0-933280-34-3. **$14.95**

Federal Lands: A Guide to Planning, Management, and State Revenues
By Sally K. Fairfax and Carolyn E. Yale
"An invaluable tool for state land managers. Here, in summary, is everything that one needs to know about federal resource management policies."—Rowena Rogers, President, Colorado State Board of Land Commissioners.

Federal Lands is the first book to introduce and analyze in one accessible volume the diverse programs for developing resources on federal lands. Offshore and onshore oil and gas leasing, coal and geothermal leasing, timber sales, grazing permits, and all other programs that share receipts and revenues with states and localities are considered in the context of their common historical evolution as well as in the specific context of current issues and policy debates.

1987. xx, 252 pp., charts, maps, bibliography, index.
Paper, ISBN 0-933280-33-5. **$24.95**

An Environmental Agenda for the Future
By Leaders of America's Foremost Environmental Organizations

". . . a substantive book addressing the most serious questions about the future of our resources."—John Chafee, U.S. Senator, Environmental and Public Works Committee. "While I am not in agreement with many of the positions the authors take, I believe this book can be the basis for constructive dialogue with industry representatives seeking solutions to environmental problems."—Louis Fernandez, Chairman of the Board, Monsanto Corporation.

The chief executive officers of the ten major environmental and conservation organizations launched a joint venture to examine goals that the environmental movement should pursue now and into the twenty-first century. This book presents policy recommendations for implementing changes needed to bring about a healthier, safer world. Topics discussed include nuclear issues, human population growth, energy strategies, toxic waste and pollution control, and urban environments.

1985. viii, 155 pp., bibliography.
Paper, ISBN 0-933280-29-7. **$9.95**

Water in the West
By Western Network

Water in the West is an essential reference tool for water managers, public officials, farmers, attorneys, industry officials, and students and professors attempting to understand the competing pressures on our most important natural resource: water. Here is an in-depth analysis of the effects of energy development, Indian rights, and urban growth on other water users.

1985. *Vol. II: Western Water Flows to the Cities*
v, 217 pp., maps, table of cases, documents, bibliography, index.
Paper, ISBN 0-933280-28-9. **$25.00**

These titles are available directly from Island Press, Box 7, Covelo, CA 95428. Please enclose $2.75 shipping and handling for the first book and $1.25 for each additional book. California and Washington, DC residents add 6% sales tax. A catalog of current and forthcoming titles is available free of charge. Prices subject to change without notice.

SALINAS PUBLIC LIBRARY

Island Press
Board of Directors

JAN 1989
Received
John Steinbeck
Library